Studies in Economic
Stabilization

Studies of Government Finance
TITLES PUBLISHED

Studies in Economic Stabilization

Edited by

ALBERT ANDO, E. CARY BROWN,

AND ANN F. FRIEDLAENDER

Studies of Government Finance

THE BROOKINGS INSTITUTION

WASHINGTON, D. C.

THE BROOKINGS INSTITUTION is an independent organization devoted to nonpartisan research, education, and publication in economics, government, foreign policy, and the social sciences generally. Its principal purposes are to aid in the development of sound public policies and to promote public understanding of issues of national importance.

The Institution was founded December 8, 1927, to merge the activities of the Institute for Government Research, founded in 1916, the Institute of Economics, founded in 1922, and the Robert Brookings Graduate School of Economics and Government, founded in 1924.

The general administration of the Institution is the responsibility of a self-perpetuating Board of Trustees. The trustees are likewise charged with maintaining the independence of the staff and fostering the most favorable conditions for creative research and education. The immediate direction of the policies, program, and staff of the Institution is vested in the President, assisted by an advisory council chosen from the staff of the Institution.

In publishing a study, the Institution presents it as a competent treatment of a subject worthy of public consideration. The interpretations and conclusions in such publications are those of the author or authors and do not purport to represent the views of the other staff members, officers, or trustees of the Brookings Institution.

Foreword

THE ECONOMIC THEORY of fiscal policy has been developing for more than three decades, but until recently little attempt was made to quantify the impact of changes in fiscal variables on the economy. The subject is still in its infancy; nevertheless, considerable progress has been made as a result of the availability of more and better data, the rapid development of the study of econometrics, and the advent of the computer. The information stemming from these sources is now being used by policymakers, and it will doubtless play a more important role in day-to-day decisions as the methodology and estimates continue to improve.

This volume contains seven studies that illustrate current research in countercyclical fiscal policy. They were prepared in a workshop in fiscal policy at the Massachusetts Institute of Technology, organized by Albert Ando and E. Cary Brown.

Other than the joint paper by Ando and Brown in which the effect on consumption of the individual income tax cut in 1964 is estimated, and that by Ando and Stephen M. Goldfeld, all of the papers in this volume are based on doctoral dissertations submitted to the Massachusetts Institute of Technology. Howard Pack investigates the effectiveness of various methods of implementing proposals for introducing "formula flexibility" into the tax system. William Oakland compares the relative effectiveness of the value-added tax and the corporate income tax as automatic stabilizers. Ann Friedlaender evaluates the role of the federal highway program in stabilization policy. Michael Spiro assesses the effect of government procurement on employment in the aircraft industry. Stephen Resnick measures the impact of changes in taxes and expenditures in one or more members of the European Economic Community on the other member nations. In the concluding paper, Ando and Goldfeld present an econometric model designed for an analysis of fiscal and monetary stabilization policy.

The volume was edited by Professors Ando, Brown, and Friedlaender. The authors wish to acknowledge the helpful suggestions and comments they received from the reading committee, which consisted of Frank deLeeuw, Lawrence R. Klein, and Warren L. Smith. They also wish to express their appreciation for the financial support from the National Science Foundation for the Ando-Goldfeld study and from the National Aeronautics and Space Administration for the Spiro study; for the unpublished data made available by the Office of Business Economics and the Bureau of Public Roads of the Department of Commerce for the Ando-Brown, Ando-Goldfeld, and Friedlaender studies; and for the simulation program provided by Gary Fromm of the Brookings Institution for the Pack study. Florence M. Robinson prepared the index.

The Ando-Brown paper is a revision of one given at the First World Congress of the Econometric Society in Rome, Italy, September 9, 1965. The authors acknowledge their indebtedness to Mrs. Marilyn Rice of the Office of Business Economics for providing them with invaluable assistance in understanding the conceptual problems involved.

This project was part of a special program of research and education on taxation and public expenditures, supervised by the National Committee on Government Finance and financed by a special grant from the Ford Foundation.

The views expressed in this book are those of the authors and are not presented as the views of the National Committee on Government Finance or its Advisory Committee, or of the staff members, officers, or trustees of the Brookings Institution or the Ford Foundation.

Kermit Gordon
President

January 1968
Washington, D.C.

Studies of Government Finance

Studies of Government Finance is a special program of research and education in taxation and government expenditures at the federal, state, and local levels. This program, which is supported by a special grant from the Ford Foundation, was undertaken and supervised by the National Committee on Government Finance appointed by the trustees of the Brookings Institution.

MEMBERS OF THE ADVISORY COMMITTEE

Contents

Tables and Figures

Pack

ALBERT ANDO AND E. CARY BROWN*

Introduction

THE STUDY of the stabilization aspects of fiscal policy has proceeded at a rapid pace since the end of World War II, but much remains to be done in order to improve knowledge on which more effective government action may be based. More specifically, the need for reliable quantitative estimates of the relationships that determine how fiscal policy will affect the economy has become more and more obvious in recent years. The papers in this volume are designed to fill some of this need.

Earlier studies of fiscal policy often focused on the automatic response of taxes and expenditures (including transfer payments) to changes in output and prices and their consequent implication for the structural stability of the economy and for discretionary changes in governmental fiscal activities. Studies of automatic stability have typically been based on annual data, but have shifted more and more to quarterly analyses as such data have become available. The Ando-Brown paper in this volume represents an updating of some work that was undertaken for the Commission on Money and Credit and the econometric model project at the Brookings Institution. It contains more satisfactory quarterly estimates of the various components of the personal income tax for use in appraising the tax reduction of 1964 and 1965 and for measuring the automatic response of the personal income tax.

* University of Pennsylvania and Massachusetts Institute of Technology.

1

One of the major changes in the operation of the existing revenue system, often suggested but not carefully analyzed, is that of formula flexibility. The appeal of this notion is that such flexibility can theoretically increase the aggregate marginal response of taxes without relying on extremely high marginal individual tax rates which may create allocational inefficiencies. However, its implementation must overcome two operational difficulties. First, the formula must be designed with the proper dynamic characteristics so that it will not add instability to the economy. Second, the formula must rely on information available sufficiently far in advance for its satisfactory operation. Howard Pack has attempted to evaluate the performance of some fairly simple formulas that use as their instrument the effective rate of the federal personal income tax and are activated by movements in the average workweek in manufacturing and in the level of gross national product (GNP). Their operation is then tested in the recessions that began in 1953, 1957, and 1960, using the model of the economy developed by Duesenberry, Eckstein, and Fromm. He finds that formula flexibility, when properly designed, can contribute substantially to the reduction of fluctuations in employment and output. At the time that Pack made his study, very few short-run models of the economy were available. Since then, a number have been developed, such as the Brookings Quarterly Model and the Ando-Goldfeld model in this volume. Pack's pioneering study now needs to be extended to these more developed models to see if his conclusions are confirmed by them.

The value-added tax has often been proposed as a new source of revenue. William Oakland's study compares the automatic stabilizing strength of this tax with the corporate income tax. Whether or not the value-added tax would provide more automatic stability than the corporate tax appears to depend crucially on the incidence of the value-added tax. If it is absorbed by business firms, or if the higher estimates of the sensitivity of corporate profits to GNP are accepted even without absorption of the tax, substitution of the value-added tax for the corporate income tax would reduce automatic stability.

Discretionary policy has also been extensively analyzed in the postwar period. The thrust of this analysis has been to point up the weakness of countercyclical variation in expenditure, and to place manipulation of revenues and transfer payments in the forefront of discretionary stabilization policy. Some argue on theoretical grounds for stability of real expenditure based on a social benefit-cost comparison; others find institutional and structural impediments to manipulation of expenditures, even though otherwise desirable. Ann Friedlaender's study of expenditure on highway construction leads her to conclude that, while present institutional arrangements leave little room for the countercyclical use of public works expenditures, it should be possible to modify these arrangements so as to make highway expenditure a countercyclical tool of some strength. These modifications would take the form of the creation of a highway stabilization fund in which would be accumulated small highway projects subject to rapid initiation and completion that could be activated by the President at his discretion.

The effectiveness of both automatic and discretionary fiscal policies depends not only on the behavior of a government's fiscal structure but also on the response of economic decision-making units—consumers and producers—to changes in fiscal variables. A useful experiment on the effect of tax reduction on consumer behavior has been provided by the tax cut of 1964, and this has been examined in some detail in the Ando-Brown paper. It is suggested there that consumers reacted to income change brought about by the tax cut quite promptly and in accordance with their past response to sustained income changes.

A similar need for knowledge of reaction time arises in connection with changes in government spending. Michael Spiro explores the aircraft industry's reactions to changes in government procurement, and Ann Friedlaender rounds out her highway study with an exploration of the impact of changes in spending on construction and related industries. A comparison of these two studies suggests that the pattern and speed of response depend critically on the nature of the production process of the industry affected, and that an accurate prediction of the changes which will take place must be based on a careful examination of the structure of the particular industry.

The operation of fiscal policy in interrelated economies, an unresolved question, has received increasing attention in recent years. Such an analysis to be definitive is particularly challenging and difficult because it requires a satisfactory model not only of one economy but of many. The problems of structural estimation and of adequate data are almost overwhelming. Especially hard to specify, even theoretically, are the demand and supply functions of one country for imports and exports of a number of other countries. In his study, which is built around the European Economic Community (EEC), Stephen Resnick shows that the import and export interrelationships among countries are a critical factor in the economic behavior of any one of them. He has developed models of the EEC countries and simulated their reactions to changes in other economies. While necessarily a preliminary analysis, the study opens up an important new area of research—that of attempting to determine the effects on the stability of one economy of stabilizing action in another.

The last paper, by Albert Ando and Stephen Goldfeld, presents an econometric model of the economy, with a detailed description of the monetary and fiscal sectors. This model provides a relatively convenient and complete method of analyzing the impact of detailed fiscal and monetary changes, and of tracing their later course through the economy. It can be used to revise earlier studies of fiscal and monetary action that were necessarily based on less satisfactory tools.

Aside from concerning themselves with stabilization policies, all papers in this volume share two features in common. One is that they are all quantitative, some less extensively than others. This reflects the conviction of the editors that economic knowledge, to be useful for stabilization policies, must be quantitative. The other is that they are all exploratory, and undoubtedly will be improved in the future with better techniques, better data, and a better theoretical framework. The momentum that studies in this general area have acquired in the past two decades is expected to continue, and at an accelerated rate.

HOWARD PACK*

Formula Flexibility:
A Quantitative Appraisal

"FORMULA FLEXIBILITY" is a fiscal action that activates a tax (or expenditure) change automatically when a certain pre-arranged signal of recession is observed. It differs from an automatic stabilizer in that the latter is built into the existing tax and transfer payment structure, while the former, when activated, changes the structure itself. The introduction of formula flexibility should increase the stability of the economy, a warranted improvement given the four postwar recessions in the United States as well as the sustained high levels of unemployment from 1957 through 1964.

During periods of low economic activity, the primary counter-cyclical policy used has been built-in flexibility, accompanied by sporadic and somewhat ineffective use of discretionary policy.[1] Both policies suffer from several disadvantages. For example, built-in flexibility can limit the severity of a cyclical movement already

* Economic Growth Center, Yale University.

[1] For a survey of recent U. S. fiscal policy, see A. E. Holmans, *United States Fiscal Policy: 1945–1959* (Oxford University Press, 1959); E. Cary Brown, "Fiscal Policy in the Post-war Period," in Ralph Freeman (ed.), *Post-War Economic Trends in the United States* (Harper and Bros., 1960), and Wilfred Lewis, Jr. *Federal Fiscal Policy in the Postwar Recessions* (Brookings Institution, 1962).

under way, but cannot reverse it;[2] also, it tends to retard recovery. As gross national product (GNP) increases from its trough, part of the rise is absorbed by tax receipts. Although some increase in tax receipts during a recovery may be desirable, an excessively high rate of growth of revenue during the early stages will hamper the expansion unless offset by higher government outlays. The effect of a restrictive budget seems to have played a major role in dampening the recoveries after the 1957–58 and 1960–61 recessions.[3]

The major drawback of discretionary policies is the time lag between the recognition of the need for a policy change and implementation. Although some rapid legislative actions on tax bills have been taken, they have not been intended primarily to combat an impending or on-going recession.[4] Therefore, these actions shed little light on the potentialities of rapid enactment of discretionary changes of a countercyclical nature. The President is allowed some flexibility in the timing of federal fiscal policies—e.g., he may delay or accelerate expenditures and tax refunds. However, the degree of flexibility available to him is limited. The objective of formula flexibility is to add another automatic, quick-acting, and quantitatively effective weapon to the countercyclical fiscal arsenal. Formula flexibility may be applied to expenditures as well as to tax changes, but this paper will be concerned only with the tax side.

Properties of Formula Flexibility

Formula flexibility combines features of both built-in flexibility and discretionary policy.[5] Tax rates would be reduced (or rates of

[2] However, Milton Friedman has shown that under certain assumptions about price flexibility this statement may be incorrect. See his "A Monetary and Fiscal Framework for Economic Stability," *American Economic Review*, Vol. 38, No. 3 (June 1948); reprinted in F. A. Lutz and L. W. Mints (ed.), *Readings in Monetary Theory* (Richard D. Irwin, Inc., 1951).

[3] *Economic Report of the President*, together with *The Annual Report of the Council of Economic Advisers* (U. S. Government Printing Office, 1962), pp. 78–82.

[4] For example, the Excise Tax Reduction Act of 1965 and the Tax Adjustment Act of 1966. The latter was intended to moderate inflationary pressures, but it merely accelerated some tax payments and delayed a number of scheduled excise tax reductions. It did not provide for any new taxes.

[5] See, for example, James E. Meade, *Consumers' Credits and Unemployment* (Oxford University Press, 1938); William Beveridge, *Full Employment in a Free Society* (W. W. Norton and Co., Inc., 1945); Albert G. Hart, *Money, Debt and Economic Activity*, 2nd ed. (Prentice-Hall, 1963): Everett E. Hagen, "Federal Taxation and Economic Stabilization,"

transfers increased) when some economic indicator forecasts a recession. The magnitude of the tax (transfer) change as well as precise details about when the change is to be activated would be embodied in prior legislation. Also, the conditions under which the rates would be restored to their previous levels or move to higher levels would be stipulated. Given such legislation, countercyclical action would not be subject to delays stemming from the need for legislative approval.

The difference between formula flexibility and built-in flexibility can be illustrated by a simple national income determination model. With built-in stabilizers alone, national product is

$$Y = \frac{C_0 + A}{1 - c(1 - \pi)},$$

where c is the marginal propensity to consume out of disposable income; C_0 is the constant in the consumption function; $(1 - \pi)$ is the percentage of net national product which becomes disposable income; and A includes all elements of net national product other than consumption, all assumed to be exogenous.

Formula flexibility may be viewed as altering the relationship between national product and disposable income, Y_d. Whereas $Y_d = Y(1 - \pi)$ under built-in flexibility, $Y_d = Y(1 - \pi + \pi')$ when formula flexibility is added, with π' reflecting the reduction in the tax rate occasioned by a recession (π' remaining in effect until "recovery" is achieved). A change in the tax rate on this account would increase the equilibrium level of the national product by

$$\frac{c\pi'}{\left[1 - c(1 - \pi)\right]\left[1 - c(1 - \pi + \pi')\right]}.^{[6]}$$

in *Federal Tax Policy for Economic Growth and Stability*, Joint Economic Committee, Papers Submitted by Panelists Appearing Before the Subcommittee on Tax Policy. 84 Cong. 1 sess. (Nov. 9, 1955).

[6] The slope of the new aggregate expenditure line is

$$\frac{1}{1 - c(1 - \pi + \pi')},$$

which is greater than the original slope. The static multiplier under formula flexibility is thus higher than that under built-in flexibility. This may seem paradoxical as the usefulness of built-in stabilizers has usually been defined in terms of their lowering the slope of the aggregate expenditure line and the inference might be that any effective stabilizer should achieve

The difficulties posed by a rapid rise in tax receipts as the economy recovers from a recession can be avoided by stipulating that the negative tax will remain in effect until actual product is within x percent of full employment product (x could, of course, be very small). Thus, although output may begin to increase, the rate structure will remain low. While it is true that, as income rises, tax receipts would increase because of the continued operation of the built-in stabilizers, the entire tax system would generate less revenue than it would in the absence of formula flexibility and therefore would offer less resistance to the return to full employment.

So far, the assumption has been made that, once the need for fiscal action was signaled, there would be a once-and-for-all change in the fiscal parameters. Alternatively, several (or continuous) changes in the fiscal parameters might be utilized, such changes depending on subsequent movements in the indicators. Both types of policy will be considered in this paper.[7]

Choice of Indicator and Policy Instruments

Derivation of Indicators

Although the goals of economic policy are numerous, the main one considered here is full employment, which is defined as the maintenance of the official U. S. rate of unemployment below a given level, say 4 percent. It is assumed that this is roughly equivalent to maintaining the rate of growth of GNP (in constant prices) at 3.5 percent a year, projected from 1955, as suggested by the Council of Economic Advisers.[8] The implications of the policies pursued upon goals other than employment will be discussed when relevant.

Since no indicator accurately predicts the target variable, GNP, a few months in advance, three alternatives may be considered,

the same result. However, the increased slope is due to the particular formulation of formula flexibility in this study, which utilizes marginal adjustments in tax rates to implement the policy. If lump-sum tax reductions were used, the new aggregate expenditure line would be higher than the prereduction line but parallel to it, i.e., the multiplier would be the same before and after the implementation of the tax cut.

[7] Most formula flexibility suggestions in the United States have embodied a one-time tax rate change as recession develops, and a restoration of the rates to prerecession levels when the economy exhibits symptoms of recovery. See, for example, Hart, *Money, Debt and Economic Activity*, and Hagen in *Federal Tax Policy*.

[8] See *Economic Report of the President*, 1962, pp. 50–53.

none of which is perfect. First, the GNP forecasts generated by one of the currently existing econometric models might be used. Without passing judgment on the merits of existing models, we chose not to deal with them in the present paper. Second, actual values of GNP in the recent past might be used as an indicator. This alternative amounts to assuming that GNP in the next period will be the same as GNP in the latest period, corrected for trend. Third, some indicator or indicators that are known to precede GNP movements might be used (these will be called *ad hoc* indicators). The last two methods are used in this paper and are discussed in turn.

A policy using the most recent GNP as a signal might be implemented by comparing actual with full employment GNP. If the former is not equal to the latter, the discrepancy may be taken as an indicator of the need for a policy change. This indicator thus triggers a shift in tax policy and also yields new information each quarter on the relative position of the economy vis-à-vis the full employment path. Full employment GNP is assumed to be the points along the 3.5 percent growth path mentioned above.[9] The insights gained from attempting to stabilize around such a growth path can be applied to other growth paths; any differences in policy would be mainly of magnitude rather than of method.

A good *ad hoc* indicator should predict turning points some time ahead of their occurrence,[10] and it should predict only those turning points which do in fact occur. For this study, several leading series[11] were examined, and four were chosen as meeting the requirements.[12] The four series are the average workweek, the gross accessions rate, and the layoff rate—all in the manufacturing sector—and new orders for durable goods.[13]

[9] For an extensive discussion of the problems involved in such a choice, see Michael E. Levy, *Fiscal Policy, Cycles and Growth* (National Industrial Conference Board, 1963), especially Chapter 5.

[10] However, correct interpretation of current movements should be considered acceptable, as often the existence of a recession has not been detected until four or five months after its onset.

[11] Selected from Geoffrey H. Moore (ed.), *Business Cycle Indicators* (Princeton University Press, 1961).

[12] For further details, see Appendix, pp. 39–40.

[13] For an analysis of the significance of these series, see Gerhard Bry, "The Timing of Cyclical Changes in the Average Workweek," Geoffrey H. Moore, "Leading and Confirming Indicators of General Business Indicators," and Victor Zarnowitz, "The Timing of Manufacturers' Orders During the Business Cycle," all in Moore (ed.), *Business Cycle Indicators*, pp. 485–505, 45–109, and 420–84, respectively.

Although the unemployment rate was not used directly, three of the series (layoffs,

To minimize false signals from disturbances that affect only a single series, three of the four series should predict a peak before a policy change is initiated. The peaks predicted by these data compare as follows with actual peaks as shown in the chronology of the National Bureau of Economic Research:

Predicted	Actual
November 1948	November 1948
October 1953	July 1953
May 1957	July 1957
May 1960	May 1960

However, because of delays in the publication of the data, these predictions would not have been made until two months after the above dates.[14]

These indicators of peaks were developed from data for the 1947–60 period. As a test of the reliability of the indicators, their performance was examined for the period between January 1961 and August 1965, a period which did not enter into the original decisions. The indicators did not predict any recession in this period and, in fact, no recession in GNP occurred. This is encouraging—especially given the widespread view during the summer of 1962 that a recession was imminent[15]—but the crucial test is whether they will accurately predict the next cyclical peak.

Choice of Stabilization Policy

Formula flexibility could be used in many ways, such as to vary the tax rates (corporate, personal, income, excise) and transfer payment rates or to change the rate of federal government expenditure.

accessions, and hours) deal with employment and they lead the unemployment rate. The layoff rate must increase or the accessions rate must decrease (or both) before unemployment can change. Moreover, before layoffs change, the average workweek will decline as employers reduce hours before beginning layoffs. In any case, use of the unemployment rate would have given approximately the same results as the indicators chosen, the unemployment rate lagging by a few months. For example, see the results obtained by the Council of Economic Advisers, using the unemployment rate, in *Economic Report of the President*, 1962, p. 74.

[14] It is necessary to work with the first revised set of series, published about eight weeks after a month is completed, rather than with the initial estimates, published four weeks after the close of the period, as the latter are subject to substantial revisions. The lag might be less, however, as the revised estimates presumably would be available within the government some time earlier than they become available to the public.

[15] See *State of the Economy and Policies for Full Employment*, Hearings Before the Joint Economic Committee, 87 Cong. 2 sess. (August 1962).

This study confines itself to the most often mentioned alternative,[16] variation in the starting rate of the personal income tax, which also has the advantage of being the simplest to implement.

The tax rates could be altered in two ways. First, they could be changed by a specific amount as soon as the signal was triggered by the indicator, and kept at this altered level until another signal was given to return it to the original. This is the "one-shot" policy. Second, the tax rates could be altered several times, or even continuously, throughout the course of a recession; the timing and magnitude of the changes would depend upon movements of the indicators. This is called a "continuous" policy.

"ONE-SHOT" POLICY. A major difficulty of the one-shot policy is the determination of the size of the tax reduction, once a recession is signaled. No indicator can provide information about the probable size of the *future* deviation of GNP from its full employment path; only a qualitative forecast is possible. Thus, the size of the tax reduction must be determined arbitrarily. The tax cut could be fixed in a dollar amount, say, $10 billion, or it could be proportional to current GNP. The former alternative seems dangerous, as the fixed figure may prove sufficient in the years immediately following the legislation but become increasingly inadequate as GNP grows. The proportionality rule is therefore preferable, and it should be so formulated that, once the indicator has signaled, tax rates would be reduced so that government revenues would decrease by 1 or 2 percent of current GNP or its previous peak. Of course, this rule is not necessarily optimal, as the severity of recessions may vary substantially and, in any given recession, the size of the tax cut may not be correct. However, some arbitrary rule is necessary, and this one is preferable to the other possibility.[17]

Another problem is the choice of an indicator to signal the restoration of the original tax rate structure. The occurrence of a

[16] See, for example, Commission on Money and Credit, *Money and Credit: Their Influence on Jobs, Prices and Growth* (Prentice-Hall, 1961): Albert G. Hart, *Defense Without Inflation* (Twentieth Century Fund, 1951); and Albert G. Hart and E. Cary Brown, *Financing Defense* (Twentieth Century Fund, 1951). Among the properties making the personal income tax the best fiscal instrument are the speed with which desired changes take effect, administrative simplicity, large yields, and a relatively small amount of uncertainty engendered by changes in the rates.

[17] The current "gap" at the time the signals occur could not be used as a measure of the required size of the tax cut as it would not provide information on the future path of demand.

trough (assuming that it could be readily identified) might serve as the restoration signal. However, this procedure might have the effect of weakening a recovery if tax rates were restored prematurely. A more useful indicator would be a capacity utilization measure (e.g., the McGraw-Hill index)[18] reaching a predetermined level, such as 94 percent. As a proxy for such a capacity measure, the ratio of actual to potential GNP is used in this study to terminate the tax reduction.

"CONTINUOUS" POLICIES. A better policy would be to continue to reduce tax rates as the recession proceeds, the changes depending on the deviation of actual from full employment GNP. This policy has two advantages: (1) The dose of additional demand can be adjusted continuously on the basis of observed changes in the gap. (2) The precise method of determining the stabilization dosage can be much more sophisticated; for instance, the dose might be based on past, as well as on current, differences between actual and desired GNP.

Consider the following policy as an example. A desired GNP level, Y^F, is determined for each period; if actual GNP, Y, differs from Y^F, a policy demand equal to $\gamma(Y^F - Y)$ is injected into the system. This may be called a proportional stabilization policy.[19] A proportional stabilization procedure by itself, however, will not completely eliminate the divergence between Y and Y^F[20] because,

[18] Annual Survey by McGraw-Hill Department of Economics, *Business Plans for New Plant and Equipment*.

[19] This terminology—as well as the terms, integral and derivative stabilizers—stems from the work of A. W. Phillips. See especially his article, "Stabilisation Policy in a Closed Economy," *Economic Journal*, Vol. 64, No. 254 (June 1954), pp. 290–323. See also his "Stabilisation Policy and the Time Forms of Lagged Responses," *Economic Journal*, Vol. 67, No. 266 (June 1957), pp. 265–77. For an exposition and elaboration of these articles, see R. G. D. Allen, *Mathematical Economics*, 2nd ed. (New York: St. Martins Press, 1959), Chapter 9.

[20] This can be shown by using the national income determination model presented above. The equilibrium level of income given there was

$$(1) \qquad\qquad Y = \frac{C_0 + A}{1 - c(1 - \pi)}.$$

Assume that if $Y \neq Y^F$, the government injects demand in proportion to their difference, i.e., $\gamma(Y^F - Y)$. Let $\bar{A}$ denote the level of $C_0 + A$ corresponding to Y^F, and consider a situation in which $C_0 + A$ is less than $\bar{A}$ by $\Delta\bar{A}$. Then, the difference between Y^F and Y becomes

$$(2) \qquad\qquad Y^F - Y = \frac{\Delta\bar{A}}{1 - c(1 - \pi)}.$$

as Y approaches Y^F the government-injected demand (which is itself a function of the gap) falls, thus causing overall demand to fall; Y^F can be approached asymptotically, but the gap cannot be closed completely.[21] The proportional policy may itself cause cyclical fluctuations, these being greater as γ increases and as the implementation lag rises.[22]

To eliminate completely the gap between Y^F and Y, an "integral stabilizer" may be introduced. This stabilizer injects demand which is opposite in sign and proportional to the sum of the differences between Y^F and Y over a number of periods; i.e., if f_i is the integral stabilization coefficient, the integral policy demand in quarter t of a cycle may be written as

$$f_i \sum_{\tau=0}^{n} (Y^F - Y)_{t-\tau},$$

where n is some predetermined constant. However, as Phillips has shown, if integral stabilizers *alone* were used to offset a decline in production, they might, themselves, introduce cycles and the approach to the desired level of production would be quite slow. For example, when Y^F is reached, the cumulated past deficiency is still forcing the integral stabilizer to impart more demand into the system.

If the integral and proportional policies are employed simul-

---

But under proportional stabilization, demand equal to $\gamma(Y^F - Y)$ is fed into the system so that the total difference between Y^F and Y is now

$$(3) \qquad\qquad Y^F - Y = \frac{\Delta \bar{A} - \gamma(Y^F - Y)}{1 - c(1 - \pi)}$$

from which it is found that

$$(4) \qquad\qquad Y^F - Y = \frac{\Delta \bar{A}}{1 - c(1 - \pi) + \gamma}.$$

If autonomous expenditures remain depressed, the deviation from full employment can be eliminated only by making γ infinite, i.e.,

$$\lim_{\gamma \to \infty} \frac{\Delta \bar{A}}{1 - c(1 - \pi) + \gamma} = 0.$$

This is based on Phillips, in *Economic Journal*, June 1954.

[21] If the government injected demand had the effect of raising A (i.e., a pump-priming effect), then the gap could be closed by proportional stabilizers alone. It is assumed that this does not occur in the example.

[22] Phillips, in *Economic Journal*, June 1954.

taneously, the results are much better than when either is used alone. A proportional stabilizer acts to limit the fluctuations caused by the integral stabilizer, and the integral helps to obtain the complete correction which the proportional alone cannot achieve. The additional correction provided by the proportional policy prevents the cyclical amplitudes from becoming as large as they would be in its absence. It is true, at least in the simple systems used by Phillips, that a combined proportional and integral stabilization policy will permit the achievement of full employment, with fairly small fluctuations resulting from the use of the integral policy. The cycles introduced by the combined policy may be further reduced in amplitude by the introduction of a "derivative" stabilization policy, i.e., a policy that injects demand which is proportional in size and opposite in sign to the rate of change of output. Thus, if demand begins to rise very rapidly, owing to the combined integral and proportional factors, a third dose of demand, i.e., $-f_d(Y_{t-1} - Y_{t-2})$, is injected. This last factor should reduce the likelihood of overshooting, and in Phillips' experiments it had precisely this effect.[23]

The effects of the three types of policies are added to obtain the net effect. For example, let $f_p = 0.5$, $f_i = 0.2$, and $f_d = 0.3$, and let $\bar{P}_t$ denote $(Y_t^F - Y_t)$; if

$$\bar{P}_t = 20, \ \sum_{\tau=0}^{n} \bar{P}_{t-\tau} = 40, \text{ and } (Y_t - Y_{t-1}) = 10,$$

the total demand injected is 15.[24]

Phillips concentrates on stabilizing around a fixed level of production while the interest of the present study is in stabilizing around a growth path. In this case, the interpretation of the proportional and integral stabilizers remains the same; i.e., the proportional acts on the current absolute deviations from the growth path, while the integral acts on the accumulated gap between the growth path GNP and actual GNP. It is essential, however, to re-

---

[23] The use of a derivative element may also mitigate or prevent cycles caused by an inventory or fixed investment accelerator. See Richard A. Musgrave, *The Theory of Public Finance* (McGraw-Hill Book Co., 1959), Chapter 21.

[24] Since $f_p \bar{P}_t = 10$, $f_i \sum_{\tau=0}^{n} \bar{P}_{t-\tau} = 8$, and $-f_d(Y_t - Y_{t-1}) = -3$.

interpret the derivative stabilizer. In this case, the derivative stabilizer operates on the rate of change of the gap rather than on the rate of change of actual output. If $(Y^F - Y)_t$ is denoted as K_t, the derivative stabilizer works on $-(K_t - K_{t-1}) = (Y_t - Y_{t-1}) - (Y_t^F - Y_{t-1}^F)$ rather than on $Y_t - Y_{t-1}$ as it previously did. While in the nongrowth case any increase in Y—i.e., $Y_t > Y_{t-1}$—implies a closing of the gap and a need for moderating the influence of the other two stabilizers, in the growth case $Y_t > Y_{t-1}$ does not necessarily imply that $K_t < K_{t-1}$, as Y^F may be growing faster than Y and the gap may become larger even though Y is increasing.

Simulation Analysis of Formula Flexibility

To analyze formula flexibility, simulation is used in this paper, and a model estimated by Gary Fromm is employed, with a slight modification.[25] The characteristics of the modified Fromm model are first reviewed briefly; then, the results of the simulation analysis are summarized.

Characteristics of the Modified Fromm Model

The modification of the model is in the consumption function. In the model, the response of consumption to an increase in disposable income is much slower than would be expected on the basis of other estimates. Therefore the following equation is substituted here for the Fromm consumption function:

$$C_t = .0005 + .4187Y_{t-1} + .5616(C_{t-1} - C_{t-2})/2$$
$$(.0782) \qquad (.0843)$$
$$R^2 = .99,$$

where C_t is aggregate consumption in quarter t and Y_{t-1} is disposable income in quarter $t - 1$. With this equation, the response in consumption to a given increase in disposable income proves to be more reasonable than that generated with the original equation.

[25] See Gary Fromm, "Inventories, Business Cycles and Economic Stabilization," in *Inventory Fluctuations and Economic Stabilization*, Part IV, Joint Economic Committee, 87 Cong. 2 sess. (1962). The choice of Fromm's model is primarily a matter of convenience. Before the results can be considered reliable, the experiments should be repeated with other models, such as the Brookings-SSRC model; see James S. Duesenberry and others (eds.). *The Brookings Quarterly Econometric Model of the United States* (Rand McNally & Co. and North-Holland Publishing Co., 1965).

Given the lagged values of the endogenous variables in period t, and the exogenous variables for the period considered, the path of endogenous variables is computed in the simulation for as many periods as the exogenous inputs are supplied.[26] Given the initial conditions for period t and the value of the exogenous variables, GNP for period t is computed by separately calculating each of the major demand components. Once GNP is computed, disposable income is obtained by generating each of the major items that account for the difference between the two. The endogenous variables thus computed for period t become predetermined variables for $t + 1$.

The GNP values computed from the Fromm model are compared in Table 1 with actual values in the national accounts for the corresponding quarters during the last three recessions. For convenience the former shall be designated "reference simulations." The decline in GNP during the 1953 recession is approximated quite closely; the actual peak to trough fall in GNP was $8.2 billion, while the computed value in the simulation shows a decrease of $7.7 billion. Also, the computed magnitudes during the recovery are close to those in the national accounts. As for timing, the actual trough and the simulation trough occur within one quarter of each other.

The results for the 1957 recession are not as good. Whereas the peak to trough fall in actual GNP was $15.4 billion, GNP in the model falls by only $4.1 billion. This is a result of the failure of the model to predict the sharp drop in business investment. Nevertheless, except for the failure to duplicate the large drop in GNP between the fourth quarter of 1957 and the first quarter of 1958, the model yields reasonable quantitative results. For example, in the periods following the trough, the simulated increases in GNP correspond fairly well to actual increases. The timing properties again are good, the model's trough occurring in the same period as that of actual GNP.

For the 1960–61 recession, computed GNP is only a fair approximation of actual GNP. The former drops by about $3 billion from its peak for one quarter but immediately rebounds and re-

---

[26] The exogenous variables are government expenditures, subsidies less current surplus of government enterprises, and excess of wage accruals over disbursements.

TABLE 1. Gross National Product (GNP) Generated in Reference Simulations Compared with GNP in National Accounts, 1953–55, 1957–59, and 1960–62

(In billions of current dollars)

Year and Quarter	Reference Simulations[a]	National Accounts[b]
1953 III	367.1	367.1
IV	364.0	361.0
1954 I	359.4	360.0
II	359.6	358.9
III	363.2	362.0
IV	368.1	370.8
1955 I	374.2	384.3
1957 III	448.3	448.3
IV	445.1	442.3
1958 I	444.2	432.9
II	450.4	437.2
III	458.4	447.0
IV	466.2	460.6
1959 I	471.1	472.2
II	477.0	487.8
III	484.1	482.7
1960 II	506.4[c]	504.1[c]
III	503.3	503.5
IV	506.7	502.1
1961 I	513.5	501.4
II	520.1	513.9
III	529.4	522.4
IV	541.5	536.9
1962 I	550.5	545.5
II	559.0	553.4

[a] Values computed from the Fromm model; see text.
[b] Estimates of U. S. Department of Commerce.
[c] The discrepancy between national account GNP in 1960-II and that in the reference simulation results from the use of revised estimates for the former, whereas the reference simulation was executed before the revised figures became available.

sumes its growth; actual GNP in the third quarter of 1960 fell only slightly from its peak and remained within $3 billion (at seasonally adjusted annual rates) of this peak for the next two quarters. After the trough in actual GNP occurs, however, computed and actual GNP rapidly begin to approach each other, suggesting that even if the model does not describe the GNP decline particularly well, it provides a fair description of the path of aggregate demand. This result may have been due to the special conditions of this period, as the economy remained substantially below capacity and the 1960 "recession" was insignificant when compared with the general shortfall from the growth path.[27]

Results of the Simulations: "Continuous" Policies

The continuous policies utilize proportional, integral, and derivative stabilizers. It is assumed that the three stabilizers come into play when actual GNP (Y) is below its growth path value (Y^F), and that the economy is allowed to run without controls during prosperity (when $Y = Y^F$). As the three periods during which ($Y^F - Y$) is positive coincide mainly with the last three postwar recessions, the policies are tested for these years only.

The initial conditions in each recession are assumed to be unaffected by any previous use of formula flexibility. The experiments for each of the three recessions should, therefore, be interpreted as indicating the performance of the economy on the assumption that the particular policy was being utilized *for the first time*.[28]

The procedure used in the simulations is to compute GNP at the end of every quarter (t) and to reduce tax rates immediately (at the end of t), according to the Phillips formulae. In the next quarter, ($t + 1$), disposable income is larger by the amount of the tax cut, GNP is again computed, and tax rates are again lowered after the end of the quarter. These steps are repeated until the GNP gap is eliminated.[29]

GAINS IN GNP. Tables 2, 3, and 4 show the principal results of the simulations. In each table, column 1 indicates the deviation of refer-

---

[27] In fact, the "recession" may have been partially the result of the steel strike which occurred during the latter part of 1959. This may be inadequately represented in the initial conditions of the 1960 simulation, thus resulting in the model's imprecise representation of the downturn.

[28] This ignores a number of considerations, e.g., (1) the structure of the economy might not be the same after the use of formula flexibility (e.g., the investment functions might shift upward in view of the increased likelihood of stable demand) and (2) the initial conditions would have been different, because of the increased growth in earlier years.

[29] This procedure assumes, first, that accurate preliminary estimates of GNP can be obtained; and, second, that tax rates can be adjusted immediately upon receipt of the GNP estimates. The assumption regarding the speed of the tax cuts is probably fairly realistic, as the experience with the 1964 tax cut indicates; the new rates went into effect within two weeks after the passage of the bill by Congress. With a two-week delay, the altered rates would be operative for five-sixths of $t + 1$, and almost the full consumption impact would be felt in this period. The assumption about the speed and accuracy with which the initial GNP estimate may be obtained is less certain.

TABLE 2. Deviation between Growth Path Gross National Product (GNP) and Simulated GNP Using Various "Continuous" Policies, 1953–55[a]

(Figures other than percentages, in billions of dollars at 1954 prices)

Year and Quarter	Reference Simulation	$f_p=.5$	$f_p=1.0$	$f_i=1.0$	$f_i=1.0$ $f_d=.5$	$f_i=.5$ $f_p=.5$	$f_i=.5$ $f_p=.5$ $f_d=.2$	$f_i=.2$ $f_p=.5$	$f_i=.8$ $f_p=.8$ $f_d=.4$
	(1)	(2)	(3)	(4)	(5)	(6)	(7)	(8)	(9)
1953 IV	− 6.3	− 6.3	− 6.3	− 6.3	− 6.3	− 6.3	− 6.3	− 6.3	− 6.3
1954 I	−15.8	−14.1	−12.5	−12.5	−10.3	−12.5	−11.6	−13.5	− 8.8
II	−19.8	−15.3	−11.5	− 8.4	− 7.0	− 9.9	− 9.3	−13.0	− 5.3
III	−20.1	−12.9	− 8.2	1.6	0.4	− 3.3	− 3.4	− 8.6	0.5
IV	−18.9	−10.2	− 5.6	10.0	6.2	2.6	1.7	3.9	3.3
1955 I	−16.8	− 7.6	− 4.0	12.3	8.6	5.8	4.7	− 0.1	4.2
Percentage of GNP loss offset by policy	—	32.0	50.8	72.1	75.8	67.2	68.7	53.5	79.1
Amount of overshooting of growth path	0	0	0	23.9	15.2	8.4	6.4	3.9	8.0

[a] f_p = value of proportional stabilizer; f_i = value of integral stabilizer; f_d = value of derivative stabilizer.

ence from full employment GNP (where the latter is defined as the 3.5 percent growth path). The remaining columns show the deviations from full employment GNP when the proportional (f_p), integral (f_i), and derivative (f_d) stabilization elements assume the values indicated at the top of each column. The reference simulation is used as a benchmark for evaluating the efficiency of the policies; i.e., for each policy, the path of GNP, after the policy parameter alteration, is compared with the reference values.

Proportional policies of .5 and 1.0 were tested. In all three recessions, the larger the value of f_p, the greater is the increase in GNP above that in the reference simulation. In the early quarters following the initiation of the policy, the differences between the two policies are substantial; but as time passes, these differences are reduced. For example, in 1958 II, when $f_p = 1.0$, GNP is $6.2 billion greater than when $f_p = .5$. By 1959 I, this difference is reduced to $3.5 billion. This result is not difficult to explain. The higher proportional element reduces the gap quickly, leading, after a short period, to an increase in taxes and a reduction in consumption. On the other hand, when $f_p = .5$, the initial decrease in the gap is small and the increase in tax revenue is negligible, thus allowing continued tax reductions and a greater gain in GNP in the later periods

TABLE 3. Deviation between Growth Path Gross National Product (GNP) and Simulated GNP Using Various "Continuous" Policies, 1957–59[a]

(Figures other than percentages, in billions of dollars at 1954 prices)

Year and Quarter	Reference Simulation (1)	$f_p = .5$ (2)	$f_p = 1.0$ (3)	$f_i = 1.0$ (4)	$f_i = 1.0$ $f_d = .5$ (5)	$f_i = .5$ $f_p = .5$ (6)	$f_i = .5$ $f_p = .5$ $f_d = .2$ (7)	$f_i = .2$ $f_p = .5$ (8)	$f_i = .8$ $f_p = .8$ $f_d = .4$ (9)
1957 IV	−20.6	−20.6	−20.6	−20.6	−20.6	−20.6	−20.6	−20.6	−20.6
1958 I	−27.2	−22.2	−17.1	−17.1	−14.9	−17.1	−16.3	−20.2	− 9.3
II	−26.8	−18.1	−11.9	− 1.9	− 2.9	− 6.9	− 7.2	−13.4	− 2.2
III	−24.7	−13.6	− 7.2	12.7	9.0	2.8	1.8	− 6.0	− 6.7
IV	−22.9	−11.5	− 6.8	17.0	12.5	6.3	5.0	− 2.1	4.4
1959 I	−24.1	−13.4	− 9.9	8.5	7.6	3.2	2.5	− 3.1	1.2
II	−24.6	−14.6	−11.5	− 3.5	0.6	− 0.5	− 0.1	− 4.1	− 2.7
III	−24.1	−15.0	−11.9	−12.3	− 5.4	− 3.1	− 2.1	− 4.5	− 2.8
Percentage of GNP loss offset by policy	—	32.0	47.5	67.6	73.2	71.2	72.0	58.6	76.2
Amount of overshooting of growth path	0	0	0	38.2	29.7	14.3	9.3	0	5.6

[a] See footnote to Table 2.

than occurs when $f_p = 1.0$. Hence, the main benefit from a high proportional stabilizer accrues in the early part of the recession (although the higher is f_p, the higher the GNP values tend to be in all quarters).

In all three recessions, the proportional policy proves to be incapable of restoring the economy to its growth path. In the 1953–55 period, the gap is reduced to a small amount ($4 billion in 1955 I when $f_p = 1.0$), but the economy, in any case, is fairly buoyant in this period, as shown by the relatively small gap between growth path and reference GNP. Even under these favorable conditions, the proportional stabilizers are not able to eliminate the gap. It is not surprising, therefore, that in the 1957–59 and 1960–62 periods, when the GNP generated in the reference simulation is far below capacity, the proportional stabilizers fail to close the gap completely. This characteristic of the proportional stabilizers is thus in accord with our earlier theoretical discussion.

The use of the proportional stabilizer does not lead to any additional cycling, although theoretically this could occur. It is possible that the rapid adjustment of taxes minimizes the instability introduced by the proportional stabilizer. However, a few simulations were run in which the tax reductions introduced at the end of $t + 1$ were dependent on the gap existing at the end of t. It was found that no additional fluctuations were caused by this lag. Further sensitivity tests along this line are certainly necessary.

Column 4 lists the results of the integral policy when $f_i = 1.0$. The rapid elimination of the gap within a year after the initiation of the policy is striking. The integral stabilizer introduces its own cycle, however, which is superimposed on the original. To dampen these cycles, derivative and proportional stabilizers are added.

The effect of the addition of a derivative stabilizer of .5 to an integral stabilizer of 1.0 is shown in column 5. As expected, the addition of the derivative element cuts down the overshooting of the growth line. Furthermore, the cycles introduced by the integral element are substantially moderated. For example, when the two policies during 1959 are compared, it is seen that the derivative stabilizer helps to keep GNP well above the level prevailing in its absence (see especially 1959 II and III). Similarly, during 1962 (see Table 4), the derivative element aids in maintaining aggregate demand near the growth path despite the downturn induced by the integral stabilizer. Even with the derivative stabilizer, overshooting

TABLE 4. Deviation between Growth Path Gross National Product (GNP) and Simulated GNP Using Various "Continuous" Policies, 1960–62[a]

(Figures other than percentages, in billions of dollars of 1954 prices)

Year and Quarter	Reference Simulation (1)	$f_p = .5$ (2)	$f_p = 1.0$ (3)	$f_i = 1.0$ (4)	$f_i = 1.0$ $f_d = .5$ (5)	$f_i = .5$ $f_p = .5$ (6)	$f_i = .5$ $f_p = .5$ $f_d = .2$ (7)	$f_i = .2$ $f_p = .5$ (8)	$f_i = .8$ $f_p = .8$ $f_d = .4$ (9)
1960 III	−30.2	−30.2	−30.2	−30.2	−30.2	−30.2	−30.2	−30.2	−30.2
IV	−33.4	−26.3	−19.1	−19.1	−16.9	−19.1	−18.2	−23.4	− 8.6
1961 I	−33.3	−22.4	−15.0	− 0.6	− 3.4	− 7.8	− 9.4	−16.2	− 3.4
II	−33.2	−19.5	−11.5	14.1	9.8	1.3	0.2	− 9.8	7.0
III	−33.1	−16.7	−10.5	19.5	15.1	6.2	4.9	− 4.6	4.7
IV	−26.8	−13.2	− 8.4	15.1	15.0	8.4	8.0	0.1	7.0
1962 I	−25.5	−14.2	−11.3	0.0	4.2	3.3	3.5	− 1.0	− 1.6
II	−25.3	−16.0	−13.3	−14.2	− 5.8	− 2.4	− 1.1	− 3.4	− 2.8
Percentage of GNP loss offset by policy	—	30.9	46.0	67.2	70.2	69.0	69.2	50.2	74.0
Amount of overshooting of growth path	0	0	0	48.7	44.1	19.2	16.6	0.1	18.7

[a] See footnote to Table 2.

still occurs and proportional stabilizers must be employed to reduce it.

Column 6 presents the results when $f_i = .5$ and $f_p = .5$. Here the amount of overshooting is fairly large, given the small size of the correction factors. This indicates the importance of a derivative element even when the values of the two other elements are relatively low. As shown in column 7, the addition of a small derivative element (.2) substantially reduces the overshooting and helps to maintain the system at levels close to those of the growth path.

The GNP profile generated when $f_i = .8$, $f_p = .8$, and $f_d = .4$ is indicated in column 9. In all three recessions, the use of the three stabilizers together closes the gap within four quarters of the initiation of the policy. Furthermore, once the growth path is attained, aggregate demand is kept within 1 percent of the GNP growth path in all three periods, except for three quarters (1958 III, 1961 II, and 1961 IV). Of course, perfect stabilization, if defined as the absence of any deviation from the growth path, is impossible in a discrete system where taxes respond with a lag to the appearance of the gap.[30] Nevertheless, the behavior of GNP under such a policy is quite good if the criterion of success is minimization of the absolute deviations of actual from growth path GNP.

Earlier, it was seen that the proportional policy used alone is incapable of restoring the system to its growth path (see columns 2 and 3). However, as shown in column 8, the addition of a small integral element (.2) permits complete correction, even with a low value (.5) for f_p. The combined policy is also more effective than the proportional policy of 1.0. This is to be expected, as the integral stabilizer will eventually increase tax reductions sufficiently to compensate for the lower proportional element. This result is important if the permissible sizes of the various elements of the policy are confined to narrow limits, for it underlines the importance of including some integral element, even if quite small, in the overall policy.[31]

---

[30] Phillips, using a continuous system, shows that perfect stabilization may be attained when the correct values for the three stabilizers are used. This is possible because, in his system, government policy demand responds instantaneously to the onset of a gap. See Phillips, in *Economic Journal* (June 1954).

[31] Of course, low boundary values for f_i might nevertheless result in enormous tax cuts. If boundaries were set, they would be more likely to appear in the form of a limit on the total size of tax reductions rather than on any one parameter.

The foregoing discussion suggests that a Phillips-type policy could have raised total U. S. output substantially.[32] The most potent policies are those which contain some integral element, used jointly with the other stabilizers. They are effective in raising output in any period of depression and in restoring the system to full employment. On the other hand, proportional stabilizers, if used alone, are most effective in periods when demand is basically buoyant and the system tends to return to full employment by itself. In such a period, the proportional stabilizers cut the interim loss in output, although even here the addition of an integral stabilizer results in closing the gap more quickly.

Thus far, the GNP profiles which the various policies generate have been compared. It would also be helpful to have one measure which summarizes the effectiveness of the policies and indicates how much is the reduction in output lost when formula flexibility is followed. To obtain such a measure, denote the full employment GNP growth path values by Y^F, the GNP values generated in the reference simulation by Y^R, and the simulated GNP values when formula flexibility is followed by Y^S. In the absence of formula flexibility, the loss in output is $\sum_t (Y^F - Y^R)$, the summation being over the quarters in the recession. When formula flexibility is followed, the loss is reduced by $\sum_t (Y^S - Y^R)$. However, this last expression overstates the gain from fiscal policy, for $Y^S - Y^R$ includes the amounts by which GNP has overshot the growth path when an integral stabilizer is present. Let

$$D_t = \begin{array}{l} Y_t^S - Y_t^R \ \text{if} \ Y_t^F - Y_t^S > 0 \\ Y_t^F - Y_t^R \ \text{if} \ Y_t^F - Y_t^S \le 0. \end{array}$$

Then $\sum_t D_t / \sum (Y^F - Y^R)_t$ is a convenient summary measure of the effectiveness of a given policy. These percentages are listed in the second from the last row in Tables 2, 3, and 4.

The last row in each of the tables gives total amounts (in billions of dollars) of overshooting for each policy during the recession. If two policies had the same percentage offset, the one which

---

[32] The assumption here is that the behavioral relations given by the model would have held under a stabilization scheme much different from the scheme which existed.

TABLE 5. Deficits under Various "Continuous" Policies, 1953–55[a]

(Quarterly figures at annual rates, in billions of dollars)

Year and Quarter	Reference Simulation	$f_p = .5$	$f_p = 1.0$	$f_i = 1.0$	$f_i = 1.0$ $f_d = .5$	$f_i = .5$ $f_p = .5$	$f_i = .5$ $f_p = .5$ $f_d = .2$	$f_i = .2$ $f_p = .5$	$f_i = .8$ $f_p = .8$ $f_d = .4$
	(1)	(2)	(3)	(4)	(5)	(6)	(7)	(8)	(9)
1953 IV	− 9.4	−12.7	−15.9	−15.9	−20.3	−16.0	−17.6	−14.0	−23.4
1954 I	−10.4	−16.8	−21.5	−27.8	−26.8	−24.7	−24.5	−20.1	−27.6
II	− 6.2	−11.9	−14.1	−28.4	−22.6	−21.3	−19.4	−16.4	−19.0
III	− 5.8	− 9.0	− 8.5	−21.4	−15.7	−15.8	−14.0	−13.2	− 9.2
IV	− 4.1	− 5.0	− 3.0	− 5.3	− 5.5	− 6.8	− 6.5	− 7.8	− 2.1
1955 I	− 4.3	− 3.3	− 1.3	8.4	2.6	− 1.0	− 1.9	− 4.8	1.5
Total deficit	40.2	58.7	64.3	90.4	88.3	85.6	83.9	76.3	79.8
Incremental total deficit	—	18.5	24.1	50.2	48.1	45.4	43.7	36.1	39.6
Incremental deficit on annual basis		4.6	6.0	12.6	12.0	11.4	10.9	9.0	9.9

[a] See footnote to Table 2.

TABLE 6. Deficits under Various "Continuous" Policies, 1957–59[a]

(Quarterly figures at annual rates, in billions of dollars)

Year and Quarter	Reference Simulation	$f_p = .5$	$f_p = 1.0$	$f_i = 1.0$	$f_i = 1.0$ $f_d = .5$	$f_i = .5$ $f_p = .5$	$f_i = .5$ $f_p = .5$ $f_d = .2$	$f_i = .2$ $f_p = .5$	$f_i = .8$ $f_p = .8$ $f_d = .4$
	(1)	(2)	(3)	(4)	(5)	(6)	(7)	(8)	(9)
1957 IV	0	−11.2	−22.5	−22.5	−27.5	−22.5	−24.5	−15.8	−40.1
1958 I	−4.2	−14.0	−18.3	−40.9	−43.3	−29.6	−27.2	−20.9	−25.1
II	−5.8	−11.4	−11.3	−36.7	−29.2	−24.0	−21.9	−18.3	−19.8
III	−5.8	− 7.1	− 3.8	−14.8	−12.8	−12.1	−11.3	−12.1	− 0.2
IV	−5.4	− 4.9	− 2.9	8.2	− 0.2	− 3.7	− 5.4	− 7.9	− 3.1
1959 I	−3.8	− 4.2	− 5.0	17.9	5.2	− 1.6	− 4.2	− 6.5	− 3.6
II	−3.0	− 4.0	− 6.1	10.3	3.7	− 3.4	− 4.8	− 6.4	− 9.7
III	−1.6	− 2.9	− 4.9	− 6.4	− 2.8	− 5.7	− 5.6	− 5.7	− 8.5
Total deficit	29.6	59.7	74.8	84.9	106.9	102.6	104.9	93.6	110.1
Incremental total deficit	—	30.1	45.2	55.3	77.3	73.0	75.3	64.0	80.5
Incremental deficit on annual basis		7.5	11.3	13.8	19.3	18.2	18.8	16.0	20.1

[a] See footnote to Table 2.

exhibited less overshooting would be the more desirable as it would tend to generate less inflationary pressure.

DEFICIT UNDER THE SEVERAL POLICIES. Of course, all of the policies which have been discussed result in deficits that exceed the reference deficits (see Tables 5, 6, and 7). It is evident that the larger the initial gap, the greater are the deficits during the earlier quarters of each recession. For example, the deficits under a proportional policy of 1.0 are much larger during the first part of the 1960 recession that in the comparable period in the 1953–55 downturn. However, once the gap begins to close there is little systematic relation between the size of the initial gap and the deficits.

Deficits associated with policies containing an integral element are higher than those associated with purely proportional policies. Whereas the multiplicand for the proportional stabilizer is $(Y^F - Y^S)_t$, the multiplicand for the integral stabilizer is

$$\sum_{\tau=0}^{n} (Y^F - Y^S)_{t-\tau},$$

and f_i is usually not sufficiently smaller than f_p to equalize the deficits. However, the differences among the deficits decline rapidly as the integral stabilizer eliminates the gap, whereas the continuing gap under the proportional policy necessitates sustained tax cuts. Nevertheless, the sum of the deficits over an entire recession is higher for policies containing an integral element.

The incremental deficit may be defined as the deficit generated when each policy is followed minus the reference deficit. Very often this magnitude is relatively small following the first stage in each recession when large deficits do occur. For example, from 1961 III through 1962 II the deficits in the reference simulation total $6 billion at an annual rate. When $f_i = .5$ and $f_p = .5$, the figure is

TABLE 7. Deficits under Various "Continuous" Policies, 1960–62[a]

(Quarterly figures at annual rates, in billions of dollars)

Year and Quarter	Reference Simulation	$f_p=.5$	$f_p=1.0$	$f_i=1.0$	$f_i=1.0$ $f_d=.5$	$f_i=.5$ $f_p=.5$	$f_i=.5$ $f_p=.5$ $f_d=.2$	$f_i=.2$ $f_p=.5$	$f_i=.8$ $f_p=.8$ $f_d=.4$
	(1)	(2)	(3)	(4)	(5)	(6)	(7)	(8)	(9)
1960 III	−2.3	−19.6	−36.9	−36.9	−42.3	−37.9	−39.1	−26.5	−62.0
IV	−2.2	−13.7	−17.0	−51.7	−40.3	−34.3	−30.1	−23.0	−32.3
1961 I	−6.3	−13.3	−13.3	−46.0	−40.2	−29.7	−28.6	−22.3	−29.0
II	−7.8	−11.0	− 8.1	−21.1	−21.4	−18.8	−18.7	−18.1	− 4.5
III	−6.1	− 6.6	− 4.6	8.4	− 1.9	− 6.9	− 8.8	−11.5	− 6.3
IV	−7.0	− 5.1	− 3.0	24.1	12.5	− 0.2	− 1.9	− 7.7	− 5.2
1962 I	−7.0	− 6.2	− 7.7	17.7	7.2	− 2.5	− 5.2	− 8.3	−13.2
II	−4.0	− 4.7	− 7.5	− 3.2	− 0.4	− 6.0	− 6.5	− 7.4	− 9.9
Total deficit	42.7	80.2	98.1	108.7	126.8	136.3	138.9	124.8	162.4
Incremental total deficit	—	37.5	55.4	66.0	123.5	84.1	96.2	82.1	119.7
Incremental deficit on annual basis		9.4	13.8	16.6	30.8	21.0	24.0	20.6	30.0

[a] See footnote to Table 2.

$3.9 billion and, when $f_i = .2$ and $f_p = .5$, it is $8.7 billion; in the former case the incremental deficit is about $-$2 billion, and in the latter case it is $2.7 billion.

It should be emphasized that the deficits required to generate full employment are closely linked to the size of the deficits in the first few periods: the larger the gap, the greater the tax cuts and the longer it takes to close the gap. This may be seen by comparing the same policies for 1953–55 and 1960–62. If an integral stabilizer is used, the deficits will become greater as the large early gaps continue to force tax reductions even as the economy approaches the full employment path. This suggests that the integral stabilizer should be modified so that the initial gap has less weight in the determination of current tax rates. The effect of such a procedure on the effectiveness of the integral policy would then have to be examined. Given the frequency with which the growth path is overshot, it is likely that the major effect of this weighting procedure would be to cut the amount of overshooting. If this is true, the deficits shown here represent high estimates of the deficits that might be incurred under formula flexibility.

There is a further reason for believing that the deficits are overstated. In each of the recessions, it is assumed that formula flexibility is being used for the first time.[33] However, if formula flexibility had first been used in 1953 and continued thereafter, the huge GNP gaps that existed at the beginning of the 1957 and 1960 recessions would not have developed, even if the downturns in GNP had occurred. Thus the large tax cuts in the early quarters of each recession would have been smaller, and the deficit would have been reduced.

PRICE EFFECTS. The effects of the various policies on prices should, of course, be considered.[34] The GNP implicit price deflator performs quite well in the model. Table 8 compares the actual ratio of the GNP price deflator in the last quarter of each recession to that in the first quarter with the ratio obtained in the reference simulation. Although there is some overstatement in the simulation, the

---

[33] This is reflected in the simulations by taking the actual data from the national accounts as the initial conditions. See page 18.

[34] Expectational effects of rapid price movements may affect the economy's behavior. However, the model presented in this paper does not include any proxy variables for price expectations.

TABLE 8. Ratio of Implicit Price Deflator in Last Quarter to That in First Quarter of 1953–55, 1957–59, and 1960–62 Recessions

Ratio Compared	1953–55	1957–59	1960–62
Actual	101.4	103.5	102.7
Reference simulation	101.8	103.5	103.7

TABLE 9. Implicit Price Deflator under Various "Continuous" Policies, 1953–55[a]

Year and Quarter	Reference	$f_p = .5$	$f_p = 1.0$	$f_i = 1.0$	$f = 1.0$ $f_d = .5$	$f_i = .5$ $f_p = .5$	$f_i = .5$ $f_p = .5$ $f_d = .2$	$f_i = .2$ $f_p = .5$	$f_i = .8$ $f_p = .8$ $f_d = .4$
	(1)	(2)	(3)	(4)	(5)	(6)	(7)	(8)	(9)
1953 III	99.1	99.1	99.1	99.1	99.1	99.1	99.1	99.1	99.2
IV	99.7	99.7	99.7	99.7	99.7	99.7	99.7	99.7	99.7
1954 I	100.2	100.2	100.2	100.2	100.2	100.2	100.2	100.2	100.2
II	100.5	100.5	100.5	100.5	100.5	100.5	100.5	100.5	100.5
III	100.6	100.7	100.8	100.8	100.9	100.8	100.8	100.7	100.9
IV	100.8	101.0	101.1	101.3	101.3	101.3	101.2	101.1	101.4
1955 I	100.9	101.3	101.5	101.9	102.0	101.7	101.8	101.5	102.0
Ratio of 1955 I to 1953 III	101.8	102.2	102.4	102.8	102.9	102.7	102.7	102.4	102.9

^a See footnote to Table 2.

simulated behavior approximates actual price performance very well. Accordingly, the behavior of prices in the various simulations is likely to be fairly reliable.

Tables 9, 10, and 11 compare the price deflators in the simulations with the reference deflators in the three recessions. In the 1953–55 recession, the inflation induced by the various policies is relatively small; prices rise at most by 1 percent more than in the reference simulation. In the two later recessions, however, the inflation is somewhat greater. For example, when $f_i = .8$, $f_p = .8$, $f_d = .4$, the price level is 3.0 percent higher than in the reference simulation from 1957 III to 1959 III, and 3.8 percent higher from 1960 II through 1962 II.[35] Thus, in the former case the rate of increase of prices is accelerated by about 1.25 percent a year and in the latter by about 1.50 percent a year. As the policies compared are extremely powerful ones, these price increases are probably outer limits.

[35] These are calculated by dividing the last figure in column 9 by the last in the reference simulation column, i.e., 106.6/103.5 and 107.6/103.7.

TABLE 10. Implicit Price Deflator under Various "Continuous" Policies, 1957–59[a]

Year and Quarter	Reference	$f_p=.5$	$f_p=1.0$	$f_i=1.0$	$f_i=1.0$ $f_d=.5$	$f_i=.5$ $f_p=.5$	$f_i=.5$ $f_p=.5$ $f_d=.2$	$f_i=.2$ $f_p=.5$	$f_i=.8$ $f_p=.8$ $f_d=.4$
	(1)	(2)	(3)	(4)	(5)	(6)	(7)	(8)	(9)
1957 III	109.1	109.1	109.1	109.1	109.1	109.1	109.1	109.1	109.1
IV	109.8	109.8	109.8	109.8	109.8	109.8	109.8	109.8	109.8
1958 I	110.3	110.3	110.3	110.3	110.3	110.3	110.3	110.3	110.3
II	110.7	110.8	110.9	110.9	110.9	110.9	110.9	110.8	110.9
III	111.1	111.3	111.5	111.6	111.6	111.6	111.6	111.4	111.8
IV	111.5	111.9	112.3	112.7	112.7	112.5	112.5	112.2	112.8
1959 I	112.0	112.7	113.2	114.1	114.0	113.6	113.6	113.1	114.0
II	112.5	113.5	114.0	115.5	115.3	114.8	114.8	114.1	115.2
III	113.0	114.2	114.9	116.7	116.6	116.0	116.0	115.2	116.3
Ratio of 1959 III to 1957 III	103.5	104.7	105.3	106.9	106.9	106.3	106.3	105.6	106.6

[a] See footnote to Table 2.

Of course, the aggregate analysis must be interpreted with caution, since it does not take into account changes in the structure of prices. Even if total demand is below overall capacity, there is no reason to believe that this condition will hold for all sectors. Some inflation that might be caused by bottlenecks in specific industries is not reflected in the results.

SUMMARY. The main results described in the preceding sections are summarized in Table 12. For each policy in each recession, the

TABLE 11. Implicit Price Deflator under Various "Continuous" Policies, 1960–62[a]

Year and Quarter	Reference	$f_p=.5$	$f_p=1.0$	$f_i=1.0$	$f_i=1.0$ $f_d=.5$	$f_i=.5$ $f_p=.5$	$f_i=.5$ $f_p=.5$ $f_d=.2$	$f_i=.2$ $f_p=.5$	$f_i=.8$ $f_p=.8$ $f_d=.4$
	(1)	(2)	(3)	(4)	(5)	(6)	(7)	(8)	(9)
1960 II	114.2	114.2	114.2	114.2	114.2	114.2	114.2	114.2	114.2
III	114.9	114.9	114.9	114.9	114.9	114.9	114.9	114.9	114.9
IV	115.4	115.4	115.4	115.4	115.4	115.4	115.4	115.4	115.4
1961 I	115.8	115.9	116.0	116.0	116.0	116.0	116.0	116.0	116.1
II	116.3	116.6	116.8	117.0	117.0	116.9	116.9	116.7	117.2
III	116.7	117.3	117.7	118.4	118.3	118.0	118.0	117.6	118.5
IV	117.2	118.1	118.7	120.1	119.9	119.4	119.4	119.7	119.9
1962 I	117.7	119.0	119.8	121.8	121.6	120.9	120.9	120.0	121.4
II	118.4	120.0	120.9	123.5	123.3	122.5	122.5	121.3	122.9
Ratio of 1962 II to 1960 II	103.7	105.1	105.9	108.1	108.0	107.2	107.1	106.2	107.6

[a] See footnote to Table 2.

table gives the percentage of GNP loss which is offset by the policy, the extent of overshooting of the full employment line, the addition to the deficit which is due to following the policy, and the ratio of the price deflator in the last quarter of the recession to that in the first quarter.

The best overall policies are those using all three stabilizers. Although similar offsets can be achieved, for example, through the use of an integral policy of 1.0 by itself, and a policy of $f_i = .5$, $f_p = .5$, and $f_d = .2$, the amount of overshooting is reduced in the latter case and the rate of price increase is also smaller.

The critical importance of the initial gap is evident. For a given policy, the percentage of GNP loss which is offset is about the same for each recession. However, to achieve this offset, increasingly large deficits are required in the later, compared with the earlier, recessions. This is due to the growing initial gap with which each recession begins, thus necessitating increasingly large tax cuts in the later recessions. One of the great advantages of sustained use of formula flexibility is precisely that, by initiating corrective action early in a recession, such large gaps might be prevented.

Finally, a given degree of GNP stabilization can be achieved in a variety of ways. For example, the percentage offsets shown in columns 5, 6, 7, and 9 of Table 12 are quite similar, as are those shown in columns 3 and 8. Each of these policies, however, has a different set of characteristics associated with it: compare the deficits and the overshooting as well as the price movements. Further, although each policy has a similar stablizing effect over the entire recession, each produces different time profiles of GNP (see Tables 2, 3, and 4). The choice of a "best" policy would require the weighting of these various characteristics in terms of a social welfare function. In the absence of a generally agreed upon function, the choice must be made by policymakers on the basis of judgment.

Results of the Simulations: "One-Shot" Policy

As was shown earlier, the signal for initiation of a change in the tax rate would have been provided by the *ad hoc* indicators (given the assumed data and implementation lags) at the beginning of the following months: February 1954, September 1957, and September 1960. In the simulations, these dates have been translated into starting dates that coincide with the end of the first quarter of 1954, the

TABLE 12. Summary of Effects of Various "Continuous" Policies[a], 1953–55, 1957–59, and 1960–62

Item	Reference	$f_p=.5$	$f_p=1.0$	$f_i=1.0$	$f_i=1.0$ $f_d=.5$	$f_i=.5$ $f_p=.5$	$f_i=.5$ $f_p=.5$ $f_d=.2$	$f_i=.2$ $f_p=.5$	$f_i=.8$ $f_p=.8$ $f_d=.4$
	(1)	(2)	(3)	(4)	(5)	(6)	(7)	(8)	(9)
1953–55									
Percentage of GNP loss offset by policy	—	32.0	50.8	72.1	75.8	67.2	68.7	53.5	79.1
Absolute amount of overshooting (billion dollars)	—	0	0	23.9	15.2	8.4	6.4	3.9	8.0
Additional deficit due to pursuing policy (annual basis, billion dollars)		4.6	6.0	12.6	12.0	11.4	10.9	9.0	9.9
Price deflator in last quarter of recession divided by price deflator in first quarter	101.8	102.2	102.4	102.8	102.9	102.7	102.7	102.4	102.9
1957–59									
Percentage of GNP loss offset by policy	—	32.0	47.5	67.6	73.2	71.2	72.0	58.6	76.2
Absolute amount of overshooting (billion dollars)	—	0	0	38.2	29.7	14.3	9.3	0	5.6
Additional deficit due to pursuing policy (annual basis, billion dollars)		7.5	11.3	13.8	19.3	18.2	18.8	16.0	20.1
Price deflator in last quarter of recession divided by price deflator in first quarter	103.5	104.7	105.3	106.9	106.9	106.3	106.3	105.6	106.6
1960–62									
Percentage of GNP loss offset by policy	—	30.9	46.0	67.2	70.2	69.0	69.2	50.2	74.0
Absolute amount of overshooting (billion dollars)	—	0	0	48.7	44.1	19.2	16.6	0.1	18.7
Additional deficit due to pursuing policy (annual basis, billion dollars)		9.4	13.8	16.6	30.8	21.0	24.0	20.6	30.0
Price deflator in last quarter of recession divided by price deflator in first quarter	103.7	105.1	105.9	108.1	108.0	107.2	107.1	106.2	107.6

[a] See footnote to Table 2.

TABLE 13. Gains in Gross National Product (GNP) under "One-Shot" Policy, 1953–55, 1957–59, and 1960–62

(Quarterly figures at annual rates, in billions of dollars)

Year and Quarter	GNP When Taxes Are Reduced by 3 Percent of Previous Peak GNP	GNP in Reference Simulations	
1953 III	370.2	370.2	
IV	365.0	365.0	
1954 I	358.7	358.7	
II	363.0	358.0	
III	369.3	360.9	
IV	377.2	365.4	
1955 I	385.0	370.9	
Percentage of GNP loss offset by policy			40.2
1957 III	411.0	411.0	
IV	405.5	405.5	
1958 I	408.5	402.6	
II	416.5	406.7	
III	426.4	412.6	
IV	434.4	418.1	
1959 I	438.5	420.7	
II	442.3	424.1	
III	446.2	428.5	
Percentage of GNP loss offset by policy			48.2
1960 II	443.4	443.4	
III	438.2	438.2	
IV	445.1	439.0	
1961 I	453.5	443.2	
II	461.9	447.4	
III	470.9	453.7	
IV	481.0	462.2	
1962 II	486.8	467.7	
III	491.0	472.2	
Percentage of GNP loss offset by policy			40.3

end of the fourth quarter of 1957, and the end of the third quarter of 1960.[36]

The procedure used in each simulation is the following. In the quarters designated as starting dates, federal personal income tax rates are reduced by an amount which decreases the yield by 3 per-

[36] In 1957, the tax change should begin at the end of the third quarter, but owing to computational problems, it is begun in the fourth quarter.

cent of the previous peak of GNP. The new tax rates are maintained at that level for the duration of the recession. Table 13 shows the GNP profiles generated by this policy and compares them with the reference simulations.

In all periods the GNP gains are quite large. In the terminal quarter of each recession, GNP is at least $14 billion greater (at annual rate) than in the reference simulation. These gains are derived mainly from increased consumption stemming from the tax reduction and the associated reduction in inventory disinvestment. These tax reductions come close to eliminating the gap between actual and potential GNP.

It is of interest to ascertain what the effect would be if the tax reduction were begun a quarter earlier in the 1953 recession (i.e., 1953 IV rather than 1954 I). This earlier start would be expected to arrest the GNP downturn earlier and to moderate its fall, and this is precisely the result obtained (Table 14). The comparison shows that the main benefit from the earlier initiation is derived in the quarters immediately after the tax reduction occurs.

As in the earlier experiments, a useful summary measure of the effectiveness of the various policies is given by

$$\frac{\sum_t D_t}{\sum_t (Y^F - Y^R)_t}.$$

TABLE 14. Effect on Gross National Product (GNP) of Initiating Tax Cut One Quarter Earlier, 1953–55

(Quarterly figures at annual rates, in billions of dollars at 1954 prices)

Year and Quarter	Tax Rates Reduced in 1954 I[a]	Tax Rates Reduced in 1953 IV	Reference Simulations[a]
1953 III	370.2	370.2	370.2
IV	365.0	365.0	365.0
1954 I	358.7	364.7	358.7
II	363.0	367.0	358.0
III	369.3	373.5	360.9
IV	377.2	380.2	365.4
1955 I	385.0	387.0	370.9
Percentage of GNP loss offset by policy	40.2	66.6	—

[a] From Table 13.

The measure still utilizes the "capacity" term Y^F although capacity does not enter explicitly into these simulations. These offsets amount to 40.2 percent in 1953–55, 48.2 percent in 1957–59, and 40.3 percent in 1960–62. The importance of beginning a tax cut early is indicated clearly by the fact that the percentage offset is 26.4 percent higher when the tax reduction in the 1953–54 recession is begun in the last quarter of 1953 rather than in the first quarter of 1954.

TABLE 15. Deficits under "One-Shot" Policy, 1953–55, 1957–59, and 1960–62

(In billions of dollars)

Year and Quarter	Deficits When Taxes are Reduced by 3 Percent of Previous Peak GNP	Deficits in Reference Simulations	Additional Deficit Due to Pursuing Policy (annual basis)
1953 IV	− 9.4	− 9.4	
1954 I	−20.6	−10.4	
II	−14.5	− 6.2	
III	−12.4	− 5.8	
IV	− 9.0	− 4.1	
1955 I	− 7.8	− 4.3	
Total deficit	73.7	40.2	8.4
1957 IV	−13.2	0.0	
1958 I	−15.0	− 4.2	
II	−14.7	− 5.8	
III	−12.8	− 5.8	
IV	−10.7	− 5.4	
1959 I	− 7.7	− 3.8	
II	− 6.1	− 3.0	
III	− 4.5	− 1.6	
Total deficit	84.7	29.6	14.0
1960 III	−17.2	− 2.3	
IV	−14.5	− 2.2	
1961 I	−16.8	− 6.3	
II	−16.2	− 7.8	
III	−12.7	− 6.1	
IV	−12.3	− 7.0	
1962 I	−11.6	− 7.0	
II	− 8.3	− 4.0	
Total deficit	109.6	42.7	16.7

In the early quarters of each recession, the deficits in the policy experiments are larger than those in the reference case by about the amount of the tax cut (Table 15). As the recession progresses, the difference between the deficits shrinks. This shrinkage results from the additional tax receipts brought in by rising GNP. Thus, in 1954 I, the deficit under formula flexibility is $10.2 billion greater than in the reference simulation; but by 1955 I, the difference is reduced to $3.5 billion.

The inflation created by the policy is quite small, the additional price increments being less than 1 percent a year (Table 16).

TABLE 16. Behavior of Implicit Price Deflator under "One-Shot" Policy, 1953–55, 1957–59, and 1960–62

Year and Quarter	Implicit Price Deflator When Taxes Are Reduced by 3 Percent of Previous Peak GNP	Implicit Price Deflator in Reference Simulations
1953 III	99.1	99.1
IV	99.7	99.7
1954 I	100.2	100.2
II	100.5	100.5
III	100.7	100.6
IV	100.9	100.8
1955 I	101.3	100.9
1957 III	109.1	109.1
IV	109.8	109.8
1958 I	110.3	110.3
II	110.8	110.7
III	111.3	111.1
IV	112.0	111.5
1959 I	112.8	112.0
II	113.8	112.5
III	114.7	113.0
1960 II	114.2	114.2
III	114.9	114.9
IV	115.4	115.4
1961 I	115.9	115.8
II	116.5	116.3
III	117.3	116.7
IV	118.1	117.2
1962 I	119.1	117.7
II	120.3	118.4

The effects of the one-shot policy are summarized in Table 17. When the percentages by which GNP losses are reduced are compared with those shown in Table 12 the stabilizing effect of the one-shot policy is seen to lie between the effect of proportional policies of .5 and 1.0. Although the overall stabilization effect is similar for each recession, which of the two policies would be more desirable

TABLE 17. Summary of Effects of "One-Shot" Policy, 1953–55, 1957–59, and 1960–62

Item	Reference	"One-shot" Tax Reduction
1953–55		
Percentage of GNP loss offset by tax reduction	—	40.2
Increment in deficit due to pursuing policy (annual rate, billion dollars)	—	8.4
Price deflator in last quarter of recession divided by price deflator in first quarter	101.8	102.2
1957–59		
Percentage of GNP loss offset by tax reduction	—	48.2
Increment in deficit due to pursuing policy (annual rate, billion dollars)	—	14.0
Price deflator in last quarter of recession divided by price deflator in first quarter	103.5	105.2
1960–62		
Percentage of GNP loss offset by tax reduction	—	40.3
Increment in deficit due to pursuing policy (annual rate, billion dollars)	—	16.7
Price deflator in last quarter of recession divided by price deflator in first quarter	103.7	105.4

if the choice were narrowed to a proportional policy of 1.0 or to the one-shot policy will depend upon society's time preference, since the GNP profile within each recession differs: The gains are larger under the proportional policy during the early part of each recession, but a reversal occurs after about five quarters; thereafter, the gain becomes larger under the one-shot policy. The total deficit generated under the one-shot policy is greater than that under a proportional policy of 1.0.

Further Considerations

Broader Stabilization Framework

Thus far in this paper, formula flexibility has been discussed without consideration of the broader stabilization framework into which it must be integrated. Now, the entire stabilization program that is envisaged and some further problems associated with formula flexibility will be considered.

It has been assumed that the sole method for implementing the desired changes under formula flexibility is to reduce taxes on personal income. Such tax changes are not envisioned as the only anti-recession weapon; they would, for example, supplement the existing automatic stabilizers. Implicitly, it also has been assumed that the discretionary powers available to the executive and legislative branches of the government are utilized to raise government expenditures as tax receipts rise.[37] Another assumption is that monetary policy will operate to increase bank reserves and to lower interest rates. In effect, it has been assumed that formula flexibility will not replace the present stabilizers but will be added to them.

Relevance of the Permanent Income Hypothesis

A crucial problem for formula flexibility is the possibility that the consumption arising out of temporary tax cuts may be relatively small, thus weakening the policy considerably. Friedman has suggested that "consumption" out of certain types of income is likely to be quite low.[38] His thesis must be considered in evaluating the stabilization potential of formula flexibility.

If it is assumed that cycles are not completely eliminated as a result of the introduction of formula flexibility, taxpayers may react to the periodic tax cuts and subsequent tax increases in two ways. First, they may assume that their permanent income has increased at the time that a policy of formula flexibility is enacted. They could then infer the likelihood of recessions from past experience, make suitable extrapolations, and deduce their new average tax rates and

[37] In the simulations, the speedup of government expenditures is already included in the exogenous variable, G. Insofar as some discretion exists concerning the speed of tax refunds, the model does not completely capture the effects of discretionary measures.

[38] See Milton Friedman, *A Theory of the Consumption Function* (Princeton University Press, 1957).

new permanent disposable income.[39] Under this hypothesis, permanent consumption (in Friedman's terminology) would rise when the plan is initiated and future consumption levels would remain higher than they would if formula flexibility were not adopted. Thus, when the anticipated tax reduction did occur, no additional consumption could be expected.[40] However, this assumes an extraordinary amount of economic sophistication and is likely to be unrealistic.

Alternatively, consumers may view each tax cut as a windfall, i.e., they make no prior changes in their behavior in anticipation of the tax reduction. In this case, the actual tax cut will be viewed as transitory, and, according to one of Friedman's main propositions, only a very small amount of "consumption" will be induced. However, Friedman does not exclude the possibility that transitory income would be spent on consumer durables, for consumption in his analysis excludes that portion of expenditure on durables that are not consumed currently, i.e., Friedman's consumption is less than total consumption expenditure. However, total consumption expenditure is the relevant magnitude for measuring the income-generating and employment-generating effects of a given policy. Thus, even the most rigid formulation of the permanent income hypothesis does not preclude formula flexibility from being effective in raising aggregate demand. The quantitative importance of these considerations is, however, still open to empirical analysis.

Conclusions

The simulations show that substantial gains in output could be realized if formula flexibility were followed. For example, in the 1953 recession, a proportional policy of 1.0 would have reduced the GNP loss for the cycle period as a whole by about $12 billion (in 1954 prices) at the "cost" of only a small additional deficit and very mild inflationary effects. A one-shot tax reduction of 3 percent of the previous peak of GNP could have achieved a similar result.

Many of the policies analyzed in this study would have gen-

[39] These subjective evaluations could be altered occasionally if new cyclical patterns occurred.

[40] The higher level of expenditure, of course, might in fact reduce the severity of future recessions.

erated larger deficits than those experienced in the United States. However, continuous use of the policies would have reduced the initial gap and thus decreased the deficits substantially below those recorded in the simulations. Further, the adoption of formula flexibility would probably have improved business expectations and increased investment. Since the investment equation used in the simulations has no such expectational variable, the tax reductions necessary to achieve a given level of demand are overstated.

The suggested use of formula flexibility should not be taken as indicating a belief in the superiority of fixed rules to intelligent decision-making. It should be viewed in the context of the difficulty of achieving full employment in the late 1950's and early 1960's, and the inertia that gripped the government during that period. The tax reduction of 1964 may have ushered in a new era of more flexible tax policy. Yet it must be remembered that this legislation was enacted after several years of deliberation, and thus does not by itself provide sufficient evidence of the willingness to respond quickly to required changes in the size of the planned deficit. Moreover, the hesitation of the Administration to propose increases in tax rates during the inflationary development in 1966 suggests that prior inertia has not been completely overcome by the 1964 experience. Clearly, formula flexibility has much to commend it over the discretionary policy that has developed in recent years in the United States.

Selection of Indicators of Turning Points in Business Cycle

IN THE TEXT, a purely empirical method has been suggested for selecting indicators of future movements in the business cycle. The method involves ascertaining whether there are any series which before a recession always decline by at least x percent from their previous peaks and remain below that level for at least n months, but never behave in this way if a recession is not imminent. To implement this procedure, monthly values in each of several series were examined, beginning with January 1947. Each monthly value in the series was denoted by s_t, and the previous peak value in the series by s_0; then $(s_0 - s_t)/s_0$ was calculated for each month.

TABLE 18. Forecasts of Downward Turning Points, 1948, 1953, 1957, and 1960[a]

Selected Indicators				NBER
Average workweek	Gross accession rate	Layoff rate	New orders for durable goods manufacturing	Date for Business Cycle Peak[b]
(1.75)	(15)	(25)	(8)	
November 1948	December 1948	November 1948	February 1949	November 1948
		July 1951	July 1951	
October 1953	October 1953	July 1953	October 1953	July 1953
June 1957	May 1957	August 1957	May 1957	July 1957
May 1960	April 1960	April 1960	September 1959	May 1960

[a] Figures in parentheses indicate the percentage change from previous peak which if maintained for three months predicts recession.
[b] National Bureau of Economic Research date. From Geoffrey H. Moore (ed.), *Business Cycle Indicators* (Princeton University Press, 1961).

After such calculations were made for many series, it was possible to determine the minimum percentage decrease that had to be maintained for three months in order to forecast accurately those recessions that had occurred, yet not to predict recessions that did not occur.

Table 18 lists the predictions made by the four "successful" series along with the business cycle peak as determined by the National Bureau of Economic Research. At the top of each column is the percentage change for each series which results in the prediction of a turning point.

One feature of these predictions calls for comment, namely, the erroneous forecasts of a downturn in 1951 indicated by the layoff and new orders series. This error is a result of the declines from previous inflated high values[41] induced by the Korean war. The figures for both series, however, were still high when compared with normal peacetime figures. This observation leads to a rather obvious conclusion—that formula flexibility would best be suspended during war periods. Sustained full employment is likely to exist under war conditions, and signals to the contrary are likely to be specious.

[41] For the series of layoffs, a rise from the previous low value would be a more accurate statement. However, as the inverse of the layoff series is being considered here, it is permissible to speak of the fall from the previous high.

WILLIAM H. OAKLAND*

Automatic Stabilization and the Value-Added Tax

THE SUBSTITUTION, at least in part, of a tax upon value-added for the present corporation income tax is one of the most significant fiscal reforms to be proposed in recent years.[1] Although the arguments put forth in favor of such a reform are numerous, three of them appear to be most popular. The first is that such a substitution would enhance the competitive position of U. S. exporters and hence ease the U. S. balance of payments difficulties.[2] This view stems in part from the fact that, under current international agreements, rebates to exporters for value-added taxes are permitted whereas rebates for corporation profits taxes are not. The proposal has also been advanced on the ground that it will have a favorable effect upon the U. S. rate of growth. Since a tax on value-added is more broadly based than a tax on income from capital, marginal rates on profits would be reduced and this would stimulate new in-

* The Johns Hopkins University.

[1] Testimony by Dan Throop Smith before the U. S. Senate Committee on Finance, in Hearings, *Revenue Act of 1963*, 88 Cong. 1 sess. (1963). Also see Conference Report of National Bureau of Economic Research and Brookings Institution, *The Role of Direct and Indirect Taxes in the Federal Revenue System* (Princeton University Press, 1964), for an extensive discussion of this proposal.

[2] R. Musgrave and P. Richman, "Allocation Aspects, Domestic and International," in *The Role of Direct and Indirect Taxes*, pp. 81–131.

41

vestment activity. Finally, the tax reform has been justified upon efficiency grounds. To quote Eckstein: "Corporations with high profits would be taxed less, unsuccessful corporations would be taxed more."[3] Thus resources would be channeled from relatively inefficient to relatively efficient firms and therefore used more effectively.

Despite these apparent advantages, such a change in fiscal structure may not prove costless but may lead to greater economic instability. To quote Eckstein again: "The value-added tax would be a weaker automatic stabilizer than the corporate income tax, since profits are more sensitive to cyclical changes than value-added. The loss in automatic stabilization would be substantial."[4] The task of this paper is to investigate the validity of this proposition. It will be shown that the effect of the proposed reform upon the degree of automatic stability cannot be deduced solely from considerations of the cyclical behavior of revenue, but depends upon the expenditure impact of the two tax structures. This in turn depends upon the set of shifting assumptions that is employed.

Characteristics of Value-Added Tax

Before the analysis is begun, certain characteristics of the value-added tax should be discussed.[5] Three fundamentally distinct versions of the value-added tax have been proposed: a value-added tax of the consumption type, of the income type, and gross product type (hereafter referred to as CVA, IVA, and GVA, respectively). The essential difference among these variants is the manner in which depreciation allowances are treated. Under the CVA, instantaneous depreciation is granted to purchasers of *new* plant and equipment and no depreciation is allowed to owners of *existing* assets. Under the IVA, deduction of economic depreciation is allowed on all physical assets, new or old. A GVA would permit no depreciation of any sort to be deducted from the tax base. It follows, therefore,

---

[3] Otto Eckstein, "European and U. S. Tax Structure," in *The Role of Direct and Indirect Taxes*, p. 247.

[4] *Ibid.*, p. 248.

[5] For a discussion of some of the allocative and distributional effects of value-added taxation, see William Oakland, "The Theory of the Value-Added Tax: I—A Comparison of Tax Bases" and "II—Incidence," *National Tax Journal*, Vol. 20, No. 2 and No. 3 (June and September 1967).

that the tax function under each of these variants is given by

$$T = \tau Y \qquad \text{(GVA)}$$
$$= \tau(Y - D) \qquad \text{(IVA)}$$
$$= \tau(Y - I) \qquad \text{(CVA)}$$

where Y is gross national product (GNP), D represents depreciation, and I is gross investment expenditure. As the form of the tax functions would suggest, and as shown elsewhere,[6] value-added taxes are essentially levies upon firms for the use of factors of production.

Since this study is an investigation of the short-run behavior of the economy under alternative tax structures and since depreciation allowances are relatively insensitive to short-run variations in income, it is evident that the IVA and the GVA will have essentially the same effects. Hence, what will be true for the GVA, will, with minor modification, also be true for the IVA. Since investment plays a central role in short-term fluctuations in income, however, the CVA may differ considerably from the GVA in its stability implications. Therefore, the effects of both variants will be considered in some detail.

Built-in Flexibility and Automatic Stability

Let the built-in flexibility of a tax structure be defined as the change in tax receipts which results from a given change in output:

$$(1) \qquad B = \frac{\Delta T}{\Delta Y}$$

where B is an index of the built-in flexibility of a tax structure. According to this definition, the built-in flexibility of a profits tax is greater than that of the value-added tax. To see this, consider the expression for B under a value-added tax (GVA):

$$(2) \qquad T = \tau^v Y \qquad B^v = \frac{\Delta T}{\Delta Y} = \tau^v.$$

Under a profits tax,

$$(3) \qquad T = \tau^P \pi \quad \therefore \quad B^P = \frac{\Delta T}{\Delta Y} = \tau^P \frac{\Delta \pi}{\Delta Y}$$

[6] *Ibid.*

where π is defined as pre-tax corporate profits. In order to provide equal revenue yield, τ^P must satisfy

$$\tau^P \pi = \tau^v Y;$$

thus equation (3) becomes

(4) $$B^P = \left(\tau^v \frac{\Delta\pi}{\pi}\right)\left(\frac{Y}{\Delta Y}\right) = \varepsilon\tau^v$$

where ε is the elasticity of profits with respect to output. As will be shown below, this elasticity is greater than 1. Thus, the profits tax provides more built-in flexibility than the value-added tax.

Before the built-in flexibility of a tax system can be related to

FIGURE 1. Cyclical Behavior of Economy under Two Tax Systems

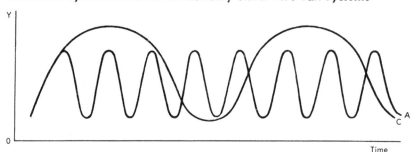

its automatic stabilizing power, the term, economic stability, must be defined. As Brown has pointed out, there is no obvious definition.[7] That this is true can readily be seen from Figure 1. Curves A and C denote the cyclical behavior of the economy under two tax systems, A and C. Tax system C gives rise to cycles of greater amplitude but of lower periodicity than tax system A. Which system provides the most stability? Clearly, this question cannot be answered without some notion of the social welfare function.

Suppose this problem is sidestepped by assuming that the tax structure which yields the smallest sum of absolute deviations from the trend line is the most desirable. Then is it possible to go directly from the size of B to the degree of automatic stability of a tax structure? The answer is, in general, no. The built-in flexibility must be related in some way to changes in expenditure. There is no reason

---

[7] E. Cary Brown, "The Static Theory of Automatic Fiscal Stabilization," *Journal of Political Economy*, Vol. 63 (October 1955), pp. 427–40.

to suppose that a dollar increase in taxes under two different tax systems will affect expenditure in the same way. More precisely, automatic stability refers to

$$\frac{\Delta E}{\Delta Y} = \frac{\Delta E}{\Delta T} B$$

where ΔE is change in expenditure. Even though tax structure A yields a larger B (a larger built-in flexibility) than tax system C, there is no reason to suppose the $\Delta E/\Delta T$ (marginal propensity to spend out of taxes) will be less under system C than under system A or will be the same under both systems. Thus it is conceivable that the value-added tax may yield a greater $\Delta E/\Delta Y$ than a profits tax while having a smaller built-in flexibility.

Even if it is ascertained that $\Delta E/\Delta Y$ is lower under a profits tax than under a value-added tax, there is no guarantee that the former provides greater automatic stability than the latter. Phillips and others have shown that the stability of the economy is very sensitive to the structure of time lags in the economy.[8] There is no necessary relationship between the size of $\Delta E/\Delta Y$ and the degree of stability in the economy. The latter is particularly true if the lag structure changes as tax systems are shifted.

In order to determine properly the effect of shifting from a corporate profits tax to a value-added tax upon short-run stability, an econometric model of the United States would have to be estimated, using the correct lag structure; then an heroic assumption would have to be made, i.e., that parameters and time lags remain constant when a value-added tax is imposed. This is a formidable task for which we have neither time, resources, nor inclination to undertake. Instead, we shall be content with a more modest approach: to study and compare the automatic stabilizing power of the two tax structures within the framework of the static Keynesian model. While it is true that this approach sheds little, if any, light upon the actual stability effects of tax substitution, it is of some interest from a purely theoretical viewpoint. More importantly, however, the results of the static model can be best translated into an estimate of the impact multiplier of an autonomous disturbance under the two tax regimes. While impact multipliers may tell little

[8] A. W. Phillips, "Stabilisation Policy in a Closed Economy," *Economic Journal*, Vol. 64 (June 1954), pp. 290–323.

about the overall stability of the economy, they provide some measure of the short-run sensitivity of the economy to random shocks.

Case I: Value-Added Tax Shifted[9]

First, consider the case where the value-added tax is fully shifted.
In other words, assume that, when a value-added tax is substituted
for a corporate profits tax, the factors of production bear the tax
according to their earnings.[10] For example, the after-tax earnings
of capital will rise from $(1 - \tau^P)\pi$ to $(1 - \tau^v)\pi - \tau^v D$ if a GVA is
substituted for a profits tax. Thus, it will be assumed that the
factors of production actually pay the value-added tax, roughly in
proportion to their earnings.[11]

Assume that

(5) $$C = C(Y_D)$$

where C is real consumption expenditure and Y_D is real disposable
income. Assume that the supply of output, Y, is infinitely elastic at
current market prices so that equation (5) holds in money terms
as well as in real terms. Also assume, for the moment, that investment expenditure is exogenous and government expenditure is
autonomous. Under these assumptions total output can be written
as

(6) $$Y = C(Y_D) + A$$

where A represents all exogeneous expenditure. Following Brown,
we take as a measure of the automatic stability of the system the following expression:

(7) $$F = \frac{1}{dY/dA} = 1 - C'(Y_D)\frac{dY_D}{dY}.$$

F is that amount of change in autonomous expenditure required
to raise income by one dollar. Clearly, the larger the F, the more
stable is the system. F is simply the reciprocal of the familiar income
multiplier.

---

[9] The following discussion draws heavily upon Brown in *Journal of Political Economy*.

[10] That this is the case in a neo-classical competitive world has been demonstrated elsewhere. See Oakland in *National Tax Journal*.

[11] This particular institutional assumption as to who is the statutory taxpayer in no way
affects the conclusions. *Ibid.*

Under any direct tax system, (6) can be rewritten more explicitly as

$$(8) \qquad Y = C(Y - T - S^c) + A$$

where T is the level of taxation and S^c represents corporate saving. Also, (7) can be reformulated as

$$(9) \qquad F = 1 - C'\left[1 - \frac{dT}{dY} - \frac{dS^c}{d\pi^n} \cdot \frac{d\pi^n}{d\pi} \cdot \frac{d\pi}{dY}\right]$$

where π is corporate profits before tax and π^n is profits after tax. It will be assumed that π is an increasing function of Y, such that $d\pi/dY \leq 1$. Furthermore, it will be assumed that corporate saving is a nondecreasing function of after-tax profits.

If the tax system is a corporate profits tax $(T = \tau^P \pi)$, equation (9) yields

$$(10) \qquad F^\pi = 1 - C'[(1 - \tau^P)(1 - \mu S) + \tau^P(1 - \mu)]$$

where

$$\mu = \frac{d\pi}{dY} \quad \text{and} \quad S = \frac{dS^c}{d\pi^n}.$$

If, on the other hand, a value-added tax (GVA) exists and the tax is shifted onto the factors of production in proportion to their earnings, F becomes

$$(11) \qquad F^v = 1 - C'(1 - \tau^v)(1 - \mu S).$$

Clearly if $\tau^P \leq \tau^v$, then $F^v > F^\pi$. In general, however, $\tau^P > \tau^v$ because the taxes should be of equal revenue. Specifically,

$$(12) \qquad \tau^v = \beta\tau^P \qquad \beta = \pi/Y < 1.$$

When (12) is substituted in (11),

$$(13) \qquad F^v = 1 - C'(1 - \beta\tau^P)(1 - \mu S).$$

Now $F^v - F^\pi \geq 0$ if

$$(14) \qquad S \geq \frac{\mu - \beta}{(1 - \beta)\mu}.$$

Clearly if $\beta \geq \mu$, (14) is satisfied. It is easy to see that $\beta > \mu$ if the elasticity of corporate profits with respect to income is less than unity; i.e.,

$$\varepsilon = \frac{d\pi}{dY}\left(\frac{Y}{\pi}\right) = \frac{\mu}{\beta}.$$

Thus, a necessary, but not sufficient, condition for Eckstein's argument to be correct is that $\varepsilon > 1$. Rewriting (14) in terms of elasticities produces

(15) $$S \geq \left(1 - \frac{1}{\varepsilon}\right)\frac{1}{1 - \beta}.$$

What has been determined empirically about the sizes of the parameters in (15)? In the long run, the share of profits in output has remained basically constant (i.e., $\varepsilon = 1$). In a static world, where adjustments occur instantaneously, it must be that the value-added tax provides more stability than a profits tax. The reason is obvious. Because the share of output accruing to profits is constant, the built-in flexibility of the profits tax is no higher than that of the value-added tax. On the other hand, retained earnings absorb a greater proportion of the change in taxes under a profits tax than under a value-added tax. Hence, disposable income will fluctuate more under a profits tax than under a value-added tax.

That a static framework is inadequate for an analysis of stability is quickly brought to light by the above discussion. The static model is incapable of incorporating into the analysis the fact that, in the short run, profits tend to vary substantially more than proportionately with output. As a consequence, the difference in the built-in flexibility of the two tax systems is passed over. Therefore, in the analysis to follow, the static model will be ignored. Instead, the first quarter response of the economy to a change in exogenous expenditure will be estimated and compared under the two tax systems; i.e., F now becomes the reciprocal of the impact multiplier.

Insofar as the inequality (15) is concerned, estimates of S have been made by Lintner,[12] and more recently by Brittain.[13] The form of the equation used to estimate S is given by

(16) $$D_t = a + (1 - S)X_t + bD_{t-1}$$

where D is quarterly dividends and X a measure of the pool of

[12] John Lintner, "Distribution of Incomes of Corporations Among Dividends, Retained Earnings, and Taxes," *American Economic Review*, Vol. 46 (May 1956), pp. 97–113.

[13] John Brittain, "The Tax Structure and Corporate Dividend Policy," *American Economic Review*, Vol. 54 (May 1964), pp. 272–87.

funds which might be used for dividend purposes.[14] In the Lintner formulation, X was profits net of both taxes and depreciation. Brittain, on the other hand, argued that, because of the arbitrary nature of depreciation allowances, profits net of taxes but gross of depreciation should be employed. Brittain estimated both of these models for the period 1942–60 and found that $S = .83$ for the Lintner formulation and .85 for his own formulation. Both parameter estimates were significant at the 1 percent level. From these estimates, a safe assumption seems to be that S is in the neighborhood of 5/6. Using this value of S in (15) yields

(17) $$\varepsilon \leq 6/(1 + 5\beta)$$

as a necessary and sufficient condition for the value-added tax to be more stable than the profits tax. In addition, β—the share of corporate profits in GNP—has been approximately 10 percent in the postwar years. Hence (17) simplifies to

(17a) $$\varepsilon \leq 4$$

as our condition.

There has been no empirical estimate of ε as such. However, separate estimates of μ have been made by Schultze[15] and by Ando and Brown.[16] Both estimates suffer from simultaneous equations bias since they were made within a single equation framework. Schultze estimated μ as the product of two terms

$$\mu = \left(\frac{\Delta \pi}{\Delta Y_c}\right)\left(\frac{\Delta Y_c}{\Delta Y}\right)$$

where Y_c is corporate product and Y is GNP. The first term was estimated as follows:

[14] Note that S now represents a measure of the first-quarter impact of a change in net profits upon the level of retained earnings; i.e.,

$$S = 1 - \frac{(D_t - D_{t-1})}{(X_t - X_{t-1})}.$$

The *total* change in retained earnings which results is given by the static solution to (16).

[15] C. L. Schultze, "Short-Run Movement of Income Shares," in National Bureau of Economic Research, *The Behavior of Income Shares* (Princeton University Press, 1964), pp. 143–82.

[16] Albert Ando and E. Cary Brown, "Lags in Fiscal Policy," Part II of "Lags in Fiscal and Monetary Policy" by Albert Ando and others, in Commission on Money and Credit, *Stabilization Policies* (Prentice-Hall, 1963), pp. 97–163.

(18)
$$\frac{\pi}{Y_c} = a + b\left(\frac{Y_c - Y_{ck}}{Y_c}\right)$$

where Y_{ck} is the capacity output level of the corporate sector. Schultze's hypothesis is that the short-run share of corporate profits in corporate product is the sum of the long-run share of profits plus a term which reflects deviations from optimum output levels. From (18), the following can be calculated:

(19)
$$\frac{\Delta\pi}{\Delta Y_c} = a + b.$$

For the postwar period, Schultze found that $a = .28$ and $b = .20$. Thus $(a + b) \doteq 1/2$.

In a similar fashion, Schultze estimated the share of corporate product in GNP:

(20)
$$\frac{Y_c}{Y} = c + d\frac{(Y - Y_k)}{Y}$$

where $Y - Y_k$ is the departure of GNP (Y) from its normal level (Y_k). From (20), equation (21) can be calculated:

(21)
$$\frac{\Delta Y_c}{\Delta Y} = c + d.$$

The value of c was estimated at 57 percent and d at .2 percent. Thus $c + d \doteq 3/5$. Multiplying $(c + d)(a + b)$ yields an estimate of μ:

$$\mu = \frac{\Delta\pi}{\Delta Y} \doteq 1/2 \cdot 3/5 = .3.$$

When this is combined with the estimate of β (10 percent),

$$\varepsilon \doteq \frac{.3}{.1} = 3$$

which, allowing for errors of estimation, appears to satisfy the inequality (17a).

Ando and Brown, on the other hand, estimated μ in a much more straightforward manner by means of the following equation:[17]

$$\pi = aY + bY_{-1} + C;$$

this yielded

---

[17] *Ibid.*, p. 102.

$$\pi = .66Y - .53Y_{-1} + 2.44.$$

It follows that $\mu = 2/3$ and $\varepsilon = \mu/\beta = 7\frac{1}{3}$, which clearly violates the inequality (17a).

On the basis of the existing evidence, therefore, it appears that little can be said about the relative degree of automatic stability generated by a value-added tax as opposed to a corporate income tax. A conclusion depends upon which of the above estimates is believed to be a better representative of the true state of the world. However, despite the fact that both models suffer from simultaneous equation bias, it is my view that the Schultze estimate more nearly approximates reality. The fact that the Schultze model allows for changes in capacity output, whereas the other model does not, means that the Schultze model suffers less from the upward bias in the coefficients that is due to a strong upward trend movement in the profit and output variables. Nevertheless, the divergence in the two estimates is so great as to preclude any definite conclusion regarding the relative automatic stabilizing effectiveness of the two tax systems.

A question to be raised in a discussion of this simplified model is whether a CVA would promote greater stability than the GVA. Recall that the difference between a CVA and GVA is that the former permits the deduction of investment expenditure whereas the latter does not. If the increase in exogenous expenditure is made by the government or by some other noninvestment source, the value of F under the CVA is given by the following:

$$(22) \qquad F^c = 1 - C'(1 - \tau^c)(1 - \mu S).$$

Now (22) is of the same form as F^v. Note, however, that $\tau^c > \tau^v$ because the base of the CVA is narrower than that of the GVA (by the amount of the investment credit). Thus $F^c > F^v$.

If, on the other hand, the increase in exogenous expenditure is caused by a rise in investment, the form of (22) must change to take into account the increase in tax credit which will result; i.e.,

$$(22a) \qquad \overline{F^c} = \frac{1 - C'(1 - \tau^c)(1 - \mu S)}{1 + C'\tau^c(1 - S)} < F^c.$$

When equation (22a) is compared with equation (11), it is clear that

$$\overline{F^c} > F^v$$

$$\text{if } \frac{1 - S}{(1 - \mu S)i}(1 - C')(1 - \mu S)(1 + \tau^c i - \tau^c) < 1$$

where I = aggregate business investment expenditure and $i = I/Y$. Empirical evidence suggests that C' is in the neighborhood of .6[18] while the ratio of business investment expenditure to GNP has been about .08 (for the period 1950–62).[19] It follows that, as long as τ^c is less than 1, this inequality is violated. Whether or not the CVA is more stable than the GVA, then, depends upon the source of the increase in exogenous expenditure. If the source is investment expenditure, the GVA has a smaller impact multiplier; if the source is government expenditure, the CVA is more stable.

Finally, when the imposition of an IVA is considered, it is found that the resulting F is of the same form as a GVA except that a higher rate of tax is necessary under the former because it exempts depreciation. Thus, the IVA provides more stability than the GVA.

Model with Induced Investment

Consideration will now be given to a model where a portion of investment expenditure is a function of the level of output. There are many forms which this function could assume; however, the "flexible accelerator" approach will be discussed here. Under this approach, investment is assumed to be equal to the difference between the actual and the desired capital stock, times a reaction coefficient which dictates the speed at which the adjustment is to take place. Furthermore, it is assumed that the desired capital stock is proportional to output in the current period. This can be expressed algebraically:

$$\dot{K} = I = b(K^d - K)$$

where K = capital stock and K^d = desired capital stock with

$$K^d = cY.$$

Thus

$$I = aY - bK \qquad a = bc.$$

[18] *Ibid.*, p. 124.
[19] U. S. Department of Commerce, *Survey of Current Business* (July issues, 1952–63), Tables 1, 37.

If employment is less than full, this hypothesis is questionable, particularly with respect to plant and equipment expenditure. Nevertheless, there may still be bottlenecks which have to be resolved and inventories which have to keep pace with sales. In any case, most short-run models of investment include some capacity measure (which is itself an accelerator concept). Under this assumption, GNP can be written as

(23) $$Y = C + aY - bK + A.$$

Furthermore, under any direct tax system F becomes

(24) $$F = 1 - C'\left(1 - \frac{dT}{dY} - \frac{dS^c}{dY}\right) - a.$$

If F is calculated for the profits tax and GVA, it is found that the analysis of the preceding section holds; i.e.,

$$F^\pi = 1 - C'[(1 - \tau^P)(1 - \mu S) + \tau^P(1 - \mu)] - a$$
$$F^v = 1 - C'[(1 - \tau^v)(1 - \mu S)] - a.$$

It is easy to see that the F's of this section are simply the F's of the preceding section minus a. Thus, the rankings of the tax systems are unaffected. The reason is obvious. Because investment is a function of output alone, the relationship between a change in exogenous expenditure and investment is unaffected by the tax structure. Under each tax system, the change in investment will be proportional to the change in output. If, on the other hand, investment were a function of internal funds, tax structure would be a crucial variable because each tax system affects internal funds in a different way. This case will be discussed in the next section.

When a CVA is considered, however, the form of F must change somewhat in order to take into account the increase in tax credit which accompanies the increase in induced investment. But this force may not be so strong as to make the CVA less stable than the GVA. To show this, consider the expression for F under the CVA when the increase in exogenous expenditures occurs through some noninvestment source:

(25) $$F^c = 1 - C'[(1 - \tau^c)(1 - \mu S) + \tau^c(1 - S)a] - a.$$

Comparing F^c with F^v yields

(26) $$F^c - F^v = C'[(\tau^c - \tau^v)(1 - \mu S) - \tau^c(1 - S)a]$$

with

$$\tau^c(Y - I) = \tau^v Y$$

or

$$\tau^v = \tau^c(1 - a - i_a)$$

where

$$i_a = \frac{bK}{Y}.$$

When (26) is rewritten,

(26a) $F^c - F^v = C'[\tau^c(i_a + a)(1 - \mu S) - \tau^c a(1 - S)].$

Clearly for any S such that $0 \leq S \leq 1$, $F^c - F^v > 0$. Even though introduction of induced investment reduces the stability of the CVA relative to the GVA, it remains that $F^c > F^v$.

If the change in exogenous expenditures occurs through a change in autonomous investment, F must be altered to include the increase in tax credit from both autonomous investment and induced investment; that is,

$$\overline{F^c} = \frac{F^c}{1 + C'\tau^c(1 - S)} < F^c.$$

Since $\overline{F^c}$ was less than F^v in the model where all investment was autonomous, it must also be less in this case. This is due to the fact that there is a change in tax credit in this model whereas in the other model there is not.

Investment As a Function of Net Profits

Thus far it has been shown that, if investment is entirely exogenous or a function of output, it is not certain that the value-added tax provides less stability (in the sense of this study) than the corporate profits tax. Now, the case where a portion of investment expenditure is determined by short-run profits as well as by output will be examined; that is,

(27) $I = I(\pi^n, Y) + I_a$

where I_a is exogenous investment.

There has been considerable controversy over the form of (27). One school of thought argues that profits are important in the expectational sense; i.e., they reflect expected rates of return on investment. Another school argues that profits are important for their cash flow effect; i.e., their effect upon the supply of internal funds. A good summary of this debate and of the state of knowledge in this area can be found in a survey article by Kuh.[20] In the present study, the effects of profits upon investment as a cash flow effect will be considered, since most of the empirical effort has been made in this area.

Under the above assumptions about investment, F can be written for any direct tax system as

$$(28) \qquad F = 1 - C'\left[1 - \frac{dT}{dY} - \frac{dS^c}{dY}\right] - a - \eta\mu\frac{d\pi^n}{d\pi}$$

where

$$\eta = \frac{dI}{d\pi^n}.$$

Solving (28) for specific tax systems leads to

$$(29) \quad F^\pi = 1 - C'[(1 - \tau^p)(1 - \mu S) + \tau^p(1 - \mu)] - a - \eta\mu(1 - \tau^p)$$

and

$$(30) \quad F^v = 1 - C'[(1 - \tau^v)(1 - \mu S)] - a - \eta\mu(1 - \tau^v)$$

for the profits tax and GVA, respectively. Hence,

$$(31) \quad F^v - F^\pi = C'[(\tau^v - \tau^p)(1 - \mu S) + \tau^p(1 - \mu S)] + (\tau^v - \tau^p)\eta\mu.$$

When $\tau^v = (1/\beta)\tau^p$ is substituted in equation (31), the result is as follows:

$$(32) \qquad F^v - F^\pi = C'(\beta - \mu) - (\eta - SC')\mu(1 - \beta).$$

Since the assumption is that $\mu > \beta$, the right-hand side of equation (32) is strictly negative if $\eta > SC'$. If all retained earnings were invested, i.e., $\eta = S$, the latter inequality would hold since $C' < 1$. In general, $F^v - F^\pi$ will be strictly positive if

$$(33) \qquad S > \frac{\eta}{C'} + \left(1 - \frac{1}{\varepsilon}\right)\frac{1}{(1 - \beta)}.$$

[20] Edwin Kuh, "Theory and Institutions in the Study of Investment Behavior," *American Economic Review*, Vol. 53 (May 1963), pp. 260–68.

It has already been concluded that

$$S > \left(1 - \frac{1}{\varepsilon}\right)\frac{1}{(1 - \beta)};$$

hence the inequality (33) depends upon η/C'. The larger the marginal propensity to invest out of net profits relative to the marginal propensity to consume, the less likely that $F^v > F^\pi$. Now η is the product of two independent terms:

$$\eta = \frac{dI}{d\pi^n} = \frac{dI}{dS^c} \cdot \frac{dS^c}{d\pi^n} = S \frac{dI}{dS^c}.$$

Given the earlier estimates of the parameters of (33)—$\varepsilon = 3$, $C = .6$, $\beta = .10$, $S = .85$—(33) holds as

(34) $\frac{dI}{dS^c} < .055.$

In a study covering the period 1950–58, Meyer and Glauber estimated $\Delta I/\Delta S_c$ at .165 for manufacturing industry as a whole.[21] A complete specification of the model they employed is given by

(35) $I = I(S^c, H, MP, r, I_{-2})$

where H is a measure of capacity (our accelerator), MP is the change in stock-market prices—included as a measure of expectations—and r is the market rate of interest. The fit of the model was good; an R^2 of .93 was obtained.

On the basis of these findings, it might be concluded that the inequality (34) is not satisfied. Even after allowance for the statistical errors of estimation, there appears to be good reason for believing that the value-added tax provides less stability than the profits tax.

However, Meyer and Glauber advanced an alternative hypothesis: that investment behavior is radically different during an expansion than during a contraction. In the expansionary phase, the primary determinant of investment expenditure is the need to increase productive capacity. During such a period, either internal funds are sufficient to meet investment requirements or, if not, firms will

[21] John Meyer and Robert Glauber, *Investment Decisions, Economic Forecasting, and Public Policy* (Division of Research, Graduate School of Business Administration, Harvard University, 1964), p. 155.

seek external funds. The primary constraint on investment is the rate of increase of output. On the downside, on the other hand, firms are loathe to use external sources to finance investment. The primary constraint on investment in a recession is the internal supply of funds. This argument was strengthened by the fact that the coefficient of S^c turned out to be statistically insignificant during expansionary phases of the business cycle. During the downswings, on the other hand, the coefficient of S^c was estimated at .40. Thus it appears that the inequality (34) is satisfied during upswings but violated during recessionary periods. If this hypothesis of investment is accepted, a direct answer to the question of the relative stability of the value-added tax versus the profits tax is not possible. In order to give an answer, the initial conditions must be known. However, the case of greatest interest here is the one where the economy is at full employment. Which tax system would bring about the smallest deviation from full employment? On the basis of Meyer and Glauber's argument, the answer is that greater stability may result from the value-added tax than from the corporate profits tax.

Case II: Value-Added Tax Unshifted

In the preceding section, it was assumed that when the corporate profits tax is replaced by a value-added tax the latter is absorbed by the factors of production in proportion to their earnings. In other words, businessmen are able to shift onto factors of production the entire burden of the value-added tax—except that portion which falls upon the return to capital. The result is, of course, a large increase in the rate of corporate profits. Notice that nothing has been said concerning the shifting behavior of corporations under the profits tax. However, nothing needs to be assumed; corporate shifting behavior under the corporate profits tax can be taken as a datum. The analysis of the preceding section is consistent with full, partial, or no shifting of the profits tax.

Whereas the aforementioned pattern of shifting of the value-added tax is consistent with the classical full employment model, it has serious deficiencies as a reasonable assumption under the Keynesian system. In the first place, the prices of productive factors are not, at least in the short run, determined by the marginal productivity principles of the classical model. Instead, the level of wages, for example, is determined by such factors as the rate of unemployment, the rate of change of consumer prices, and the level of profits. Secondly, money wages are extremely sticky in the downward direction. Thus, firms could only shift the value-added tax by raising prices. Given the current political setting, this might prove quite difficult, since firms could not point to a lower level of profits as their justification for raising prices. (Indeed, firms have found it difficult to raise prices even when profits are falling.) The average level of profits would have remained the same because the two taxes are of equal yield.

Even if firms succeeded in raising prices, money wages might rise sufficiently to wipe out any increase in real profits.[22] Wages might rise in response to the higher levels of consumer goods prices. Furthermore, the higher level of corporate profits would provide labor unions with a potent bargaining weapon when making subsequent wage demands. Thus, a different set of shifting assumptions appears to be called for in an analysis of the Keynesian model. The alternative model of shifting that will be adopted here is that firms bear the entire burden of the value-added tax. This is equivalent to assuming that, in the short run, firms do not distinguish between the corporate profits tax and the value-added tax.

While this new shifting assumption appears to be as unreasonable as the earlier assumption, there is considerable merit for this approach. First, and most important, rigid money wages make it unlikely that part of the tax could be shifted backward onto labor (at least in the short run). Second, it is also unlikely that firms would try to pass the tax forward in the form of higher prices; the pressure of public opinion, and hence the threat of government intervention, would present a great obstacle. Third, in the aggregate, firms would enjoy the same average level of profits under the value-added tax as under the corporate profits tax; hence there would be no sense of urgency for shifting the tax. Finally, this shifting assumption is of the opposite extreme to our original shifting assumption; combined with our earlier assumption, this approach enables us to put limits on the possible outcome of the shift in tax structure.

[22] For evidence concerning this possibility, see George Perry, *Unemployment, Money Wage Rates, and Inflation* (Massachusetts Institute of Technology Press, 1966.)

Let F^v be the stability factor of a system where the GVA is shifted. Similarly, let F^π and F^v_2 represent the stability factors for a profits tax and nonshifted GVA, respectively. From the preceding analysis, on the assumption that investment was exogenous,

$$F^v = 1 - C'[(1 - \tau^v)(1 - S\mu)]$$

and

$$F^\pi = 1 - C'[(1 - \tau^p)(1 - S\mu)\tau^p].$$

Since

$$\pi^n = \pi - \tau^v Y$$

in the nonshifted value-added tax case, it can be deduced that

$$(36) \qquad F^v_2 = 1 - C'[(1 - \tau^v)(1 - S\mu) + S\tau^v(1 - \mu)].$$

Clearly, $F^v_2 < F^v$; that is, the nonshifted value-added tax provides less stability than the shifted value-added tax. Furthermore,

$$(37) \qquad F^v_2 - F^\pi = C'[(1 - \tau^p)(1 - S\mu) + (1 - \mu)\tau^p] \\ - C'[(1 - \beta\tau^p)(1 - \mu S) + S\beta\tau^p(1 - \mu)]$$

which is less than zero as

$$(38) \qquad Z = (1 - \mu S)(\beta - 1) - (1 - \mu)(\beta S - 1) < 0.$$

Now Z is a function of S, and the latter must fall into the range $0 \le S \le 1$. Evaluated at $S = 1$, Z becomes

$$(\beta - 1) - (\beta - 1) = 0.$$

At $S = 0$, it becomes

$$(\beta - 1) - (1 - \mu) < 0$$

because $\mu > \beta$. Furthermore,

$$\frac{dZ}{dS} = (1 - \beta)\mu - (1 - \mu)\beta > 0.$$

By the mean value theorem, it can be deduced that $F^\pi > F^v_2$. *Q.E.D.*

Thus, if the value-added tax is fully absorbed by business, it will provide less stability than the corporate profits tax. On the other hand, it has been shown above that, if the value-added tax is shifted backward, it may provide greater stability than the corporate profits tax. The reason for this turnabout is straightforward. When the value-added tax is fully absorbed by firms, it falls completely upon profits. Therefore, it must have exactly the same effect upon expenditure (per dollar of tax) as does a profits tax. Recall, however, that the profits tax has greater built-in flexibility than the value-added tax. Since the attempt is being made to isolate

$$\frac{\Delta E}{\Delta Y} = \frac{\Delta E}{\Delta T} B$$

for each tax system, it must be that $\Delta E/\Delta Y$ is less under the profits tax than under the nonshifted value-added tax. In our analysis of the shifted value-added tax, on the other hand, a dollar's change in tax had a greater effect upon expenditure under a value-added tax than under the profits tax (i.e., $\Delta E/\Delta T$ was greater in absolute value). This, of course, was due to the fact that the bulk of the value-added tax affects disposable income directly, whereas a good deal of the profits tax is absorbed by retained earnings.

Thus, the relative stability of the value-added tax and profits tax largely depends upon how the value-added tax is shifted. Since the value-added tax probably cannot be shifted in the short run, its immediate effect will be to reduce the stability of the economy. In the long run, however, firms will tend toward the position dictated by the classical full employment model. Firms will tend to substitute capital for labor because, at the prevailing wage-profit ratio, the existing capital-labor ratio is too low. This will have the effect of increasing the sensitivity of before-tax profits to changes in output (i.e., μ). This in turn will tend to increase the stability of the economy. To see this, simply consider the expression for F under the nonshifted value-added tax:

$$F_2^v = 1 - C'[(1 - \tau^v)(1 - S\mu) + S\tau^v(1 - \mu)].$$

Now

$$\frac{dF_2^v}{d\mu} = - C'[-(1 - \tau^v)S - S\tau^v\mu] > 0.$$

Thus in the long run, the system will become more stable. Whether or not this force can be so strong as eventually to make the value-added tax more stable than the profits tax cannot be determined here. It is, however, a possibility. If it should occur, the nonshifting model might have greater applicability in the short run, whereas the shifting model would have greater validity in the long run.

ANN F. FRIEDLAENDER*

The Federal Highway Program as a Public Works Tool

PUBLIC WORKS PROGRAMS have played an obvious, if not altogether important, role in combating economic downturns in the United States ever since the Great Depression of the 1930's. However, because of the lags of recognition and action that are typically involved in initiating the programs, there has been a tendency to question their usefulness.[1] Thus, given the generally short duration of the postwar recessions, it is felt that public works programs may actually be destabilizing if their lags are so great that the programs cannot be initiated until the recovery is well advanced. If, however, it can be shown that the lags are primarily institutional and that some government construction projects could be manipulated in a countercyclical fashion without creating serious distortions or losses through their postponement, then there is a clear case for the countercyclical role of public works programs of this type. Thus, in order to evaluate their role in stabilization policy, it is desirable to submit the programs to a careful analysis to determine if they are in fact as inherently inflexible as their critics claim.

* Boston College.
[1] See, for example, Commission on Money and Credit, *Money and Credit: Their Influence on Jobs, Prices and Growth* (Prentice-Hall, 1961), Chapter 5.

This paper attempts to undertake such an analysis for highway construction expenditures and shows that, with a few modifications in the federal highway program, highway construction expenditures could become a fairly potent countercyclical tool. Thus, to dismiss public works programs because they are too inflexible under the current institutional arrangements may be too hasty.

This paper begins by considering the determinants of all highway construction expenditures. It is found that annual expenditures can be determined by a capital stock adjustment process in which an effort is made to close the gap between a desired highway capacity and actual capacity. However, as the expenditures at any one moment in time may deviate from this norm because of short-run pressures, an effort is made to estimate the short-run determinants of highway construction expenditures. The finding is that the expenditures are sensitive to such short-run factors as available revenues, unemployment, etc., and show slight pro-cyclical tendencies. Next, the study is concerned specifically with the possibility of using the federal highway program to counteract the pro-cyclical tendencies of highway construction expenditures and to help to stabilize the economy. The actual and potential flexibility of that program is analyzed; the finding is that, with certain institutional changes, it could be used as a stabilization measure. Then the impact of highway construction expenditures upon the economy is considered, and it is shown that they could exert a significant, if not major, stabilizing influence. Finally, the results are summarized, and ways in which expenditures might respond to a change in national income, both under the existing institutional framework and under some proposed modifications, are discussed.

Determinants of Highway Construction Expenditures

Long-Run Determinants

Annual highway construction expenditures are determined by a capital stock adjustment mechanism in which an effort is made to close the gap existing between the desired or optimal highway facilities—which would permit the traffic to flow through the highway system with some permissible amount of congestion, accidents, and strain—and the actual facilities—marked by excessive congestion, accidents, and strain. Highway construction expenditures since the Clay Committee's reports on highway deficiencies[2] give a good example of this process of adjustment. After obtaining estimates from each state about the number of miles of highway then existing, which clearly were inadequate to meet the present and projected travel demands, and the cost of correcting the deficiencies, the Clay Committee determined that a ten-year construction program to modernize all the necessary roads and streets would require $101 billion. Although expenditures were not raised by the amount suggested, Congress did initiate the interstate program and increased the rest of the federal-aid program. Hence, over a fifteen-year period, additional highways costing $55 billion should be built as a result of the Clay Committee's recommendations.

To state this adjustment process formally, let E_t represent the real value of highway construction in year t, H_t^* represent the real value of highway facilities desired at the end of year t, and H_t represent the real value of existing highway facilities at the end of year t. The following model describes the relationship between the three variables:

$$E_t = \gamma(H_t^* - H_{t-1}) + \varepsilon_t$$

where γ is a constant that reflects the speed of adjustment of the existing to the desired stock of highways and ε_t is a random disturbance.

The optimal or desired value of the highway stock, H_t^*, should permit present and future traffic to flow through the highway system at some minimum attainable vehicular cost. Since vehicular cost depends on highway use, the desired stock of highway facilities must depend on the current and projected use of the highway system. Use is reflected in traffic volume, congestion, and accident rates. The optimal stock of highways is, then, an increasing function of all of these variables. However, congestion and accidents also depend upon traffic volume. Therefore, it is sufficient to consider the optimal stock of highway facilities as related to traffic volume alone. This can be represented by vehicle miles of travel, fuel con-

[2] The President's Advisory Committee on a National Highway Program, *A 10-Year National Highway Program: A Report to the President* (Government Printing Office, 1955).

sumption, and registrations.[3] Thus, as a first approximation, it was assumed that

$$H_t^* = \beta_0 + \beta_1 D_t$$

where D_t represents the expected value of each of the variables that reflect the future demand for highway services, respectively taken to be fuel, registrations, and vehicle miles.

The actual stock of highway facilities existing at the end of the previous period, H_{t-1}, should reflect the services that the existing highway system actually provides. The depreciated real value of the stock of highway facilities that are actually in use should give the best approximation of these actual services.

Lagged expenditure was added to the estimated equation as a variable in order to introduce a somewhat more complex reaction. The regression equation that was finally estimated took the following form:

$$E_t = \gamma[(a_0 + a_1 D_t) - a_2 H_{t-1}] + a_3 E_{\text{lagged}} + \eta_t$$

where E_t equals the value, in billions of dollars, of real highway construction of state and local roads during year t;[4] H_t represents the depreciated real value, in billions of dollars, of the miles of surfaced highway existing at the end of year t; D_t is a proxy for the desired stock of highways and is represented by, respectively, F_t (billions of gallons of motor fuel consumed in year t), V_t (billions of miles of vehicular travel during year t), and R_t (millions of total vehicular registrations at the end of year t);[5] and η is a new random

---

[3] Of these variables, fuel probably is the best proxy for highway use, since it gives a heavier weight to the large vehicles that impose greater wear and congestion upon the highways.

[4] The dollar value of construction was deflated by the construction bid price index of a composite mile, which is composed of the average quantities used in a typical highway project and includes the cost of a standard bundle of excavation, paving, reinforcing and structural steel, and structural concrete. The composite mile does not represent the quantities involved in the actual construction of any particular type of road. By deflating construction expenditures by this index, technical change is implicitly incorporated into highway construction and, therefore, can be neglected. Since 1940, the index has been adjusted downward to eliminate the effect of increased design standards. Therefore, the increasing standards of highways will be reflected in increased construction expenditures.

[5] In these equations, there may be considerable interaction between the lagged mileage variable and the proxies for the desired stock of highway facilities. Specifically, if the desired mileage is a function of total highway use, highway use is also a function of the existing mileage. However, the correlation matrices do not indicate much multicollinearity of this type.

TABLE 1. Regression Coefficients for Annual Highway Equations[a]

Demand Variable	Constant	D_t	H_{t-1}	E_{t-1}	R^2	Vn[b]
Fuel (F)	.309	.036	−.024	.815	.908	1.99
	(.181)	(.012)	(.015)	(.116)		
Vehicle miles (V)	.248	.0032	−.0285	.823	.908	1.99
	(.176)	(.0011)	(.0168)	(.117)		
Registrations (R)	.040	.0301	−.0197	.802	.908	1.98
	(.174)	(.0100)	(.0142)	(.118)		

[a] D_t = proxy for the desired stock of highways and is represented by the following:
F_t = billions of gallons of motor fuel consumed in year t
V_t = billions of miles of vehicular travel in year t
R_t = millions of total vehicular registrations at end of year t
H_t = depreciated real value, in billions of dollars, of the miles of surfaced highway existing at end of year t
E_t = value, in billions of dollars, of real highway construction of state and local roads during year t.
[b] Von Neumann statistic.

disturbance. Since D_t represents the desired stock, the equation implies that highway construction expenditures are a function of the current and all past values of the gap between the desired and the actual stock of highway facilities. The estimated relationships are given in Table 1.[6]

Since highway construction expenditures in any one year create the change in the value of the stock of highway facilities in that year, the ultimate value of the stock of highway facilities associated with an increase in the demand for travel services can be calculated from the following equations:

$$H = 12.5420 + 1.500F$$
$$H = .8702 + .1123V$$
$$H = 2.0304 + 1.528R .$$

Thus, if the consumption of highway fuel were to increase by one billion gallons per year and remain at that level forever after, the total value of the highway stock would finally increase by $1.5 billion; if the amount of travel were to increase by one billion miles per year, the value of the stock of highways would ultimately in-

[6] Because of the presence of the lagged dependent variable on the right-hand side of the equation, estimates reported in Table 1 may be biased if serial correlation of the residuals is present. In this paper, no attempt was made to determine the order of magnitude of these biases, but that question must be thoroughly investigated before the results reported in this paper can be accepted as definitive.

crease by $112 million; if the number of registered vehicles increased by one million vehicles each year, the value of the highway stock would ultimately increase by $1.5 billion. These relationships imply the following steady-state elasticities of demand for the stock of highways:[7]

> Fuel: $E = 1.581$
> Vehicle miles: $E = 1.554$
> Registrations: $E = 2.370$.

Hence, the highway stock is most sensitive to changes in the total number of registrations.

Table 2 indicates that there is a certain amount of overexpansion of the stock of highways in response to a steady increase in the demand for travel before the highway stock reaches its equilibrium level. Nevertheless, the response is extremely slow, and ten years after the initial increase in the demand for automotive transportation the new highway stock has reached only 60 to 70 percent of its equilibrium value. Thus, even though the estimated elasticities indicate that the highway stock is ultimately quite responsive to changes in the demand for highway services, the stock is not very responsive in any one year. Construction does not react substantially, on an annual basis, to changes in demand. This can be seen from the following annual elasticities:[8]

> Fuel: $E = .330$
> Vehicle miles: $E = .396$
> Registrations: $E = .379$.

Short-Run Determinants

While annual highway construction expenditures are probably determined by the divergence between the actual and the desired

---

[7] The elasticities were calculated by using the long-term or steady-state coefficients and the average values of the relevant variables. The elasticities calculated by using these coefficients are referred to as steady-state elasticities, in contrast to elasticities calculated by using the coefficients based on annual or quarterly relationships. These latter elasticities are referred to as annual or quarterly elasticities, respectively.

[8] These elasticities were computed by using the short-term coefficients and the average values of the variables. A steady-state solution for the level of expenditures would not make sense since expenditures are the first difference of the highway stock, which is also included in the equation.

TABLE 2. Value of the Highway Stock After a Unit Increase in the Demand for Automotive Travel

(In billions of dollars)

Year After Increase	Demand Proxies		
	Fuel	Registrations	Vehicle miles
1	.0360	.0301	.0032
2	.1005	.0838	.0089
3	.1866	.1555	.0166
4	.2883	.2403	.0257
5	.4003	.3340	.0356
6	.5180	.4334	.0459
7	.6374	.5354	.0563
8	.7555	.6378	.0665
9	.8696	.7385	.0761
10	.9777	.8362	.0851
11	1.0783	.9297	.0933
12	1.1705	1.0181	.1005
13	1.2535	1.1009	.1062
14	1.3271	1.1777	.1122
15	1.3918	1.2483	.1166
16	1.4460	1.3127	.1201
17	1.4920	1.3709	.1228
18	1.5297	1.4232	.1247
19	1.5597	1.4697	.1259
20	1.5827	1.5109	.1264
Equilibrium value	1.5000	1.5280	.1123

highway facilities, other factors must determine actual expenditures within a period as short as a quarter of a year. In particular, the short-run behavior of highway construction expenditures should be particularly sensitive to the availability of funds, seasonal weather conditions, and the state of the economy. Data on expenditures can, of course, be seasonally adjusted to eliminate the influence of the weather; after such adjustment the data reflect the dependence of expenditures upon the available funds and the state of the economy.

Nevertheless, quarterly highway construction expenditures are clearly linked to annual expenditures, and some recognition of this fact must be made. This is not difficult, however, for user tax revenues themselves depend on the demand for automotive travel. Specifically, there are three types of federal user excise taxes: those imposed on the purchase of (1) gasoline and lubricating oil, (2) motor vehicles and parts, and (3) tires and tubes. The revenues from each of these must be increasing functions of the demand for automotive travel and are, specifically, respective functions of the amount of motor fuel consumed, the number of new registrations, and tire and tube sales. However, data limitations made it necessary to estimate the automobile and tire excise revenues on the basis of consumer purchases of automobiles and parts and to relate tire excises to tire production rather than to sales. Both of these variables should be fairly good proxies. Because the tax rates were not constant over the period, they were also included as determinants of the level of taxes.

The estimated relationships took the following form:[9]

Fuel Taxes:

$$\ln T_t = 7.089 + .828 \ln F_t + .9135 \ln R_t$$
$$(.596) \quad (.133) \qquad (.0765)$$
$$R^2 = .99$$

where T is quarterly tax revenues from sales of gasoline and oil in thousands of dollars, seasonally adjusted; F is quarterly fuel consumption in millions of gallons, seasonally adjusted; R is gasoline tax rate in dollars per gallon.

Automobiles and Parts Taxes:

$$\ln T_t = 6.868 + .916 \ln C_{t-1} + .918 \ln R_{t-1}$$
$$(.375) \quad (.108) \qquad (.055)$$
$$R^2 = .95$$

where T is quarterly tax revenues from sales of motor vehicles and parts in millions of dollars, seasonally adjusted; C is quarterly consumer purchases of automobiles and parts in billions of dollars, seasonally adjusted; R is ad valorem tax rate.

[9] See Albert Ando, E. Cary Brown, and Earl W. Adams, Jr., "Government Revenues and Expenditures," in James Duesenberry and others (eds.), *The Brookings Quarterly Econometric Model of the United States* (Rand McNally & Co. and North-Holland Publishing Co., 1965), pp. 544–47, for a full discussion of the specific form of the equations.

Tire and Tube Taxes:

$$\ln T = .973 + .206 \ln P_t + .405 \ln P_{t-1} + .190 \ln R_t + .771 \ln R_{t-1}$$
$$(1.257) \quad (.124) \qquad (.120) \qquad\qquad (.143) \qquad\quad (.143)$$
$$R^2 = .94$$

where T is quarterly tax revenues from sales of tires and tubes in millions of dollars, seasonally adjusted; P is quarterly tire production in thousands of tires at annual rates, seasonally adjusted; R is tax rate in dollars per pound.

The coefficients of these equations indicate that the excise tax revenues are quite sensitive to changes in the demand for automotive travel as reflected by fuel consumption, automobile purchases, and tire and tube production.

In addition to user excise taxes,[10] the funds available for highway construction are determined by the amount of state and local government and turnpike bond flotations[11] and of property tax revenues.[12] The connection between user excises and highway construction should be fairly close since states are very responsive to changes in the revenues available for highway construction. However, because the flotation of highway bonds is only the first step in

---

[10] In 1959, 28 states used all of their user excises for highway purposes; only Delaware, Georgia, New York, New Jersey, and Rhode Island placed all of their highway user tax revenues into the state general fund. Furthermore, 11 states diverted less than 10 percent of their highway excises to nonhighway uses. See P. Burch, *Highway Revenue and Expenditure Policy in the United States* (Rutgers University Press, 1962), p. 64.

[11] In 1955, the total receipts from user taxes were approximately $4 billion, while the receipts from bond issues were only $0.66 billion. Of the nonrevenue bonds floated for highway purposes, well over 80 percent are usually general obligation bonds, backed by the taxing power of the state. Limited obligation bonds, backed by user tax receipts, have become increasingly popular since World War II, while reimbursement obligations, which are local bonds backed by a reimbursable portion from the states, are used very little. See H. C. Duzan, W. R. McCallum, and T. R. Rodd, "Highway Bond Financing," *Public Roads*, Vol. 27, No. 4 (October 1957), p. 73.

[12] In the urban areas, approximately 55 percent of the local roads are financed through property taxes, while in the rural areas only 40 percent are financed through such taxes. Although there are a few special assessments on property, based on the assumption that the landowner ought to pay for some of the increased valuation of his property caused by its increased accessibility, most of the property taxes are straight *ad valorem* taxes on the value of the land and buildings and are not specifically linked to highways. Most of the remaining cost of the local highways is financed by state grants-in-aid to the local communities; approximately 26.2 percent of local urban roads and 41.5 percent of local rural roads are financed through these grants. However, these local roads account for only a small percentage of total highway construction. (See Burch, *Highway Revenue*, pp. 69 and 132.)

the construction of bond-financed highways, the response of highway construction to changes in the highway-bond rate must be fairly slow. Because property taxes form such a small percentage of the available funds, they can safely be ignored.

The link between highway construction expenditures and economic activity can be analyzed by including an unemployment variable in the estimated quarterly equation. But since lags in recognition and in action may prevent an immediate response to an increase in employment, the unemployment variable should be introduced only with a lag.

The quarterly behavior of highway construction expenditures was postulated to be determined by the following relationship:

$$E_t = a_0 + a_1 T_{\text{lagged}} + a_2 N_{\text{lagged}} + a_3 r_{\text{lagged}} + a_4 E_{\text{lagged}} + u_t$$

where E equals the quarterly expenditures in millions of current dollars, seasonally adjusted,[13] T represents quarterly federal user excise taxes in millions of current dollars, seasonally adjusted,[14] N is the quarterly excess of unemployment over 4 percent, seasonally adjusted,[15] r is the quarterly municipal bond rate, seasonally adjusted,[16] and u_t represents a random disturbance variable.

[13] It seemed desirable to estimate quarterly highway construction expenditures in terms of their current money value instead of in real terms, since the hypothesis is that these expenditures are a function of the current value of the revenues available (and not the real value of the funds). This formulation implicitly assumes a short-term money illusion on the part of governments, but not a long-term money illusion, since the annual construction expenditures are estimated in real terms.

[14] Unfortunately, data are lacking on the quarterly revenues from state and local user taxes. However, using the value of only federal excises probably does not affect the results of the estimations, although its use is theoretically difficult to justify. Before the formation of the federal highway trust fund, only half of the federal user excise revenues were used for highway purposes. However, the unused half was approximately equal to the state and local user tax revenues. Since the formation of the trust fund, federal revenues have tended to swamp state and local revenues. Thus, the sum of federal excises is probably not a bad proxy for the sum of all excises.

[15] An unemployment rate above 4 percent was taken to indicate a depressed state of the economy, which might be expected to make the government increase its expenditures on highway construction.

[16] The highway bonds issued are mostly state and local government general obligation bonds and turnpike bonds. In a paper on the effect of credit tightening on state and local capital outlays, Charlotte Phelps showed that there is no apparent difference in the behavior of the rates on state and on local general obligation bonds. Therefore, using the municipal bond rate to represent the behavior of both the state and local general obligation bonds is justified. However, revenue (turnpike) bonds do yield a higher rate than these other bonds, partly because they are not tax exempt and partly because they have somewhat higher risks of flotation and default. Consequently, using the municipal bond rate to reflect the cost of

Experimentation with the actual lags yielded the following relationship:[17]

$$E_t = 95.291 + .428T_{t-1} + 51.18N_{t-1} - 53.04r_{t-4} + .742E_{t-1}.$$
$$\quad (96.60) \quad (.139) \quad\quad (36.77) \quad\quad (68.11) \quad\quad (.109)$$
$$R^2 = .933 \quad Vn = 2.09.$$

The equilibrium relationship given by this equation is

$$E = 369.345 + 1.659T + 198.37N - 205.58r.$$

Thus, a million-dollar increase in federal user excises will lead to an increase of \$1.66 million in highway construction expenditures; an increase in the unemployment rate of 1 percentage point above 4 percent will raise highway construction expenditures by almost \$200 million; and an increase of 1 percentage point in the municipal bond rate will ultimately reduce highway construction expenditures by slightly more than \$200 million.

The following elasticities are implied by these relationships:[18]

Taxes: $\qquad\qquad\qquad E = \varepsilon_T = \quad 1.152$
Unemployment rate: $\; E = \varepsilon_N = \quad .091$
Interest rate: $\qquad\quad\; E = \varepsilon_r \; = \; -.551.$

Hence, in the short-run, changes in highway construction expenditures are primarily determined by changes in the availability of funds. Moreover, the speed of adjustment is quite rapid, and three-fourths of the ultimate impact from an increase in any of the variables will have worked itself out within a year.

Some idea of the consistency of the annual and quarterly estimates can be obtained from a comparison of the elasticities of highway construction with respect to a change in travel demand estimated on a quarterly basis and on an annual basis. In particular, two comparisons are relevant: a comparison of the annual elasticity of construction expenditures with respect to a change in fuel con-

---

turnpike capital will underestimate this cost. No other alternative seemed to be available, however. See Charlotte Priscilla Demonte Phelps, "The Impact of Tightening Credit on Municipal Capital Expenditures in the United States," in Commission on Money and Credit, *Impacts of Monetary Policy* (Prentice-Hall, 1963), pp. 642–43.

[17] Because the interest rate coefficient is insignificant, its value should not be taken too seriously. The insignificance may be due to statistical difficulties involved with introducing the interest rate variable into the equation in linear form.

[18] The elasticities were computed by using the long-term equilibrium or steady-state coefficients and the means of the variables.

sumption estimated on the basis of quarterly data with that estimated on the basis of annual data; and a comparison of the steady-state elasticity of construction expenditures with respect to a change in fuel consumption estimated on the basis of quarterly data with that estimated on the basis of annual data.

Although the quarterly elasticity of highway construction with respect to changes in fuel consumption was not directly estimated, it can be inferred from other estimated relationships. The quarterly elasticity of construction with respect to a shift in available revenues is .297[19] while the quarterly elasticity of revenues with respect to a shift in fuel consumption is .828. Hence the inferred elasticity of construction expenditures with respect to a shift in fuel consumption is .246. To be compared with the annual elasticity of .33, this figure must be converted to an annual basis. By estimating the annual impact on highway construction expenditures of an increase of taxes, an annual elasticity of .681 can be derived.[20] Multiplying this by .828, the elasticity of tax revenues with respect to fuel consumption,[21] yields an annual elasticity of .564 for highway construction expenditures with respect to changes in fuel consumption.

This figure is considerably greater than the annual elasticity of .33 estimated directly. However, this latter figure probably underestimates the true elasticity since it accounts only for the influence of an increase in fuel consumption on the demand for highway services, while the other takes into account the influence of fuel consumption on both the demand for and supply of highway services. Hence the two estimates seem to be reasonably consistent, with the estimate of .564 probably being closer to the true annual elasticity of highway construction with respect to a shift in fuel consumption.

An alternative measure of the consistency of the relationships can be derived by comparing the steady-state elasticities of construction with respect to changes in fuel consumption estimated by using quarterly data with those estimated by using annual data. The short-run elasticity of fuel tax collections with respect to fuel consumption was found to be .828, while the steady-state elasticity

[19] This was calculated by using the quarterly revenue coefficient and the averages of the relevant variables.

[20] This calculation is based on the assumption that the ratio of the quarterly averages of taxes and expenditures does not differ from the annual ratio.

[21] Biases may be introduced since .828 is a quarterly figure. However, the annual and the quarterly elasticities should vary only if the rate changes.

of highway construction with respect to highway taxes was found
to be 1.152. As long as total highway tax collections move proportionately with fuel tax collections, the product of the above two
elasticities, .954, can be taken as the minimum steady-state elasticity
of highway construction with respect to fuel consumption. This
figure is a minimum for two reasons: first, an increase in fuel consumption may increase highway construction over and above the
effects obtained through an increase in taxes; second, an increase
in fuel consumption, representing an increase in the demand for
highway services, might induce the government to raise the rate at
which fuel consumption is taxed. Since neither of these considerations was included in the above calculation, it is likely that the true
steady-state elasticity of highway construction with respect to fuel
consumption is greater than the estimated elasticity of .954. If it is
assumed that the stock of highways increases at a steady exponential
rate, the expenditures on highway construction must necessarily
grow at the same rate. This implies, however, that the steady-state
elasticity of construction with respect to fuel consumption should be
the same as the steady-state elasticity of the highway stock with
respect to fuel consumption. This latter elasticity was found to be
1.58, which is not inconsistent with the estimated steady-state
construction elasticity of .954 because of the underestimation connected with the quarterly steady-state elasticity. Nevertheless, the
higher figure is probably a better indication of the true elasticity.

   Although the quarterly estimates indicate that highway construction expenditures are insensitive to changes in the unemployment rate, they may be sensitive to changes in national income.
Since the remainder of this paper is specifically concerned with the
countercyclical effectiveness of the federal highway program, it is
desirable to determine if highway construction expenditures have
responded to such changes.

   In spite of the low elasticity of quarterly highway construction
expenditures with respect to the unemployment rate in excess of 4
percent, which indicates that changes in highway construction are
not very sensitive to changes in employment, the general level of the
expenditures has been tied to economic activity throughout the
postwar period. This is true because highway construction depends
upon available revenues, which are closely tied to economic activity.
The major portion of highway construction takes place through the

state highway departments, which administer the local federal-aid highway funds and the state grants-in-aid to the county and local governments. Before 1956, the federal-aid highway program accounted for a little less than one-half of all highway construction. This program was financed on a fifty-fifty sharing basis between the states and the federal government. Hence, the latter's contribution represented only about one-fourth of all funds available for highway construction. Consequently, the states (with some help from the local governments) had to finance three-fourths of the total highway construction expenditures from their available tax revenues, which are largely determined by the tax revenues in their highway trust funds.[22] As the equations relating highway user excise revenues to the demand for automotive transportation indicate, these user excises are quite sensitive to fluctuations in the demand for automotive transportation; therefore, the revenues available will vary as the demand for automotive transportation varies. Consequently, the sensitivity of the revenues available for highway construction will largely depend upon the responsiveness of automotive transportation to changes in national income.

The Federal-Aid Highway Act of 1956, which initiated the interstate program and created a federal highway trust fund, changed the structure of financing highway construction without changing the dependence of the available revenues upon the general demand for automotive transportation. The formation of the interstate program enlarged the share of the federal highway program, which currently accounts for approximately two-thirds of all highway construction expenditures. Because the interstate program is 90 percent financed by federal funds, the role of the state revenues has been reduced more than proportionately, and the federal government now accounts for over one-half of all highway construction expenditures.[23] However, the increase in federal participation has not lessened the dependence of highway construction funds upon user

[22] See Burch, *Highway Revenue*, p. 64.
[23] The interstate program accounts for approximately two-thirds of all federal-aid highway expenditures and thus accounts for approximately four-ninths of all highway construction expenditures. Since the federal government contributes 90 percent of the cost of the interstate program, the federal government currently finances approximately 40 percent of all highway construction expenditures through that program. The remaining one-third of the federal-aid program is shared equally by the states and the federal government. Thus, the federal government finances somewhat over 50 percent of all highway construction expenditures.

excises, because the 1956 Highway Act also created a highway trust fund, whose revenues are determined solely by user excises. Moreover, Congress imposed a pay-as-you-go requirement on the trust fund, which makes it impossible to run a deficit in the fund unless Congress specifically removes the pay-as-you-go requirement for a specified length of time.[24] Thus, to the extent that driving and automobile and tire purchases are sensitive to the state of the economy, user tax revenues will be affected, which will, in turn, affect the amount of highway construction.

Instead of estimating the relationship between highway construction expenditures and national income directly, an indirect approach was used, which would take into account the chain of events outlined above. Consequently, the demand for automotive transportation was first estimated as a function of national income in three equations:

$$F_t = a_0 + a_1 GNP_t$$
$$C_t = a_0 + a_1 GNP_t$$
$$P_t = a_0 + a_1 GNP_t$$

where F is quarterly fuel consumption, C represents quarterly consumer expenditures on automobiles and automotive parts, P equals quarterly production of tires and tubes, and GNP is quarterly gross national product (GNP); all are seasonally adjusted. After calculating the elasticity of each of the demand parameters with respect to GNP, it is possible to relate this to the elasticity of each type of tax, in order to obtain a measure of the elasticity of automotive taxes with respect to GNP. This can then be applied to the elasticity of highway construction expenditures with respect to highway excise revenues, to obtain a measure of the sensitivity of highway construction expenditures with respect to changes in GNP.

The estimated relationships between the demand proxies and GNP are as follows:

$$F_t = 1.309 + .027\ GNP_t \qquad R^2 = .936$$
$$(.001)$$

where F is quarterly fuel consumption in millions of gallons,

[24] This was done in the 1958 Highway Act when Congress created the special counter-cyclical D Program. See pp. 93–98, below.

TABLE 3. Derivation of Elasticity of Highway Construction Expenditures with Respect to Gross National Product (GNP)

Specific User Excise	Elasticity of Travel Demand with Respect to GNP[a] $\dfrac{\partial D}{\partial Y}\left(\dfrac{Y}{D}\right)$	Elasticity of User Tax Revenues with Respect to Travel Demand[b] $\dfrac{\partial T}{\partial D}\left(\dfrac{D}{T}\right)$	Elasticity of Taxes with Respect to GNP $\dfrac{\partial T}{\partial Y}\left(\dfrac{Y}{T}\right)$	Elasticity of Highway Construction Expenditures with Respect to User Excises[c] $\dfrac{\partial E}{\partial T}\left(\dfrac{T}{E}\right)$	Elasticity of Highway Construction Expenditures with Respect to GNP $\dfrac{\partial E}{\partial Y}\left(\dfrac{Y}{E}\right)$	Specific User Excise Revenue as a Proportion of All Highway User Excise Revenue[d]	Weighted Elasticity of Highway Construction Expenditures with Respect to GNP
	(1)	(2)	(3)=(1)×(2)	(4)	(5)=(3)×(4)	(6)	(7)=(5)×(6)
Fuel	.515	.828	.426	1.152	.491	.464	.228
Autos	1.002	.916	.917	1.152	1.054	.456	.481
Tires and tubes	.501	.611	.306	1.152	.353	.080	.028
Total							.737

Note:
D = Travel demand proxy and represents fuel consumption, consumer purchases of automobiles and automotive parts, and tire and tube production
Y = GNP
T = All tax revenues from federal highway user excises
E = Highway construction expenditures
[a] See p. 77.
[b] See pp. 68–69.
[c] See p. 71.
[d] Derived from data in Albert Ando, E. Cary Brown, and Earl W. Adams, Jr., "Government Revenues and Expenditures," in James S. Duesenberry and others (eds.), The Brookings Quarterly Econometric Model of the United States (Rand McNally & Company and North-Holland Publishing Co., 1965).

seasonally adjusted; *GNP* is quarterly real value of GNP (in 1958 dollars) at annual rates, seasonally adjusted.

$$P_t = 3.303 + .057\,GNP_t \qquad R^2 = .625$$
$$(.006)$$

where *P* is quarterly tire production (in millions of tires), at annual rates, seasonally adjusted; *GNP* is quarterly real value of GNP (in 1958 dollars) at annual rates, seasonally adjusted.

$$A_t = -.021 + .037\,GNP_t \qquad R^2 = .719$$
$$(.003)$$

where *A* is quarterly consumer purchases of automobile and automobile parts, in billions of current dollars, seasonally adjusted; *GNP* is quarterly current value of GNP at annual rates, seasonally adjusted.

These equations imply the following elasticities:[25]

Fuel: $\qquad\qquad E = \varepsilon_F = .515$
Auto purchases: $E = \varepsilon_A = 1.002$
Tire production: $E = \varepsilon_p = .501.$

Table 3 gives the calculations used to estimate the elasticity of highway construction expenditures with respect to GNP. This elasticity is approximately .74, which implies that for every 1 percent change in GNP there is a .74 percent change in highway construction expenditures. Thus, the experience of the postwar period indicates that highway construction expenditures are somewhat sensitive to changes in national income and have moved in the same direction as the business cycle. Whether this is a rigid relationship will be the subject of the next section.

Lag Relationships in the Federal Highway Program

Of the many public works programs undertaken by the federal government, the federal highway program should be particularly

---

[25] The elasticities were calculated by using the average value of the relevant variables. Since quarterly highway expenditures were being estimated in terms of current value, it was necessary to adjust the estimated elasticities of fuel consumption and tire production to put them in terms of current dollars. This was done by multiplying the estimated elasticities by the ratio of the percentage change in real GNP to the percentage change in money GNP over the period of estimation, using the average values of GNP as a base.

well suited to countercyclical manipulation. It is composed of a large number of projects, many of which are sufficiently small to be easily initiated and completed within a year. Moreover, the total dollar value of these projects is sufficiently large to stimulate considerably both output and employment in the affected industries and regions. Postponing these projects to periods of low employment should cause substantial savings in their social costs, while the losses in the total benefits caused by postponing their construction should be negligible. Thus, the creation of a stock of small highway projects, which would be released for construction in a countercyclical fashion, would give the government a fairly potent tool to help to stabilize the economy.

Unfortunately, past efforts to use highway construction expenditures in a countercyclical fashion were not particularly successful.[26] This, however, can be blamed on institutional rigidities rather than on any lags inherent in the highway construction program itself. Under present arrangements, most federal-aid highway construction is planned far in advance and, in addition to being based upon the highway needs in each state, the amount of programmed construction is heavily influenced by the revenues available in the highway trust fund. Each state highway department works closely with the Bureau of Public Roads (BPR) and continuously submits various projects for approval by the BPR's field representative. Once a project has been initially approved or programmed, the BPR considers that the funds for the share of the federal government are obligated, although these funds will not be used for several years. After the initial approval, the project must be sent back to the state highway department for further development before it can be formally approved. Only after formal approval has been given can bids on a project be sought and construction begin. However, the BPR does not have to use the funds earmarked for the project until its construction is well advanced, since the BPR reimburses the state only for funds that the state has actually paid to the contractor. As the usual lag between initial approval and payment of funds to the states is between one and two years,[27] the BPR must plan its obligations far in advance. If it feels

[26] See pp. 93–98, below.

[27] The BPR has estimated that the lags between the initial programming and the payments of funds to the states are fifteen months for the federal-aid primary system; twelve months for the federal-aid secondary system; and twenty-two months for the urban exten-

that there may not be sufficient revenues in the highway trust fund to cover the required expenditures for projects currently approved, it will postpone the programming of any additional projects until it believes that the projected revenues will be adequate to cover the projected expenditures.[28] Thus, the BPR views the pay-as-you-go requirement as a real restraint upon its freedom of action.

Consequently, any special countercyclical highway program must be initiated by Congress. However, the lags in congressional recognition and action are so long that the actual construction expenditures of such a highway program will only begin to enter the income stream when the recovery is well advanced. Congressional action of this type is at best ineffective and at worst may be actively destabilizing. Nevertheless, with a few changes in the institutional structure of the highway program, highway construction could become a fairly potent countercyclical weapon, for there is little inherent in its lag structure to make it unmanageable. In particular, the small highway projects in the federal-aid secondary system, which account for approximately $500 million of annual highway construction, can typically be completed within a year after construction begins. Thus, if a highway stabilization fund containing these small projects were established and these projects were released in a countercyclical fashion, their construction expenditures should enter into the income stream in a stabilizing way. The impact of these expenditures upon the economy would certainly not be insignificant since $1.5 billion worth of projects could accumulate in this fund during an upswing of three years.[29]

Institutional Setting

The Federal-Aid Highway Act of 1956 divided the federal highway program into two parts: the ABC program whose funds are distributed among the federal-aid primary system, the federal-aid secondary system, and the urban extensions of these systems;[30] and the interstate program whose funds are divided approximately

---

sions of these systems. The interstate lag was estimated to be somewhere between the lags for the federal-aid primary and the urban projects.

[28] This happened in 1959 when virtually no projects were programmed for three or four months.

[29] See pp. 98–101, below.

[30] The federal-aid primary system receives 45 percent of the ABC authorizations, the federal-aid secondary system 30 percent, and the urban extensions 25 percent.

FIGURE 1. Total Federal-Aid Highway Program: Authorizations and Apportionments, 1952–61

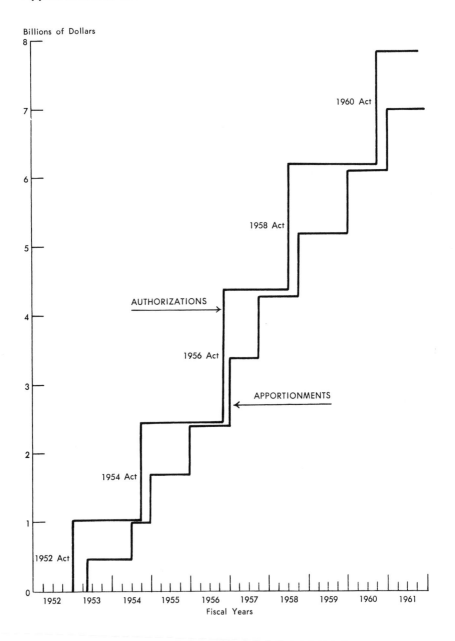

equally between the rural and the urban interstate systems. Because ABC projects are typically smaller and less complex than interstate projects, the lag structure of the ABC program should be somewhat different from that of the interstate program. Hence the lag structure of each program should be quantified separately.[31] Before estimating the lags, however, it is desirable to outline the nature of each step between the initial authorization of funds and the time when they actually enter the income stream as construction expenditures.

AUTHORIZATION-TO-APPORTIONMENT LAG. In order to facilitate the planning of the highway program, Congress tries to make authorizations well in advance of the time when the funds are actually to be used. The funds for the ABC program are usually authorized at the beginning of every other fiscal year. Hence ABC funds are authorized one year in advance of the first fiscal year in which they are to be made available to the states and two years in advance of the second year. Prior to 1956, Congress also followed this same procedure for the interstate program, but with the 1956 Highway Act, it authorized the entire estimated cost of completing the interstate system over a period of thirteen years.[32]

The BPR apportions these funds to the states at least six months before the beginning of the fiscal year for which they are authorized so that, for example, funds authorized for fiscal 1958 must be apportioned by January 1957. Usually, however, the BPR apportions these funds even earlier, as Figure 1 shows.[33] If Congress authorizes

[31] Similarly, the lag structure of each type of project within each program should be different. Unfortunately, data limitations made it impossible to estimate the lag structure within each program.

[32] Congress initially authorized $24.825 billion for the federal share of the interstate system to be spent in the fiscal years 1957–69 as follows: fiscal 1957, $1 billion; fiscal 1958, $1.5 billion; fiscal 1959–67, $2.2 billion each year; fiscal 1968, $1.5 billion; fiscal 1969, $1.025 billion. However, the 1958 Highway Act increased the authorizations for fiscal 1960 and 1961 to $2.5 billion a year, and the 1959 Highway Act then decreased the 1960 authorizations to $2 billion. The 1961 Highway Act made new authorizations based on a final cost estimate of $41 billion required to construct the interstate system, with a federal share of $37 billion. The period of authorizations was extended to 1972 and the following funds were authorized for each fiscal year: 1962, $2.2 billion; 1963, $2.4 billion; 1964, $2.6 billion; 1965, $2.7 billion; 1966, $2.8 billion; 1967, $2.9 billion; 1968–71, $3 billion a year; and 1972, $2.885 billion.

[33] Funds authorized for fiscal 1958 were apportioned on August 1, 1956; for fiscal 1959, on August 1, 1957; for fiscal 1960, on August 1, 1958; and for fiscal 1961, on October 8, 1959. Thus, the BPR usually apportions these funds a little less than a year before the fiscal year for which they are authorized.

additional funds belatedly, the BPR can apportion them immediately. Once the funds are apportioned, they remain available for two years after the close of the fiscal year for which they were authorized; e.g., funds authorized for fiscal 1960 were apportioned on August 1, 1958 and remained available for use by the states through June 1962. Consequently, the states know the amount of funds available for their use at least three years in advance of the time when they must actually be used.

APPORTIONMENT-TO-PROGRAMMING LAG. After the funds are apportioned to the states, each state highway department can program these funds for individual projects, whose construction can start only after the beginning of the relevant fiscal year. Because ABC authorizations and apportionments have remained relatively constant since the war, the state highway departments have a fairly clear notion of the funds available several years in advance. Consequently, there is a fairly steady stream of ABC projects coming into the BPR offices for initial approval.

However, this situation is not true for the interstate program, which was made a separate entity in the 1956 Federal Highway Act. The interstate system was formally established in 1944; but prior to 1956, Congress authorized funds for its construction as part of a single federal-aid highway program. These authorizations usually amounted to less than $100 million for annual construction. Therefore, the 1956 Highway Act, which was passed on June 29, 1956, led to an immediate tenfold increase in interstate authorizations, which jumped to $1 billion for fiscal 1957, $1.7 billion for fiscal 1958, and $2.0 billion a year for fiscal 1959–67. Since the BPR apportioned the 1957 authorization immediately, on July 1, 1956, there were $1 billion of apportioned funds available for interstate projects, in addition to whatever funds remained from past apportionments. The reaction of the state highway departments to their enlarged apportionments should give some indication of their probable response to additional authorizations and apportionments for a countercyclical highway program.

Because the interstate system had, in fact, been in existence for twelve years prior to the formation of the separate program to accelerate construction, there was a large backlog of potential projects. The Federal-Aid Highway Act of 1954 had directed the states to estimate the cost of completing the system in each state. This estimate required origin and destination studies, traffic projection studies, tentative route selection, and preliminary surveys for most of the system. Thus, by 1956, many projects had reached the programming stage and could be submitted to the BPR for initial approval when funds became available. Therefore, the response to the increased authorizations was almost instantaneous. In June 1956, programmed funds amounted to $5 million; in July, the figure rose to $74.3 million; in August to $122 million; by October it reached $224.7 million; and it has remained at approximately that amount every month since then.

Thus, within one month after the increased interstate apportionments, programmed funds responded substantially, and within three months, they reached a new high. This can be taken to represent the general lag between a sudden increase in apportionments and the resulting increase in programmed funds for both the ABC and the interstate programs when plans are already in existence. Therefore, if a countercyclical highway program were authorized in any given month, the BPR could apportion these funds immediately; and within four to six weeks a substantial portion of these funds could be programmed.

PROGRAMMING-TO-APPROVAL LAG. By the time a given project has been programmed, the state highway departments have made preliminary estimates of the costs of surveying, right-of-way acquisition, engineering services, and the actual construction of the roadway and structures. Before the project can be submitted for final approval, however, it is necessary to make detailed surveys, engineering studies, specifications, and cost estimates, and to acquire any needed right of way. Only when a state highway department believes that a project is ready to go out for bids does it submit the project to the BPR for final approval, which is usually given without requiring substantial modifications. The time between the initial and the final approval usually is anywhere from two or three months to a year, depending upon the size and complexity of the project. Small rural projects, which may require resurfacing or grade reduction and use standard engineering techniques, can be made ready for final approval within a few months, while a large interstate project, which may require special bridge types and structures and complicated grading, may take a year or more. In general, the less engineering time required in a project, the faster it can be made ready for approval.[34]

APPROVAL-TO-CONTRACTS LAG. After a project has been approved by the BPR, it is ready for bids. Usually at least three weeks must elapse between the time when the contract is advertised and the bids are opened. After the low bidder is determined, the BPR must approve his qualifications before the contract can be signed. The time between the approval of a project and the signing of the contract should take about four weeks.

CONTRACTS-TO-CONSTRUCTION LAG. Once the contract has been signed, construction begins as soon as the contractor can mobilize his workforce. As soon as the contractor begins to pay his men, the construction funds enter the income stream. However, this is recorded with a lag, since the monthly measure of construction only comes when the contractor submits a record of his expenses to the state, which pays him upon verification that the work has actually been completed.

Estimation of Structural Lags in the Highway Program

The structure of the lags in the federal highway program was estimated in this study by employing distributed lags. This procedure makes it possible to determine the response of construction expenditures to an increase in the programmed or approved funds and to trace the time path of this reaction.

ESTIMATION OF THE DISTRIBUTED LAGS. The following time series were available monthly for the years 1956–62: the federal share of the total highway funds programmed; the federal share of the total highway funds approved; the total value of the contracts awarded; and the federal share of construction put in place. Because each of these series forms a definite progression in time, each variable was estimated as a function of the previous variable; e.g., construction put in place was separately estimated as a function of contracts

---

[34] To minimize the design time, 78 percent of the state highway departments have developed standard plans for drainage structures and small bridges, and 72 percent have developed plans for superstructures. See the American Road Builders' Association, Task Force Report, *The Highway Construction Industry in a Long Range National Highway Program* (ARBA, April 1956), p. 16.

let, funds approved, and funds programmed. Each equation took the following general form:

$$Y_t = a_0 + a_1 X_t + a_2 Y_{t-1} + a_3 Y_{t-2} + a_4 X_{t-1} + u_t.$$

This implies that the dependent variable Y is a weighted sum of the current and all past values of the independent variable X, with a particular pattern of weights that specifically depend upon the estimated values of the lagged coefficients.[35]

However, there is a strong seasonal component in most of the variables. The BPR does less work in the summer months and around the Christmas holidays, causing the flow of programmed and approved funds to diminish during these periods. Moreover, adverse weather causes highway construction to decline during the winter. Because it is important to know if a public works highway program would respond differently if the additional funds were authorized in January or July, the data were not seasonally adjusted, but the model was altered to account for the seasonal variations explicitly by introducing seasonal dummy variables into the lagged dependent variable terms. The model was estimated using monthly and bi-monthly data. In the first case, the model took the following specific form:[36]

$$Y_t = a_0 + a_1 X_t + a_2\left[Y_{t-1} + d_1 Y_{t-1} + d_2 Y_{t-1} + d_3 Y_{t-1}\right]$$
$$+ a_3\left[Y_{t-2} + d_1 Y_{t-2} + d_2 Y_{t-2} + d_3 Y_{t-2}\right] + a_4 X_{t-1} + u_t$$

where

$d_1 = 1$ for the first quarter; otherwise 0;
$d_2 = 1$ for the second quarter; otherwise 0;
$d_3 = 1$ for the third quarter; otherwise 0.

---

[35] Specifically, a distributed lag of this type assumes that $Y_t = \sum_\tau w_\tau X_{t-\tau}$, where $w_\tau = k_1 \lambda_1^\tau + k_2 \lambda_2^\tau$; thus, w_τ is the sum of two geometric series, $k_1 \lambda_1^\tau$ and $k_2 \lambda_2^\tau$. The equation then takes the form

$$Y_t - (\lambda_1 + \lambda_2)Y_{t-1} + (\lambda_1\lambda_2)Y_{t-2} = (k_1 + k_2)X_t - (k_1\lambda_2 + k_2\lambda_1)X_{t-1}.$$

[36] Because the behavior of the dependent variable varies seasonally, it will respond cyclically to a steady unit increase in the independent variable. Consequently, the weighting function will be composed of trigonometric terms to permit a cyclical reaction function. Specifically,

$$Y_t = \sum_\tau w_\tau X_{t-\tau}, \text{ where } w_\tau = k_1 \lambda_1^\tau + k_2 \lambda_2^\tau, \text{ and } \lambda_1 = Re^{i\theta}, \lambda_2 = Re^{-i\theta}.$$

Since $a_2 = (\lambda_1 + \lambda_2)$ and $a_3 = -(\lambda_1\lambda_2)$, the elements of the a_2 term determine the periodicity of the reaction while the elements in the a_3 term determine its amplitude.

In the second case, the model took the following form:

$$Y_t = a_0 + a_1 X_t + a_2 [Y_{t-1} + d_1 Y_{t-1} + d_2 Y_{t-1}]$$
$$+ a_3 [Y_{t-2} + d_1 Y_{t-2} + d_2 Y_{t-2}] + a_4 X_{t-1} + u_t$$

where

$d_1 = 1$ for the first four months of the year; otherwise 0;

$d_2 = 1$ for the second four months of the year; otherwise 0.

Because of random fluctuations in the data, only the relationship between approved and programmed funds yielded meaningful results in the model using monthly data. Consequently, all the other relationships were estimated by using bimonthly data and the second model. Table 4 gives the estimated relationships, and Table 5 summarizes the most important aspects of the lag relationships. From these tables, the following conclusions can be drawn.

Because authorizations and apportionments occur only sporadically, it makes little sense to estimate the relationship between these variables and construction by means of distributed lags. An increase in highway construction authorizations could be apportioned immediately, and within a month or two these increased apportionments would be reflected in an increased flow of programmed funds. Consequently, in order to estimate the lags between actual construction and authorizations of funds, a month or two should be added to the programming-construction lag.

Relative speeds of the ABC and interstate responses. (1) The response of approved interstate funds is somewhat slower than the response of ABC funds to an increase in programmed funds. Thus, after six months, the approved funds in the ABC program settle down to their equilibrium pattern of behavior, while the approved funds in the interstate program require somewhat more than a year to do this. This difference should be expected because of the larger size of the interstate projects.

(2) However, the reaction of contracts let is almost identical in both the ABC and the interstate programs, and within a year both reaction patterns reach their equilibrium patterns. This similarity of behavior is also expected because the lag between the final approval of a project and the letting of the contract is largely independent of the project's size.

(3) Construction in the ABC program responds much more

rapidly to an increase in the flow of funds than does construction in the interstate program. While interstate construction usually takes several years to reach its equilibrium peak, the typical behavior of the ABC program is to overshoot its equilibrium peak before settling down to its equilibrium cycle. Consequently, a counter-cyclical highway program should be limited to the ABC program, whose projects are typically smaller than those in the interstate program.

Timing relationships. (1) The response of approved funds is essentially invariant to the date when the flow of programmed funds is increased. This occurs because the response of approved funds has a seasonal peak in April and in October of approximately equal magnitude. Consequently, it does not matter when the flow of programmed funds is initiated, since virtually all of the reaction will work itself out within a year.

(2) The reaction of contracts let is somewhat sensitive to the date of the initial increase in the flow of approved funds. The reaction path of the ABC program has a cyclical peak in the May–June period and also in the November–December period. However, unlike the behavior of approved funds, the speed of the reaction of ABC contracts does vary with the date of the initial increase in the flow of approved funds, and the maximum impact is achieved if the increase begins in the January-February period. The reaction function of the interstate program has one peak in the July–August period and a trough in the March–April period. The interstate reaction responds the most rapidly to an increase in the January–February period. Thus, for both the ABC and the interstate programs, the reaction of contracts let is the most sensitive to an increase in the flow of approved funds initiated in the beginning of the year.

(3) For maximum rapid impact, the flow of funds should be increased in the May–June period for the ABC program and in the January–February period for the interstate program. This will permit the maximum amount of construction to take place before the seasonal decline of construction during the winter months.[37]

---

[37] Table 5 actually indicates that slightly more impact is attained if the flow of ABC funds is increased in the September–October period. This, however, should not be taken too seriously, since it largely reflects the overshooting of the reaction function.

TABLE 4. Regression Coefficients for Lag Relationships in Interstate and ABC Programs

Lag Relationship	Constant	X_t	Y_{t-1}	$d_1 Y_{t-1}$	$d_2 Y_{t-1}$
Y=Federal funds approved X=Federal funds programmed					
Interstate[a]	.246 (14.030)	.690 (.066)	.334 (.160)	−.291 (.162)	−.075 (.236)
ABC[a]	24.486 (9.061)	.497 (.065)	.294 (.156)	−.128 (.247)	.065 (.243)
Y=Total contracts let X=Federal funds approved					
Interstate[b]	66.897 (33.407)	.235 (.055)	−.284 (.220)	−.286 (.279)	.207 (.248)
ABC[b]	147.440 (74.24)	.496 (.199)	.197 (.184)	−.505 (.280)	.123 (.311)
Y=Federal funds put in place X=Total contracts let					
Interstate[b]	−72.084 (54.66)	.454 (.212)	−.437 (.311)	.565 (.347)	.810 (.386)
ABC[b]	76.43 (61.38)	.109 (.142)	.473 (.347)	−.653 (.477)	.121 (.456)
Y=Federal funds put in place X=Federal funds approved					
Interstate[b]	−26.502 (26.044)	.266 (.076)	−.392 (.283)	.658 (.315)	1.046 (.341)
ABC[b]	81.69 (50.66)	.219 (.189)	.758 (.356)	−.733 (.506)	−.064 (.492)
Y=Federal funds put in place X=Federal funds programmed					
Interstate[b]	−9.736 (8.390)	.161 (.041)	−.282 (.229)	.513 (.276)	.821 (.298)
ABC[b]	87.67 (45.59)	.142 (.149)	.683 (.384)	−.793 (.496)	−.669 (.491)

[a] Based on monthly data where
$d_1 = 1$ for 1st quarter; otherwise 0
$d_2 = 1$ for 2nd quarter; otherwise 0
$d_3 = 1$ for 3rd quarter; otherwise 0
[b] Based on bimonthly data where
$d_1 = 1$ for 1st four months of the year; otherwise 0
$d_2 = 1$ for 2nd four months of the year; otherwise 0

88

TABLE 4 (concl.). Regression Coefficients for Lag Relationships in Interstate and ABC Programs

d_3Y_{t-1}	Y_{t-2}	d_1Y_{t-2}	d_2Y_{t-2}	d_3Y_{t-2}	X_{t-1}	Y_{t-3}	R^2
−.244	−.109	.081	.228	.153	−.186	.265	.731
(.161)	(.137)	(.159)	(.248)	(.161)	(.104)	(.073)	
−.132	−.034	.093	.147	.071	−.115	—	.554
(.170)	(.263)	(.156)	(.246)	(.263)	(.172)	—	
—	.367	.289	−.073	—	.211	—	.792
	(.229)	(.263)	(.246)	—	(.067)	—	
—	−.107	.344	−.112	—	.675	—	.704
	(.176)	(.247)	(.381)	—	(.237)	—	
—	1.245	−1.151	−.747	—	.350	—	.863
	(.345)	(.371)	(.479)	—	(.216)	—	
—	−.516	.235	−.417	—	.249	—	.823
	(.371)	(.427)	(.681)	—	(.138)	—	
—	1.401	−1.238	−.861	—	—	—	.908
	(.318)	(.338)	(.427)	—	—	—	
—	−.548	.345	.128	—	—	—	.753
	(.396)	(.460)	(.702)	—	—	—	
—	1.333	−1.113	−.517	—	—	—	.891
	(.136)	(.136)	(.229)	—	—	—	
—	−.518	.415	1.088	—	−.341	−.312	.825
	(.415)	(.455)	(.692)	—	(.147)	(.155)	

TABLE 5. ABC and Interstate Programs: Date of Equilibrium Peak, Initial Peak as Percentage of Equilibrium Peak, and Period After Initial Increase by Different Lag Relationships

Lag Relationship	Date of Equilibrium Peak	Initial Peak as Percentage of Equilibrium Peak, When Increase Initiated in						
		1st quarter	2nd quarter	3rd quarter	4th quarter	1st third	2nd third	3rd third
Federal funds approved on federal funds programmed								
ABC[a]	April	98.2	100.0	100.0	99.9	—	—	—
	October	100.0	100.0	100.0	99.9	—	—	—
Interstate[a]	April	86.0	98.8	97.4	93.3	—	—	—
	October	97.4	92.1	84.0	99.0	—	—	—
Total contracts let on federal funds approved								
ABC[b]	May–June	—	—	—	—	71.3	69.5	62.4
	Nov.–Dec.	—	—	—	—	89.2	74.9	80.0
Interstate[b]	July–Aug.	—	—	—	—	86.7	75.3	92.0
	July–Aug.	—	—	—	—	98.0	95.6	98.8
Federal funds put in place on total contracts let								
ABC[b]	Nov.–Dec.	—	—	—	—	101.0	127.2	117.5
Interstate[b]	Nov.–Dec.	—	—	—	—	20.7	20.2	13.5
	Nov.–Dec.	—	—	—	—	55.8	39.1	32.0
Federal funds put in place on federal funds approved								
ABC[b]	Sept.–Dec.	—	—	—	—	96.2	14.9	116.8
Interstate[b]	Nov.–Dec.	—	—	—	—	63.9	51.7	29.6
	Nov.–Dec.	—	—	—	—	84.9	79.5	70.0
Federal funds put in place on federal funds programmed								
ABC[b]	Sept.–Dec.	—	—	—	—	94.3	110.2	112.8
Interstate[b]	Nov.–Dec.	—	—	—	—	48.9	38.3	21.0
	Nov.–Dec.	—	—	—	—	71.3	64.7	54.9

[a] Based on monthly data and quarterly dummy variables.
[b] Based on bimonthly data and triyearly dummy variables.

(4) ABC construction expenditures will respond most rapidly to an increased flow of contracts let. However, the flow of contracts cannot be managed in a countercyclical manner, for contractors would be too disrupted if they were not sure of receiving the BPR's

TABLE 5 (concl.). ABC and Interstate Programs: Date of Equilibrium Peak, Initial Peak as Percentage of Equilibrium Peak, and Period After Initial Increase by Different Lag Relationships

Months After Initial Increase Before Initial Peak is Reached, When Increase Initiated in

1st quarter	2nd quarter	3rd quarter	4th quarter	1st third	2nd third	3rd third
4	13	10	7	—	—	—
10	7	4	13	—	—	—
4	13	10	7	—	—	—
10	7	4	13	—	—	—
—	—	—	—	8	8	8
—	—	—	—	14	14	14
—	—	—	—	6	6	14
—	—	—	—	20	18	24
—	—	—	—	12	4	4
—	—	—	—	12	8	4
—	—	—	—	24	20	16
—	—	—	—	12	6	4
—	—	—	—	12	8	4
—	—	—	—	24	20	16
—	—	—	—	12	6	4
—	—	—	—	12	8	4
—	—	—	—	24	20	16

approval for a year or more after the signing of the contract. Consequently, the BPR should regulate the flow of highway projects at the approval stage. Since the lag between the approval of funds and the letting of the contract is quite small, this policy would be almost as

FIGURE 2. ABC Program: Cumulative Totals of Funds for Highway Projects, 1956–62

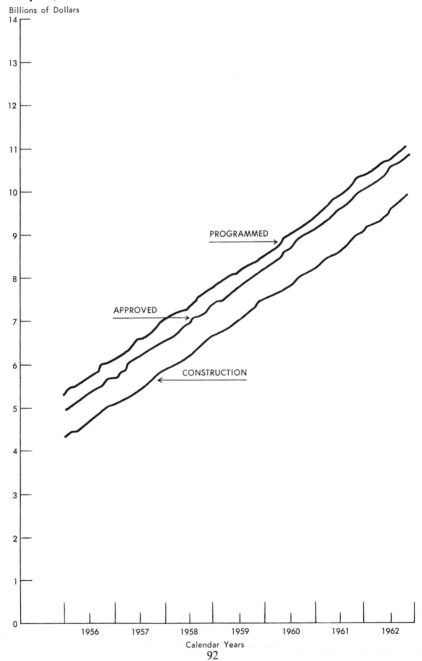

Billions of Dollars

PROGRAMMED

APPROVED

CONSTRUCTION

Calendar Years

effective as controlling the flow of actual contracts let and would reduce many of the lags that currently exist in the federal highway program.

ACTUAL LAGS. Although the above analysis outlines the structure of the lags inherent in the federal highway program, it does not give a satisfactory answer to the question of exactly how many months must elapse before an additional countercyclical authorization of funds will enter the income stream as construction expenditures, and of how many more months must elapse before these funds will have been spent. The problem arises because the distributed lag structure was generated by a permanent increase in the flow of funds, while any countercyclical program must be limited to a single addition to the flow of funds. Thus, to determine the actual lags that would exist if Congress were to make a single authorization of highway funds, a different approach must be used.

By plotting the cumulative totals of the programmed, approved, and construction funds, it is possible to get a rough notion of the lags involved from measuring the time elapsed before construction reaches the same level as programmed or approved funds. Figures 2 and 3 give these relationships for the ABC and the interstate programs, respectively. Since the BPR could regulate the flow of approved funds, the important lag is the one between approval and construction. It is obvious from the figures that the time required for construction to reach the same level as approved funds is much shorter for the ABC than for the interstate program. This lag is usually less than a year for the ABC program and between one and one-half and two years for the interstate program.

The D Program

In instituting the D program in April 1958 to counteract the 1957–58 recession, Congress experimented with using highway construction as a countercyclical tool. Because, however, the trough of the recession occurred before the D program was initiated, the usefulness of the program was obviously limited. Nevertheless, the experience of the program does indicate that the lags inherent in the programming of projects can be substantially reduced and that, once a project has received final approval, construction can take place quite rapidly.

FIGURE 3. Interstate Program: Cumulative Totals of Funds for Highway Projects, 1955–62

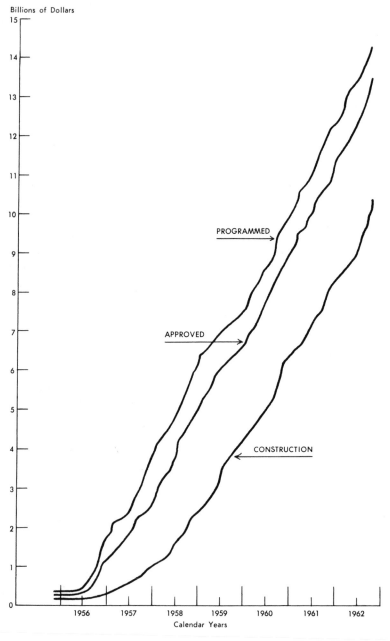

94

Under Section 2 of the 1958 Highway Act, Congress authorized an additional $400 million of ABC funds, which were to be matched by the states on a one-third to two-thirds state-federal basis instead of the usual fifty-fifty sharing. Consequently, a total of $600 million was made available for highway construction. To ensure the short-term nature of the program, Congress stipulated that all D contracts must be let by December 1, 1958 and that all construction must be put in place by December 1, 1959.

Every effort was made to induce the states to take advantage of these additional funds. Apportioning the funds to the states immediately, the BPR waived the usual requirement that the ABC funds be rigidly divided between the primary, secondary, and urban systems. Moreover, to stimulate the states to take further advantage of the additional authorizations, Congress set aside an additional $115 million in the L fund, from which each state could borrow up to two-thirds of its D apportionment, with the borrowed funds to be deducted from the state's ABC apportionments in fiscal 1960 and 1961.[38] Finally, to ensure that the D program would not interfere with the regular federal highway program, Congress suspended the pay-as-you-go requirement in the highway trust fund, which limits the amount of expenditures to the amount of revenues. This suspension appears to have been effective, because, during the period when the D funds were fully obligated, the ABC obligations amounted to 113 percent and the interstate obligations amounted to 118 percent of their project goals.[39]

Faced with a sudden increase in apportioned funds and given extremely attractive matching arrangements, the states responded immediately, and by the end of April, only two weeks after the final approval of the D program, they had programmed $28.7 million worth of projects; by the end of June, they had programmed over three-fourths of the available funds; and by the end of August, they had programmed 95 percent of the available funds.

Figure 4 indicates that the D program somewhat reduced the lags inherent in the ABC program. In the D program, the lags be-

---

[38] The importance of the L fund is indicated by the fact that only three states did not utilize it to finance part of their share of the D program. See testimony of Bertram D. Tallamy, Federal Highway Administrator, in *Hearing, Highway Amendment Act of 1959*, House Committee on Public Works, 86 Cong. 1 sess. (May 1959), p. 15.

[39] Tallamy, in *Hearing, Highway Amendment Act of 1959*.

FIGURE 4. D Program: Cumulative Percentage of Funds Utilized for Highway Projects from Date of Initiation of Program, 1958–60

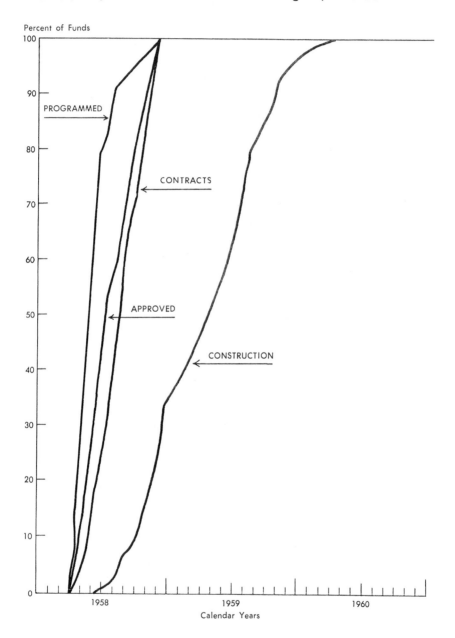

tween programming and construction were approximately eleven months and the lags between approval and construction were approximately eight months. This should be compared with comparable lags of fourteen and eleven months in the ABC program. This reduction in the lags should probably be attributed to the small size of the projects utilized in the D program, rather than to any basic changes in the lag structure of the highway program.

Even though construction reacted relatively rapidly in response to the initial increase in funds, the lags inherent in starting the program at the authorization stage were too long to permit the construction funds to enter the income stream until the recovery was well along. GNP reached a peak of $448.3 billion in the third quarter of 1957 and fell in the next two quarters, hitting a low of $432.9 billion in the first quarter of 1958. It then began to rise, just as Congress was authorizing the D program, and reached its previous peak by the third quarter of 1958. At that time, however, only 8 percent of the D funds had actually been put in place. Thus, only after the recovery was well along did the D program begin to affect the economy.

However, because of the seasonal nature of highway expenditures and the prolonged steel strike of 1959, the D program was able to exert a stabilizing influence. During the first and second quarters of 1959, when income was rising rapidly, D construction expenditures remained relatively low in response to the adverse weather conditions that prevailed in the winter and spring months. Over this period, only 20 percent of the D funds entered the income stream. In the second half of 1959, GNP fell sharply in response to the steel strike, while the bulk of the D construction actually took place.[40] By the first quarter of 1960, when income had recovered from the adverse effects of the strike, D construction expenditures had virtually ceased. Thus, Figure 5 indicates that the timing of the D program was ideal in mitigating the adverse impact of the steel strike upon the economy, although its effectiveness was certainly fortuitous and unplanned.

---

[40] The steel strike did not seem to cause any bottlenecks in the D program. This was probably due to the relatively small steel requirements of small rural highway projects.

FIGURE 5. Comparison of D Program Construction Expenditure and GNP, Quarterly, 1957–60

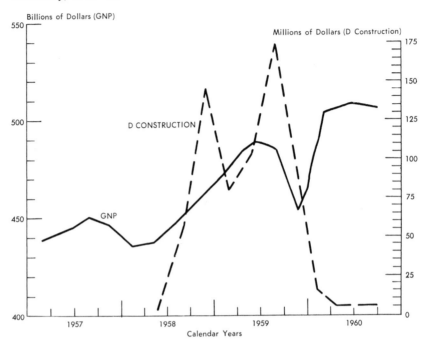

Highway Programs for Countercyclical Purposes

The experience of the D program and the lag relationships estimated for the ABC program indicate that institutional rather than
structural limitations are the factors that make highway construction expenditures currently unmanageable for countercyclical purposes. As long as a countercyclical highway program must be
initiated in Congress, there is little likelihood that highway construction expenditures can be a useful stabilization device. Since
Congress is effectively in session only between March and September, a downturn in economic activity must occur in the fall or winter
if Congress is to be able to take any useful action. However, each
of the last three cyclical peaks occurred in the summer or spring:
July 1953, July 1957, and May 1960. Thus, by the time it became
apparent that the economy was in recession, Congress had ad-
journed for the year. Another six months had elapsed before Con-

gress could reconvene and take action, and by this time, recovery was underway.[41] In view of the relatively mild nature of the post-war recessions, there is little more than a year between downturn and recovery. Since at least three months must elapse before a downturn is recognized,[42] there is at most a period of nine months to a year when a public works program can be effective.

If Congress did not have to initiate a public works program, highway construction expenditures could be quite a useful stabilizing device. The experience under the ABC and D programs indicates that, once projects have received final approval, construction can begin quite rapidly. Therefore, if Congress were to establish a special program of small projects that could be completed within a year and were to direct the BPR to regulate its approval of these projects in a countercyclical fashion, these highway construction expenditures could exert a considerable stabilizing force upon the economy. As the usual recognition lag is between three and four months, the BPR should be able to release these approved projects within five months after the downturn. Depending upon the season, highway construction expenditures would react more or less rapidly. Since, as pointed out above, the last three peaks occurred in the early summer, a countercyclical highway program could not have been initiated until autumn. Because of the slowdown in construction that occurs in the winter, autumn is probably the worst time to initiate a countercyclical highway program, for just as construction is getting underway it must be curtailed. Nevertheless, even under such relatively adverse conditions, almost all of the construction projects should be completed within a year. Consequently, the entire public works program could be completed within a year and a half after the initial downturn.

The efficacy of such a program must depend upon the existence of a large number of projects that could be completed in a relatively short time. Although virtually none of the interstate projects could

---

[41] Since Congress now seems to be in session for most of the year, this consideration may no longer be relevant. Nevertheless, any congressional program must still be faced with the lags of legislation and initiation that limited the effectiveness of the D program.

[42] See Rendigs Fels, "The Recognition-Lag and Semi-Automatic Stabilizers," *Review of Economics and Statistics*, Vol. 45, No. 3 (August 1963), pp. 280–85.

meet this requirement, most of the projects in the federal-aid secondary system could.[43] Since 30 percent of the $1.5 billion of annual ABC construction expenditures are allocated to these projects, approximately $500 million should accumulate in the highway stabilization fund during any one year.[44] Thus, during an upswing at least $1 billion should accumulate in the stabilization fund.

Suppose, for example, that Congress had established such a fund in the 1956 Highway Act. Then by the July 1957 peak, at least $500 million should have accumulated in the fund. Because of the recognition lags, another $100 million would probably have accumulated before the approved projects could have been released in October 1957. Thus, $600 million would have been available, the same amount that was authorized in the D program. With a stabilization fund available, the flow of construction expenditures could have begun by the first of the year and have been completed by December 1958. At that time, however, only 20 percent of the D funds had entered the income stream. It seems clear that, if public works expenditures had been freed from congressional initiative, their effectiveness would have been increased considerably. Any new projects coming into the fund after October 1957 would have been earmarked for the next recession. Since the peak in May 1960 was not recognized until October of that year,[45] $1.5 billion would have accumulated in the highway stabilization fund to help to offset the mild recession of 1960.

There should be relatively little loss from postponing small projects from periods of high employment to periods of low employment because such projects tend to be rather marginal. Thus, a postponement of two to three years out of a project's useful life

[43] The BPR has estimated that there are about 10,000 projects initiated in any one year. Many of them must be quite small, since less than 1,000 interstate projects account for two-thirds of the federal-aid highway construction expenditures. Because the projects in the federal-aid secondary system are predominantly small, it was assumed that all of the projects in that system would meet the size requirements and that none of the other ABC projects would.

[44] A slight complication may arise because of the requirement that the states match federal funds. Congress usually authorizes between $750 million and $1 billion for the annual ABC program, and these funds must be matched by the states. Consequently, if a highway stabilization fund is to be operative, the states must have the matching funds available. Nevertheless, as long as the states are required to put funds earmarked for the special projects into the stabilization fund, there is no reason why any complication should arise.

[45] Fels, in *Review of Economics and Statistics.*

of twenty to thirty years should not cause much reduction in the discounted benefits. Any losses resulting from the postponement should be more than offset by the gains caused by the reduction in the social cost of the resources used in the project and the multiplier effects of the construction expenditures. Thus, as long as the projects are built in areas of labor surplus where resources would have remained idle in the absence of the project, postponement should lead to an increase in the discounted stream of income. Therefore, the existence of a countercyclical highway fund should increase the total discounted value of highway construction to society, while permitting it to have a considerable stabilizing impact upon economic activity.

Impact of Highway Construction Expenditures on the Economy

To evaluate the efficacy of highway construction expenditures as stabilization tools, it is not enough to show that they can be regulated in a countercyclical fashion. It is necessary, in addition, to show that these expenditures will generate a demand for labor and materials in a stabilizing fashion. Thus, the lags between the initiation of construction and the peak of employment and of materials output should not be so long that they cause highway-generated demand to move with aggregate demand.

Impact on Employment

The direct labor required for a highway project must obviously be utilized while construction is taking place. If the construction projects financed from a countercyclical highway fund are undertaken in a stabilizing fashion, the demand for on-site employment must also occur in a stabilizing fashion, provided, of course, that the construction expenditures take place in areas of labor surplus.[46]

---

[46] This should usually be the case, since the expenditures are postulated to take place during periods of low aggregate demand. However, under the existing arrangements, there is no guarantee that funds will go to areas of relatively large labor surplus, since funds are allocated to the states on the basis of their population, area, and postal mileage. A countercyclical fund would be more effective if projects were screened to make sure that projects in areas of high unemployment were chosen first.

TABLE 6. Indirect and Direct Labor Requirements per Billion Dollars of Federal-Aid Highway Construction Expenditures, by Type of Highway Program

(In thousands of man-years)

Type of Labor Requirement	Interstate			ABC			Total Federal-Aid		
	Rural	Urban	Total	Rural	Urban	Total	Rural	Urban	Total
Indirect									
Aggregates	11.9	6.6	10.1	18.8	11.5	15.9	14.4	9.1	12.0
Lumber and timber	2.6	4.2	3.3	2.1	2.8	2.4	2.8	3.5	3.0
Explosives	1.3	0.3	1.0	1.5	0.5	1.1	1.3	0.5	1.0
Bitumens and petroleum	18.5	9.5	14.9	36.8	11.0	29.2	24.6	12.7	19.5
Cement	13.3	6.8	10.8	9.8	10.3	10.1	12.2	8.2	10.5
Structural clay	0.4	0.1	0.3	0.1	0.3	0.1	0.3	0.1	0.2
Concrete	10.2	17.5	13.2	9.1	18.7	13.0	9.6	17.8	13.0
Structural steel	27.2	37.8	31.4	16.2	28.5	21.1	23.5	32.7	28.1
Misc. steel	1.6	1.9	1.8	1.0	1.7	1.4	1.4	1.9	1.6
Total	87.1	84.8	86.7	95.6	85.3	94.4	90.1	86.5	89.1
Direct	45.8	45.8	45.8	46.3	44.8	45.8	45.9	45.4	45.8
Total	132.9	130.6	132.5	141.9	130.1	140.2	136.0	131.9	134.9

Note: Totals will not necessarily equal sums of items because of rounding.

The impact of highway construction expenditures on the labor employed in the materials-producing industries depends upon the timing of the increased demand for the products of these industries. Although the available evidence is somewhat sketchy, it suggests that the lags between increased construction and increased output are sufficiently short to permit a countercyclical highway program to affect these industries in a stabilizing fashion.[47] Hence, it must affect the demand for labor in these industries in a stabilizing fashion.

Of the various types of highway projects, those in the rural ABC program generate the greatest demand for labor per dollar of construction expenditures. Table 6 indicates, for example, that projects in the rural ABC system require approximately 11,300 more man-years of labor per billion dollars of construction expenditures than those in the urban interstate system. However, for the total ABC program the amount of on-site labor utilized is about equal to that of the interstate program. Hence, the difference in labor utilization arises from the differences in indirect labor re-

[47] See pp. 103–6, below.

quirements, for the small ABC projects utilize relatively more labor-intensive materials—particularly aggregates and bitumens— than the larger interstate projects.[48] As long as materials production responds to increased construction, the differential labor demand created by the small ABC projects increases their countercyclical effectiveness relative to other types of highway projects. Since these ABC projects are also the easiest to complete rapidly, it seems clear that a countercyclical fund should be limited to these projects.

Impact on Materials-Producing Industries

If highway construction expenditures are to help to stabilize the construction materials industries, two conditions must be fulfilled: the highway demand must be a sufficiently large percentage of the total demand for these materials to affect their output significantly, and the lags between the increased construction expenditures and increased materials output must be short enough to permit the additional output to occur when production would otherwise be low.

The materials used in highway construction are aggregates (the fill—composed of crushed stone, gravel, etc.—needed for the base of the highway), structural steel, cement, bitumens (asphalt and road oil), other petroleum products (such as lubricating oil and gasoline), structural clay and concrete pipes, explosives, and lumber and wood. Table 7 indicates that the demand for these materials for use in highway construction constitutes a substantial portion of the total demand. Consequently, highway construction expenditures should be able to influence output in these industries.

---

[48] Table 6 was derived by applying the direct and indirect labor requirements estimated for the 1947, 200 × 200 input-output table to the cost distribution of highway materials that is given in *Highway Statistics.* For these figures to be valid, it is necessary to assume that each affected industry will in fact produce all the additional demand. Hence, there can be no excessive inventories in any of the affected industries. The credibility of this assumption is clearly strained in view of the postulated depressed state of the economy. Consequently, these figures should not be taken to be anything more than rough orders of magnitude. See Wassily Leontief," Factor Proportions and the Structure of American Trade: Further Theoretical and Empirical Analysis," Appendix III, *Review of Economics and Statistics,* Vol. 38, No. 4 (November 1956), pp. 403–7, and U. S. Department of Commerce, Bureau of Public Roads, *Highway Statistics,* 1960, Table PT-2A, p. 202 (Government Printing Office, 1961).

TABLE 7. U. S. Production of Selected Materials and Their Use in Highway Construction, 1960

Type of Material	Units	Total Production	Highway Use	Highway Use as Percentage of Total Production
Structural steel	thousands of tons	15,581	2,049	13.1
Wide flange shapes, etc.	thousands of tons	5,085	776	15.3
Sheet piles	thousands of tons	286	33	11.5
Wide plate, etc.	thousands of tons	7,450	202	2.7
Reinforcing bars	thousands of tons	2,358	830	35.2
Reinforcing wire	thousands of tons	402	208	51.7
Cement	millions of barrels	319	69	21.6
Bitumens[a]	thousands of tons	19,566	8,000	40.9
Aggregates[b]	millions of tons	1,351	568	42.0
Lumber	millions of board feet	34,000	377	1.1
Petroleum products	millions of gallons	3,197	792	24.8
Explosives	millions of pounds	1,123	131	11.7

[a] Petroleum asphalt, road oil, bituminous asphalt.
[b] Sand, gravel, crushed stone, and slag.
Source: "Materials Requirements for Highway Construction, 1960–1962," U. S. Department of Commerce, Construction Review, Vol. 8, No. 3 (March 1962), p. 10.

Moreover, the expenditures should affect the output in a stabilizing fashion, since they should begin to influence the materials-producing industries shortly after a contract has been signed. If an industry produces for order (which is true of structural steel, aggregates, and cement), output should respond as soon as a contract is let and the contractor orders the needed materials. Moreover, even if an industry produces for inventory but has not accumulated excessive inventories, the time between the letting of the contract and the increase in production should be fairly close. Once the inventories are depleted below some acceptable level, production will be increased to replenish the stocks;[49] but in this case, the lag between the letting of the contract and the increase in output will be greater than it would be if the industry were producing for order.

Because the output of the materials-producing industries is linked to orders for materials, the impact of highway construction expenditures upon these industries should be determined by esti-

[49] See Michael C. Lovell, "Manufacturers' Inventories, Sales Expectations, and the Acceleration Principle," *Econometrica*, Vol. 29, No. 3 (July 1961), pp. 293–314, for a full discussion of the stock adjustment model implied here.

mating the following relationship between contracts let and the indices of production of the relevant materials:

$$P_t = a_0 + a_1 C_t + a_2 P_{\text{lagged}} + u_t$$

where P_t represents the relevant index of quarterly production, seasonally adjusted, C_t represents the quarterly real value in billions of dollars of highway contracts let and seasonally adjusted, and u_t represents a random disturbance.

Although the available indices do not precisely represent the materials used in highway construction, some index representing the production of the relevant material could be used for each industry. Indices of production were available for the following industries, and the relationship between them and contracts let was estimated: stone, clay, and glass products; concrete and plaster products; portland cement; structural clay products; petroleum products; earth minerals; structural steel products; and a composite of all materials.

Table 8 gives the results of the estimations and Table 9 summarizes the lag patterns. These tables indicate that the reaction of the materials-producing industries to an increased flow of contracts is quite rapid. In most cases, over 80 percent of the impact has been felt within a year after the initial increase in contracts; and virtually all of the impact has been felt within eighteen months. Thus, if a countercyclical highway program were initiated at the first sign of a recession and approved funds were released at an increased rate, the contracts could be signed within a month or two and construction begun. Within a year, most of the impact upon the materials-producing industries would have worked itself out. Therefore, if there is a three-month recognition lag, the impact from a countercyclical highway program would be almost totally spent within a year and a half after the downturn. This is well within reasonable limits for an effective public works program, since the recovery should be gaining strength just as the highway program is reaching completion.

Investment Effects of Highway Program

Besides influencing the materials-producing industries in a stabilizing manner, additional highway construction expenditures

TABLE 8. Regression Coefficients for the Materials Equations

Materials Index (P)	Constant	C_t	P_{t-1}	P_{t-2}	R^2	Vn
Composite materials	35.862 (10.264)	13.752 (6.405)	.647 (.099)	—	.830	1.96
Stone, clay, and glass products	14.910 (4.129)	9.386 (3.831)	1.207 (.130)	−.419 (.129)	.958	2.07
Concrete and plaster products	5.978 (2.142)	14.168 (3.613)	1.432 (.117)	−.579 (.119)	.988	2.15
Portland cement	43.854 (13.061)	34.212 (14.099)	.553 (.124)	—	.719	2.32
Structural clay products	13.644 (7.371)	4.993 (7.502)	.878 (.071)	—	.924	1.73
Petroleum products	23.176 (6.739)	21.264 (6.772)	.621 (.098)	—	.879	2.50
Earth minerals	4.225 (2.111)	6.904 (3.865)	.920 (.043)	—	.990	1.85
Structural steel products	16.839 (5.214)	15.535 (4.818)	.718 (.079)	—	.935	2.15

could possibly induce additional investment in these industries through accelerator effects. This possibility was particularly true in 1957, after the 1956 Highway Act raised total highway construction expenditures by more than 75 percent.[50] In view of the generally low economic activity that prevailed between 1957 and 1961, any investment induced by the enlarged highway program was certainly a net gain for the economy.

Whether the enlarged highway program could have induced any additional investment was estimated in the following way: The dollar value of the materials needed per million dollars of highway construction was obtained from the cost distribution of construc-

---

[50] Before the 1956 Highway Act, highway construction expenditures had averaged approximately $4.5 billion annually, of which $1.5 billion was spent on the federal highway program. The 1956 Act raised ABC expenditures by approximately $1 billion and instituted the interstate program with annual expenditures of approximately $2.5 billion, raising the total of highway construction expenditures by approximately $3.5 billion.

TABLE 9. Proportion of Reaction of Materials Production Obtained After a Unit Increase in Contracts Let for Highway Construction

Quarter After Increase in Contracts	Proportion of Reaction Obtained After Each Period for							
	Composite materials	Stone, clay, glass	Concrete and plaster	Portland cement	Structural clay products	Petroleum products	Earth minerals	Structural steel
0	.000	.000	.000	.000	.000	.000	.000	.000
1	.353	.212	.147	.447	.122	.389	.008	.282
2	.581	.468	.356	.694	.229	.614	.154	.484
3	.729	.688	.574	.831	.323	.761	.221	.630
4	.825	.847	.762	.908	.406	.841	.284	.744
5	.886	.946	.906	.949	.478	.908	.341	.809
6	.927	.998	1.003	.972	.542	.943	.394	.863
7	.953	1.021	1.059	.984	.598	.964	.462	.902
8	.969	1.027	1.083	.991	.647	.978	.487	.929
9	.980	1.023	1.084	.995	.690	.986	.528	.949
10	.987	1.017	1.073	.997	.727	.991	.566	.964
11	.992	1.011	1.056	.999	.761	.995	.601	.974
12	.995	1.006	1.037	1.000	.790	.997	.633	.981
13	.997	1.001	1.022	1.000	.816	.998	.663	.986
14	.998	1.000	1.009	1.000	.838	.999	.690	.990
15	.999	1.000	1.001	1.000	.858	1.000	.714	.993
16	1.000	1.000	.996	1.000	.875	1.000	.736	.995
17	1.000	1.000	.994	1.000	.891	1.000	.758	.996
18	1.000	1.000	.993	1.000	.904	1.000	.778	.997
19	1.000	1.000	.994	1.000	.916	1.000	.795	.998
20	1.000	1.000	.996	1.000	.926	1.000	.819	.999

tion expenditures published by the BPR.[51] Then, by treating these data as increased outputs to be produced by the economy and utilizing the inverse of the 1947 200 × 200 input-output table, the total additional output required from every industry affected by the additional highway construction was computed.[52] This estimate was then added to the actual 1957 output of these industries. If the sum of actual output and the output required to sustain the additional highway construction expenditures was greater than capac-

[51] *Highway Statistics*, 1957, p. 198. The 1957 distribution was used because this was the first year that the enlarged program had any impact.

[52] Although using the 1947 table undoubtedly introduces biases by failing to account for technical change, the errors are probably not too great.

TABLE 10. Investment Effects on Industries of the Enlarged Federal Highway Program

Industries	Estimated Capacity Output in 1957[a] ($ mil.)	Actual Peak Output in 1957 at Annual Rate[a] ($ mil.)	Percentage of Capacity Utilized at Peak[a]	Additional Output Needed $2.5 billion interstate ($ mil.)	Additional Output Needed $1.0 billion ABC ($ mil.)	Actual 1957 Output plus Additional Highway Output ($ mil.)	Expanded Output as Percentage of Capacity Output
Motor vehicles	17,225	11,552	67	9.0	3.6	11,565	67.1
Nonferrous products	4,632	3,715	80	7.3	2.9	3,725	80.4
Stone, clay, glass	5,614	4,303	77	321.8	122.8	4,748	84.6
Rubber products	4,014	3,331	83	19.0	7.7	3,358	83.7
Iron and steel	10,388	8,936	86	278.8	99.3	9,314	89.7
Paper and allied products	5,892	4,909	83	52.3	21.0	4,982	84.6
Machinery, excluding electric	14,638	13,365	91	618.5	261.0	14,245	97.3
Lumber and wood	2,816	2,297	82	76.8	22.0	2,396	85.1
Fabricated metals	10,529	8,940	85	522.0	158.6	9,621	91.4
Petroleum and coal	22,692	20,614	91	300.8	135.7	21,051	92.8
Chemicals and allied products	15,176	14,695	97	25.0	7.5	14,728	97.5
Printing and publishing	4,790	4,655	97	11.5	4.4	4,671	97.5

[a] From Daniel Creamer, "Capital Expansion and Capacity in Postwar Manufacturing," in National Industrial Conference Board, *Studies in Business Economics*, No. 72 (1961), Table 5, p. 25.

ity, the need for additional investment was indicated. However, Table 10 shows that the demand generated by the highway program alone could not have induced any additional investment. But when coupled with possible increases in demand from other sources, the highway program might induce new investment in the stone, clay, and glass industry, the fabricated metals industry, and the machinery industry.

Conclusion

It is now desirable to summarize the main points of this study and to analyze how highway construction expenditures could be expected to react to a change in national income, first under the present institutional framework and then under some postulated changes in the procedure of the BPR.

If the BPR takes no positive action, there is a fairly close relationship between national income and highway construction expenditures. Thus, if national income falls by 1 percent, highway construction expenditures will fall by approximately 0.7 percent. The average decrease in GNP during the postwar recessions has been between 2 and 3 percent, which means that highway construction expenditures should have fallen by between 1.5 and 2 percent. With the total value of highway construction currently at about $6 billion, the implication is that highway construction expenditures might fall by between $90 million and $120 million. This decline could easily be offset by a countercyclical highway program.

However, the purpose of a public works program is not merely to offset the forces working against highway construction expenditures during a recession, but to increase the expenditures sufficiently to take up the slack existing elsewhere in the economy. Yet the existing institutional arrangements, which require that Congress initiate any public works program, make highway construction expenditures an unwieldy tool to use against the typically mild postwar recessions. In addition to the lags in recognition, the lags of congressional action are so long that the trough of a recession is likely to be reached before any program can be initiated. This is exactly what happened in the D program.

With a few modifications, however, the federal highway program could become a fairly potent countercyclical tool. Assume that Congress passed a law creating a highway stabilization fund into which the BPR placed all projects at the approval stage that could be completed in less than a year. The President would be given discretionary power to release the projects in this fund whenever he had determined that a recession had developed. Such a finding could be made with the aid of the Council of Economic Advisers, which would inform the President that the economy was entering a recession. Under the usual recognition lags, the President would be able to instruct the BPR within three or four months after a downturn to release the projects in this highway stabilization fund. Since the states would also be required to accumulate sufficient funds to cover their share of the cost, there should be no financing problems, although the pay-as-you-go requirement in the trust fund would clearly have to be waived or eliminated. Under these conditions, special antirecession highway construction expenditures could begin to enter the income stream within four or five months after the beginning of a recession and could be completed within eighteen months after the downturn. The response of the materials-producing industries to the letting of highway contracts is sufficiently rapid so that within a year to a year and a half virtually all of the impact of such a program would have been felt in these industries. Thus, highway construction expenditures could be timed in such a way that within a year and a half after the initial downturn virtually all of their direct effect would have been completed, and within another six months all of their indirect effect upon the materials-producing industries would have been completed. This is well within the time limits of a desirable public works program.

Moreover, there are a sufficient number of small projects to enable a countercyclical highway fund to have considerable impact upon the economy. Since all projects in the federal-aid secondary system should meet the size requirements of a countercyclical highway program, approximately $500 million worth of projects could be accumulated in the highway stabilization fund in any one year.[53] Suppose that on a given date the President decreed that all projects currently in the fund should be released for construction. Then any new projects reaching the approval stage would begin to accumulate until the next recession. The length of time between the downturn and the peak of most recoveries is at least three years and in most of the postwar recessions has been considerably longer. Thus, a minimum of $1.5 billion should accumulate in the highway stabilization fund during an upswing. Obviously, this could exert a not inconsiderable stabilizing influence on the economy. Consequently, the formation of such a highway stabilization fund should be a high priority recommendation to Congress, for it would help to stabilize the economy, while creating few, if any, losses due to the postponement of the small, marginal highway projects.

---

[53] By law, the federal-aid secondary system receives 30 percent of funds spent on the ABC program. Since the volume of ABC construction is currently over $1.5 billion, expenditures on the federal-aid secondary system should be approximately $500 million. See pp. 100–1.

Data Used in Regression Equations

A. Interstate, ABC, and D Programs

Monthly data, 1956–62, for federal funds programmed, federal funds approved, total contracts let, and federal construction put in place were provided by the U. S. Department of Commerce, Bureau of Public Roads.

B. Indices of Highway Construction Materials, Quarterly, 1949–59

(1) Composite Materials Index. 1949–57 data from U. S. Department of Commerce (USDC), *Construction Materials Statistics, 1947–1957*, Table 1; 1958–59 data from USDC, *Construction Review*, various issues, Table F-1. The data were aggregated from monthly series and then seasonally adjusted by the ratio to centered moving average method with the following adjustment factors:

1st quarter	1.023
2nd quarter	0.994
3rd quarter	0.958
4th quarter	1.025

(2) Stone, Clay, and Glass Index. Board of Governors of Federal Reserve System, *Indices of Industrial Production, 1959*. The data were aggregated from monthly series and then seasonally adjusted by the ratio to centered moving average method with the following adjustment factors:

1st quarter	0.958
2nd quarter	1.009
3rd quarter	1.021
4th quarter	1.010

(3) Concrete Index. From *Indices of Industrial Production, 1959.* Adjustment factors:

1st quarter	0.919
2nd quarter	1.010
3rd quarter	1.069
4th quarter	1.002

(4) Cement Index. 1949–57 data from *Construction Materials Statistics,* Table 22; 1958–59, data from *Construction Review,* Table F-1. Adjustment factors:

1st quarter	0.793
2nd quarter	1.067
3rd quarter	1.120
4th quarter	1.020

(5) Clay Construction Products Index. 1947–57 data from *Construction Materials Statistics,* Table 14; 1958–59 data from *Construction Review,* Table F-1. Adjustment factors:

1st quarter	0.889
2nd quarter	1.027
3rd quarter	1.052
4th quarter	1.028

(6) Petroleum Products Index. From *Indices of Industrial Production, 1959.* Adjustment factors:

1st quarter	0.995
2nd quarter	0.970
3rd quarter	1.012
4th quarter	1.020

(7) Earth Minerals Index. From *Indices of Industrial Production, 1959.* Adjustment factors:

1st quarter	0.904
2nd quarter	1.022
3rd quarter	1.061
4th quarter	1.012

(8) Structural Steel Index. From *Indices of Industrial Production, 1959.* Adjustment factors:

1st quarter	0.993
2nd quarter	0.996
3rd quarter	0.993
4th quarter	1.018

C. Highway Construction, Annually, 1921–60

(1) Real Value of Highway Construction (billions of dollars). 1919–56 data from U. S. Department of Commerce (USDC), *Construction Volume and Costs, 1915–56: A Statistical Supplement to Construction Review*, Table 3, p. 8; 1957–61 data from USDC, *Construction Review*, various issues, Table A-3. The data were deflated by a construction bid price index on a 1957–59 base. (See, for example, USDC, Bureau of Public Roads, *Highway Statistics*, 1960, Table PT-1, p. 200.)

(2) Annual Consumption of Highway Fuel (billions of gallons). 1919–55 data from *Highway Statistics, Summary to 1955*, Table G-221, p. 2; 1956–61 data from *Highway Statistics*, various issues, Table G-23.

(3) Total Vehicular Registrations (millions of vehicles). 1919–55 data from *Highway Statistics, Summary to 1955*, Table MV-201, p. 18; 1956–61 data from *Highway Statistics*, Table MV-1.

(4) Vehicle Miles of Travel (billions of miles). From E. H. Holmes, "Highway Transportation," in *U. S. Transportation: Needs, Sources, and Utilization* (National Academy of Sciences, National Research Council, 1961).

(5) Depreciated real value of the miles of surfaced highway (billions of dollars). From E. H. Holmes in *U. S. Transportation*.

D. Highway Construction, Quarterly, 1949–61

(1) Money Value of Highway Construction (millions of dollars). Quarterly sums of monthly totals given in U. S. Department of Commerce (USDC), *Construction Review*, various issues, Table A-2. Seasonally adjusted by the ratio to centered moving average method with the following adjustment factors:

1st quarter	0.518
2nd quarter	1.050
3rd quarter	1.445
4th quarter	0.987

(2) Real Value of Highway Construction (millions of dollars). Series (1) above was deflated by a construction bid price index on a 1957–59 base. (See USDC, Bureau of Public Roads, *Highway Statistics*, 1960, Table PT-1, p. 200.)

(3) Federal User Tax Revenues (millions of dollars). This series is the sum of gasoline taxes, lubricating oil taxes, motor vehicle and parts taxes, and tire and tube taxes. All these data are from U. S. Treasury, *Annual Report of the Commissioner of Internal Revenue*. Seasonally

adjusted by the ratio to centered moving average method with the following adjustment factors:

Gasoline taxes

	1947–53	1954–61
1st quarter	0.942	1.013
2nd quarter	0.938	0.888
3rd quarter	1.071	1.012
4th quarter	1.047	1.087

Oil taxes

	1947–53	1954–61
1st quarter	0.916	0.944
2nd quarter	1.117	0.962
3rd quarter	0.963	1.110
4th quarter	1.004	0.984

Motor vehicle and parts taxes

	1947–53	1954–61
1st quarter	0.925	1.000
2nd quarter	1.056	1.122
3rd quarter	0.949	1.070
4th quarter	1.067	0.804

Tire and tube taxes

1st quarter	0.917
2nd quarter	0.974
3rd quarter	1.036
4th quarter	1.073

(4) Fuel Consumption (billions of gallons). From *Highway Statistics*, Table G-23. Seasonally adjusted by the ratio to centered moving average method with the following adjustment factors:

1st quarter	0.907
2nd quarter	1.034
3rd quarter	1.062
4th quarter	0.994

(5) Unemployment Rate Greater than Four Percent. Figures on total employment and the civilian labor force for the years 1947–59 are from *Survey of Current Business*, April 1960, p. 23, and for later years from various issues of the *Survey*. Seasonally adjusted by the

ratio to centered moving average method with the following adjustment factors:

	Labor Force	Employment
January	0.998	0.968
February	0.980	0.969
March	0.984	0.976
April	0.986	0.985
May	0.999	0.999
June	1.023	1.019
July	1.027	1.023
August	1.020	1.022
September	1.004	1.002
October	1.004	1.012
November	1.001	1.004
December	0.989	0.991

The differences between the seasonally adjusted monthly figures of these two series were recorded as monthly unemployment. The percentages of unemployment of the total labor force were computed and then averaged to obtain quarterly unemployment rates.

(6) Municipal Bond Rate (Standard and Poor's). From USDC, *Business Statistics*, various issues. Seasonally adjusted by the ratio to centered moving average method with the following adjustment factors:

1st quarter	1.0166
2nd quarter	0.9965
3rd quarter	0.9812
4th quarter	1.0030

(7) Contracts Let for Highway Construction (millions of real dollars). 1949–54 data from USDC, *Construction Volume and Costs, 1915–54*, Table 22; 1955–60 data from *Construction Review*, various issues. Seasonally adjusted by the ratio to centered moving average method with the following adjustment factors:

1st quarter	0.78025
2nd quarter	1.16844
3rd quarter	1.14260
4th quarter	0.90830

The data were deflated to real dollars by using a deflator for period t

equal to the average of the construction bid price index for periods $t, t-1, t-2, t-3$. (See *Business Statistics*.) The construction bid price index was given for different base years, as follows:

1st quarter 1947–3rd quarter 1952	1925–29 = 100
1st quarter 1949–4th quarter 1960	1946 = 100
1st quarter 1959–4th quarter 1961	1957–59 = 100

These series were spliced by averaging the overlapping years in each series and adjusting the 1925–29 = 100 and 1957–59 = 100 series to the 1946 = 100 series by multiplying each observation in the former two series by the ratio of the averages.

(8) Tire Production (millions of tires, seasonally adjusted quarterly totals). From *Survey of Current Business*, various issues, Table, "Rubber and Rubber Products," line, "Pneumatic Casings, Production." Seasonally adjusted by the ratio to centered moving average method with the following adjustment factors:

1st quarter	1.0119
2nd quarter	1.0349
3rd quarter	0.9655
4th quarter	0.9875

(9) Purchases of Automobiles and Parts (seasonally adjusted quarterly totals at annual rates, in billions of dollars). From *Survey of Current Business*, various issues, Table, "General Business Indicators," line, "Personal Consumption Expenditures, Automobiles and Parts."

(10) GNP (seasonally adjusted quarterly totals at annual rates in billions of 1958 dollars). From *Survey of Current Business*, August 1965, Table 2, pp. 26–27.

(11) GNP (seasonally adjusted quarterly totals at annual rates in billions of current dollars). From *Survey of Current Business*, August 1965, Table 1, pp. 24–25.

ALBERT ANDO AND E. CARY BROWN*

Personal Income Taxes and Consumption Following the 1964 Tax Reduction

TAX REDUCTION on a major scale, without the accompaniment of an equal or greater reduction in government expenditures, was undertaken in the United States in 1964 for the first time in the country's post-Keynesian fiscal history. This cut was not undertaken for short-run stabilization purposes, but to reduce the longer-run fiscal drag exerted by the federal government's budget on total demand for output. This drag arose because government expenditures were less income-elastic than government revenues under a constant tax structure. The growing full-employment income expanded full-employment budget surpluses and exerted increasingly contractive pressure on demand. This fiscal drag could, of course, be offset in a number of ways, such as an easing of money, increased government expenditures, or tax reduction, depending on the tastes of the public.

In 1963 and 1964, expansive policies to cope with fiscal drag were considered to be constrained or less desirable than tax reduction. Enactment of the Revenue Act of 1964 was a consequence,

* University of Pennsylvania and Massachusetts Institute of Technology.

lopping approximately 13 percent off the personal income tax for 1964 and 20 percent for 1965, and making smaller percentage reductions in the corporate income tax, with which this paper will not be concerned.

Despite the fact that the tax reduction was not undertaken for countercyclical purposes, it does provide an interesting and rare experiment that can shed light on the use of the fiscal mechanism as a stabilization instrument. How quickly do tax collections fall when rates are cut? How promptly do consumers respond to the new flow of disposable income? Of what type are the added consumer expenditures? How quickly does production react to the expanded flow of demand?

These questions require answers if the results of fiscal action on the level of economic activity, and especially the short-run responses to that action, are to be predicted.[1] While the preponderance of economic opinion had few doubts about the direction and long-run consequences of the 1964–65 tax reduction, there was considerable difference of opinion as to the time profile of its impact. Some believed that consumers would anticipate the reduction in 1963 and not spend much more in 1964; others thought that consumers' reaction would be slow indeed; still others anticipated a large increase in demand for output through the induced effects on business spending.

This paper is not designed to answer the general question of the effects of the tax cut on total output. That, of course, would require a complete model of the economy. Instead, the focus is limited to the two questions first posed: what was the tax response, and how did consumers react to the change, given the levels of income that were actually generated in 1964 and 1965? Thus, only a partial answer is supplied, to be sure, but it is an important step toward an answer to the general question. It can be considered as a further refinement of earlier work carried out by the present authors for the Commission on Money and Credit[2] and the econometric model project of the Brookings Institution.[3]

---

[1] Complete analysis would also require analysis of the effects of the tax cut on the supply side, such as on personal effort.

[2] Commission on Money and Credit, *Stabilization Policies* (Prentice-Hall, 1963).

[3] James S. Duesenberry and others (eds.), *The Brookings Quarterly Econometric Model of the United States* (Rand McNally & Co. and North-Holland Publishing Co., 1965), Chapter 14.

Behavior of Tax Revenues

The first task is to determine the pattern of tax reduction arising from the tax changes in the Revenue Act of 1964. First, the new rate structure altered tax liabilities. In addition, the modification in liabilities, combined with the withholding changes, altered the pattern of tax payments. These in turn induced changes in disposable income.

Tax Liabilities

The comprehensive concept of tax liabilities can be estimated only on an annual basis.[4] It is the product of the tax base—taxable income—and the effective tax rate.

An explanation of the tax base—annual taxable income—is similar to the one used in the present authors' earlier studies, but it covers the period 1946–63. The dependent variable is the fraction of total personal income that did not enter the tax base; the independent variables are personal income, the aggregate value of personal exemptions available to the entire population, and the population. The relationship was estimated in logarithmic form as follows:[5]

$$(1) \qquad \ln\left(1 - \frac{Z}{Y}\right) = -.820 - .303 \ln\frac{Y}{P} + .261 \ln\frac{E}{P}.$$
$$\qquad\qquad\qquad\quad (.069) \ \ (.017) \qquad\quad (0.41)$$

$R^2 = .96$ Standard Deviation $= .01$ Durbin-Watson $= 2.1$

In this relationship, Z represents taxable income, Y is personal income (Office of Business Economics concept), P is population, and E represents aggregate exemptions of the population. When actual personal income, population, and exemptions in 1964 and

---

[4] The tax liabilities concept used is that of individuals as shown in U. S. Treasury Department, *Statistics of Income, Individual Income Tax Returns*, plus that of fiduciaries, less the social security self-employment tax.

[5] When a concept of taxable income that excludes fiduciaries is used, this relationship is as follows for the period 1929–63:

$$\ln\left(1 - \frac{Z}{Y}\right) = -.580 - .267 \ln\frac{Y}{P} + .124 \ln\frac{E}{P}.$$
$$R^2 = .99 \qquad SD = .02 \qquad DW = 1.1$$

The forecasts presented in this study are based on the more recent period, 1946–63.

TABLE 1. Comparison of Predicted with Actual Taxable Income and Tax Liabilities, 1964 and 1965

(In billions of dollars)

Year	Taxable Income		Tax Liabilities	
	Actual[a]	Predicted	Actual[a]	Predicted
1964	231.2	230.4	47.3	47.1
1965	255.8	254.6	49.7	49.4

[a] U. S. Treasury Department, *Statistics of Income—Individual Income Tax Returns,* 1964 and 1965. Taxable income and the liabilities shown here are increased by $1.3 billion and $0.4 billion, respectively, in order to account for fiduciaries—the same amount as in 1962.

1965 are used in equation (1), predictions of taxable income for those years are obtained, as shown in Table 1. The error in the predictions for the two years is less than one-half of 1 percent.

The second factor determining tax liabilities—the effective tax rate—is much more difficult to predict than is taxable income. Under the tax structure in operation from 1954 through 1963, the effective tax rate was remarkably constant, despite a near doubling of total taxable income (from $115 billion to $209 billion). The 1964 legislation changed the rate structure. The bottom bracket, for example, which accounts for over half of taxable income, was divided into four equal parts. This reduced the effective rate and may also have made it vary with variations in income. Such evidence as is available, scanty to be sure, shows this to be the case.

The simplest assumption to make is that every rate was proportionately reduced and, thus, the new effective rate exhibits the same remarkable constancy as before, but at a proportionately lower level. Estimates prepared at the time of the tax legislation showed a reduction of 19.5 percent in the effective rate for 1965, and of two-thirds that amount for 1964, on the basis of income levels ruling in 1962 or 1963.[6] This would indicate a reduction from the effective rate of 23 percent in 1963 to 19.94 percent in 1964 and to 18.5 percent in 1965 and subsequent years. But since that time, statistics for these years show the actual effective rate to have been higher—

[6] Joseph A. Pechman, "Individual Income Tax Provisions of the Revenue Act of 1964," *Journal of Finance,* Vol. 20 (May 1965), p. 261; and U. S. Senate, 88 Cong. 2 sess., Committee on Finance, *Report on The Revenue Act of 1964,* pp. 14, 15, 28.

20.43 percent in 1964[7] and 19.38 percent in 1965[8]—on the basis of a taxable income that was, respectively, 10 percent and 22 percent higher than in 1963. This evidence certainly suggests that the effective tax rate generated by the new rate structure is responsive to the amount of taxable income. The evidence is incomplete as to just why this is the case.[9] In the present study, a predicted effective rate is not used, but instead the actual rates as tabulated by the Treasury. The product of these rates and predicted taxable income are shown in Table 1.

Tax Payments

One of the concepts of disposable income used here to predict consumer behavior is based on the tax liabilities estimated above and interpolated on a quarterly basis.[10] However, disposable income as calculated by the Office of Business Economics (OBE), Department of Commerce, is based on tax payments, which ultimately depend, of course, on tax liabilities. Since there is no clearcut case for favoring one concept over the other, an attempt is made in this section to explain the pattern of payments.

Tax payments can be divided into three parts: (1) current withholding on wages and salaries, (2) payment of up to four additional installments throughout the year, and (3) final settlement of tax liability through additional payment or refund of overpayment by the government. Ideally, we would like to explain each of these components separately, but statistical difficulties prevent it. While data on withholding are in adequate detail, a separation of the different types of nonwithheld tax payments is not available.

[7] U. S. Treasury Department, *Statistics of Income—1964, Individual Income Tax Returns.*

[8] *Ibid., 1965.*

[9] If it is assumed that the reduction in the effective rate from 1963 to 1964 is approximately one-third of the reduction from 1963 to 1965, the actual rate for 1964—20.43 percent—implies a rate of 19.1 percent for 1965. However, if it is further assumed that the change in the effective rate that is due to the change in income from 1964 to 1965 is the same as that from 1963 to 1964, and that the effective rate in 1964 would have been 19.94 percent in the absence of any

income change, then an effective rate of 19.1 percent $\times \dfrac{20.43}{19.94} = 19.6$ percent is obtained for

1965. This is very close to the actual effective rate obtained in 1965, 19.38 percent. This calculation is merely a speculation, but it might provide some clue to the relationship between income change and the effective rate. At any rate, much work is needed to clarify this question.

[10] See page 127, footnote 15, for the method of interpolation.

WITHHELD TAX PAYMENTS.[11] The withheld tax has been estimated on both a seasonally adjusted and unadjusted basis. However, because there seems to be no clear basis for seasonally adjusting the nonwithheld portion of the tax, only the unadjusted results are used here. Since taxes are withheld only on wages and salaries, they are the obvious explanatory variable when multiplied by the withholding tax rate. However, data for seasonally unadjusted wages and salaries are not available. Hence we have had to use a derived seasonally unadjusted personal income as an independent variable.[12] Aggregate exemptions available to the population were tried as a variable, as in the case of liabilities, but they did not improve the explanation. A reasonable result, in logarithmic form, with the coefficient of the withholding tax rate constrained to unity, for the period covering the second quarter of 1948 through the fourth quarter of 1963 is as follows:

$$(2) \quad \ln T^w = \ln r_w + 1.546 \ln Y - 3.255 - .009 S_2 - .047 S_3 - .127 S_4.$$
$$\quad (.016) \qquad (.069) \quad (.011) \quad (.011) \quad (.011)$$
$$\quad R^2 = .994 \qquad SD = .0009 \qquad DW = 1.3$$

In the equation, T^w represents withholding taxes (quarterly totals in billions of dollars); r_w is the withholding tax rate; Y equals seasonally unadjusted personal income (quarterly totals in billions of dollars); and S_2, S_3, and S_4 are seasonal dummies for the indicated quarter. The equation indicates that the income elasticity of withholding taxes is about 1.5—a result that has appeared in a wide variety of relationships we have computed, whether the independent variable is income or wages and salaries.[13]

[11] The data for withheld tax payments are from OBE, based on business returns, rather than receipts as reported by the Treasury, which would ordinarily lag actual withholding.

[12] It is obtained by working through the seasonally unadjusted relation of personal income to gross national product. Thus, our concept of personal income is inaccurate to the extent of the statistical discrepancy in the national income statistics.

[13] For purposes of comparison, the equation for seasonally adjusted withheld taxes, OBE definition, for the same period is

$$\ln T^{w*} = \ln r_w + 1.478 \ln W - 2.410,$$
$$\quad (.607) \qquad (.029)$$
$$\quad R^2 = .999 \qquad SD = .015 \qquad DW = 1.1$$

where T^{w*} represents seasonally adjusted withheld taxes in billions of dollars at annual rates; r_w is the withholding tax rate; and W equals seasonally adjusted wages and salaries in billions of dollars at annual rates. Again, the wage elasticity of the tax is 1.5.

TABLE 2. Actual and Predicted[a] Tax Payments, Quarterly, 1964–66

(In billions of dollars)

Year and Quarter	Withheld		Nonwithheld		Total	
	Actual	Predicted	Actual	Predicted	Actual	Predicted
1964						
I	9.6	10.1	1.2	}5.4	10.8	}24.3
II	8.7	8.8	5.0		13.7	
III	8.9	9.0	2.5	2.5	11.4	11.5
IV	9.4	9.4	0.7	0.7	10.1	10.1
Total	36.6	37.3	9.4	8.6	46.0	45.9
1965						
I	8.9	9.1	2.1	}8.4	11.0	}27.3
II	9.6	9.8	6.4		16.0	
III	10.1	10.1	2.7	2.3	12.8	12.4
IV	10.3	10.9	0.8	0.7	11.1	11.6
Total	38.9	39.9	12.0	11.4	50.9	51.3
1966						
I	10.4	10.7	2.2	}8.6	12.6	}30.4
II	11.2	11.1[b]	6.8		18.0	
III	12.0	11.8[b]	2.7	2.5	14.7	14.4
IV	12.6	12.2[b]	0.7	0.7	13.3	12.9
Total	46.2	45.8	12.4	11.9	58.6	57.7

[a] Predictions are based on equations (2), (3), and (4).
[b] The withholding tax rate for the period after May 1966 is calculated as 14 percent times the ratio of estimated withheld taxes before and after the change in the withholding methods of May 1966. See *Statement of the Secretary of the Treasury Before the Ways and Means Committee*, January 19, 1966, and *The Budget of the U. S. Government*, 1967, p. 60.

This equation satisfactorily predicts withheld taxes for the 1964–66 period (Table 2). The largest quarterly errors are an overestimate of $0.5 billion in the first quarter of 1964, an overestimate of $0.6 billion in the fourth quarter of 1965, and an underestimate of $0.4 billion in the fourth quarter of 1966.

NONWITHHELD TAX PAYMENTS. The *first and second quarters* of the year merge a wide variety of nonwithheld taxes; therefore, we have combined them. In these quarters are found (1) the final installment of the previous year, (2) the final payment for the previous year when separate from the final installment, (3) refunds of overpayments of the previous year (a subtraction), and (4) the first and second quarterly installment of the current year. As in every quarter, there are also miscellaneous payments for back taxes, fiscal year returns, and the like.

The first three items above, represented by X, are given by the identity

$$X = L_{t-1} - T^w_{t-1} - (Q_1 + Q_2 + Q_3)_{t-1}$$

where L_t is the tax liability for the year t, T^w_t represents total withheld taxes for the year t, and Q_i is the ith quarterly installment of year t.

The fourth item depends on the way that taxpayers estimate their final liability for the current year and the amount that they think will be withheld. A variety of hypotheses are possible in explaining how these estimates are formed. One hypothesis would be that last year's tax liability, adjusted for changes in the tax law, is used as a proxy for that of the current year. Alternatively, the liability estimate may be made by reference to income in the first two quarters and the effective tax rate. The estimate of withholding which would enter negatively in the relationship may be formed by reference to actual withholding in the first two quarters or to estimated withholding based on estimated annual income.

Since we have no data for $(Q_1 + Q_2 + Q_3)_{t-1}$, we let T^w_{t-1} act as a proxy, both for itself and for $(Q_1 + Q_2 + Q_3)_{t-1}$, and run the regression in the form

$$T^n_{(1+2)t} = \alpha_1 L_{t-1} + \alpha_2 T^w_{t-1} + \alpha_3 r_t Y_{(1+2)t}$$
$$+ \alpha_4 T^w_{(1+2)t} + \alpha_5 L_{t-1} + \alpha_0,$$

where $T^n_{(1+2)t}$ represents nonwithheld taxes in the first two quarters in year t, r_t is the average effective tax rate, $Y_{(1+2)t}$ is personal income in the first two quarters of year t, and $T^w_{(1+2)t}$ represents withholding taxes in the first two quarters in year t. We should expect that $\alpha_1 = 1$, $\alpha_2 < -1$, $\alpha_3 > 0$, $\alpha_4 < 0$, and $\alpha_1 + \alpha_5 > 1$.

The statistical results satisfy the second and third condition, but not the first and fourth. The sum of $\alpha_1 + \alpha_5$ is slightly less than unity, and α_4 is positive and insignificant. We have, therefore, restricted the coefficient so that $\alpha_1 + \alpha_5 = 1$, and have eliminated

$T^w_{(1+2)t}$ from the regression. The result is

(3) $\quad T^n_{(1+2)t} = L_{t-1} - 1.139T^w_{t-1} + .036r_t Y_{(1+2)t} - .881.$
$$\qquad\qquad (.037) \qquad (.017) \qquad\qquad (.481)$$
$$R^2 = .999 \qquad SD = .32 \qquad DW = 2.2$$

Estimated nonwithheld taxes have not been separated as between the first and second quarters. There seems to be no reasonable basis on which this can be done. In the estimates of consumption behavior, the actual tax figures for each quarter are used, so that this division is unnecessary for that purpose.

The *third-quarter* payment is composed almost entirely of the third quarterly installment of taxpayers, plus the usual miscellaneous back taxes. The problem, then, is to determine how taxpayers arrive at the amount of their installment payment.

A sophisticated taxpayer would estimate his tax liability for the year at a particular point in time and then would subtract the amount of withholding he estimates for the year and the installments he has paid so far in the year. This type of relationship would be complicated indeed to estimate, even if the data were subdivided in such a way as to make an estimate possible. Instead, a simple form was used, which depended only on income in the quarter and the effective tax rate for that year. The use of withholding taxes in the current quarter as another independent variable yielded the correct sign but was not very significant. The relationship found for the period 1948–63, all variables referring to the third quarter, was

(4) $\qquad\qquad T^n_{(3)t} = .041r_t Y_{(3)t} - .174T^w_{(3)t} - .161,$
$$\qquad\qquad (.013) \qquad\qquad (.107) \qquad (.330)$$
$$R^2 = .95 \qquad SD = .10 \qquad DW = 1.3$$

where $Y_{(3)t}$ is seasonally unadjusted personal income for the third quarter of year t (annual rate in billions of dollars); $T^w_{(3)t}$ is the withheld tax in the third quarter (quarterly totals in billions of dollars); and r_t is the average effective tax rate.

The nonwithheld tax collection in the *fourth quarter* consists completely of miscellaneous items, such as back taxes and delayed payments, and payments by persons who are on a fiscal-year basis other than the calendar year. There is no way to relate these miscellaneous payments in an orderly manner to any meaningful variables determining them. We have tried to relate the nonwithheld taxes of the fourth quarter to those of the preceding year, but found that the fit of the regression was not particularly good. Therefore, we have simply assumed that fourth quarter payments in any year are the same as those for the preceding year.

The *predictions of tax payments* based on equations (1), (2), and (3), for the period 1964–66, using actual personal income and the effective tax rates of those years, are given in Table 2. The actual tax payments are also given in the table for comparison.

The predictions of tax payments for the years 1964 through 1966 are remarkably close, in total, to the actual amounts, although the error is somewhat larger for the withheld and the nonwithheld components, separately. It appears clear from these results that a reasonably precise prediction of tax payments can be made, once personal income and effective tax rates are given. The major uncertainty at the present time centers around the behavior of the average effective tax rate with respect to changes in income. Research effort should be directed at filling this gap.

Responses of Consumer Expenditure

In an earlier article, we tentatively concluded that the responses of consumers to changes in disposable income consequent upon tax changes do not differ materially from those consequent on changes in income before tax.[14] This conclusion is restricted to tax changes which consumers believe to be permanent. We cannot say anything about temporary, short-run tax changes simply because there has not been any experience with them. But as the tax changes enacted by the Revenue Act of 1964 were believed to be permanent, we rely on our earlier findings in assuming that an ordinary consumption function will reflect the effects on consumer expenditure of income changes induced by taxes.

One question that must be settled at the start is the concept of income. As is well known, disposable income is defined in the na-

---

[14] Albert Ando and E. Cary Brown, "Lags in Fiscal Policy," Part II of "Lags in Fiscal and Monetary Policy" in Commission on Money and Credit, *Stabilization Policies* (Prentice-Hall, 1963).

tional income statistics as net of personal income tax payments rather than of liabilities. If our dependent variable were consumption rather than consumer expenditure (the difference is in the treatment of depreciation of, and expenditure on, consumer durables), we would be inclined to argue that the liability concept of disposable income is the more relevant one. However, since we are more concerned with the effects of income changes on consumer expenditure rather than on consumption, the case for choosing either of the concepts is an ambiguous one. Therefore, we have tried both. However, we have worked with seasonally adjusted data in the case of the liability concept,[15] and with seasonally unadjusted data in the case of the cash-flow concept. Because seasonal adjustment of cash-flow data is problematical and difficult to extend into the future, we have not attempted such adjustment. On the other hand, if consumers are sophisticated enough to base their expenditure on tax liabilities rather than on cash payments, it seems reasonable to assume that they adjust for regular seasonal variations in their income in determining their expenditure.

The consumption function utilized is a very simple one, with disposable income, net worth of consumers, and lagged consumer expenditure as independent variables, all deflated by the implicit deflator of consumer expenditure.

Seasonally Adjusted (Tax Liabilities Basis)

The behavior of consumer expenditure with respect to disposable income, with taxes on a liabilities basis, and wealth is estimated as follows:

(5a)
$$C = .764D_L + .179C_{-1} - 4.374$$
$$(.209) \quad (.227) \quad \quad (2.599)$$
$$R^2 = .996 \quad SD = 2.62 \quad DW = .75$$

and

(5b)
$$C = .636D_L + .031A + .142C_{-1} + 1.125.$$
$$(.177) \quad (.012) \quad (.216) \quad \quad (2.908)$$
$$R^2 = .997 \quad SD = 2.52 \quad DW = .72$$

[15] Quarterly tax liabilities have been estimated by inserting in equation (1) personal income for the quarter at an annual rate. The resulting estimates have then been adjusted slightly so that the implied annual totals match the actual annual liabilities.

In these equations, C is consumer expenditure, D_L is disposable income (net of personal income tax liability), and A is consumer net worth—all measured in billions of 1958 dollars at annual rates. The data cover the period 1948 through 1963, with the third and fourth quarter of 1950 and the first and second quarter of 1951 excluded in order to eliminate the unusual behavior of households during the early part of the Korean conflict.

The estimates are obtained by the method suggested by Liviatan[16] in order to avoid a least squares bias arising from the simultaneous presence of lagged consumption as an independent variable and the serial correlation of residuals.[17] The ordinary least squares (OLS) estimates are given by

(6a)
$$C = .214D_L + .773C_{-1} - .176$$
$$(.065) \quad (.072) \quad (1.602)$$
$$R^2 = .998 \quad SD = 2.02 \quad DW = 1.27$$

and

(6b)
$$C = .182D_L + .018A + .705C_{-1} + 2.546.$$
$$(.065) \quad (.082) \quad (.076) \quad (1.970)$$
$$R^2 = .998 \quad SD = 1.96 \quad DW = 1.28$$

When equations (5) and (6) are compared, the differences in their coefficients are seen to be quite dramatic. The OLS estimates of the coefficients of C_{-1} in both equations (6a) and (6b) are four times those estimated by the Liviatan method in (5a) and (5b). The speed of adjustment of consumer expenditure to changes in income is thus substantially different in the two estimates.[18]

Very low Durbin-Watson statistics indicate the presence of substantial serial correlation in the residuals. Under these circum-

---

[16] N. Liviatan, "Consistent Estimation of Distributed Lags," *International Economic Review*, Vol. 4, No. 1 (January 1964).

[17] See, for instance, Zvi Griliches, "Distributed Lags: A Survey" (mimeo., June 1965).

[18] Similar estimates reported by Arthur Okun resemble our ordinary least squares estimates. However, the comparison of our results with Okun's is not exact because of two substantial differences in our data: (1) We used data expressed in 1958 dollars while those used by Okun are expressed in current dollars. (2) Our data cover the period 1948–63 while his are for the period 1954–64. See Arthur Okun, "Measuring the Impact of the 1964 Tax Reduction" (Paper delivered at the meeting of the American Statistical Association, Philadelphia, Pa., Sept. 10, 1965).

stances, Liviatan's estimation procedure is known to be consistent but inefficient, and there are now some suggestions for improving its efficiency.[19] Preliminary results of further analysis indicate that our results will not be altered substantially.

Actual consumer expenditure and predictions obtained by using equations (5) and (6) are shown in Table 3. One set of predictions uses actual lagged consumer expenditure as a variable; the other uses predicted lagged consumer expenditure.

The data for net worth for 1964–66 are our own extrapolation of figures reported by Goldsmith, Lipsey and Mendelson,[20] and there is some indication that they may be underestimated. If they are adjusted upward (by $15 billion for 1964, $30 billion for 1965, and $45 billion for 1966) to allow for underestimate, the annual figures in equation (6b) will be raised for 1964 by $0.4 billion, for 1965 by $0.7 billion, and for 1966 by $1.1 billion, while the corresponding adjustments in equation (5b) will be, respectively, $0.7 billion, $1.3 billion, and $2.0 billion. The predictions thus adjusted, using equation (5b), are very close to the actual figures for all three years.

One feature of the predictions is that the OLS estimates for the first quarter of 1964 (equations (6a) and (6b)), the first time that the tax reduction became effective, substantially underestimate the effects of the tax cut on consumer expenditure. The reason is that the coefficient of current income is very small in the OLS estimates, reflecting the bias due to the simultaneous presence of C_{-1} as an independent variable and the serial correlation of the residuals. In addition, because the coefficient of C_{-1} is very large in the OLS estimates, the behavior of the predictions after the first quarter of 1964 differs substantially, depending on whether actual or predicted consumer expenditure is used as the predicting variable, C_{-1}. If actual values are used as C_{-1}, the underestimate is corrected im-

---

[19] The more efficient method of estimation applicable to the first-order autoregressive specifications of the residuals, such as that due to Clifford Hildreth and John Y. Lu (*Demand Relations with Autocorrelated Disturbances*, Michigan State University Agricultural Experimental Station, Technical Bulletin 276, November 1960), does not converge in our case, indicating that serial correlation of the residuals is of a more complex nature. Further analysis of this problem is being undertaken by Ando in connection with the joint econometric model project of the Federal Reserve Board and Massachusetts Institute of Technology.

[20] Raymond W. Goldsmith, Robert E. Lipsey, and Morris Mendelson, *Studies in the National Balance Sheet of the United States* (Princeton University Press, 1963).

TABLE 3. Actual and Predicted Consumer Expenditure, Seasonally Adjusted at Annual Rate, 1964–66

(In billions of 1958 dollars)

Year and Quarter	Actual	A. Using Equations (5a) and (6a)			
		Predicted			
		Using actual C_{-1} in equation		Using predicted C_{-1} in equation	
		(5a)	(6a)	(5a)	(6a)
1964					
I	366.3	365.9	362.1	—	—
II	370.7	371.2	369.7	371.1	366.5
III	378.6	377.4	374.7	377.4	371.4
IV	379.3	381.7	381.9	382.5	376.3
Average	373.7	374.3	372.1	—	—
1965					
I	389.1	389.8	384.4	390.4	382.1
II	394.1	395.6	393.2	395.9	387.0
III	400.7	404.4	399.2	404.8	393.8
IV	409.9	411.6	405.9	412.4	400.6
Average	398.4	400.4	395.7	400.9	390.9
1966					
I	416.2	416.1	414.1	417.0	406.9
II	415.2	419.7	419.4	419.8	412.2
III	420.4	424.4	420.0	425.2	417.7
IV	420.4	429.5	425.3	430.3	423.2
Average	418.0	422.6	419.7	423.1	415.0

mediately; but if predicted consumer expenditure is used, under-estimation persists for a very long time.

When estimates by Liviatan's method (equations (5a) and (5b)) are used, these problems do not arise. Thus, it seems safe to conclude that the coefficient of income is better given by the Liviatan method. It is, therefore, more likely to lie between .65 and .70 than it is to be the .2 given by OLS. We would conclude, therefore, that some 70 percent, rather than 20 percent, of the additional income provided by tax reduction, on the liability basis, is used for expenditure by consumers within the first quarter.

TABLE 3 (*concl.*). Actual and Predicted Consumer Expenditure, Seasonally Adjusted at Annual Rate, 1964–66

(*In billions of 1958 dollars*)

Year and Quarter	Actual	B. Using Equations (5b) and (6b)			
		Predicted			
		Using actual C_{-1} in equation		Using predicted C_{-1} in equation	
		(5b)	(6b)	(5b)	(6b)
1964					
I	366.3	365.4	361.6	—	—
II	370.7	370.5	369.0	370.4	365.7
III	378.6	376.3	373.8	376.3	370.3
IV	379.3	381.2	380.6	380.8	376.4
Average	373.7	373.4	371.3	—	—
1965					
I	389.1	388.1	383.3	388.3	381.3
II	394.1	393.1	391.3	392.9	385.8
III	400.7	400.4	396.7	400.2	390.9
IV	409.9	407.4	403.5	407.3	396.6
Average	398.4	397.3	393.7	397.2	388.7
1966					
I	416.2	411.3	410.7	410.9	401.3
II	415.2	413.8	415.3	413.0	404.8
III	420.4	416.3	415.1	415.9	407.8
IV	420.4	420.0	419.5	419.4	410.6
Average	418.0	415.4	415.2	414.8	406.1

While this is a very tentative result requiring further confirmation using more efficient methods of estimation, it suggests that the speed of adjustment of consumer expenditure to income changes is much faster than it is generally thought to be.[21] If this finding is confirmed by further work, it will have a major implication on the effectiveness of the variation of income tax liability as a counter-cyclical tool; its effect will be felt much more quickly and decisively than is indicated by the Okun study.

[21] See, for instance, Okun, "Measuring the Impact of the 1964 Tax Reduction."

TABLE 4. Actual and Predicted Consumer Expenditure, Seasonally Unadjusted at Annual Rate, 1964–66

(In billions of 1958 dollars)

Year and Quarter	Actual	A. Using Equation (7a)	
		Predicted	
		Using actual C_{-1}	Using predicted C_{-1}
1964			
I	350.0	346.0	—
II	366.4	369.6	366.4
III	367.6	365.2	365.2
IV	410.8	410.0	408.0
Average	373.7	372.7	—
1965			
I	367.6	365.2	363.2
II	390.0	387.2	384.0
III	390.0	389.2	384.8
IV	445.6	437.6	433.2
Average	398.4	394.8	391.3
1966			
I	400.0	396.8	388.4
II	415.6	420.4	411.2
III	413.2	412.8	410.0
IV	443.2	458.8	456.0
Average	418.0	422.2	416.4

Seasonally Unadjusted (Tax Payments Basis)

Estimates of the consumption function using disposable income net of the OBE cash concept of personal income taxes, seasonally unadjusted, are as follows:

(7a) $C = .194D_p + .705C_{-1} - .379 + .143C_{-1}S_2$
          (.094)   (.089)   (.908)   (.017)
          $+ .080C_{-1}S_3 + .176C_{-1}S_4$
          (.015)   (.029)
          $R^2 = .99$ $SD = 1.11$ $DW = .61$

TABLE 4 (*concl.*). **Actual and Predicted Consumer Expenditure, Seasonally Unadjusted at Annual Rate, 1964–66**

(In billions of 1958 dollars)

Year and Quarter	Actual	B. Using Equation (7b)	
		Predicted	
		Using actual C_{-1}	Using predicted C_{-1}
1964			
I	350.0	346.4	—
II	366.4	372.0	369.6
III	367.6	366.8	368.8
IV	410.8	410.8	412.0
Average	373.7	374.0	—
1965			
I	367.6	366.0	366.8
II	390.0	389.2	388.8
III	390.0	388.4	387.6
IV	445.6	436.4	434.8
Average	398.4	395.0	394.5
1966			
I	400.0	393.2	386.8
II	415.6	417.2	407.6
III	413.2	407.2	402.4
IV	443.2	452.4	444.4
Average	418.0	417.5	410.3

(7b)
$$C = .144D_p + .008A + .585C_{-1} + .571 + .132C_{-1}S_2$$
$$(.078) \quad (.004) \quad (.114) \quad\quad (.983) \quad (.056)$$
$$+ .073C_{-1}S_3 + .173C_{-1}S_4.$$
$$(.014) \quad\quad (.024)$$
$$R^2 = .995 \quad\quad SD = .85 \quad\quad DW = .64$$

In these equations, C, D_p, C_{-1} are, respectively, consumer expenditure, disposable income net of tax payments, and lagged consumer expenditure, all quarterly totals in billions of 1958 dollars, and A is net worth of consumers, in billions of 1958 dollars. The estimates are obtained by the Liviatan method. The OLS estimates appear to have a bias similar to that of the seasonally adjusted data, but its magnitude is much smaller, and the two sets of estimates are much closer together than they are when based on seasonally adjusted data. They are not presented here.

The predictions of seasonally unadjusted consumer expenditure are compared in Table 4 with actual figures for 1964, 1965, and 1966. In general, these equations seem to perform well.

When all the predictions based on various methods and concepts are compared, it is clear that the use of ordinary least squares in this type of analysis is very dangerous. The bias that is due to the simultaneous presence of the lagged dependent variable and the serial correlation of the residuals may be very large; and if estimates containing such a bias are used for making predictions for a period not covered by the data used in estimation, the accumulated error is likely to be very large. When the comparative advantage of including or excluding consumer net worth in the consumption function is considered, it appears that its inclusion improves the prediction, particularly if allowance is made for the likely underestimate of the net worth data. However, the advantage does not seem to be large enough to make a clear-cut case for inclusion, particularly in view of the present unreliability of the net worth estimates themselves.

The crucial question is whether the liability or the cash payment of taxes influences consumer expenditure more directly. Unfortunately, our results do not provide an obvious answer to this question. As far as the prediction of consumer expenditure for 1964 is concerned, the liability concept seems to be more accurate, although both concepts perform well. This is so in spite of large differences in income coefficients, coefficients of lagged consumption, and the implied speed of adjustment in equations (5) and (7). This is due in part to the fact that changes in cash payments tend to lag behind changes in the liability when the provisions of the tax law are changed, and the movement of payments is somewhat blurred because of the complex payment structure in the tax system, as indicated in Table 5.

If a future study using more detailed data confirms that the coefficient of income defined on the tax liability basis is much larger

TABLE 5. Comparison of Time Patterns of Tax Liability (Seasonally Adjusted) and Tax Payment (Seasonally Unadjusted), 1963–66
(Annual rates in billions of dollars)

Year and Quarter	Tax Liability[a]	Tax Payment
1963		
I	47.6	45.6
II	48.1	56.8
III	49.0	51.2
IV	50.0	45.2
Average	48.7	49.8
1964		
I	45.8	43.2
II	46.8	54.8
III	47.8	45.6
IV	48.7	40.4
Average	47.3	46.0
1965		
I	47.6	44.0
II	48.7	64.0
III	50.4	51.2
IV	51.7	44.4
Average	49.7	50.9
1966		
I	(54.6)[b]	50.4
II	(55.7)[b]	72.0
III	(57.2)[b]	58.8
IV	(58.8)[b]	53.2
Average	(56.6)[b]	58.6

[a] For the methods of obtaining quarterly liabilities, see footnote 15, page 127.
[b] Preliminary estimates based on equation (1) and the guess that the average effective rate for 1966 would be 19.85 percent.

than that of income defined on the tax payment basis, the policy implication of this finding is quite significant. It suggests that policies which merely change the payment pattern and keep the liability constant—such as the manipulation of refunds and a change in the withholding rate, as done in 1966—will not affect consumer spending very significantly.

Implications for Fiscal Policy

What implications can be drawn from these findings for the manipulation of the personal income tax to stabilize effective demand? How rapid is the response to variation in taxes? Strictly speaking, our results are applicable only to situations in which a permanent tax reduction takes place. The government's policy position was that the tax reduction of 1964 was not a temporary change taken to shore up cyclical demand, but a move to affect the long-run budgetary drag. Therefore, all that we can say is that if consumers expect the tax change to continue indefinitely we would expect them to act in the way predicted.

A tax change can be effected speedily—waiving the length of time it takes to propose and enact the change. Changes in the withholding rate can be implemented almost immediately, and this covers the great bulk of total liabilities. Moreover, quarterly installments are somewhat sensitive to rate changes and would also be modified—more slowly to be sure. The speed of the tax variation itself, therefore, certainly seems adequate, particularly if consumers respond quite promptly to changes in tax liabilities, as our findings suggest. The predicted speed of response of consumers, as implied by the relationships found in this study, varies; it depends upon which consumption function best describes consumer behavior. Taking equation (5b) as an example, we find that 64 percent, 72 percent, and 74 percent of changes in disposable income will be spent by consumers in the first, the second, and the third quarter, respectively.

This does not mean that a unit reduction in taxes would lead to an expansion of demand by only these amounts, however, because the calculations are based on the assumption that income changes by one unit and remains at that level throughout the year. The expansion in consumer demand itself generates income in the familiar multiplier pattern, affecting investment adversely at first, by reducing inventories, and then expanding it as demand is increased. The usual multiplier-accelerator process would push up total demand, expressed as a percent of the initial tax cut, by considerably more. The response seems sufficiently prompt, however, so that optimism may be expressed about the flexibility of the personal income tax as an instrument of fiscal policy, once the initial problems of implementing it are overcome.

However, since genuine countercyclical action must necessarily be considered temporary, consumer response to it will almost surely be less marked than the kind of reduction experienced in 1964–65. Indeed, as consumers become used to the manipulation of rates, they may begin to ignore the short-run variation completely and base their consumption decisions on the longer-run average rate around which variation was being made. Were this to be the case—and only experience will show whether or not it is—consumption-tax variations might have to be substituted for those under the personal income tax. Intertemporal substitution of consumption could be encouraged by exaggerating the cylical variation in prices of consumer goods. Variations of, say, 10 percent in the rate of a general consumption tax would have an effect far beyond anything that could be achieved through interest rate manipulation.

MICHAEL H. SPIRO*

The Impact of
Government Procurements on
Employment in the Aircraft Industry

THIS STUDY investigates some aspects of the impact of government procurements on employment in the aircraft industry and in its supplying industries. The inquiry is an extension and a refinement of a study by Ando, Brown, Kareken, and Solow, who measured various structural lags of monetary and fiscal policy, including preliminary estimates for the aircraft industry.[1]

First, a very simple model of the aircraft industry is constructed; it describes the response of the industry to changes in orders placed with it by the federal government. This model is based on the assumption that aircraft manufacturers set their employment policies so as to minimize labor costs while filling government orders. From this model, a relationship is derived which should prevail between employment, backlogs of orders, and other variables if the above assumption about the aircraft manufacturers is approximately correct. Then, by use of the available time-series data, the parameters of this relationship are estimated, and some inferences are made about the time pattern of reactions of employment in the aircraft industry to changes in government orders. Also, a relation-

* University of Pittsburgh.

[1] Albert Ando and others, "Lags in Fiscal and Monetary Policy," in Commission on Money and Credit, *Stabilization Policies* (Prentice-Hall, 1963).

138

ship is postulated, describing the response of shipments to changes in the size of the work force, and its parameters are estimated. Since orders are the only stimulus of the model, it is relatively easy to perform a simulation with the objective of determining whether the model, given actual orders, would succeed in generating an employment time-series which would approximate the actual employment pattern in the period studied. Such an analysis is reported toward the end of this paper. The study closes with some estimates of the impact of government procurements from the aircraft industry on employment in industries which are the leading suppliers of intermediate goods to the aircraft industry.

In the past few years, a number of studies pertaining to the potential impact of a significant change in the size or composition of the defense budget have been made. The Leontief-Hoffenberg and the Hansen-Tiebout studies are excellent examples.[2] These studies employ input-output models of national or of regional economies and are designed to estimate the ultimate change in the composition of output and employment that would result from a change in the defense budget. The present study differs from the Leontief-Hoffenberg and Hansen-Tiebout studies in two respects: first, it is narrow in scope and focuses on the aircraft industry and related industries rather than on the whole economy; second, it is concerned with the time pattern of variables and not only with their ultimate change.

The results of this inquiry should facilitate the design of policies which will alleviate stresses that may result from a rapid increase or decrease in government procurements from the aircraft industry. Economists engaged in the design of models of the national economy will find in this study descriptions of mechanisms and estimates of lags in the aircraft industry which could serve as a component in their models. Economists engaged in planning in government and business may find in this study a tool for making projections of employment and sales in response to assumed streams of government obligations.

[2] Wassily W. Leontief and Marvin Hoffenberg, "The Economic Effects of Disarmament," *Scientific American*, Vol. 240, No. 4 (April 1961), pp. 47–55, and W. Lee Hansen and Charles M. Tiebout, "An Intersectoral Flow Analysis of the California Economy," *Review of Economics and Statistics*, Vol. 45, No. 4 (November 1963), pp. 409–18.

Models of Manufacturers of Aircraft

The discussion begins by considering a short-run decision of an aircraft manufacturer whose plant facilities are fixed, for the time being; he must decide how to change the size of his labor force when a new order is received from a customer. A survey of the financial statements of a leading aircraft manufacturer suggests that a new order is added to the backlogs of unfilled orders and that

FIGURE 1. A Model of the Aircraft Industry

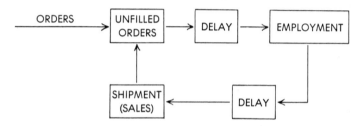

current production and employment depend on the backlogs rather than directly on current new orders.[3] Furthermore, the available information indicates that there are virtually no finished goods inventories and, therefore, the rate of shipment is roughly equal to the rate of output.[4] Thus, it appears reasonable to postulate that there are two major lags in this process: first, the lag between changes in unfilled orders and changes in employment; second, the lag between changes in employment and changes in shipment. The model is illustrated by Figure 1.

Before these lags are estimated, the cost structure of aircraft production which leads to the existence of the lags will be con-

---

[3] Boeing Airplane Company, Annual Reports, 1950–60.

[4] The decision to ignore finished goods inventories in this analysis is based on the following evidence: The data reveal that in 1960 finished goods inventories amounted to less than $300 million while total inventories exceeded $3 billion. Total shipments for the year were $13.7 billion. This evidence suggests that finished goods inventories probably do not constitute a significant variable in the employment decision of the industry. However, the "in process" inventory variable, which is by far the largest component of total inventories, is included in the unfilled orders variable. The source for the above data is U. S. Department of Commerce, Bureau of the Census, *Annual Survey of Manufactures: 1962* (Government Printing Office, 1964), pp. 47 and 357.

sidered, and an attempt will be made to identify factors that determine their specific characteristics.

Models of Short-Term Employment

Perhaps the simplest and most flexible formulation of the cost structure underlying production scheduling and inventory control is the quadratic approximation developed by Holt, Modigliani, Muth, and Simon.[5] Their formulation is based on the assumption that production scheduling and inventory control are a result of balancing two kinds of costs, both of which are approximated by quadratic functions: costs of the first type—cost of holding inventory, implicit costs associated with delays in shipment and with the accumulation of blacklogs of orders—increase as production is smoothed, given the pattern of orders; costs of the second type—set-up costs, overtime and idle time costs, and hiring and firing costs of labor—tend to decrease as production is smoothed. That formulation in its simplest form will be adapted to aircraft production.

It will be assumed that the aircraft manufacturing firm takes the following costs into account in its employment decisions: regular payroll costs, hiring and firing costs, and costs due to operations at over or under capacity. If the average wage and the size of the work force at time t are W_t and L_t, respectively, then the costs of the general payroll may be expressed as follows: $W_t L_t$.

When a firm hires new employees, it incurs a number of costs, such as those related to training, recruiting, and moving. Also, when a firm lays off personnel, it incurs severance pay costs, reorganization costs, and intangible costs that are due to loss of morale among its employees, a possibly bad reputation in the labor market, and a loss in capacity which may impair its chances of getting new contracts. The weak assumption that the average of these costs per man increases as the number of employees involved increases, and the strong assumption that hiring and layoff costs are symmetrical, will be made here.[6]

[5] Charles C. Holt and others, *Planning Production, Inventories, and Work Force* (Prentice-Hall, 1960).

[6] Actually, the assumption of symmetry in our model is not necessary, but since the parameter which would introduce asymmetry could not be identified, little would be gained by such a complication. Furthermore, it is not evident that this assumption is an unreasonable first approximation.

On the basis of the above considerations, the costs of changes in the size of the work force will be approximated by a quadratic function:

$$C_2(L_t - L_{t-1})^2.$$

C_2 is a constant and L_t and L_{t-1} are employment at time t and $t - 1$, respectively.

Finally, the costs that the firm would incur if it operated at over or under capacity need to be specified. Assume that the firm has a desired employment level which, if attained, would enable it to meet its contractual requirements at minimum cost. The desired employment level, L_t^d, is defined in terms of the desired production rate, Q_t^d, and is related to it by means of a linear homogeneous production function in labor. If b is the average and marginal productivity of labor, then

$$L_t^d = Q_t^d/b.$$

The desired production rate is determined by two factors: the backlog of orders at the end of the previous period, U_{t-1}, and the delivery commitments of the firm. The delivery commitments of the firm may be expressed in terms of a leadtime, g, which is defined as the interval of time that may elapse between the receipt of an order and the shipment of goods. The desired production rate may be approximated by dividing the backlog of orders by the leadtime:

$$Q_t^d = \frac{U_{t-1}}{g}.$$

Deviations of the actual employment level from the desired level will result in costs above the minimum level because of the need for overtime, or because the labor force is not fully utilized.[7] The cost of the deviation is assumed to increase with the square of the deviation. Thus, this cost is

$$C_1(L_t^d - L_t)^2.$$

When all the cost components are combined, and the appropriate

---

[7] For a discussion of labor-hoarding, see Robert M. Solow, "Distribution in the Long and Short Run" (International Economic Association, Conference on the Distribution of National Income, September 1964), pp. 7–15.

substitutions are made, the following current cost expression is derived:

$$(1.0) \qquad C_t = C_1\left(\frac{U_{t-1}}{bg} - L_t\right)^2 + C_2(L_t - L_{t-1})^2 + W_t L_t.$$

Assume that the firm has a short planning horizon and chooses an employment level, L_t, which will minimize these costs. Thus, the cost equation is differentiated with respect to L_t, and the resulting expression is equated to zero:[8]

$$\frac{\partial C_t}{\partial L_t} = -\frac{2C_1}{gb}U_{t-1} + 2C_1 L_t + 2C_2 L_t - 2C_2 L_{t-1} + W_t = 0.$$

Thus,

$$L_t = \frac{C_1}{(C_1 + C_2)bg}U_{t-1} + \frac{C_2}{C_1 + C_2}L_{t-1} - \frac{1}{2C_1 + 2C_2}W_t$$

and the change in the labor force is

$$(1.1) \qquad \Delta L_t = L_t - L_{t-1} = \frac{C_1}{(C_1 + C_2)bg}U_{t-1}$$

$$+ \left(\frac{C_2}{C_1 + C_2} - 1\right)L_{t-1} - \frac{1}{2C_1 + 2C_2}W_t.$$

For the purpose of statistical estimation, the equation is rewritten and an error term, e_t, is added:[9]

$$(1.2) \qquad \Delta L_t = a_0 + a_1 U_{t-1} + a_2 L_{t-1} + a_3 W_t + e_t.$$

The model imposes some restrictions on the values that the coefficients may take. Since all the components of a_1 and a_3 are positive, the model requires that a_1 will turn out to be positive and a_3 to be negative. Furthermore, the theory restricts the value of a_2:

$$a_2 = \frac{C_2}{C_1 + C_2} - 1 = -\frac{C_1}{C_1 + C_2}.$$

The expression suggests that a_2 must fall into the following range:

$$-1 \leq a_2 \leq 0.$$

---

[8] The positive quadratic nature of the function assures the fulfillment of second-order conditions.

[9] The only parameter which cannot be identified is either b or g.

The proposition just derived will constitute the basic hypothesis of this study. However, a number of extensions will also be considered. The first of these involves the assumption that the manufacturer incurs a cost that is due not only to hiring and firing but also to changes in the rates of hiring and firing. An economic justification for introducing this cost component is that the personnel and training facilities in the firm are geared to processing a certain number of prospective and current employees and that any departure from this rate will result in costs above and beyond those mentioned so far. The derivation of this hypothesis, presented in detail in Appendix A (p. 176), results in the following equation:

$$(3.5) \quad \Delta L_t = a_0 + a_1 U_{t-1} + a_2 L_{t-1} + a_3 L_{t-2} + a_4 W_t + e_t.$$

A second extension of the basic hypothesis is derived from a model based on the cost function specified in equation (1.0) and on the assumption that the employment decisions are based not only on the current state of affairs but also on the expectations of the firm for the foreseeable future. That is, the firm adjusts its labor force so as to minimize the present value of the stream of estimated future costs rather than only current costs. The detailed specifications of the model and the derivation of a testable hypothesis are given in Appendix A. The resulting equation is

$$(4.10) \quad \Delta L_t = a_0 + a_1 L_{t-1} + a_2(U_{t-1} + O_t)$$
$$+ a_3 \sum_{i=1}^{\infty} z^i O_{t+i} + a_4 \sum_{i=0}^{\infty} z^i W_{t+i}.$$

Current orders and forecasts of orders are represented by O; z is the weight that the firm attaches to the variables—orders and wages—which are forecast; it is a complex function of the leadtime, the rate of interest, and the various cost components.

Thus far, the discussion has been concerned with the derivation of hypotheses which are designed to explain changes in employment. Next, a function relating shipment to employment will be described.

Determinants of Rate of Shipment

Concern with the rate of shipment is motivated by two considerations: first, an estimate of the lag between changes in employment and changes in shipment is necessary if the results of this study are to be compared with those of Ando and Brown, who measured the lag between obligations and expenditures;[10] second, this relationship (which is described in the lower portion of Figure 1) is necessary for our simulation experiments.

The two primary inputs affecting the rate of production are assumed to be labor and plant and equipment. Since the production cycle of the industry spans a number of quarters, an increase in inputs, when allocated among the products in various stages of completion in the "in process" inventory, will not result in an immediate proportional increase in shipments; rather, shipments will rise only gradually in response to an increase in production. The equations specifying this description of the production and shipment process are

(5.0)
$$Q_t = aK_t + bL_t$$

and

(5.1)
$$S_t = \sum_{i=1}^{T} a_i Q_{t-i}.$$

Equation (5.0) specifies that the production rate, Q, is a linear function of plant and equipment, K, and of labor, L. Equation (5.1) states that current shipment is a function of the production rates of the previous periods. The exact nature of the function is determined by the weights, $a_i's$.[11] The assumption is that the weights decline geometrically, which implies that the current rate of shipment is much more dependent on production in the previous quarter than on production in earlier quarters.[12] Thus, let

$$a_i = \lambda^i \quad \text{and} \quad 0 < \lambda < 1.$$

If it is assumed that $T \to \infty$, which is a rather weak assumption

---

[10] Albert Ando and E. Cary Brown, "Lags in Fiscal Policy," Part II of "Lags in Fiscal and Monetary Policy," in Commission on Money and Credit, *Stabilization Policies* (Prentice-Hall, 1963).

[11] For a discussion of these concepts, see Leendert Koyck, *Distributed Lags and Investment Analysis* (Amsterdam: North-Holland Publishing Co., 1954) and Robert M. Solow, "On a Family of Distributed Lags," *Econometrica*, Vol. 28, No. 2 (April 1960).

[12] Estimates based on an alternative assumption about the weights are presented below in the section, "Estimation of Determinants of Shipments."

considering the assumed weights, and if the proper substitutions are made, the following expression is derived:

(5.2) $$S_t = \sum_{i=1}^{\infty} \lambda^i(aK_{t-i} + bL_{t-i}).$$

Upon the specification of a similar expression for S_{t-1} and the subtraction of λS_{t-1} from S_t,

(5.3) $$S_t = \lambda aK_{t-1} + \lambda bL_{t-1} + \lambda S_{t-1}$$

and

(5.4) $$\Delta S_t = S_t - S_{t-1} = \lambda aK_{t-1} + \lambda bL_{t-1} + (\lambda - 1)S_{t-1}.$$

All the parameters in this equation can be identified, and the only restriction imposed by the model on the estimated coefficient is

$$-1 < \lambda - 1 < 0.$$

Estimation of Employment Adjustment

Evidence will now be presented in support of the models for explaining changes in the size of the work force in the aircraft industry. First, estimation problems and the data will be discussed. Then, experiments which are based on the linear models will be analyzed. Next, some alternative hypotheses will be considered and tested. And finally, details will be given for (1) estimates of the speeds of response of production and nonproduction workers to changes in order backlogs and (2) estimates based on the data of a particular firm rather than on aggregate industry data.

Estimation Problems and the Data

The theories that have been advanced contain assumptions which are stated as descriptions (1) of the objectives and behavior of entrepreneurs and (2) of the cost structures of firms. The primary objective of this investigation, however, is to measure the aggregate response of employment in the industry to changes in backlogs of orders. The results of Grunfeld and Griliches will be used to justify the use of a micro model for explaining macro behavior.[13]

[13] Yehuda Grunfeld and Zvi Griliches, "Is Aggregation Necessarily Bad?" *Review of Economics and Statistics*, Vol. 42, No. 1 (February 1960), pp. 1–13.

Grunfeld and Griliches argue that, in situations where the aggregation error is likely to be smaller than the specification error, and the investigator is interested in explaining aggregate behavior, he is advised to use aggregate data for estimation purposes. These conditions appear to hold for the model presented in the present paper. This view is supported by the argument that the model, as specified, does not account for the effects on employment resulting from the interaction of firms in the industry. Specifically, the model does not contain a description of the state of the labor market at the time the firm wishes to hire. It is expected that the speed of hiring of any one firm will be dependent on whether other firms are in the process of hiring or firing.[14] On the basis of these considerations, and on the basis of the practical difficulties of gathering data of companies and of the analytical difficulties of devising a composite response from individual responses, a micro model will be applied to macro data.

The data for the regressions are derived from a variety of sources. The quarterly data on unfilled orders in the aircraft industry for the period 1948–63 were made available by the Aerospace Industries Association and reported by the U. S. Department of Commerce, Bureau of the Census, in *Facts for Industry*, Series M42D. However, the method of sampling was changed in 1961. Consequently, the data from 1961 on are not consistent with the data for prior years. The Department of Commerce could not suggest a procedure for adjusting the data; and as the consistent time series covers a span of 12 years and provides 48 observations, it was decided to limit most of the study to the period 1948–60 and not attempt to manipulate the data.

Since the models are formulated in real terms and the backlog data are measured in current dollars, the question of an appropriate price index arises. The specification of a price index for the aircraft industry is a difficult problem for at least two reasons. First, the products of the industry changed substantially during the decade of the 1950's. Aircraft which were constructed in the late part of the

[14] Attempts to support this assertion with at least one example did not prove successful. The experiment that was conducted involved the addition of aggregate industry backlogs and employment as explanatory variables for employment at Boeing Airplane Company. However, the coefficient of the aggregate unfilled orders variable was insignificant. This failure is attributed to a specification error. These results are discussed in some detail below in the company versus industry analysis.

decade could hardly be considered the same as the product constructed in the early part. In addition, the product mix of the industry changed. While at the beginning of the decade most of the output consisted of aircraft, in later years an increasing portion consisted of missiles and research and development. The Department of Labor does not seem to publish a price index for the aircraft industry, and all attempts to locate one were unsuccessful. Levinson, who studied price movements in numerous manufacturing sectors, indicated that a price index for the transportation industry as a group was not available and limited his discussion of prices in transportation to motor vehicles only.[15] In the absence of a price index for the aircraft industry, experiments with the Department of Labor wholesale price index for electrical machinery and with average hourly earnings of production workers in aircraft will be reported. The data on employment and wages are from publications of the Department of Labor.[16] The wage data are average hourly earnings of production workers. Sources of the remaining data will be cited when the regressions utilizing the data are presented.

Linear Models of Employment Change

This section—which reports the results of experiments testing the hypotheses set forth above in the discussion, "Models of Manufacturers of Aircraft—is divided into two parts. The first examines the evidence in support of the first-order lag models; the second contains the results of the estimation of the second-order lag models.

FIRST-ORDER LAG MODELS. In the absence of a price deflator for the aircraft industry, the naive assumption is made that the prices of the output of the industry remained constant during the 1950's. The results of the regressions are as follows:[17]

---

[15] Harold M. Levinson, *Postwar Movement of Prices and Wages in Manufacturing Industries*, Study Paper No. 21, Joint Economic Committee, 86 Cong. 2 sess. (1960).

[16] U. S. Department of Labor, *Employment and Earnings Statistics*, Bulletin No. 1312-1, Standard Industrial Classification (SIC) 372, pp. 257, 258.

[17] S_e is the standard error of the estimates, DW is the Durbin-Watson statistic, L is employment, U is unfilled orders, W is the wage rate, and T is a trend variable. The estimates are based on quarterly data for the period 1948–60.

$$\Delta L_t = 61.04 + .013U_{t-1} - .325L_{t-1}$$
$$(10.33) \quad (.002) \qquad (.048)$$
$$R^2 = .49 \qquad S_e = 22.44 \qquad DW = .83$$

$$\Delta L_t = 60.572 + .013U_{t-1} - .339L_{t-1} + 1.105\sqrt{T}$$
$$(10.549) \quad (.002) \qquad (.067) \qquad (3.730)$$
$$R^2 = .49 \qquad S_e = 22.66$$

$$\Delta L_t = 64.646 + .012U_{t-1} - .315L_{t-1} - 3.223W_t$$
$$(18.653) \quad (.002) \qquad (.065) \qquad (13.822)$$
$$R_2 = .49 \qquad S_e = 22.66 \qquad DW = .84$$

$$\Delta L_t = 138.367 + .012U_{t-1} - .338L_{t-1} - 77.040W_t + 20.920\sqrt{T}$$
$$(46.127) \quad (.002) \qquad (.065) \qquad (44.521) \qquad (12.019)$$
$$R^2 = .52 \qquad S_e = 22.20 \qquad DW = .89$$

Additional information common to all of these estimates is $\bar{L} = 631.332$, $r(L_{t-1}, U_{t-1}) = .9579$. Furthermore, the results obtained using the square root of the variable T were superior to those obtained when the variable T was included in the regression.[18]

A number of comments on the meaning of these results are appropriate. The explanatory power of the unadjusted unfilled orders variable is very significant. The coefficients of unfilled orders and lagged employment are very stable and are affected only slightly by the introduction of additional variables into the regression. Furthermore, the introduction of a trend variable alone or wages alone does not improve the fit, and only the joint introduction of these two variables results in a significant coefficient for either, though neither coefficient is as large as twice the size of its standard error. The positive sign of the coefficient of $\sqrt{T}$ is puzzling and leads us to question the assumption of a constant leadtime. Our interpretation of these results is that the assumptions of fixed prices, technology, and leadtime are probably not correct but that these variables interact in such a way as to compensate for each other's effect on employment and consequently make the assumptions appear correct

---

[18] The trend variable is supposed to account for possible long-term changes in leadtime and productivity. It is conceivable that the square root of the trend variable results in estimates that are superior to the variable proper because the leadtime decreases at a declining rate while productivity increases at a constant rate.

FIGURE 2. Aircraft Industry: Leadtime, 1952–61

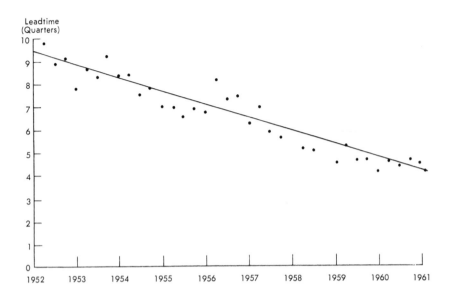

in the first regression. An increase in productivity, *ceteris paribus*, decreases the labor force requirements, given a certain backlog, in comparison with what the requirements would have been without the productivity increase. An increase in the leadtime, *ceteris paribus*, also decreases labor requirements, and so does the effect of a price increase provided that the backlog is measured in current dollars. Thus, the interpretation that either prices actually remain constant while productivity increases and the leadtime decreases, or that productivity remains constant while prices and leadtime change, or that all three variables change, is consistent with the empirical results cited above. Thus, the only conclusion that can be drawn is that, if these variables change, they neutralize each other's effect on employment.

In the hope of gaining some insight into these questions, estimates for leadtime and productivity are plotted as a function of time (Figures 2 and 3). The estimate for leadtime (Figure 2) is derived by dividing unfilled orders by sales which are taken as an indication of shipments. Under the strict conditions that the firm ships a fraction of its order backlog in each period, it can be demonstrated that

FIGURE 3. Aircraft Industry: Average Annual Labor Productivity, 1947–59

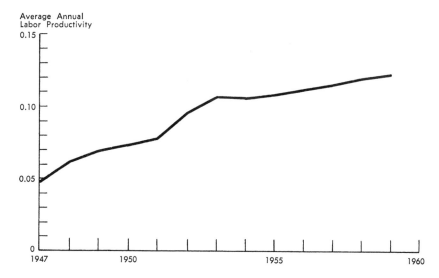

the average leadtime is the inverse of this fraction.[19] Even if these conditions were not strictly maintained, the data strongly suggest that the leadtime declined between the beginning and the end of the decade of the 1950's. The change in the composition of the output of the industry, and the shift from manufacturing and hardware goods to research and development, may account for this phenomenon. Thus, the decline in the leadtime could explain the positive sign of the coefficient of $\sqrt{T}$ in the last regression.

The estimate for productivity is inferred from the judgment of economists at the Federal Reserve Board, as manifested in their construction of the index of industrial production for the aircraft industry. Thus, productivity estimates are derived here by dividing production by employment.[20] The results are presented in Figure 3; they suggest that the economists who constructed the production index rejected the assumption of constant productivity. Therefore, the evidence presented so far suggests that the leadtime de-

[19] For a proof, see George Hadley, Memorandum D-28, Industrial Dynamics Research Project (School of Industrial Management, Massachusetts Institute of Technology, Jan. 16, 1959).

[20] Manhours rather than employment were used in the construction of the production index.

clined and productivity increased during the period under study.

The next set of experiments is designed to test the implication of the relaxation of the assumption of constant prices. As a deflator of unfilled orders and wages, the wholesale price index for electrical machinery is used. The results follow:

$$\Delta L_t = 36.334 + .0076U_{t-1} - .153L_{t-1}$$
$$(11.197) \quad (.002) \quad\quad\quad (.032)$$
$$R^2 = .33 \quad\quad S_e = 25.87$$

$$\Delta L_t = 34.651 + .0083U_{t-1} - .178L_{t-1} + 2.319\sqrt{T}$$
$$(12.012) \quad (.0025) \quad\quad\quad (.069) \quad\quad\quad (5.626)$$
$$R^2 = .33 \quad\quad S_e = 26.09$$

$$\Delta L_t = 242.148 + .0058U_{t-1} - .093L_{t-1} - 141.300W_t$$
$$(67.808) \quad (.002) \quad\quad\quad (.036) \quad\quad\quad (46.012)$$
$$R^2 = .44 \quad\quad S_e = 23.82$$

$$\Delta L_t = 402.761 + .0106U_{t-1} - .268L_{t-1} - 262.051W_t + 21.044\sqrt{T}$$
$$(75.994) \quad (.002) \quad\quad\quad (.059) \quad\quad\quad (53.646) \quad\quad (5.986)$$
$$R^2 = .56 \quad\quad S_e = 21.33$$

The simple correlation between unfilled orders and employment is .8560 and is lower than its value when unadjusted unfilled orders are used. In comparing these results with the first set of results obtained by using unadjusted data for orders and wages, it is evident that, except for the last case of the second set, the fit in the first set of regressions is better than that in the second set. In our judgment, however, the most striking result is that in the second set of regressions the coefficient of L_{t-1} is quite sensitive to the presence of wages and a trend variable in the regression, and that in the last regression in which the best fit is obtained this coefficient is quite similar to the one obtained fairly consistently in the first set of regressions when unadjusted unfilled orders are used. The values of the coefficient of L_{t-1} in the first and the second set are .338 and .268, respectively, and imply an average lag between the change in unfilled orders and the change in employment of 3 and 3.7 quarters.[21]

[21] While the manuscript was undergoing its final revision, an additional experiment employing a two-stage least-squares estimating procedure was conducted. This experiment, which resulted in estimates of average lags of about 1.4 quarters, is reported in Appendix B.

Although the assumptions of constant technology and leadtime may not be correct, the analysis thus far suggests that variations in these assumed parameters have opposite effects on the rate at which employment is adjusted and that their net effect may be small. The deflation of unfilled orders by the wholesale price index for electrical machinery improves the fit slightly over what it is when unadjusted variables are used. However, the improvement is not significant enough to exclude further estimates using unadjusted data.[22]

The last experiment in this sequence tests the hypothesis (4.10) that was derived from the multiperiod horizon model in which the assumption is made that the manufacturers of aircraft adjust their labor force so as to minimize costs over the foreseeable horizon rather than only current costs. The equation which is derived from this model includes forecasts of orders in addition to the variables mentioned thus far. As a survey of the literature did not yield information about an appropriate forecasting method, the assumption was made that orders were forecast accurately by the industry. The results of the estimates were disappointing and were not superior to the ones obtained from a simpler model in which only current costs were minimized.

A number of explanations can be offered. First, the assumption made about the forecasts is incorrect. This explanation is supported by the results of a number of surveys conducted by the Department of Labor and which suggest considerable uncertainty in the aircraft industry about future labor requirements.[23] Given this level of uncertainty, and given the leadtime in the industry which is quite long in comparison with the average response time of employment to changes in backlogs of orders, a question arises concerning the supposition that the industry looks beyond its order backlogs in determining its labor requirements. Furthermore, it can be argued that the incorporation of order backlogs rather than orders into the decision rule may be viewed as the implicit introduction of a

---

[22] Hourly earnings of production workers in the aircraft and parts industry were also used as a deflator for unfilled orders. The results, however, were inferior to the ones cited. A possible explanation is that the rise in marginal productivity of labor caused prices to rise more slowly than wages, and that the use of wages as a deflator eliminated the effects of technological change.

[23] See, for instance, U.S. Bureau of Employment Security, Industry Manpower Survey, *Aircraft and Parts Manufacturing*, No. 2 (October 1955), p. 4, and No. 85 (February 1958), p. 5.

multiperiod horizon into the model in a way which best describes the behavior of the industry.

Prior to concluding the discussion of first-order models, the response pattern implied by these models will be examined. For this purpose the first model using the unadjusted data will be used. The transient solution to this system, on the assumption that the system starts from rest and a unit order is injected at time t_0, is as follows:

$$L_t = L_0(.67^t).$$

The percentage of total change in employment that takes place in each quarter is determined by dividing the coefficient in each period by the sum total of all coefficients which is a measure of the total change.[24] The total change is

$$\sum_{t=0}^{\infty} .67^t = \frac{1}{1 - .67} = 3.03.$$

The percentage effect and the cumulative effect are as follows:

Lag	0	1	2	3	4	5
Coefficient	1	.67	.45	.30	.21	.14
Percentage of total response	33	23	15	10	7	5
Cumulative percentage of response to date	33	56	71	81	88	93

Thus, more than 50 percent of the total change in employment resulting from a unit input in order backlogs, or a shipment of one unit without a new one coming in, takes place within less than 6 months of the change in order backlogs.

Not only the distribution over time of the change in employment but also the magnitude of the total change is of interest. This information is derived by solving the equation for its steady-state solution:

$$\Delta L_t = 138.367 + .012U - .338L - 77.040W + 20.920\sqrt{T} = 0$$

and

$$L = 411.6 + .036U - 227.9W + 62.0\sqrt{T}.$$

[24] Percent of total response $= \dfrac{L_0(.67)^t}{\displaystyle\sum_{t=0}^{\infty} L_0(.67)^t} = \dfrac{.67^t}{\displaystyle\sum_{t=0}^{\infty} (.67)^t}.$

Since employment is measured in thousands of men and unfilled orders in millions of dollars, it follows from the preceding equation that an increase of $1 million in the order backlogs of the industry will result in an increase of 36 employees in the size of the labor force of the industry. The long-range elasticity of employment with respect to backlogs of unfilled orders is .68.[25] This elasticity implies increasing returns to labor.[26] An elasticity coefficient of .58 is derived from the estimates of the regression in which the data were deflated by the wholesale price index for electrical machinery. The elasticity of employment with respect to wages can also be computed in a similar way; the results are $-.76$ and -2.45 for the un-

---

[25] In the computations of the elasticity, the mean values of the variables are used.

[26] Actually, the decline in the leadtime implies that the returns to scale are greater than what the above coefficient of elasticity suggests.

Proof: Let $E_{L,Q}$ be the elasticity of employment with respect to output and $E_{L,U}$ the elasticity of employment with respect to backlogs. Thus,

$$E_{L,Q} = \frac{\partial L/L}{\partial Q/Q}$$

and

$$E_{L,U} = \frac{\partial L/L}{\partial U/U}.$$

Assume now that output is a fraction of the order backlogs and that the inverse of the fraction is the average leadtime.

$$Q = \frac{U}{g}$$

$$\therefore \quad U = gQ$$

and

$$dU = g\,dQ + Q\,dg.$$

It follows that

$$\frac{dU}{U} = \frac{dQ}{Q} + \frac{dg}{g}$$

and

$$E_{L,Q} = \frac{\partial L/L}{\partial U/U - \partial g/g}.$$

Thus, if the leadtime is constant, $E_{L,Q} = E_{L,U}$. However, it was demonstrated earlier that the leadtime is declining and therefore $E_{L,Q} < E_{L,U}$. Hence, the observation that the coefficient $E_{L,U}$ underestimates the extent to which the returns to scale are increasing.

adjusted data and the data adjusted by the price index for electrical machinery, respectively. These results suggest that, while considerable confidence can be placed on the explanatory power of the unfilled orders variable, only very limited confidence can be placed on the explanatory power of wages. The results may be an indication of the inadequacy of the theory or of the inappropriate choice of data for the wage-rate variable.

SECOND-ORDER LAG MODELS. All the experiments presented in this section are designed to test the same basic logical structure; the differences among them are due to different assumptions about the behavior of prices.

The result of the estimation when unadjusted data are used is

$$L_t - L_{t-1} = 87.586 + .0078U_{t-1} + .215L_{t-1} - .459L_{t-2}$$
$$(40.552) \quad (.0022) \qquad (.148) \qquad (.114)$$
$$- 48.875W_t + 16.496\sqrt{T}$$
$$(37.922) \qquad (10.109)$$
$$R^2 = .64 \qquad S_e = 19.33 \qquad DW = 1.87$$

The result of the estimation when unfilled orders and wages are deflated by the wholesale price index for electrical machinery is

$$L_t - L_{t-1} = 288.341 + .0073U_{t-1} + .148L_{t-1} - .351L_{t-2}$$
$$(82.604) \quad (.0023) \qquad (.162) \qquad (.129)$$
$$- 188.149W_t + 17.172\sqrt{T}$$
$$(57.068) \qquad (5.779)$$
$$R^2 = .62 \qquad S_e = 19.958$$

The fit in all of these cases is an improvement over the fit for the corresponding first-order lag models. Furthermore, all the signs in the equations are consistent with the theory. The transient solutions to the two equations are oscillatory, but the transient practically vanishes before L_t assumes negative values in response to a positive input at U_t. The two equations imply fairly similar lag structures.

The response of employment in the first system to a unit input into backlogs is as follows:

Lag	0	1	2	3	4	5	6
Coefficient	1	1.22	1.03	.71	.41	.17	.02
Percentage of total effect	24	29	25	17	9	6	0
Cumulative percentage of total effect[27]	24	53	78	95	104	109	109

The response of the second system in which unfilled orders and wages are deflated by the wholesale price index for electrical machinery is as follows:

Lag	0	1	2	3	4	5	6	7	8
Coefficient	1	1.15	.99	.74	.50	.32	.21	.14	.09
Percentage of total effect	18	21	18	14	8	6	4	3	3
Cumulative percentage of total effect	18	39	57	71	79	85	89	92	95

The first of these two estimates of the lag suggests that by the end of the second quarter about half of the total adjustment in the labor force will have taken place in response to a unit change in backlogs. The second estimate yields a slightly slower response and suggests that by the middle of the third quarter an adjustment of comparable magnitude will have taken place. The long-range elasticities of employment with respect to unfilled orders and wages when computed from the second-order model are about 10 percent smaller than the corresponding values which were computed from the first-order lag models.

It is our view that the results of the estimates of the second-order lag models support our earlier contention that the evidence does not contradict the assumption of constant prices. Thus, in the absence of a price index for the aircraft industry, this assumption will be adopted for future estimates in this study. A number of alternative hypotheses about the determinants of employment will now be examined.

---

[27] The cumulative percentage exceeds 100 because of the oscillatory nature of the solution to the difference equation and the fact that the transient does not vanish completely before turning negative.

Estimation of Alternative Hypotheses

Experiments reported thus far have tested variants of hypotheses specified above. In the present section, a number of alternative hypotheses will be examined, and their explanatory powers will be compared with those of the linear models. The first set of experiments assumes that the correct variables have been selected for explaining changes in employment but that the function has been specified incorrectly. The second experiment tests an hypothesis which implies a relationship that differs from the one described in the model of the aircraft industry. This hypothesis states that employment is adjusted in response to sales rather than unfilled orders.

LOGARITHMIC MODEL OF EMPLOYMENT CHANGE. Thus far, lags which were derived from linear models have been investigated. An issue of interest, however, is the sensitivity of the results and inferences about the response of employment to the structure of the assumed model. In order to gain some insight into this question, a logarithmic model will be postulated and tested.

Assume the following adjustment mechanism:

$$\frac{L_t}{L_{t-1}} = \left(\frac{L_t^d}{L_{t-1}}\right)^{\alpha}.$$

L_t and L_t^d are the desired and actual levels of the workforce and α is a parameter indicating the speed of adjustment. Let the desired level of the workforce be directly related to the level of unfilled orders, U_{t-1}, and inversely related to the wage rate, W_t:

$$L_t^d = A U_{t-1}^{\beta} W_t^{-\gamma}.$$

β and γ are the elasticities of the desired labor force with respect to unfilled orders and wages, respectively, and A is an arbitrary constant. Thus,

$$\frac{L_t}{L_{t-1}} = \left[\frac{A U_{t-1}^{\beta} W_t^{-\gamma}}{L_{t-1}}\right]^{\alpha}.$$

Following a logarithmic transformation and the inclusion of a trend variable, T, to account for long-term changes in productivity and leadtime, the equation is estimated. The results of the estimation of this model are as follows:

$$\ln L_t - \ln L_{t-1} = .328 + .233 \ln U_{t-1} - .138 \ln W_t$$
$$\phantom{\ln L_t - \ln L_{t-1} = } (.116) \quad (.039) \qquad\quad (.077)$$
$$\phantom{\ln L_t - \ln L_{t-1} = } - .387 \ln L_{t-1} + .034 \ln T$$
$$\phantom{\ln L_t - \ln L_{t-1} = } (.062) \qquad\quad (.019)$$
$$R^2 = .61 \qquad S_e = .036$$

The long-term elasticity of employment with respect to unfilled orders and with respect to wages can readily be computed. The first elasticity is β and the second is γ. The elasticities which are computed from various models are presented below for comparative purposes:

Steady-State Elasticity of Employment with Respect to	Linear Model[28]		Logarithmic Model
	Unadjusted Data	Data Adjusted by Wholesale Price Index for Electrical Machinery	Unadjusted Data
Unfilled orders	.68	.58	.61
Wages[29]	−.76	−2.45	−.35

Again, these results point out the fact that the unfilled orders variable leads to fairly stable inferences; this is not the case with the wage variable.

The study of the lag structure that is implied by the logarithmic model is more complex than the one implied by the linear model, since a unit input into unfilled orders cannot be assumed and the employment response be studied while the model is in its logarithmic form. Thus, a number of approximations will have to be made. These are presented in detail in Appendix C.

---

[28] The elasticity computation of the linear model uses sample means.

[29] The wage elasticity of the linear model depends significantly on the sample observation at which it is computed. The following additional long-term elasticities of employment with respect to wages were computed from the linear models:

Sample Point	Unadjusted Data	Data Adjusted by Wholesale Price Index for Electrical Machinery
First quarter 1950	−1.4	−6.1
First quarter 1960	− .87	−2.5

The logarithmic model implies the following response pattern of employment to a unit change in unfilled orders:

Lag	0	1	2	3	4	5
Coefficient	1.0	.61	.37	.23	.14	.08
Percentage of total response	39	24	14	9	5	3
Cumulative percentage of total response	39	63	77	86	91	94

When this response was compared with the one computed from the estimates of the linear model using identical data, the logarithmic model seemed to imply a slightly faster response than the linear model. The logarithmic model suggests that 63 percent of the total effect will have taken place by the end of the second quarter, while the linear model suggests 56 percent. The real process is probably neither linear nor purely logarithmic and probably contains both linear and nonlinear elements. Our view is that the results of the estimate of the logarithmic model reinforce our confidence in the results derived from the linear model concerning the speed of response of employment to changes in unfilled orders in the aircraft industry.

RESPONSE OF EMPLOYMENT TO SALES. The primary motivation in measuring the response of employment to sales is to test the supposition implied in our model that it is unsuitable to use sales by the private sector, which correspond to expenditures by the public sector, as a variable for measuring the impact of procurements on the aircraft industry. This statement is supported by the argument that the initial impact takes place prior to the expenditure phase. The objective of the present experiment is to test this contention.

In measuring the response of employment to sales, the model used is similar to the linear models which have already been discussed at length. The only difference between this model and previous models is that the desired employment level is specified in terms of sales rather than in terms of backlogs of orders. *Ceteris paribus*, an increase in sales results in a decrease in unfilled orders. Therefore, if the theory that unfilled orders is the relevant variable for explaining employment in the aircraft industry is correct, it would be expected that, in the absence of finished goods inventories, an increase in sales would result in a decrease in employment. The results of the estimation are as follows:[30]

$$L_t - L_{t-1} = 105.02 - .036S_{t-1} - .022L_{t-1}$$
$$(42.534) \ (.009) \qquad (.054)$$
$$R^2 = .35 \qquad S_e = 24.977$$

Two aspects of these results are noteworthy. First, the sign of the coefficient of the sales variable is consistent with our expectations. Second, the coefficient of L_{t-1} is insignificant. Therefore, the conclusion is that the sales variable is not appropriate for measuring the timing of the impact of government procurements on employment in the aircraft industry.

Production, Nonproduction, and Company Employment

The analysis of the time pattern of reactions of employment in the aircraft industry to changes in unfilled orders will be completed by examining a "less aggregate" group of employees than has been examined thus far. First, the responses of production and nonproduction workers to changes in unfilled orders will be measured, and the speeds of response of these two groups will be examined, to determine whether a significant difference exists between them. Second, the response in one particular firm, the Boeing Airplane Company, will be compared with the response estimated for the industry.

RESPONSE OF PRODUCTION AND NONPRODUCTION WORKERS TO CHANGES IN ORDER BACKLOGS. The data for nonproduction workers are obtained by subtracting the data for production workers from those for total employment in the aircraft industry. Because of results reported and discussed earlier, order backlogs at current prices are used as the explanatory variable. The results for nonproduction workers are as follows:[31]

$$L_t = 6.72 + .0013U_{t-1} + .91L_{t-1}$$
$$(2.55) \ (.0003) \qquad (.019)$$
$$R^2 = .994 \qquad S_e = 6.74 \qquad \bar{L} = 206.3$$

---

[30] This estimate, and also the remaining estimates in this investigation, are based on data unadjusted for possible price changes.

[31] The high multiple correlation coefficient is due in part to the use of L_t rather than ΔL_t as the dependent variable in the regressions in this section.

and

$$L_t = 4.50 + .0006U_{t-1} + 1.43L_{t-1} - .48L_{t-2}$$
$$(2.57)\ \ (.0003)\qquad\quad (.15)\qquad\ (.14)$$
$$R^2 = .994\qquad S_e = 6.59$$

The coefficients are significant, and all fall into ranges which are consistent with the theory. The partial correlation coefficient between unfilled orders and nonproduction workers is .837, which is significantly lower than the partial between total employment and unfilled orders. Probably the explanation is that, in estimates of total employment, the leadtime change neutralizes, in part, the effect of the technological change and the resulting decline in employment per given backlog of orders. However, for nonproduction workers this may not be true. It is quite possible that effects generated by the technological change may have combined forces with the declining leadtime to suggest a larger change in nonproduction employment in 1960 per change in backlog of orders than would have been expected in 1950. In any case, a more refined theory may well be in order for explaining the behavior of nonproduction workers. The response implied by the first-order lag model is as follows:

Lag	0	1	2	3	4	5	6	7
Coefficient	1	.91	.83	.76	.69	.63	.57	.52
Percentage of total effect	9	8	7	7	6	6	5	5
Cumulative percentage of total effect	9	17	24	31	37	43	48	53

Clearly, the response is very slow since it takes 7 quarters for 50 percent of the effect to take place.

The following response is derived from the second-order equation:

Lag	0	1	2	3	4	5	6	7
Coefficient	1	1.33	1.45	1.42	1.35	1.23	1.14	1.06
Percentage of total effect	5	7	8	8	7	6	6	5
Cumulative percentage of total effect	5	12	20	28	35	41	47	52

The response is as slow as the previous one although the time pattern is different.

The steady-state solution of the above equations is

$$L = 74.6 + .014\ U,$$

which suggests that an order of \$1 million would result in the hiring of 14 nonproduction workers.

When similar experiments are performed for the production workers, the results are as follows:

$$L_t = 54.2 + .0099 U_{t-1} + .61 L_{t-1}$$
$$(12.67)\ (.0027) \qquad (.1)$$
$$R^2 = .978 \qquad S_e = 21.63 \qquad \overline{L} = 441.35$$

and

$$L_t = 40.73 + .0072 U_{t-1} + 1.22 L_{t-1} - .51 L_{t-2}$$
$$(10.94)\ (.0023) \qquad (.15) \qquad (.11)$$
$$R^2 = .984 \qquad S_e = 18.04$$

The statistical results of both equations are good and the magnitude of the coefficients is consistent with the theory.

The response for the first-order difference equation is shown below:

Lag	1	2	3	4
Coefficient	1	.61	.37	.22
Percentage of total effect	39	23	15	9
Cumulative percentage of total effect	39	62	77	86

The second-order lag model yields the following response:

Lag	0	1	2	3	4
Coefficient	1	1.22	.97	.54	.17
Percentage of total effect	30	37	29	16	5
Cumulative percentage of total effect[32]	30	67	96	112	117

The steady-state solution is

$$L = 139.0 + .026 U$$

and suggests that 26 production workers will be hired or fired with a long-term increase or decrease of \$1 million in the order backlogs of the aircraft industry.

---

[32] The percentages in excess of 100 are due to the fact that the transient response is oscillatory and does not quite taper out before going into the negative range.

These results also suggest that the number of production workers affected by a change in order backlogs will be greater than the number of nonproduction workers, and that production workers will be affected by the change much earlier than nonproduction workers. About 50 percent of the total change of production workers occurs within less than 6 months, while more than 20 months may pass before a similar percentage of nonproduction workers is affected.

COMPANY VERSUS INDUSTRY ANALYSIS. Prior to the availability of data for the entire industry, this inquiry utilized data of the Boeing Airplane Company.[33] The results of the analysis based on company data differ enough from those based on industry data to merit some consideration.

When the single-period model is applied to Boeing data, the results for the period 1950–60 are as follows:

$$L_t = 5.77 + .0033U_{t-1} + .835L_{t-1}$$
$$(2.08) \quad (.0012) \qquad (.045)$$
$$R^2 = .964 \qquad S_e = 3.599$$

The response pattern indicated by these estimates is given below:

Lag	0	1	2	3	4	5	6
Coefficient	1	.835	.693	.582	.486	.406	.339
Percentage of total effect	16	14	12	10	8	7	6
Cumulative percentage of total effect	16	30	42	52	60	67	73

An estimation of the model containing a second-order lag results in the following estimates:

$$L_t = 4.8979 + .0028U_{t-1} + 1.1173L_{t-1} - .2596L_{t-2}$$
$$(2.02) \qquad (.0012) \qquad (.1301) \qquad (.1131)$$
$$R^2 = .968$$

The response pattern is as follows:

Lag	0	1	2	3	4	5	6	7
Coefficient	1.00	1.12	.99	.85	.69	.56	.45	.36
Percentage of total effect	13	15	13	11	9	7	6	4
Cumulative percentage of total effect	13	28	41	52	61	68	74	78

[33] The data were made available by Dr. Murray L. Weidenbaum, then Corporate Economist, Boeing Airplane Company, and now Professor of Economics, Washington University, St. Louis.

The steady-state solution for these equations is

$$L = 5.77 + .0033U + .835L$$
$$L = 34.7 + .02U.$$

The long range elasticity is .59.

When these results are compared with those derived from industry data, it appears that the Boeing Company was slower than the industry as a whole in adjusting its work force to changes in backlogs of orders.[34] While more than 4 quarters elapsed before 50 percent of the total adjustment at Boeing took place, only 2 quarters were required for the corresponding adjustment for the industry. An examination of the raw data suggests that, while Boeing was slower than the industry in its response throughout the whole decade of the 1950's, the major difference was in the speed of the buildup of employment following the outbreak of the Korean war. A possible explanation of these results is that the Boeing management is more conservative in the sense that its aversion to risk is greater than that of the industry as a whole, or that difficulties in recruiting personnel may have been greater for Boeing than for the industry because of its geographic location; therefore the company responded more slowly.[35]

Earlier in this study, the view is expressed that the aggregation error in this investigation is believed to be smaller than the specification error. In hope of supporting this belief with evidence, an additional experiment is conducted. The theory postulates that the cost of changing the level of the work force in the firm increases with the square of the change and is independent of any other variable. This assumption, which is of doubtful truth on the macro level, appears wrong when applied to the firm. Surely, the cost of changing the level of the work force would be expected to be a function of the scarcity of labor in this industry, if not of general business conditions. As a possible indicator of the scarcity of labor in the industry, the difference is taken between desired aggregate employment, which is a function of aggregate unfilled orders, and actual aggre-

---

[34] Boeing data are, of course, a subset of the industry data. Mean employment for Boeing for the period was about 11 percent of industry employment, and mean Boeing backlogs were about 16 percent of industry backlogs.

[35] In terms of our cost function, this statement would mean that Boeing attached a larger cost to C_2, the cost parameter which is proportional to the change in the size of the work force, than did the industry as a whole.

gate employment. When these variables are incorporated in the model, the results of the estimation are as follows:[36]

$$L_t - L_{t-1} = 10.556 + .0075U_{t-1} - .140L_{t-1}$$
$$\quad\quad (2.925) \quad (.0020) \quad\quad (.056)$$
$$\quad\quad + .0004U^a_{t-1} - .0323L^a_{t-1}$$
$$\quad\quad (.0005) \quad\quad (.0165)$$
$$R^2 = .36 \quad S_e = 3.423 \quad \bar{L} = 69.17$$

The insignificance of the coefficient of the variable for aggregate unfilled orders may be due to a specification error. The model specifies that the macro variable be related in a nonlinear way to the micro variable, but in the estimation a linear relationship is used. While the lag structure of the firm is practically unchanged from the previous estimate, the coefficient of the Boeing variable for unfilled orders more than doubles with the introduction of the macro variable. Consequently, the long-range elasticity of employment with respect to unfilled orders increases from .59 to 1.58. The long-range elasticities of employment with respect to orders in the industry, which are reported in this study, have values ranging from .58 to .68. A possible conclusion is that the industry incurs increasing returns to labor while Boeing incurs decreasing returns. This conclusion, which is based on a limited investigation, raises some interesting questions about aggregation; these questions, however, will be left as subjects for future studies.

Estimation of Determinants of Shipments

As stated earlier in this study, there are two reasons for examining the factors that determine the rate of shipments:[37] first, to estimate the lag between the receipt of an order and the receipt of payments which corresponds to the lag between obligations and expenditures in the public sector; second, to close the model so that simulation experiments may be conducted.

[36] U^a and L^a indicate aggregate industry variables less Boeing variables.

[37] The assumption is made that sales data reflect shipments. Advance and progress payments as a percentage of total sales to the government by 16 leading aerospace companies were 28 percent in 1947–51; 25.8 percent in 1952–56; and 14.9 percent in 1957–61. Source: Stanford Research Institute, *The Industry-Government Aerospace Relationship*, Vol. 2 (1963), p. 187.

A number of versions of the assumed relationship between changes in sales and the factors of production in the industry are tested with available data. The Securities and Exchange Commission has been collecting quarterly data on net plant and equipment since 1956.[38] Furthermore, some annual data of 12 leading airframe producers are also available.[39] Thus, it appeared feasible at first glance to construct a time-series for plant and equipment. However, further study revealed that the aircraft industry leased a large portion of its plant and equipment from the government throughout most of the decade; therefore, all the available "plant and equipment" data tend to underestimate this input into production.[40] Because of this difficulty, it was decided to use a time-trend variable as a substitute for the capital-stock variable in the regression equation. The second difficulty pertains to the deflation of the sales variable which is measured in current dollars. In the absence of a price deflator for the industry and on the basis of the conclusions reached earlier in this study to the effect that the evidence does not contradict the assumption of price stability, it was decided to maintain this assumption in this portion of the investigation.

Two versions of the sales function were estimated, a linear and a logarithmic version; first-order and second-order lags were assumed for both versions. The results for the linear model are[41]

$$\Delta S_t = -249.51 + 1.51L_{t-1} - .72S_{t-1} + 25.15T$$
$$(85.33) \quad (.28) \quad\quad (.12) \quad\quad\quad (5.44)$$
$$R^2 = .44 \quad\quad DW = 2.21$$
$$\Delta S_t = -196.19 + 1.34L_{t-1} - .91S_{t-1} + .33S_{t-2} + 17.68T$$
$$(81.90) \quad (.26) \quad\quad (.13) \quad\quad (.12) \quad\quad\quad (5.75)$$
$$R^2 = .53 \quad\quad DW = 1.49$$

---

[38] Federal Trade Commission-Securities and Exchange Commission, *Quarterly Financial Report for U. S. Manufacturing Corporations*, various years.

[39] Standard and Poor's Corporation, Industry Survey, *Aircraft*, Jan. 2, 1958, p. A18.

[40] Stanford Research Institute estimates that, in the 1957–61 period, gross property reported on balance sheets of 13 of 19 aerospace companies, representing approximately 85 percent of the sales of the industry, was slightly less than government-supplied property at cost. See *The Industry-Government Aerospace Relationship*, p. 119.

[41] The definitions of the variables are S = Sales, L = Employment, T = Trend, and $\Delta S_t = S_t - S_{t-1}$.

The results for the logarithmic model are

$$\ln S_t - \ln S_{t-1} = .0793 + .71 \ln L_{t-1} - .66 \ln S_{t-1} + .0099T$$
$$\quad\quad\quad\quad (.24)\quad (.13)\quad\quad (.12)\quad\quad\quad (.0027)$$
$$R^2 = .48 \quad DW = 2.18$$

$$\ln S_t - \ln S_{t-1} = .03 + .66 \ln L_{t-1} - .81 \ln S_{t-1}$$
$$\quad\quad\quad\quad (.23)\quad (.13)\quad\quad (.14)$$
$$+ .0081T + .20 \ln S_{t-2}$$
$$\quad (.0028)\quad (.12)$$
$$R^2 = .51 \quad DW = 1.65$$

The statistical measurement does not provide an obvious choice between the logarithmic and the linear model. The first-order logarithmic model enables an easy determination of the long-range elasticity of shipments with respect to employment which is $.71/.66$ and is equal to 1.08, implying increasing returns to labor. The average response of shipments to employment can readily be computed from the first-order linear model. The computed average lag is about 1.4 quarters. The trend variable, which is a substitute for the capital-stock variable, has a positive coefficient. This result is consistent with our expectation which is based on the argument that, *ceteris paribus*, an increase in the capital stock should result in an increase in shipments. Experiments with the use of the square root of T instead of T resulted in estimates inferior to the ones cited above.

The results presented here could probably be improved significantly if data on capital stock were available. A more detailed separation of sales according to product mix, namely, missiles and aircraft, and details of employment according to occupational category would probably also have contributed to better estimates.

Simulation of Employment and Analysis of Simulation

This inquiry has been devoted so far to the specification and estimation of models describing the behavior of short-term employment and shipments in the aircraft industry. From these relationships, the model which was described in Figure 1 is now constructed, and employment in the aircraft industry for the period 1948–60 is simulated. The objective is to determine whether the various estimated relationships are capable, when combined into a model, of generating an employment time-series which approximates actual employment. Actual orders serve as the only input into the model, and actual values in 1948 serve as initial conditions for the endogenous variables, U, L, and S. The output of the simulation consists of the following time series: employment, unfilled orders, and sales. While, in the regression, actual values of these variables are used as the independent variables, in the simulation the endogenously determined values are used in computing the values of these variables for the next period.[42]

Figures 4 and 5 describe the input and output of two alternative models. Figure 4 describes the actual order time-series, which serves as the only input for the simulation. Figure 5 presents the actual employment time-series, the employment time-series generated by a linear model, and the employment time-series generated by a logarithmic model. It is judged that, given the simplicity of these models, the results are surprisingly good. As a further test for the goodness of fit of these models, an experiment suggested by Cohen and Cyert was conducted.[43] The actual employment data were regressed against the computer-generated data. The reason for estimating the regressions is that, if the computer-generated employment approximates actual employment, then the correlation coefficient should be high, the constant should be insignificant, and the value of the coefficient of the computer-generated variable should approach unity. The results are as follows:

Linear model:

$$L_t^{\text{actual}} = - 215.15 + 1.27 L_t^{\text{linear model}}$$
$$(52.43) \quad (.07)$$
$$R^2 = .87 \quad DW = .22$$

Logarithmic model:

$$L_t^{\text{actual}} = 23.91 + .92 L_t^{\text{logarithmic model}}$$
$$(25.00) \quad (.03)$$
$$R^2 = .94 \quad DW = .24$$

[42] For a full discussion of this approach, see Kalman J. Cohen, *Computer Models of the Shoe Leather, Hide Sequence* (Prentice-Hall, 1960), pp. 8–17.

[43] Kalman J. Cohen and Richard M. Cyert, "Computer Models in Dynamic Economics," *Quarterly Journal of Economics*, Vol. 75, No. 1 (February 1961), p. 120.

FIGURE 4. Aircraft Industry: Actual Orders, 1948–60

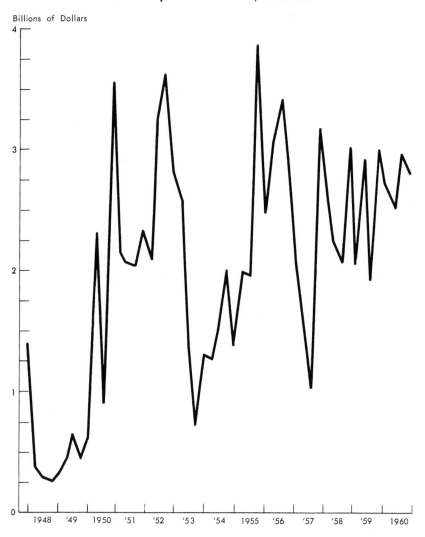

These regressions strongly suggest that the logarithmic model is superior in its explanatory power to the linear model. The high serial correlation of the residuals suggests that the deviation of the computer-generated employment series and the actual employment series is due not to random fluctuations but to some systematic errors in the model. These errors may be due to changes in productivity, leadtime, and the lack of good data on plant and equipment.

FIGURE 5. Aircraft Industry: Simulated and Actual Employment, 1948–60

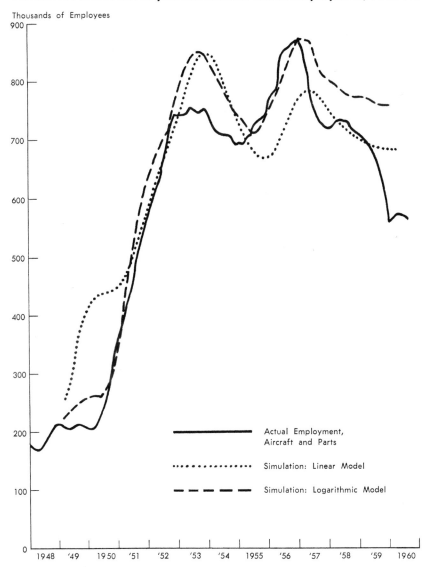

The results of the simulations are of interest for two reasons: First, it is reassuring that the equations describing the changes in employment and in sales generate an employment time-series for a period of about 50 quarters which approximates reasonably well the actual employment pattern. Second, while the estimated equation describing changes in employment could be used for making one-period predictions for the level of employment, it could not by itself predict employment for more than one period. The reason for its limited predictive power is, of course, that unfilled orders—one of the explanatory variables in the equation—are strongly affected by the size of the workforce. The closed model, consisting of the employment response and sales response equations, is, however, capable of making quarterly predictions for a fairly long horizon. Thus, it can serve as a useful tool for economists engaged in planning in government or industry who may wish to determine the time pattern of employment and sales in response to assumed streams of government obligations.

Response of Indirect Employment to Changes in Order Backlogs

The present section reports the results of some experiments designed to investigate the impact of government procurements from the aircraft industry on employment in industries supplying the aircraft industry. In measuring this impact, two primary lags have to be considered. The first is the one elapsing between the receipt of orders by the aircraft industry and the placement of orders for raw materials and subassemblies by the prime contractors with the supplying industries. The second lag is between the receipt of orders by the supplying industries and the response of employment in these industries to the orders. The interest here is in measuring the sum total of these lags; their separate values are of only secondary interest. Furthermore, practical considerations suggest that these lags be combined, since to the best of our knowledge no data are available on the various sources of orders received by an industry. Thus, essentially, the only choice is to measure the response of employment in the supplying industries to changes in the aircraft industry's backlogs of orders. In pursuing this study, numerous difficulties were encountered, and the results of the investigation are hardly conclusive.

Since the 1958 input-output model for the national economy was not available when this study was undertaken, the best guide for identifying industries supplying the aircraft industry was the input-output model for California.[44] In this model, the aircraft industry falls under the category of transportation; but since only 0.2 percent of the output of the industry goes to final private consumption, and since 61.7 percent goes to the government, it is assumed that aircraft manufacturers predominate in the transportation industry. The two major suppliers to the aircraft industry are the ordnance and instruments industry and the electrical machinery industry. Of total employment in the ordnance and instruments industry, only 16.7 percent is on transportation account; the corresponding number for the electrical machinery industry is as low as 4.8 percent.

Two other difficulties must be reported. While sufficient data are available on the electrical machinery industry as a whole, very little data are available on the subordinate sectors. As a matter of fact, most time-series on employment in subgroups of the electrical machinery industry are available only from 1958 on. A similar problem arises in relation to ordnance equipment. Furthermore, a problem with aircraft data must be reiterated. As pointed out earlier in this study, the size of the sample and the sampling procedure were changed in 1961 and, consequently, the data prior to and after 1961 are inconsistent. The differences between the two series is revealed in the respective values of backlogs for the fourth quarter of 1960, which were $12.5 billion and $15.3 billion. As a result, there was practically no choice but to adjust the new series, since this was the only way of getting, at least, a span of about 5 years and 20 observations for the analysis.[45]

The first experiment involves a measure of the response of employment in the ordnance industry to changes in order backlogs in the aircraft industry. The results were unsatisfactory because the sign of the coefficient of unfilled orders is negative and, therefore, inconsistent with the theory. A possible explanation is that, while some employment in the ordnance industry is dependent on orders from the aircraft industry, most of the employees work on projects which are substitutes for projects in the aircraft industry. Thus, there arises the situation of two industries primarily competing for

---

[44] Hansen and Tiebout, in *Review of Economics and Statistics.*

[45] The adjustment consisted of the construction of a time-series from the components of the aerospace data.

the defense dollar and complementing each other only to a very limited extent.[46]

The next experiment involves the use of data on a subsection of the ordnance industry which supplies the sighting and fire control equipment for the aircraft industry (SIC 194). The results of this experiment are unsatisfactory too, insofar as the coefficient of unfilled orders in the aircraft industry is highly insignificant. The final experiment with employment in the ordnance industry involves the measurement of the response of employment in the fire control industry to backlogs of aircraft and parts only, that is, exclusive of missiles. The results are as follows:

$$L_t = -.251 + .0009U_{t-1} + .821L_{t-1}$$
$$(1.97) \quad (.0004) \quad (.11)$$
$$R = .989 \quad S_e = 1.055 \quad \bar{L} = 36.6$$

The response pattern implied by this equation is significantly slower than the corresponding pattern in the aircraft industry. It is not known whether this is due to the lag which exists between the receipt of an order by the aircraft industry and the placement of an order with the fire control industry, or whether it is due simply to a slower response by the fire control industry. Attempts to secure information about backlogs in the sighting and fire control industry were unsuccessful; if such information were available, it could clarify the picture.

The results of experiments with the response of employment in electrical machinery and subgroups of this industry to changes in backlogs of orders in the aircraft industry and its subgroups were inconclusive. The experiments included such subgroups as SIC 3662 which combines radio and television communications equipment and includes, according to a Department of Labor publication, the military space and commercial products categories.[47] The failure to obtain significant results is attributed, in large measure, to the high level of aggregation of the employment data. The results of

---

[46] This interpretation is also implied by Hitch who stated that the large increase in ordnance reflected both the increase in the so-called conventional weapons as well as the ordnance industry's expanding missile work. See Charles J. Hitch, "January 1961, Economic Report of the President and the Economic Situation and Outlook," Hearings before the Joint Economic Committee, 87 Cong. 1 sess. (1961).

[47] U. S. Department of Labor, *Employment Outlook and Changing Occupational Structure in Electronic Manufacturing*, Bulletin 1363, p.48.

these experiments are disappointing, and it is doubtful that significant results can be obtained by using the data presently available.

Conclusions

The investigation of the impact on employment of government procurements from the aircraft industry indicates that the major change in employment occurs after the obligation phase and prior to the expenditure phase in the government procurement cycle. Thus, any fiscal policy designed to compensate for changes in procurements from the aircraft industry should take account of the time pattern of obligations rather than that of expenditures. The estimated average lag between the receipt of an order and the increase in employment is 9 months, with more than 50 percent of the change occurring within 6 months. The total net change in employment resulting from an increase of $1 million in government obligations is about 35–40 workers. The number of workers hired or fired in any period will, however, depend on whether the backlogs of orders are large or small relative to the size of the work force. Production workers appear to be affected much faster and in larger numbers than nonproduction workers by a change in backlogs.

Other results indicate that shipments respond to changes in the size of the work force with an average lag of $4\frac{1}{2}$ months. The estimated average lag between obligations and expenditures is about 13 months and the estimated total lag is about 20 months.[48] This estimate is in close agreement with that of Ando and Brown.[49]

The inquiry into the impact of government procurements from the aircraft industry on employment in industries supplying that industry yields only fragmentary evidence because of the high level of aggregation of the employment data.

The simulation experiments demonstrate that the estimated equations are capable, when combined into a model, of generating a pattern of employment which approximates the actual employment pattern in the period studied. Thus, the model may serve economists who are engaged in planning in government and in industry as a tool for examining the implications of alternative streams of government obligations for employment in the industry.

---

[48] Total lag is defined in terms of the time elapsing between the receipt of an order and the receipt of 95 percent of the payment.

[49] *Stabilization Policies*, p. 145.

Second-Order Lag and Multiperiod Horizon Models

THE DERIVATION of second-order lag and multiperiod horizon models are presented in this Appendix.

Second-Order Lag Model

Assume that the firm incurs all the costs specified in the original equation (1.0), namely, wages, the cost of operating at over and under capacity, and the cost of changing the level of the labor force. However, in addition to these costs the firm incurs a cost which is related to changes in the rate of accessions and separations.

$$(3.1) \quad C_3[(L_t - L_{t-1}) - (L_{t-1} - L_{t-2})]^2 = C_3(L_t - 2L_{t-1} + L_{t-2})^2.$$

This cost is incorporated in the model, and the following cost function is derived:

$$(3.2) \qquad C_t = W_t L_t + C_1\left(\frac{U_{t-1}}{bg} - L_t\right)^2 + C_2(L_t - L_{t-1})^2$$
$$+ C_3(L_t - 2L_{t-1} + L_{t-2})^2.$$

Upon differentiation with respect to L_t, setting $\partial C_T/\partial L_t$ equal to zero, and solving for L_t for a minimum cost employment level, an expression is derived for L_t:

$$(3.3) \quad L_t = \frac{C_1}{(C_1 + C_2 + C_3)bg} U_{t-1} + \frac{C_2 + 2C_3}{(C_1 + C_2 + C_3)} L_{t-1}$$

$$- \frac{C_3}{(C_1 + C_2 + C_3)} L_{t-2} - \frac{1}{2(C_1 + C_2 + C_3)} W_t$$

and

$$(3.4) \quad \Delta L_t = \frac{C_1}{(C_1 + C_2 + C_3)bg} U_{t-1} + \left(\frac{C_2 + 2C_3}{C_1 + C_2 + C_3} - 1 \right) L_{t-1}$$

$$- \frac{C_3}{(C_1 + C_2 + C_3)} L_{t-2} - \frac{1}{2(C_1 + C_2 + C_3)} W_t.$$

For estimation purposes, this equation is rewritten as follows:

$$(3.5) \quad \Delta L_t = a_0 + a_1 U_{t-1} + a_2 L_{t-1} + a_3 L_{t-2} + a_4 W_t + e_t.$$

The theory imposes some restrictions on the range of values that the coefficients may adopt. Since the institutional, technological, and cost parameters used are all nonnegative, it can readily be seen that a_1 must be positive and a_3 must be negative. In addition, since $-1 \leq a_2 + a_3 \leq 0$ and $-1 \leq a_3 \leq 0$, it follows that $-1 \leq a_2 \leq 1$.

The coefficient a_3 attains its maximum value of zero when the cost of changes in the rate of accession and separation is zero. In this case, the second-order difference equation collapses into a first-order difference equation.

Multiperiod Horizon Model

Assume that the firm has the cost function specified in equation (1.0). In addition, suppose that the firm has as its objective the minimization of total costs over the anticipated horizon, and that it discounts future costs by the rate of interest, i. The cost function of the firm is

$$C_T = \sum_{t=0}^{n} \left\{ \left(\frac{1}{1+i} \right)^t \left[C_1 \left(L_t - \frac{U_{t-1}}{gb} \right)^2 + C_2 (L_t - L_{t-1})^2 + W_t L_t \right] \right\}.$$

However, the firm is constrained in its cost minimization by the following structural identity:

$$U_t = U_{t-1} + O_t - S_t$$

where O_t represents incoming orders and S_t represents shipments. Earlier in this inquiry it was assumed that production is proportional to the work force. Now, the additional assumption is made that shipments equal production. Thus, $S_t = bL_t$ and the constraining equation is[50]

---

[50] This particular model assumes that there is no lag between changes in employment and changes in shipments.

$$U_t = U_{t-1} + O_t - bL_t.$$

Next, the constraint is incorporated in the model by means of the Lagrangean multiplier, λ_t. Also, by letting $r = 1/1 + i$, an expression for total cost is derived:

$$(4.0) \qquad C_T = \sum_{t=0}^{n} r^t \left[W_t L_t + C_1 \left(\frac{U_t}{gb} - L_t \right)^2 + C_2 (L_t - L_{t-1})^2 \right.$$

$$\left. + \lambda_t (U_t - U_{t-1} - O_t + bL_t) \right].$$

The first-order conditions for minimum costs are that the partial derivatives of the endogenous variables and the Lagrangean multipliers are equated to zero:[51]

$$\frac{\partial C_T}{\partial L_T} \cdot \frac{\partial C_T}{\partial U_t} \cdot \frac{\partial C_T}{\partial \lambda_t} = 0 \qquad t = 1, 2, \ldots n.$$

C_T is a positive quadratic function and, therefore, second-order conditions for a minimum are satisfied.

Next, let $n \to \infty$ and apply the generating function transform

$$X(z) \equiv \sum_{t=0}^{\infty} X_t z^t \quad \text{where} \quad |z| < 1$$

to the three sets of equations. The resulting three equations have five unknowns: $U(z)$, $L(z)$, $\lambda(z)$, λ_0, and L_0. Two equations and two unknowns, $U(z)$ and $\lambda(z)$, are eliminated. The remaining equation contains three unknowns: $L(z)$, L_0, and λ_0. The coefficient of $L(z)$ is a second-order polynomial and, thus, the variable is eliminated by equating its coefficient to zero through an appropriate choice of values for z. The values for z are found by solving the polynomial for its two roots. A demonstration that the roots meet the condition that their absolute value is less than unity can be provided. The two roots are now substituted in the remaining equation, yielding two equations and two unknowns, λ_0 and L_0. These equations when solved for L_0 result in the following expression:

[51] For descriptions of rigorous derivations of linear decision rules, see any of the following: Holt and others, *Planning Production, Inventories, and Work Force;* Gerald L. Childs, "Linear Decision Rules for Explaining Finished Goods Inventories and Unfilled Orders" (unpublished Ph.D. thesis, Massachusetts Institute of Technology, September 1963); Charles C. Holt and Franco Modigliani, in *Inventory Fluctuations and Economic Stabilization*, Part II (Joint Economic Committee, 87 Cong. 1 sess., 1961), pp. 51–53; and Charles C. Holt, "Linear Decision Rules for Economic Stabilization and Growth" (Carnegie Institute of Technology, August 1960, mimeo.), pp. 57–65.

$$L_0 = \frac{z_1 z_2}{r^2} L_{-1} + \left\{ \frac{C_1 z_1 z_2 [(1 - z_2)g(r - z_1) - (1 - z_1)g(r - z_2) - z_2]}{C_2 r^2 g^2 b(1 - z_1)(1 - z_2)(z_2 - z_1)} \right\} U_{-1}$$

$$+ \left\{ \frac{C_1 z_1 z_2 [g(r - z_1) - z_1]}{C_2 r^2 g^2 b(1 - z_1)(z_2 - z_1)} \right\} O(z_1) - \left\{ \frac{C_1 z_1 z_2 [g(r - z_2) - z_2]}{C_2 r^2 g^2 b(1 - z_2)(z_2 - z_1)} \right\} O(z_2)$$

$$- \left[\frac{z_1 z_2 (r - z_1)}{2 C_2 r^2 (z_2 - z_1)} \right] W(z_1) + \left[\frac{z_1 z_2 (r - z_2)}{2 C_2 r^2 (z_2 - z_1)} \right] W(z_2).$$

It should be remembered that

$$O(z_1) \equiv \sum_{t=0}^{\infty} O_t z_1^t.$$

Upon the completion of this and similar substitution in the equation, and upon the introduction of appropriate definitions for the coefficients, the following equation results:

$$L_0 = \frac{z_1 z_2}{r^2} L_{-1} + a_1(U_{-1} + O_0) + \sum_{t=1}^{\infty} (a_{21} z_1^t - a_{22} z_2^t) O_t$$

$$- \sum_{t=0}^{\infty} (a_{31} z_1^t - a_{32} z_2^t) W_t.$$

For estimation purposes, this equation is further approximated:

$$L_0 = \frac{z_1 z_2}{r^2} L_{-1} + a_1(U_{-1} + O_0) + a_2 \sum_{t=1}^{\infty} z^t O_t - a_3 \sum_{t=0}^{\infty} z^t W_t.$$

Since this expression is applicable to other periods, it can be written more generally:

$$(4.1) \qquad L_t = \frac{z_1 z_2}{r^2} L_{t-1} + a_1(U_{t-1} + O_t) + a_2 \sum_{i=1}^{\infty} z^i O_{t+1} - a_3 \sum_{i=0}^{\infty} z^i W_{t+1}.$$

Additional Experiment
To Estimate Employment Adjustment

THIS APPENDIX reports the results of an additional experiment which was conducted while the manuscript was undergoing its final revision. The ordinary least-squares procedure that has been used in this study leads to biased estimates if the model contains endogenous variables as explanatory variables, and if the residuals are correlated. Liviatan discusses this problem and argues that the bias can be eliminated by resorting to a two-stage least-squares estimating procedure.[52] Thus, an additional experiment was conducted in which the proposed procedure of Liviatan was used.[53] The results of the regressions are as follows:

First stage:

$$L_{t-1} = 190.1 + .0059U_{t-1} + .0126U_{t-2} + .0147U_{t-3}$$
$$(.0070) \qquad (.0012) \qquad (.0069)$$
$$- 106.7W_t + 56.61\sqrt{T}$$
$$(99.9) \qquad (27.76)$$
$$R^2 = .976$$

---

[52] N. Liviatan, "Consistent Estimation of Distributed Lags," *International Economic Review*, Vol. 4, No. 1 (January 1964).

[53] The model is identical to the one reported above (p. 149).

Second stage[54]

$$\Delta L_t = 199.7 + .0203U_{t-1} - .6117L_{t-1}^* - 130.08W_t + 46.41\sqrt{T}$$
$$(.0027) \qquad (.0819) \qquad (52.52) \quad (15.42)$$
$$DW = 1.87$$

The lag in the response of employment to changes in unfilled orders which is implied by the two-stage least-squares procedure is considerably shorter than the one implied by ordinary least squares. The two-stage least-squares estimate implies an average lag of about $4\frac{1}{2}$ quarters, with more than 60 percent of the total response occurring within 3 months. The ordinary least-squares estimate implies an average lag of about 9 months, with more than 50 percent of the total response occurring by the end of 6 months. This discrepancy in estimates is a matter of concern. While the large sample properties of the two-stage least-squares estimates are demonstrably superior to the ordinary least-squares estimates, we cannot help expressing skepticism that employment responds as rapidly as is indicated by the two-stage least-squares estimate. The little evidence that is available is provided by the estimates of Ando and Brown, which are in much closer agreement with the ordinary least-squares estimates than they are with the two-stage least-squares estimate.[55] Furthermore, a plot of actual employment predicted by the first stage suggests that predicted employment appears to lead actual employment over the later portion of the period; this could possibly account for the quicker response of the two-stage estimate. However, it must be admitted that the lead is not very obvious and, even if it were, this would not be a completely satisfactory resolution to the problem.

The issues raised by the sensitivity of the results to the estimating procedure are important; unfortunately, sufficient time was not available to allow them to be fully explored in this study.

[54] L_{t-1}^* is computed from the first stage.

[55] Ando and Brown estimated the response of the Federal Reserve index of industrial production, which is constructed from man-hours, to government obligations to the aircraft industry. They estimated that production increased by approximately 0.2 unit by the end of the second quarter in response to a unit increase in obligation. Thus, they estimated the lag to be considerably longer than the one derived in this study when ordinary least squares are used. The Ando and Brown estimate is not based on a distributed lag model, and their estimate is unbiased; see *Stabilization Policies*, p. 145.

Linear Approximation to Logarithmic Model of Employment Change

THIS APPENDIX presents the approximations made in transforming the logarithmic model into a linear model. This transformation is necessary if the response pattern implied by this model is to be investigated, using the techniques employed thus far.

Assume that the model is

$$\frac{L_t}{L_{t-1}} = \left(\frac{L_t^d}{L_{t-1}}\right)^{\alpha}.$$

L_t^d is the desired employment level and is a function of unfilled orders, wages, technology, and leadtime. The steady-state solution of the model is $L_s = L_s^d$.

Assume a unit increase in the desired employment level:

$$L_t^d = L_s^d + \Delta L_t^d$$
$$\Delta L_t^d = \varepsilon \quad \text{when} \quad t = 0$$
$$= 0 \quad \text{when} \quad t \neq 0.$$

Let $L_t = L_s + \Delta L_t$. The deviations of employment from the steady-state level at times t and $t - 1$, respectively, are ΔL_t and ΔL_{t-1}. Then,

$$\frac{L_s + \Delta L_t}{L_s + \Delta L_{t-1}} = \left(\frac{L_s^d + \Delta L_t^d}{L_s + \Delta L_{t-1}}\right)^{\alpha}.$$

The steps that follow are based on routine algebraic operations and approximations.

$$\frac{1 + \dfrac{\Delta L_t}{L_s}}{1 + \dfrac{\Delta L_{t-1}}{L_s}} = \left(\frac{1 + \dfrac{\Delta L_t^d}{L_s^d}}{1 + \dfrac{\Delta L_{t-1}}{L_s^d}} \right)^\alpha ;$$

$$\left(1 + \frac{\Delta L_t}{L_s}\right)\left(1 - \frac{\Delta L_{t-1}}{L_s}\right) = \left[\left(1 + \frac{\Delta L_t^d}{L_s^d}\right)\left(1 - \frac{\Delta L_{t-1}}{L_s^d}\right)\right]^\alpha ;$$

$$1 + \frac{1}{L_s}(\Delta L_t - \Delta L_{t-1}) = \left[1 + \frac{1}{L_s^d}(\Delta L_t^d - \Delta L_{t-1})\right]^\alpha$$

$$= 1 + \frac{\alpha}{L_s^d}(\Delta L_t^d - \Delta L_{t-1}).$$

Now, $L_s = L_s^d$. Therefore, $\Delta L_t - \Delta L_{t-1} = \alpha(\Delta L_t^d - \Delta L_{t-1})$ or $\Delta L_t = \alpha(\Delta L_t^d)$ + $(1 - \alpha)\Delta L_{t-1}$.

Using this approximation, the response of employment to a unit input into desired employment which is a function of unfilled orders is computed. The results are presented in the main text, where a logarithmic model of employment change is discussed.

STEPHEN A. RESNICK*

An Empirical Study of Economic Policy in the Common Market

THE RECENT HISTORY of econometric research is characterized by various attempts to use economic models to estimate the effect of changes in government policy.[1] These models have dealt primarily with a single country or region and have not attempted to deal with the flows between two or more systems. Clearly, the typical econometric application of fiscal policy to a model of one country will not be realistic if that country has close economic relations with one or more other countries. The multicountry case requires the development of a model that takes into account the various feedback relationships among them. The purpose of this study is to investigate empirically the effect of changes in economic policy within such a system, taking as the example the European Economic Community (EEC or Common Market). The trade linkages among the member countries are such that fiscal action by one or more will probably have measurable effects on all.

* Yale University.

[1] In particular, see L. R. Klein and A. S. Goldberger, *An Econometric Model of the United States* (Amsterdam: North-Holland Publishing Co., 1955); A. S. Goldberger, *Impact Multipliers and Dynamic Properties of the Klein-Goldberger Model* (Amsterdam: North-Holland Publishing Co., 1959); James S. Duesenberry, Otto Eckstein, and Gary Fromm, "A Simulation of the United States Economy in Recession," *Econometrica*, Vol. 28 (1960).

Multicountry Model

Purpose

The model used in this paper represents the economy of each member country of the Common Market by a set of aggregate demand functions, consisting of consumption and investment equations and a domestic price equation. To study the implications of the simultaneous feedbacks among the members, the model also includes a separate equation for imports from and exports to every other member country. In total, there are 50 structural equations to be estimated.

Both the external and internal trade equations of the respective Common Market countries are treated as determined endogenously within the context of the entire simultaneous system. Thus, given the estimated parameters in such a model, it is possible to predict the outcome of fiscal action by a respective member, both on the country whose government institutes the initial policy and on the other countries of the Common Market. To make such predictions, the model is solved in terms of policy parameters and other exogenous variables. From this solution, the long-run equilibrium multipliers of some of the endogenous variables with respect to policy parameters are computed.[2] For example, a 5 percent increase in government expenditure in Germany is expected to raise German income by 1.64 percent and incomes of France, Italy, Belgium, and the Netherlands by 1.53, 0.56, 0.49, and 0.24 percent,

---

[2] All variables in the model are transformed into index numbers based on 100 for 1953. Therefore, the coefficients in the estimated equations are elasticities for 1953 magnitudes, and, in the reduced form, equilibrium multipliers in elasticity form are computed. Actually, the procedure followed in deriving these elasticities is somewhat involved. From the Appendix (p. 201), it can be seen that the system is nonlinear. The method employed was to take the total differential of the equations and substitute the structural estimates of the coefficients for the relevant partial derivatives. After some simplification, a system of differential equations resulted which was then put into reduced form by the usual matrix inversion program. In evaluating the nonlinear structure at some set of points (the sample means over the period), it was assumed that the reduced form was valid for small changes about this set of points. In terms of this reduced form solution, it is possible numerically to compute the percentage change of any endogenous variable, say gross national product of any member country, in response to a percentage change of any policy parameter of one or more member countries. For further discussion see Stephen Resnick, "An Econometric Study of the Common Market" (unpublished Ph.D. thesis, Massachusetts Institute of Technology, 1964), pp. 176–81 (hereinafter cited as "An Econometric Study").

respectively. The change in German income in this example reflects not only the usual direct impact of a change in government expenditure but also all the indirect effects through the trade linkages among all five countries.

Qualifications

The estimates in this paper are subject to a variety of qualifications which must be reviewed before the estimates can be presented and analyzed.[3]

Because the system is one in which several subsystems are linked tightly together, the whole system inevitably becomes quite large even when each subsystem is fairly small. Conversely, in order to keep the size of the whole system small enough, the level of sophistication which could be built into the subsystems to reflect the peculiarities of each country is severely limited. This is particularly true because the number of observations usable for the study is small.

It is commonly accepted that until 1951 the productive facilities in Western Europe had not recovered from the effects of World War II sufficiently to satisfy the basic needs of the population. As a consequence, the levels of economic activity in Western Europe prior to 1952 were determined largely by production and supply conditions rather than by demand conditions. Beginning in 1952, however, recovery was practically completed so that year-to-year fluctuations in economic activity may be represented by a Keynesian type model.[4] Since the subsystems representing each country in our framework are essentially of the Keynesian type, the inclusion of observations from the 1948–51 period to estimate the parameters might introduce some bias in the results. Nevertheless, since the parameter estimates of this model are consistent with *a priori*

---

[3] For a detailed discussion of the theoretical foundations of the model and the empirical relevancy of the estimates, see "An Econometric Study."

[4] The hypothesis that by 1952 recovery had been achieved and supply was no longer an important constraint can be supported, first, by the statistical record which indicates that by 1952 prewar levels of production, consumption, trade, etc. had been surpassed; second, by evidence which indicates that the stock of industrial capital was up to prewar levels; and finally, by signs that inflationary problems had assumed a more "normal" posture. See "An Econometric Study," Chapter 1.

expectations, the model can be expected to hold as a partial description of economic behavior over the period 1948–61.[5]

In addition, there were a number of structural changes in the trade and other institutional arrangements during the period of estimation. These should be taken into account if the model is to be realistic enough to be considered for detailed policy use. However, if this had been done, the number of parameters to be estimated would have been increased, a luxury that could not be afforded because of the small number of observations at our disposal.[6]

Thus, the estimates reported here must be considered tentative, and the purpose of the study should be thought of primarily as providing an analytical framework for the behavior of an interrelated system with several independent fiscal authorities. In spite of this, the estimates appear to conform to the economic history of the respective Common Market Countries. Also, the model gives some interesting insights into the behavior of a rather complex system, and may be useful as a guide for further study when more data are available.

---

[5] A discussion of the possible introduction of different types of statistical bias in the individual equations will be found in "An Econometric Study," Chapter 2. Comments are made there concerning the effects that shifts in supply conditions (and other institutional changes) may have had on both the internal and external equations of the system. For example, observations are made on the potential effects of, say, price rationing and production constraints on the consumption and investment equations of the respective member countries, and implications are drawn concerning the possible coefficient bias of these (and other) individual equations. (Tables 9, 10, and 13 in the Appendix to this paper show that the income elasticity of the consumption equation and the reaction coefficient of the investment equation are both much smaller at the beginning [1948] than at the end [1961] of the period, thus reflecting the influence of various constraints on expenditures.) In Chapter 4 of "An Econometric Study," the empirical validity of the estimates in terms of the time-series experience of the EEC countries is analyzed (e.g., capital-output ratios, marginal propensity to consume, growth rates, etc.) and it is concluded that the estimates do provide a fair degree of structural information on the postwar history of the respective countries.

[6] The internal recovery of the member countries was accomplished concomitantly with the progressive establishment of a de facto regional trade area. The effects that certain institutions (e.g., Organization for European Economic Cooperation, European Payments Union, General Agreement on Tariffs and Trade, etc.) may have had on the general system, as well as on the specification of the external trade equations, cannot be minimized. For example, quota and tariff reductions as well as shifts in export supply equations should have been incorporated within the system. The neglect of these institutional changes qualify the estimates of the model, especially in the external trade equations.

Operation

Suppose government expenditure in France increases by a given percentage. This change is assumed to be exogenous to the model or, more explicitly, not dependent on the government expenditure of any other EEC country. There will now be a multiplier impact on France's national income whose size depends on the coefficients of the structural equations describing the economy. In this study, however, the government expenditure multiplier is the generalized foreign trade multiplier that makes allowance for the French impact on the incomes of the other EEC countries. Furthermore, the multiplier allows for the foreign trade leakages indicated by increased French imports generating income in the other member countries, and takes into account the feedback relationship on French exports. This circular flow of spending induced by an autonomous increase in a policy instrument is at the core of this study.

The exact impact on national income of any EEC country which is due to a policy change depends on the structural equations describing the behavior of the internal and external demand equations. A Keynesian type of aggregate demand behavior is assumed for each member country, characterized by a consumption and investment function, a price equation, and demand equations for imports disaggregated by trading country. For example, the structural model of the French economy depicts consumption as a function of disposable income, a current endogenous variable. After substitution and simplification (see the Appendix), consumption is determined by gross national product (GNP), an endogenous variable, and two predetermined variables, lagged consumption and total taxes less tranfers. The second important demand variable, investment, is assumed to depend upon the difference between the desired and actual capital stock—the simple accelerator hypothesis. Once again, after simplification (see Appendix), the final equation shows that investment behavior depends on two predetermined variables, lagged GNP and the lagged actual capital stock. The price equation assumes that prices can be determined by two exogenous variables, wages lagged one period and indirect business taxes.

The external trade equations which are crucial to the linkage arguments of the generalized foreign trade multiplier are broken down by country so that for each member country a separate equation exists for imports from each of its trading partners. Thus, for France, there are 5 import equations depicting the imports of France from Belgium, Germany, Italy, the Netherlands, and the rest of the world taken as one trading block. For the system as a whole, there must be 20 such import equations (for each of the five Common Market countries there are 4 trade equations) and 5 rest-of-the-world import equations, giving a total of 25 trade equations. Each of these trade equations assumes that imports are determined by two endogenous variables, the GNP of the home country and the export price of the exporting country deflated by the domestic price of the importing country. Thus, for example, imports of France from, say Germany, depend on the GNP of France and the export price of Germany deflated by the domestic price of French goods.

Each endogenous variable is dependent on all the predetermined variables in the entire system. What is involved, of course, is the distinction between a structural system and the derived reduced form. The model for France has been specified in terms of a set of structural equations. Since a similar model is assumed to hold for the other four countries, a set of structural equations is obtained describing economic behavior in the Common Market. For policy purposes, however, the reduced form is the relevant version of the model. To discover the explicit workings of the model, each of the endogenous variables must be solved in terms of the predetermined variables. Because of the foreign trade linkages, this means that a given endogenous variable, say national income of France, is dependent on the predetermined variables for France as well as on all the other exogenous variables for the remaining four countries. In the present study, the reduced form coefficients associated with the set of structural equations describing the Common Market serve to indicate the quantitative direct and indirect magnitude of a change in any predetermined variable on any endogenous variable. Thus, the assumed change in government spending of France will affect all the endogenous variables of the system. In this way, it is possible to trace how a change in fiscal policy in one country can affect the economy of any other country. Specifically, there will be an impact not only on France but on the national incomes of the four other countries as well. This influence, in turn, can be traced back to the set of trade equations postulated for each Common Market member. In fact, the stronger the estimated trade linkages among the countries, the greater the impact on any given country's national income. Of course, the trade linkages will vary from country to country so that the final effect need not be the same across the Common Market. But the important element to note in this analysis is how policy changes can be transmitted throughout the Common Market via changing import and export demands.

The circular flow of spending, or the generalized foreign trade multiplier, can best be determined from this reduced form. The reduced form is also used to predict new levels of income from a given change in a policy instrument. Confidence in the results of the policy, however, depends crucially on the specification of the model, especially the trade equations describing Common Market export and import behavior. Given the somewhat simple Keynesian model used, the results of this study must be regarded as tentative if not crude.

The various uses to which such a model can be put are discussed in the following sections. Details of the model itself are given in the Appendix.

Application of the Model
to Economic Policy

The quantitative implications of changes in government expenditures and taxes on the equilibrium level of income of the five EEC countries will be discussed in this section. The results support the proposition that the member countries' trade linkages are strong enough so that a change in policy by one country becomes a matter of concern to the remaining Common Market countries.

General Policy Effects

While there are many combinations and permutations of policy changes that can be tried in the model, rather modest policy changes were considered. Although there are 55 endogenous variables in the system, the policy targets were narrowed to the GNP's of the

TABLE 1. EEC Countries: Effect on Gross National Product of 5 Percent Increase in Government Expenditure in One Country

(In percent)

Country	Countries Increasing Government Expenditure				
	Belgium (1)	France (2)	Germany (3)	Italy (4)	Netherlands (5)
Belgium	0.81	0.34	0.49	0.28	0.30
France	0.31	2.57	1.53	1.07	0.67
Germany	0.14	0.88	1.64	0.47	0.30
Italy	0.21	0.69	0.56	1.81	0.86
Netherlands	0.16	0.20	0.24	0.22	0.92

five countries. For the first example, a 5 percent change in government spending (G) by any one country of the EEC is assumed while the policy variables of the remaining nations are kept unchanged. The results are presented in Table 1.

Reading down column (1) in the table shows that a 5 percent increase in Belgium's government expenditure causes a change of 0.81 percent in GNP in Belgium, 0.31 percent in France, 0.14 percent in Germany, 0.21 percent in Italy, and 0.16 percent in the Netherlands. Column (2) indicates the results of a 5 percent increase in the government expenditure of France; and so forth for Germany, Italy, and the Netherlands in the remaining three columns.[7]

Two interesting relationships emerge from Table 1: the first deals with the economies of all five countries and the second deals with the economies of France, Germany, and Italy. First, the results for all five countries show that, although the impact on individual countries differs substantially, the overall effect of a change in any one country's government expenditure (with the possible exception of Belgium) has effects on the economies of the other four that cannot be disregarded.

The second interesting point concerns the interrelationship among France, Germany, and Italy. A given 5 percent change in

---

[7] The actual equilibrium multipliers associated with these elasticities, calculated from the reduced form, are as follows: Belgium, 1.29; France, 3.26; Germany, 2.27; Italy, 2.90; and the Netherlands, 1.36. These are the long-run generalized foreign trade multipliers associated with a change in government expenditure, *ceteris paribus*.

government expenditure by any one of the three will have rather large effects on the GNP of the other two. For example, a change of 5 percent in expenditure of Germany will lead to a change of 1.53 percent in GNP for France and of 0.56 percent for Italy. A similar percentage change in the expenditure of France will lead to changes of 0.88 percent and 0.69 percent in GNP for Germany and Italy, respectively. And a 5 percent change in the expenditure of Italy will cause a change of 1.07 percent in France's GNP and of 0.47 percent in Germany's. Thus, it seems that these three economies are closely related.[8]

Finally, of all the countries in the Common Market, France is the most susceptible to a change in the government expenditure of the other four and Germany is the most influential in its effects on the others.

A brief intuitive explanation of the results of Table 1 with respect to the underlying model can be given. The income effects represent the stimulating influence on each country's imports and exports of the originating country's increase in government expenditure. The final outcome depends entirely upon the structural coefficients estimated for both the internal and external set of demand equations. Furthermore, it is known that the implicit foreign trade multiplier must be somewhere between the limits of the foreign trade multiplier with no feedbacks and the national multiplier with no trade effects; in fact, it must be smaller than the latter multiplier but larger than the former. France, for example, has the largest generalized foreign trade multiplier according to Table 1 (see also footnote 7). This means that a rise in government expenditure of France not only may have a relatively large effect on that country's GNP, but the induced expansion of her imports may also cause a relatively large secondary increase in French exports. In fact, the trade leakage to France indicated by reading across the row for France in Table 1 is, in every case but one, larger than that for any other country. In short, the effect of an expansion of government expenditure by France is to spread the stimulus throughout the Common Market, thereby giving rise to a feedback on France or a secondary rise in French exports of a fairly significant amount.

[8] The relationship between Belgium and the Netherlands, shown in Table 1, is not so close as might have been expected.

TABLE 2. EEC Countries: Effect on Gross National Product of 5 Percent Tax Reduction in One Country

(In percent)

Country	Countries Reducing Taxes				
	Belgium (1)	France (2)	Germany (3)	Italy (4)	Netherlands (5)
Belgium	0.67	0.32	0.61	0.32	0.38
France	0.25	2.44	1.92	1.21	0.86
Germany	0.11	0.84	2.05	0.53	0.39
Italy	0.18	0.66	0.70	2.04	1.10
Netherlands	0.13	0.19	0.30	0.25	1.18

Table 2 gives the long-run impact on GNP of a change in the tax variable, $T^*_{x_t}$.[9] The organization of Table 2 is similar to that of Table 1. It may be useful at this point to repeat that the policy results are in terms of elasticities. When the effects on income, shown in Tables 1 and 2, for Germany, Italy, and the Netherlands are compared, the implication is that the effect on GNP of a 5 percent change in $T^*_{x_t}$ is greater than the effect of a 5 percent change in government expenditure. This, however, does not mean that the associated tax multiplier in nonelasticity form is greater than the similar government expenditure multiplier. In fact, as shown in footnotes 7 and 9, the multiplier for expenditure is larger than the tax multiplier.

The elasticities in Table 2 indicate that a tax/transfer change in any one nation will have repercussions on the economies of the other four. There is also an interesting relationship among the economies of France, Germany, and Italy. For example, a 5 percent decrease in taxes by France leads to an increase of 2.44 percent in GNP for France, 0.84 percent for Germany, and 0.66 percent for Italy. Correspondingly, a 5 percent decrease for Germany leads to GNP increases of 2.05 percent for Germany, 1.92 percent for

[9] The tax variable used in the model is defined to be $T^*_x = T^D_{x_t} + T^I_{x_t} - T_{R_t}$ where $T^D_{x_t}$ includes total direct taxes, $T^I_{x_t}$ total indirect taxes, and T_{R_t} total transfers. Since a given percentage change in $T^*_{x_t}$, rather than in its individual components, is postulated, the individual effects from a tax and/or transfer change cannot be isolated. For example, a 5 percent decrease in $T^*_{x_t}$, as in Table 2, is really composed of a combination tax/transfer change, each of which should have its own multiplier.

As with the numerical expenditure multipliers shown in footnote 7, the following tax multipliers are associated with the elasticities in Table 2: Belgium, 0.81; France, 1.70; Germany, 1.15; Italy, 2.21; Netherlands, 0.65.

TABLE 3. EEC Countries: Effect on Gross National Product of Simultaneous Changes in Government Expenditure or Taxes in All Five Countries

(In percent)

Country	Increase in Government Expenditure			Reduction in Taxes		
	1 Percent (1)	5 Percent (2)	10 Percent (3)	1 Percent (4)	5 Percent (5)	10 Percent (6)
Belgium	0.43	2.21	4.44	0.45	2.29	4.61
France	1.19	6.15	12.39	1.31	6.66	13.42
Germany	0.67	3.43	6.92	0.77	3.91	7.88
Italy	0.80	4.14	8.33	0.93	4.65	9.38
Netherlands	0.34	1.74	3.51	0.41	2.05	4.11

France, and 0.70 percent for Italy. Finally, a similar 5 percent change in Italy causes a 1.21 percent increase in GNP for France and a 0.53 percent increase in that for Germany. As with the effects associated with a change in government expenditure in Table 1, the tax effects for France, Germany, and Italy indicate how closely these economies are interrelated.

The above examples assume a *ceteris paribus* change in taxes or government expenditure; however, it is probably more realistic to assume simultaneous changes among the member countries. Table 3 shows the effects of such changes; the results are in terms of 1 percent, 5 percent, and 10 percent changes in the two fiscal instruments.

The impact on the GNP of the five countries is now more striking than the previous findings. For example, the effect of a simultaneous 5 percent increase in government spending by all the member countries ranges from a high of 6.15 percent (in France) to a low of 1.74 percent (in the Netherlands). A simultaneous 10 percent increase will lead to effects ranging from 12.39 percent to 3.51 percent.[10] These effects are significant enough to warrant serious

[10] The results in Table 3 indicate that a 1 percent change in government spending by all five countries raises France's GNP by more than 1 percent. This, however, does not mean that the (calculated) French economy is unstable. As the five countries increase their government expenditure, the effect on the French economy is such that the expansion effect on her exports significantly dilutes her own foreign trade leakages to the other EEC members. Thus, the results of Table 3 confirm what was found in Table 1 where France was most susceptible to Common Market changes.

TABLE 4. EEC Countries: Effect on Gross National Product of Changes in the Rest of the World's Gross National Product

(In percent)

Country	Increase in Rest of World's Gross National Product		
	1 Percent (1)	5 Percent (2)	10 Percent (3)
Belgium	0.63	3.23	6.47
France	1.24	6.30	12.64
Germany	0.89	4.52	9.07
Italy	0.85	4.32	8.69
Netherlands	0.54	2.73	5.48

consideration of fiscal harmonization by the members of the Common Market.[11]

The model used in this paper can be considered to be nearly block recursive (see the Appendix). GNP in the United States and the United Kingdom were used as proxy variables for the rest of the world. Table 4, which presents the results of a change in these assumed exogenous variables on the Common Market countries, shows that the effects are quite large. For example, the effect on GNP of a 5 percent change in GNP of the rest of the world ranges from 6.30 percent (in France) to 2.73 percent (in the Netherlands).

The policy implications of the elasticities shown in Table 4 cannot be minimized. If the model is reasonable, the Common Market countries are quite sensitive to income changes in the United States and United Kingdom. In fact, the effect on GNP for any member country is similar in magnitude (compare Tables 3 and 4 for the same percentage change in income). Thus, the Common Market countries are closely related to the United States and the United Kingdom as well as to Common Market members. The importance of this relationship will be made clearer when the combined effect of a change in government expenditure in the EEC countries and a change in the rest of the world's GNP is discussed below.

---

[11] "In particular, one must examine whether, how, when, and to what extent the abolition of the 'custom frontiers' can be complemented by the abolition of the 'fiscal frontiers'." F. Neumark, *Tax Harmonization in the Common Market* (Commerce Clearing House, 1963).

TABLE 5. EEC Countries: Effect on Gross National Product of Simultaneous Increase in Government Expenditure in All Five Countries Accompanied by Changes in Other Variables

(In percent)

Country	5 Percent Tax Increase by All Five Countries (1)	5 Percent Reduction in Rest of World's Gross National Product (2)	5 Percent Tax Reduction by All Five Countries (3)
Belgium	−0.09	−1.02	4.52
France	−0.54	−0.16	12.89
Germany	−0.49	−1.09	7.39
Italy	−0.52	−0.22	8.84
Netherlands	−0.30	−0.99	3.80

Table 5 presents the effects of several policy combinations. For example, column (1) indicates that a simultaneous 5 percent increase in government spending by all five countries coupled with a 5 percent increase in taxes or decrease in transfers *reduces* GNP in all member countries. Once again, the reader is reminded that this result is to be interpreted in terms of elasticities and not numerical magnitudes. As indicated before, the implied numerical tax multiplier for any given country is smaller than the government expenditure multiplier. What column (1) implies is that the percentage change in government expenditure must be larger than that of taxes to obtain a greater equivalent percentage change in GNP.

Column (2) in Table 5 shows that a simultaneous 5 percent increase in government spending by all five member countries coupled with a 5 percent reduction in the GNP of the rest of the world will reduce GNP in the Common Market countries. Therefore, if the member nations knew that the rest of the world's GNP was going to decline, they would have to increase government expenditure (or decrease taxes) by a greater percentage than the decline in GNP in the rest of the world.

Column (3) indicates a combined increase in government expenditure and decrease in taxes for all five countries. In this experiment, the effects on GNP turn out to be sizable, the increases ranging from 12.89 percent (France) to 3.80 percent (the Netherlands).

In summary, the results presented in Tables 1–5 indicate that a policy change in one (or all) of the Common Market countries will, in general, have a significant impact on the other countries in the community. This is a consequence of the strong trade linkages among these countries. As a result of these linkages, the economic policy decisions of one member country are a matter of concern for all the other members.

Specific Policy Effects

The evidence on the effects of policy changes presented in Tables 1–5 is, of course, not all inclusive. For example, the final effects when one nation increases its government expenditure while the other four decrease theirs have not been investigated.

Table 6 shows the results of a 5 percent increase in government expenditure by one member country and a 5 percent decrease by the other four countries. The impression derived from this table is that any one country in the Common Market cannot pursue its own policies independent of the actions of the other members, since the policies of the other members may frustrate the objectives of a single member. If, for example, Belgium decides to raise its GNP by increasing government expenditure by 5 percent and, at the same time, the other four countries want to counter some slight inflationary pressures and reduce their respective government expenditures by 5 percent, the net effect would be a decline in

TABLE 6. EEC Countries: Effect on Gross National Product of 5 Percent Increase in Government Expenditure in One Country and 5 Percent Decrease in Other Four Countries

(*In percent*)

Country	Countries Increasing Government Expenditure				
	Belgium (1)	France (2)	Germany (3)	Italy (4)	Netherlands (5)
Belgium	−0.62	−1.55	−1.24	−1.66	−1.62
France	−5.62	−1.02	−3.13	−4.05	−4.88
Germany	−3.21	−1.69	−0.15	−2.52	−2.87
Italy	−3.77	−2.80	−3.06	−0.51	−2.46
Netherlands	−1.45	−1.36	−1.28	−1.32	−0.10

Belgium's GNP.[12] A similar situation, differing in degree only, is indicated for the other Common Market countries. Fiscal co-operation in a complex system like the Common Market may be a necessary condition for a member's attainment of various stabilization goals.

Comparison of Table 6 with Table 3 indicates the importance of France and Germany in the interrelated system. Column (2) of Table 3 shows the effects of a 5 percent simultaneous change in government expenditure by all nations. In Table 6, the entries on the principal diagonal are much smaller, reflecting each member country's own increase in government expenditure. This is to be expected. However, there is a significant difference in the results of the two tables for France and Germany. If France (or Germany) moves in a direction opposite to that of the other four countries, the percentage reduction in the GNP of the remaining four countries will be significantly less than it would be if all five countries moved together, as shown in Table 3. This is the result of the relative size of these two countries in the Common Market. If the situation in the above example is reversed—i.e., a 5 percent decrease in Germany's (or France's) government spending is combined with a 5 percent increase in government expenditure of the other four countries—the effects on the GNP of those countries desiring to increase their respective levels of income will be much smaller than otherwise. Because of the strong influence of both France and Germany, the other member countries should be aware of the intentions of France or Germany before they decide to pursue a particular economic policy.[13]

To emphasize the importance of France and Germany, assume that both countries decide simultaneously to increase their government expenditure by 5 percent while the other three countries decrease their government expenditure by 5 percent. The results of

---

[12] Since the Common Market countries are interrelated, it is not reasonable to expect that any one country can be completely out of phase with the rest. Therefore, the examples in the text will refer to "slight" inflationary or deflationary gaps for member countries because of the effective transmission of economic change throughout the system.

[13] Table 6 indicates that France is also sensitive to changes in the policies of the other Common Market countries. Along the principal diagonal, the largest impact in absolute value is on France. This result is to be expected from Table 1 and the discussion concerning the generalized foreign trade multiplier of France.

TABLE 7. EEC Countries: Effect on Gross National Product of 5 Percent Increase in Government Expenditure in France and Germany and 5 Percent Decrease in Belgium, Italy, and the Netherlands

Country	Percentage Change in GNP
Belgium	−0.56
France	2.09
Germany	1.64
Italy	−1.66
Netherlands	−0.87

this experiment are presented in Table 7. Although France and Germany are hardly affected by the expenditure reductions in the other three countries (compare Table 7 with the diagonals in Table 1), the reductions in GNP in the other countries are moderated significantly by the expansionary policies of France and Germany.[14]

Some Final Comments on Coordination of Policy

In an interrelated system like the Common Market, an oligopolistic framework is quite possible, especially in the determination of foreign exchange rates.[15] This suggests, by analogy, the possibility of some type of "fiscal collusion" among the Common Market countries.[16] Various forms of fiscal cooperation are possible; e.g., there could be a mutual exchange of information on potential policy changes, or limited coordination of actual plans, or, perhaps, full coordination of economic policy by some kind of supra Common Market fiscal authority.[17] The empirical results in this study shed some light on these questions.

Assume that France was facing a minor deflationary situation while the other four countries were facing an inflationary situation.

---

[14] Other combinations of countries with either France or Germany have been tried, but only the combination of these two gives as clear and marked results.

[15] See "An Econometric Study," pp. 101–6.

[16] "Fiscal collusion" is probably not the appropriate term to use. What is meant is a kind of policy coordination among countries.

[17] Fiscal cooperation is, of course, not the only alternative open to the member countries. The possibility of fiscal warfare or more sophisticated types of game strategies cannot be ruled out. If government policies of member countries tend to depend on the initiating country's government actions, then the dynamics of a given policy change could be investigated by placing appropriate "reaction coefficients" or decision rules in the model.

Table 6 indicates that, if France moved in one direction and the other four moved in another, the net effect would be to the disadvantage of France. If France were informed that the other countries intended to reduce their government expenditure, France could plan a larger increase in its own expenditure. For example, on the basis of the model, if the other countries reduce their government expenditure by 5 percent, France must increase its government expenditure by about 15 percent in order to obtain a 2.5 percent increase in its GNP.[18] A similar qualitative result differing only in degree holds for the other nations as well.

The model used in this paper is subject to various qualifications, but the estimates of the equation system are not unreasonable. Using this model, we conclude that a change in a fiscal instrument by one or more subsystems can have important effects on all the subsystems. For example, it was shown that a country can be frustrated in its attempt to gain a specific goal if the other countries move in an opposite direction. It can also be inferred from these results that an uncoordinated national fiscal policy will require larger policy changes to achieve specific goals than would be required if there were some kind of fiscal cooperation among the countries. In other words, the cost of uncoordinated economic policy among the Common Market countries may be quite high.

---

[18] This approach is most closely connected with the work of Tinbergen. In this formulation, a specific target is set for a nation in terms of endogenous variables and the value of the policy instrument needed to obtain that given target is computed. Although G_t is the assumed policy instrument of France, $T_{x_t}^*$, or a combination of both, could be used.

Econometric Model and
Estimated Results

THE ECONOMETRIC MODEL used in this study and the estimated results are presented in this Appendix.

The Model

The definitions of all the variables are as follows:

$Y_i \equiv$ gross national product

$Y_i^d \equiv$ disposable income

$C_i \equiv$ personal consumption

$I_i \equiv$ gross domestic investment

$G_i \equiv$ government expenditures

$M_i^j \equiv$ imports of j from i

$M_w^j \equiv$ imports of j from the rest of the world

$M_i^w \equiv$ imports of the rest of the world from i

$k_i \equiv$ capital stock

$k_i^d \equiv$ desired capital stock

$S_i^c \equiv$ corporate savings gross of depreciation and dividends but net of corporate taxes

$T_{x_i}^D \equiv$ total personal and corporate direct taxes plus contributions to social insurance

$T_{x_i}^I \equiv$ total indirect taxes net of subsidies

$T_{R_i} \equiv$ total transfer payments

$p_{c_i} \equiv$ consumer price level

$p_{c_w} \equiv$ consumer price level of the rest of the world

$p_{x_i} \equiv$ export price level

$p_{x_w} \equiv$ export price level of the rest of the world

$W_i \equiv$ average hourly earnings

$\pi_i^j \equiv$ foreign exchange rate of i to j

$\pi_i^w \equiv$ foreign exchange rate of i to the rest of the world

$\pi_w^j \equiv$ foreign exchange rate of the rest of the world to j

$Y_w \equiv$ gross national product of the rest of the world.

In all of the above variables, the running indices i and j go from Belgium to France, Germany, Italy, Netherlands; the expression $i = B, \cdots, N$ indicates that the index i runs over all five countries listed above.

The system of equations can be written as shown below. The μ's are random disturbances; w is defined to be the rest of the world; and t is, of course, a time subscript.

(1) $\qquad C_{it} = \alpha_{i0} + \sum_{n=0}^{\infty} \lambda^n \alpha_{i1} Y_{it-n}^d + \mu_{i1}$ $\qquad\qquad i = B, \cdots, N$

(2) $\qquad I_{it} = \beta_{i0} + \beta_{i1}(K_{it-1}^d - K_{it-1}) + \mu_{i2}$ $\qquad\qquad i = B, \cdots, N$

(3) $\qquad M_{B_t}^j = \delta_{j0} Y_{jt}^{\delta_{j1}} \left(\dfrac{p_{xB}^j}{p_{c_j}} \right)_t^{\delta_{j2}} \mu_{j3}$ $\qquad\qquad j = F, \cdots, W$

(4) $\qquad M_{F_t}^j = \delta_{j4} Y_{jt}^{\delta_{j5}} \left(\dfrac{p_{xF}^j}{p_{c_j}} \right)_t^{\delta_{j6}} \mu_{j7}$ $\qquad\qquad j = B, G, \cdots, W$

(5) $\qquad M_{G_t}^j = \delta_{j8} Y_{jt}^{\delta_{j9}} \left(\dfrac{p_{xG}^j}{p_{c_j}} \right)_t^{\delta_{j10}} \mu_{j11}$ $\qquad\qquad j = B, F, I, \cdots, W$

(6) $\qquad M_{I_t}^j = \delta_{j12} Y_{jt}^{\delta_{j13}} \left(\dfrac{p_{xI}^j}{p_{c_j}} \right)_t^{\delta_{j14}} \mu_{j15}$ $\qquad\qquad j = B, F, G, N, W$

(7) $\qquad M_{N_t}^j = \delta_{j16} Y_{jt}^{\delta_{j17}} \left(\dfrac{p_{xN}^j}{p_{c_j}} \right)_t^{\delta_{j18}} \mu_{j19}$ $\qquad\qquad j = B, \cdots, I, W$

(8) $\qquad M_{W_t}^j = \delta_{j20} Y_{jt}^{\delta_{j21}} \left(\dfrac{p_{xW}^j}{p_{c_j}} \right)_t^{\delta_{j22}} \mu_{j23}$ $\qquad\qquad j = B, \cdots, N$

(9) $\qquad p_{c_{it}} = \varepsilon_{i0} + \varepsilon_{i1} W_{it-1} + \varepsilon_{i2} T_{x_{it}}^I + \mu_{i24}$ $\qquad\qquad i = B, \cdots, N$

(10) $\qquad p_{x_{it}} = \varepsilon_{i00} + \varepsilon_{i3} W_{it-1} + \varepsilon_{i4} T_{x_{it}}^I + \mu_{i25}$ $\qquad\qquad i = B, \cdots, N$

(11) $\qquad S_{it}^c = \phi_{i0} + \phi_{i1} Y_{it} + \mu_{i26}$ $\qquad\qquad i = B, \cdots, N$

(12) $\quad K_{it-1}^d = \eta_i Y_{it-1} + \mu_{i27}$ $\qquad\qquad\qquad\qquad\qquad i = B, \cdots, N$

(13) $\quad Y_{it}^d = Y_{it} - S_{it}^c - (T_{x_{it}}^D + T_{x_{it}}^I) + T_{R_{it}}$ $\qquad\quad i = B, \cdots, N$

(14) $\quad Y_{it} = C_{it} + I_{it} + G_{it} + M_{it}^* - M_{*t}^i + M_{it}^w - M_{wt}^i$ $\quad i = B, \cdots, N$

(15) $\quad M_{it}^* \equiv \sum\limits_{j=1}^{5} M_{it}^j$ $\qquad\qquad j \neq i$ $\qquad\qquad\qquad i = B, \cdots, N$

(16) $\quad M_{*t}^i \equiv \sum\limits_{j=1}^{5} M_{jt}^i$ $\qquad\qquad j \neq i$ $\qquad\qquad\qquad i = B, \cdots, N$

(17) $\quad p_{x_{it}}^j \equiv \pi_{it}^j p_{x_{it}}$ $\qquad\qquad\quad j \neq i$ $\qquad\qquad\qquad i = B, \cdots, N$

$\qquad\qquad\qquad\qquad\qquad\qquad\qquad\qquad\qquad\qquad\qquad\qquad j = B, \cdots, N$

(18) $\quad p_{x_{it}}^w \equiv \pi_{it}^w p_{x_{it}}$ $\qquad\qquad\qquad\qquad\qquad\qquad\qquad i = B, \cdots, N$

(19) $\quad p_{x_{wt}}^i \equiv \pi_{wt}^i p_{x_{wt}}$ $\qquad\qquad\qquad\qquad\qquad\qquad\qquad i = B, \cdots, N$

Equations (1) through (14) constitute a system of 70 equations in 70 unknowns, viz., C_i, Y_i^d, I_i, K_i^d, M_i^j, p_{x_i}, p_{c_i}, M_i^w, M_w^i, S_i^c, Y_i, where $i = 1, \cdots, 5$ and $j = 1, \cdots, 5$; $j \neq i$. Equations (15) through (19) define, respectively, M_i^*, M_*^i, p_{xi}^j, p_{xi}^w, and p_{xw}^i.

Consumption Equation

There has been considerable discussion in recent years concerning the specification of a consumption function. In this model, consumption in constant prices, C_t, is specified to be a function of disposable income in constant prices, Y_t^d, in the form of a distributed lag. By combining equations (1), (11), and (13) and by performing the usual kind of transformation on the distributed lag equation, the following equation is derived:[19]

(1a) $\qquad C_t = A_i + \alpha_{i1}(1 - \phi_{i1})Y_{it} - \alpha_{i1}T_{x_{it}}^* + \lambda_i C_{it-1} + V_{i1}$

$\qquad\quad$ where $T_{x_t}^* = T_{x_t}^d + T_{x_t}^I - T_{r_t}$ and $T_{x_t}^d + T_{x_t}^I > T_{r_t}$

Investment Equation

As with the consumption function, the theory of investment behavior has undergone major changes in recent years. The investment equation in this model, however, is a simple form of the acceleration principle. It is assumed that investment, I_t, is a function of the difference between the desired capital stock (of last period), K_{t-1}^d, and the actual capital stock

---

[19] Tables 9–12 present the estimates of equation (1a). Two of the more interesting results should be pointed out: the long-run marginal propensity to consume out of GNP for the EEC member countries averages about 0.60 and for disposable income about 0.90. For the detailed derivation of equation (1a) along with a full discussion of the assumption involved, and for a discussion of the estimates, see "An Econometric Study," pp. 64–71 and pp. 140–50.

(of last period), K_{t-1}, all in constant prices. By substituting equation (12) in (1), the following structural equation is obtained:[20]

(2b) $I_t = \beta_i + \beta_{i1}\eta_i Y_{it-1} - \beta_{i1}K_{it-1} + V_{i2}$

Import Equation

When an attempt is made to estimate import-export demand elasticities, there does not seem to exist a satisfactory model that would meet all the general criticisms leveled at these kinds of econometric frameworks. The classical problem has been one of having an under-identified system by not taking into account the remaining equations of the system. It is usually argued that unreliable export-import price elasticities are estimated by relying on simple least-squares regression techniques. In view of the voluminous work that has been done on estimating simultaneous equations, it should be possible to deal with this criticism, and, in this study, a serious attempt has been made to take into account a simultaneous equation system.

It is assumed that the quantity demanded of imports by the jth country from the ith country, M_i^j, is a function of (1) the ratio of the export price level of the ith country to the jth country, p_{xi}^j, divided by the home price level of the jth country, p_{cj}, and (2) the level of real income in the jth country, Y_j. Equations (3)–(8) are specified to be nonlinear of the constant elasticity type. For purposes of estimation, the logarithm of both sides of each import equation is taken and a linear equation in the parameters is then derived:[21]

$$\ln M_{it}^j = \delta_n + \delta_{n+1} \ln Y_{jt} + \delta_{n+2} \ln\left(\frac{p_{xi}^j}{p_{cj}}\right)_t + V_{n+3}.$$

---

[20] Tables 13 and 14 present the estimates of equation (2b). In examining the results of these tables, one of the interesting things to note is that the estimates are surprisingly good. A simple accelerator model tends to explain much of the variance over the period with fairly significant coefficients. Also, the estimated capital-output ratios do not seem unreasonable (Table 14). For assumptions involved in deriving equation (2b) and a discussion of estimates, see "An Econometric Study," pp. 71–74 and pp. 151–65.

[21] Table 8 presents the estimates of the import equation for the five countries. The results are interesting in that rather high price elasticities of the "right" sign are obtained and, of the 30 price elasticities, 26 are significant at least at the 10 percent level. One other thing should be pointed out: The definition of P_{xi}^j is the export price of the ith country, multiplied by the exchange rate, π_i^j, between the trading countries. From definitions (17)–(19), it is seen that π_i^j is taken to be exogenous. This assumption is crucial to the model, and it relates to the general analysis of demand and supply equations for traded goods as well as capital movements. For present purposes, however, it is sufficient to realize that exchange rate devaluations or appreciations have been incorporated in the model. For a full discussion of the trade equations, see "An Econometric Study," pp. 74–86, 110–19, 166–71, and 218–21.

The supply of traded goods from the ith to the jth country is assumed exogenous over the relevant range. From the model, it can be seen that the export price, although still an endogenous variable, is determined without knowing the quantity of exports, and this, in turn, implies that the supply curve of exports is nearly perfectly elastic, or approximately so in the relevant range of quantities actually supplied. It is then assumed, from equation (10), that shifts in the supply curve are governed by wages and indirect taxes, and this in turn implies that, given the domestic wage rate and the level of indirect taxes, the export price can be determined without knowledge of the actual quantity of exports. Thus a mark-up equation over costs has been specified for determining the export price level in any member country. These *a priori* restrictions on the specification of the model imply that, for the ith country, the import price level it faces [recall the identities given in (17)–(19)] is determined by the domestic wage rate and the level of indirect taxes in the exporting country.

Price Equation

In the equations discussed thus far, i.e., the consumption, investment, and trade equations, fairly well known and by now traditional functional forms were relied upon. Now, however, a somewhat controversial equation is introduced. It is assumed that price behavior can be explained by an equation that shows how prices are set in terms of costs. In effect, as noted above, price behavior in the model is in terms of an equation that indicates a mark-up over prime costs: wage earnings and indirect taxes both in money terms [see equations (9) and (10)].[22]

One of the first things to note about the price equations is the possibility that they may be part of a wage-price subsystem, e.g., there may exist a feedback equation relating wages to prices. For the present model, it has been shown elsewhere[23] that, by assuming a simplified wage-price subsystem where the crucial equation consists of a wage-bargaining equation, the price equations can be estimated directly, as has been done in the present study.

However, various factors influenced the behavior of prices in the Common Market countries over the postwar period. The influence of monetary factors on prices was exemplified by the excess liquidity inherited from

---

[22] Table 8 contains the estimates of the price equations. It seems that the results of the consumer price equations are satisfactory, but those of the export price equations are less than satisfactory. One is left with the impression that, although export prices are important in the system, an adequate structure has not been provided to explain their determination (an attempt was made to take into account both demand and supply elements to determine the export price but the results were poor). See "An Econometric Study," pp. 87–92 and 171–75.

[23] *Ibid.*

World War II. In our model, the lack of connection between the monetary and real sector is evident. Rather than become involved in a discussion of how the effects of a change in the money supply would affect the real system of equations, it seems sufficient to state that some kind of connection between the monetary and real sector should have been included in the model. This, however, was not done, and our system, especially the price equation, needs to be qualified by this neglect of monetary influences.

Final Comments on the Model

For the sake of convenience, the final model to be estimated after all substitutions and logarithmic transformations is as follows:

(1a) $C_{it} = A_i + \alpha_{i1}(1 - \phi_{i1})Y_{it} - \alpha_{i1}T^*_{x_{it}} + \lambda_i C_{it-1} + V_{i1}$

(2b) $I_{it} = \beta_i + \beta_{i1}\eta_i Y_{it-1} - \beta_{i1}K_{it-1} + V_{i2}$

(3c) $\ln M^j_{Bt} = \delta_{j0} + \delta_{j1} \ln Y_{jt} - \delta_{j2} \ln \left(\dfrac{p^j_{xB}}{p_{cj}}\right)_t + V_{j3}$

(4d) $\ln M^j_{Ft} = \delta_{j4} + \delta_{j5} \ln Y_{jt} - \delta_{j6} \ln \left(\dfrac{p^j_{xF}}{p_{cj}}\right)_t + V_{j7}$

(5e) $\ln M^j_{Gt} = \delta_{j8} + \delta_{j9} \ln Y_{jt} - \delta_{j10} \ln \left(\dfrac{p^j_{xG}}{p_{cj}}\right)_t + V_{j11}$

(6f) $\ln M^j_{It} = \delta_{j12} + \delta_{j13} \ln Y_{jt} - \delta_{j14} \ln \left(\dfrac{p^j_{xI}}{p_{cj}}\right)_t + V_{j15}$

(7g) $\ln M^j_{Nt} = \delta_{j16} + \delta_{j17} \ln Y_{jt} - \delta_{j18} \ln \left(\dfrac{p^j_{xN}}{p_{cj}}\right)_t + V_{j19}$

(8h) $\ln M^j_{w_t} = \delta_{j20} + \delta_{j21} \ln Y_{jt} - \delta_{j22} \ln \left(\dfrac{p^j_{xW}}{p_{cj}}\right)_t + V_{j23}$

(9i) $p_{c_{it}} = \varepsilon_{i0} + \varepsilon_{i1}W_{it-1} + \varepsilon_{i2}T^I_{x_{it}} + V_{i24}$

(10j) $p_{x_{it}} = \varepsilon_{i00} + \varepsilon_{i3}W_{it-1} + \varepsilon_{i4}T^I_{x_{it}} + V_{i25}$

From our final system, there are, in total, 50 structural equations to be estimated; 15 of them, the investment and price equations, are in recursive form. The block of 35 simultaneous equations is estimated by the method of instrumental variables.[24]

[24] The formal estimating procedure was as follows: using a principal component analysis, a set of instrument variables was chosen for the first-stage regressions. The method used followed closely the procedure outlined in an article by T. Kloek and L. B. M. Mennes, "Simultaneous Equation Estimation Based on Principal Components of Predetermined Variables," *Econometrica*, Vol. 28 (1960), pp. 45–61. Once the corrected values for all jointly dependent variables were obtained, the second-stage results were estimated. In addition, it is shown elsewhere that the model satisfied the identifiability criteria for nonlinear systems. For discussion of both of the above problems, see "An Econometric Study," Appendix 4.

It is interesting to note that in the above model the economic system can be divided into two highly simplified blocks, the EEC as one and the rest of the world as the other. Within this classification, it is assumed that the block defined to be the EEC can be represented by a system of simultaneous equations, whereas in this study it is assumed that the block defined to be the rest of the world need not be specified as to internal structure (that is, within block structure), but that the variables within the latter block need only be taken as approximately exogeneous to those of the former block. Thus our system can be characterized as being nearly block recursive. (In "An Econometric Study," Chapter 3 and Appendix 2, it is shown that the restrictions on the variance-covariance matrix of error terms can be used for identifiability, and that the feedback in the nearly block recursive system is sufficiently weak so that nearly consistent estimates result.)

TABLE 8. EEC Countries: Estimated Results for System of Equations, Elasticities Evaluated at Base Year, 1953[a]

Country or Variable	Results			
	Consumption Equation			
	$\alpha_1(1 - \phi_1)\,_0Y_t$	$\lambda\,_0C_{t-1}$	$\alpha_1\,_0T_x^*{}_t$	$\bar{R}^2$
Belgium	.819 (.135)	.205 (.109)	−.120 (.042)	.976
France	.526 (.114)	.447 (.153)	−.131 (.054)	.995
Germany	.520 (.264)	.422 (.209)	−.182 (.101)	.995
Italy	.431 (.134)	.510 (.238)	−.082 (.107)	.993
Netherlands	.371 (.127)	.633 (.208)	−.121 (.061)	.962
	Investment Equation			
	$\beta_1\,\eta\,_0Y_{t-1}$	$\beta_1^*\,_{0_i}\sum_i^{t-1} I_i$		$\bar{R}^2$
Belgium	1.222 (.149)	−.232 (.009)		.879
France	1.216 (.530)	−.389 (.200)		.893
Germany	1.068 (.367)	−.386 (.101)		.963
Italy	1.155 (.505)	−.375 (.157)		.971
Netherlands	2.116 (1.080)	−.541 (.290)		.828

Continued on page 208.

Country or Variable	Results		
	Import Equation		
$_0M^j_{i_t}$	$\delta_{n+1} \ln \left(\dfrac{p^j_{xi}}{{}_0p_{cj}}\right)_t$	$\delta_{n+2} \ln {}_0(Y_j)_t$	$\bar{R}^2$
M^F_B	-2.072 (1.03)	2.208 $(.470$	$.89$
M^G_B	$-.636$ $(.096)$	1.65 $(.181)$	$.88$
M^I_B	-1.70 (1.45)	2.19 $(.683)$	$.73$
M^N_B	$-.617$ $(.150)$	2.41 $(.378)$	$.87$
M^W_B	$-.355$ $(.014)$	1.330 $(.305)$	$.93$
M^B_F	-1.97 $(.062)$	4.757 (1.062)	$.87$
M^G_F	-1.57 (1.27)	1.88 $(.217)$	$.91$
M^I_F	-1.429 $(.769)$	2.06 $(.708)$	$.79$
M^N_F	-1.50 $(.72)$	$.55$ $(.203)$	$.48$
M^W_F	-6.485 (1.141)	1.990 $(.76)$	$.96$
M^B_G	-12.047 $(2.637$	1.74 $(.903)$	$.96$
M^F_G	-2.305 $(.764)$	3.34 $(.274)$	$.95$
M^I_G	$-.833$ $(.958)$	2.36 (1.04)	$.79$
M^N_G	$-.314$ $(.144)$	1.151 $(.308)$	$.74$
M^W_G	-5.804 (1.528)	2.243 (1.07)	$.90$
M^B_I	-2.515 $(.684)$	1.65 $(.730)$	$.97$
M^F_I	$-.907$ $(.387)$	2.43 $(.954)$	$.81$
M^G_I	$-.327$ $(.004)$	2.57 $(.324)$	$.94$
M^N_I	-1.26 $(.599)$	2.52 $(.685)$	$.96$
M^W_I	-3.684 $(.630)$	1.520 $(.746)$	$.97$
M^B_N	-10.445 (1.496)	2.917 $(.986)$	$.99$

Concluded on page 209.

TABLE 8 (*concl.*). EEC Countries: Estimated Results for System of Equations, Elasticities Evaluated at Base Year, 1953[a]

Country or Variable	Results		
M_N^F	−1.67 (.500)	2.92 (.239)	.96
M_N^G	−5.68 (2.41)	3.25 (.634)	.89
M_N^I	−1.48 (.380)	2.08 (.705)	.96
M_N^W	−2.356 (.472)	1.210 (.428)	.97
M_W^B	−1.31 (.456)	.65 (.058)	.84
M_W^F	− .678 (.242)	.68 (.048)	.89
M_W^G	− .876 (.209)	1.04 (.092)	.95
M_W^I	−1.333 (.655)	.73 (.101)	.97
M_W^N	− .112 (.054)	.55 (.032)	.88

Consumer Price Equation

	$\epsilon_1 \, _0W_{t-1}^E$	$\epsilon_2 \, _0T_{x_t}^I$	$\bar{R}^2$
Belgium	.312 (.107)	.009 (.008)	.93
France	.498 (.034)	.658 (.176)	.97
Germany	.267 (.121)	.05 (.08)	.93
Italy	.642 (.398)	.07 (.02)	.94
Netherlands	.184 (.08)	.308 (.103)	.92

Export Price Equation

	$\epsilon_3 \, W_{t-1}^E$	$\epsilon_4 \, _0T_{x_t}^I$	$\bar{R}^2$
Belgium	.65 (.18)	1.69 (.41)	.53
France	.397 (.03)	.60 (.12)	.97
Germany	.108 (.04)	.28 (.14)	.32
Italy	.619 (.101)	.903 (.238)	.78
Netherlands	.09 (.04)	.50 (.108)	.64

[a] All variables in form $_0X_t$ are defined to be volume indices where $0 \equiv 1953$.
  M_i^j indicates exports of i to j; $n = 14$.
  $\bar{R}^2$ is corrected for degrees of freedom.
  For investment equation, see notes to Table 13.

TABLE 9. EEC Countries: Short-Run Elasticities for Consumption Equation Evaluated at 1953 (the Base Year), 1948, 1961, and Sample Mean for Period 1948–61[a]

Country	Short-Run Elasticities			
	At 1953			
	$\alpha_1(1 - \phi_1)\, _0Y_t$	$\lambda\, _0C_{t-1}$	$\alpha_1\, _0T_{xt}^*$	$\bar{R}^2$
Belgium	.819	.205	−.120	.976
	(.135)	(.109)	(.042)	
France	(.526)	(.447)	−.131	.995
	(.114)	(.153)	(.054)	
Germany	.520	.422	−.182	.995
	(.264)	(.209)	(.101)	
Italy	.431	.510	−.082	.993
	(.134)	(.238)	(.107)	
Netherlands	.371	.633	−.121	.962
	(.127)	(.208)	(.061)	
	At 1948			
	$\alpha_1(1 - \phi)\, _{48}Y_t$		$\alpha_1\, _{48}T_{xt}^*$	
Belgium	.757		−.101	
France	.505		−.084	
Germany	.527		−.206	
Italy	.425		−.063	
Netherlands	.315		−.104	
	At 1961			
	$\alpha_1(1 - \phi_1)\, _{61}Y_t$		$\alpha_1\, _{61}T_{xt}^*$	
Belgium	.835		−.127	
France	.574		−.140	
Germany	.520		−.183	
Italy	.574		−.113	
Netherlands	.371		−.107	
	At Sample Mean			
	$\alpha_1(1 - \phi_1)\, \bar{x}Y_t$		$\alpha_1 \bar{x}T_{xt}^*$	
Belgium	.810		−.118	
France	.549		−.122	
Germany	.526		−.174	
Italy	.456		−.097	
Netherlands	.360		−.109	

[a] The symbols $_0Y_t$, $_0C_t$, and $_0T_{xt}^*$ denote volume indices as defined earlier.

210

TABLE 10. EEC Countries: Long-Run Elasticities for Consumption Equation Evaluated at 1953 (the Base Year), 1948, 1961, and Sample Mean for Period 1948–61

Country	Long-Run Elasticities	

At 1953

Country	$\dfrac{\alpha_1(1-\phi_1)}{1-\lambda}\,_0Y_t$	$\dfrac{\alpha_1}{1-\lambda}\,_0T_{x_t}$
Belgium	1.030	−.151
France	.951	−.237
Germany	.900	−.315
Italy	.880	−.167
Netherlands	1.011	−.330

At 1948

Country	$\dfrac{\alpha_1(1-\phi_1)}{1-\lambda}\,_{48}Y_t$	$\dfrac{\alpha_1}{1-\lambda}\,_{48}T_{x_t}^{*}$
Belgium	.952	−.127
France	.914	−.153
Germany	.912	−.357
Italy	.869	−.128
Netherlands	.859	−.283

At 1961

Country	$\dfrac{\alpha_1(1-\phi_1)}{1-\lambda}\,_{61}Y_t$	$\dfrac{\alpha_1}{1-\lambda}\,_{61}T_{x_t}^{*}$
Belgium	1.051	−.159
France	.971	−.253
Germany	.900	−.317
Italy	.998	−.231
Netherlands	1.011	−.293

At Sample Mean

Country	$\dfrac{\alpha_1(1-\phi_1)}{1-\lambda}\,_{\bar{x}}Y_t$	$\dfrac{\alpha_1}{1-\lambda}\,_{\bar{x}}Y_{x_t}^{*}$
Belgium	1.019	−.148
France	.929	−.221
Germany	.911	−.301
Italy	.931	−.198
Netherlands	.981	−.297

TABLE 11. EEC Countries: Coefficients from Tables 9 and 10 Transformed into Marginal Propensities To Consume out of Gross National Product and Disposable Income

Country	Marginal Propensity To Consume out of Gross National Product		Long-run Marginal Propensity To Consume out of Disposable Income
	Short-run	Long-run	
Belgium	.586	.737	.913
France	.355	.642	.824
Germany	.313	.542	.881
Italy	.304	.620	.904
Netherlands	.216	.587	.911

TABLE 12. EEC Countries: Rate of Growth of Gross National Product, Average Propensity to Consume, and Long-Run Marginal Propensity To Consume out of Gross National Product and Disposable Income[a]

Country	Annual Growth Rate of Gross National Product, 1950–61[a]	Average Propensity To Consume, 1948–61[a]	Long-run Marginal Propensity To Consume out of	
			Gross national product	Disposable income
Belgium	2.96	.72	.737	.913
France	4.42	.67	.642	.824
Germany	7.53	.59	.542	.881
Italy	6.10	.66	.620	.904
Netherlands	4.65	.59	.587	.911

[a] In 1953 prices.

TABLE 13. EEC Countries: Elasticities for Investment Equation Evaluated at 1953 (the Base Year), 1948, 1961, and Sample Mean for Period 1948–61[a]

Country	Elasticities for Investment Equation		
	At 1953		
	$\beta_1\, \eta\,_0 Y_{t-1}$	$\beta_1^*\,_0 \sum_i^{t-1} I_i$	$\bar{R}^2$
Belgium	1.222	−.232	.879
	(.149)	(.009)	
France	1.216	−.389	.893
	(.530)	(.200)	
Germany	1.068	−.386	.963
	(.367)	(.101)	
Italy	1.155	−.375	.971
	(.505)	(.157)	
Netherlands	2.116	−.541	.828
	(1.08)	(.290)	
	At 1948		
	$\beta_1\, \eta\,_{48} Y_{t-1}$	$\beta_1^*\,_{48} \sum_i^{t-1} I_i$	
Belgium	1.129	−.066	
France	1.178	−.107	
Germany	1.335	−.132	
Italy	1.236	−.148	
Netherlands	1.619	−.142	
	At 1961		
	$\beta_1\, \eta\,_{61} Y_{t-1}$	$\beta_1^*\,_{61} \sum_i^{t-1} I_i$	
Belgium	1.046	−.403	
France	1.096	−.674	
Germany	.857	−.645	
Italy	.911	−.539	
Netherlands	1.549	−.790	

Concluded on page 214.

TABLE 13 (concl.). EEC Countries: Elasticities for Investment Equation Evaluated at 1953 (the Base Year), 1948, 1961, and Sample Mean for Period 1948–61[a]

Country	Elasticities for Investment Equation	
		At Sample Mean
	$\beta_1 \eta \, \bar{x} Y_{t-1}$	$\beta_1^* \, \bar{x} \sum_{i}^{t-1} I_i$
Belgium	1.124	—.268
France	1.079	—.431
Germany	.954	—.476
Italy	1.060	—.432
Netherlands	1.720	—.569

[a] Definitions:

$n = 14$.

$\bar{R}^2$ corrected for degrees of freedom.

Note that the capital stock variable is written as $\sum_{i}^{t-1} I_i$ and the associated coefficient as β_1^*; this differs from the presentation in the text (see system of equations). Basically, what is involved is first defining capital stock at time t as $K_t = \bar{K} + \sum_{i=1}^{t} I_i$ where $\bar{K}$ denotes the stock at the beginning of the period, and then transforming the equation so that part of the unknown variable, e.g., $\bar{K}$, is absorbed in the constant term. However, it is shown in "An Econometric Study," pp. 151–65, that there still remains an unknown variable in the denominator of the last term (note that it is an index number). It is shown in the above thesis that an estimate of β_1^* will be biased. The desired capital-output ratio in Table 14 is corrected for this bias.

TABLE 14. EEC Countries: Incremental Capital-Output Ratios Computed from Time Series, Equilibrium Capital-Output Ratios Computed from Regression Equations, and Rates of Growth of Gross National Product in Constant Prices

Country	Capital-Output Ratio		Annual Growth Rate of Gross National Product, 1960–61[c] (percent)
	Incremental[a]	Desired[b]	
Belgium	5.61	5.30	2.96
France	4.29	3.42	4.42
Germany	3.21	2.99	7.53
Italy	3.46	3.64	6.10
Netherlands	5.05	5.13	4.65

[a] Computed as follows: ratio of capital formation in constant prices (1953) to annual rate of growth of gross national product in constant prices (1953).

[b] Computed from the regression equation. See notes to Table 13.

[c] In 1953 prices.

ALBERT ANDO AND STEPHEN M. GOLDFELD*

An Econometric Model for Evaluating Stabilization Policies

THIS PAPER PRESENTS an aggregative econometric model of the U. S. economy specifically designed to evaluate short-run impacts of stabilization policies, both fiscal and monetary. The model is based on quarterly data from 1950 through 1964 (except where indicated otherwise), and is used to trace the effects of once-for-all policy actions. Dynamic multipliers associated with these policy changes for four quarters are presented, on the assumption that the changes were initiated at the end of 1964.

This paper is a natural outgrowth of the interdependent research interests pursued by the authors during the past few years. Recently, one of us reported on a study of commercial bank behavior in the context of an aggregate econometric model of the postwar U. S. economy.[1] That study had a number of limitations. Among the more important ones was the treatment of both revenues and expenditures of the government sector as exogenous to the model. It seems fruitful to improve this aspect of the model by drawing on recent work in this area to which the other author has contributed.[2] This op-

* University of Pennsylvania and Princeton University.

[1] Stephen M. Goldfeld, *Commercial Bank Behavior and Economic Activity* (Amsterdam: North-Holland Publishing Co., 1966).

[2] Albert Ando and E. Cary Brown, "Lags in Fiscal Policy," Part II of "Lags in Fiscal and Monetary Policy," in Commission on Money and Credit, *Stabilization Policies* (Pren-

portunity has also been taken to extend all previous work to include data up to 1964.[3] This extension seemed particularly important in view of a number of significant developments in the economy, such as the growth of negotiable certificates of deposit and other structural changes in the money market, the tax cut of 1964, and the near full employment conditions which prevailed in the latter part of this period.[4]

Although improvement of the model in a few other respects was attempted, there remain, of course, a number of shortcomings which will be mentioned before the model itself and its implications for stabilization policy are discussed.

The model presented here is strictly a demand model, designed to reflect the behavior of the economy in the short run. It takes the capacity of the economy to produce—both the capital facilities and the labor force—as given. More specifically, the contribution of investment, both in productive facilities and in technical change, to the productive capacity of the economy is treated as a trend factor. Furthermore, the response of the labor-force-participation rate to the level of economic activity is not dealt with in this model, and the labor force is assumed to be strictly exogenous.

This means that the behavior of the model when the economy is operating at very near capacity cannot be expected to be completely satisfactory. In particular, when effective demand exceeds the economy's capacity to produce (somehow defined), the interaction between real output and wage-price behavior cannot be inferred adequately from this model. The price equation presented here is merely a stopgap formulation, pending a thorough investigation of this problem.[5] Wages do not even appear in this model explicitly.

tice-Hall, 1963); Albert Ando, E. Cary Brown, and Earl W. Adams, Jr., "Government Revenues and Expenditures," in James S. Duesenberry and others (eds.), *The Brookings Quarterly Econometric Model of the United States* (Rand McNally & Co. and North-Holland Publishing Co., 1965); Albert Ando and E. Cary Brown, "Personal Income Taxes and Consumption Following the 1964 Tax Reduction," in this volume.

[3] The model in Goldfeld, *Commercial Bank Behavior*, was estimated by using data through the second quarter of 1962.

[4] In addition, Mr. George Jazsi of the Office of Business Economics (OBE), U. S. Department of Commerce, kindly made available seasonally unadjusted figures corresponding to the 1965 revision of national income statistics. These revised data were used for the estimation in this model; the older model was, of course, estimated by using the unrevised data.

[5] During the academic year 1966–67, a major effort is being devoted to constructing a more satisfactory model for the use of monetary policymakers. The project is being under-

A related problem is the behavior of corporations in their decisions as to pricing, distribution of dividends, investment, employment, and financing. Theoretically, corporate profits should be obtained as the residual after behavioral equations are estimated for the items listed in the preceding sentence. For the purposes of this model, however, fairly traditional and *ad hoc* formulations for corporate profits and dividends were adopted. As a result, this model is not completely adequate for analyzing the effects on investment of changes in corporate and excise taxes.

The work required to remedy any of these deficiencies would be quite formidable. Solving some of them does appear possible, however, and the project mentioned in footnote 5 is being undertaken largely in order to deal with them. Thus, one of the purposes of this paper is to set down, as precisely as possible at this time, just how far we can go in evaluating the implications of various monetary and fiscal policy measures, and how seriously any one of the defects of our model is likely to affect our conclusions.

Despite our awareness of these limitations, we feel that the results contained in this study do provide some useful information for policymakers, provided that the limitations of the model are always kept in mind in interpreting these results.

In the following sections, the estimated model will be described briefly; then an analysis of various multipliers with respect to a number of policy changes will be presented.

Description of the Model

As indicated above, the primary aim of this study is to investigate the short-run impacts of alternative monetary and fiscal policies on the economy. Naturally, the equations presented below have been designed with this in mind, and this predisposition largely accounts for the imbalanced structure of the model. Of the fifty equations, five are demand functions for real consumption and investment; nine are equations necessary to relate disposable income to gross national product (GNP); four are demand functions

taken by the members of the staff of the Division of Research and Statistics, Board of Governors of the Federal Reserve System, and by a team organized at the Massachusetts Institute of Technology under the sponsorship of the Social Science Research Council and supported by the Federal Reserve Board. Albert Ando, Daniel Brill, Frank deLeeuw, and Franco Modigliani are jointly responsible for directing the project.

for financial assets; twelve are bank behavioral equations; two explain the structure of interest rates and the formation of prices; and the remaining eighteen are definitional identities.

Before discussion of the equations, some general comments are in order. The sources of data and the adjustments that are made are described in the Appendix. Unless otherwise specified in the description of individual equations, all flow variables are seasonally unadjusted quarterly totals, in billions of dollars. All stock variables are in billions of dollars, the tax rates and the required reserve ratios in actual fractions, and the interest rates in percent per annum. In a few cases where the data are seasonally adjusted, the variables so adjusted are denoted by the superscript "s".[6]

The model is generally estimated by using the method of two-stage least squares. In certain equations, the method of ordinary least squares is applied, and this is indicated explicitly in the description below. Because of the presence of numerous nonlinearities in the model, the meaning of two-stage least squares becomes ambiguous. We follow the interpretation of this method as specified in the study by Goldfeld and Quandt.[7] In most cases, we assume that the structural equation contains an exponentially distributed lag, which is estimated through the presence of the lagged dependent variable in the equation. Although this procedure may lead to serious biases in estimated parameters if the residuals are serially correlated, there are now a number of methods for dealing with this problem.[8] However, to adopt any of the more efficient methods in the context of a fairly large structural system, such as ours, requires more work, both theoretical and computational, than we could devote to the project. Therefore, the study was confined to a few experiments in which we corrected on an *ad hoc* basis what appeared to be serious biases in our estimates as a result of this procedure and examined the implication of these corrections for the behavior of the system.

[6] The case for or against using seasonally unadjusted data is ambiguous and far from settled. A brief discussion of the implications of using unadjusted data in the analysis of the system is given in the Appendix (pp. 282–85).

[7] Stephen M. Goldfeld and R. E. Quandt, "Non-Linear Simultaneous Equations: Estimation and Prediction," *International Economic Review*, Vol. 9 (February 1968).

[8] See, for instance, P. J. Dhrymes, "Efficient Estimation of Distributed Lags with Autocorrelated Errors" (Discussion Paper No. 23, Department of Economics, University of Pennsylvania, 1966) and references given there.

Before the individual equations are discussed, it should be reiterated that many of them have their predecessors in earlier published works; as they are described extensively in those sources, the present discussion will be brief. Equations that constitute the model are given on pages 238–46.

The first group of equations (1 through 6), those dealing with consumption and investment expenditures, are, with a few exceptions, relatively standard specifications. Consumption expenditures were divided into durable and nondurable categories, and gross private domestic investment was separated into plant and equipment, inventory, and a residual category. In addition, all variables were expressed in real terms by use of the implicit GNP deflator. This allows for general price effects but not for relative price changes.[9]

The specification for nondurables makes consumption a function of disposable income, lagged consumption, and wealth. As all three variables are sufficiently commonplace in consumption functions, they require no elaboration. In the specification for durables, the same set of variables was tried, but wealth yielded a perverse negative coefficient. This may have been due to the fact that the stock of consumer durables was not separated from other assets.[10] In any event, the sum of currency and demand deposits ("money") was substituted for wealth, and it yielded a positive coefficient. It is impossible to say whether this should be interpreted strictly as a proxy for wealth or as reflecting other considerations as well (e.g., timing of expenditures or a liquid asset effect). Finally, the change in GNP as an explanatory variable is meant to account for some of the volatility of durable expenditures.

Several general comments should be made about the investment functions.[11] First, the form of the three investment equations can be derived from a flexible version of the capital-stock adjustment

---

[9] We do not mean to imply that relative price changes are unimportant. Moreover, in terms of making price an endogenous variable, a more satisfactory formulation would make the components of the GNP deflator depend on different sets of factors. However, at this point, as with several others in the paper, time constraints necessarily limited the extent of disaggregation.

[10] The stock of durables is one component of wealth and, if a stock adjustment model is relevant, would be expected to yield a negative coefficient.

[11] The construction of the variables is such that the three investment components do not exactly add up to gross private domestic investment. In particular, inventory investment

principle. Thus, each equation is a distributed-lag specification with current investment depending on lagged investment, output, interest rates, and other variables to be elaborated upon. Second, the traditional, and perhaps too restrictive, Keynesian assumption that some market rate of interest represents the cost of capital for firms is adopted. This view is tempered somewhat by including in each investment equation a variable measuring the change in commercial and industrial loans at commercial banks. This variable was viewed as a constraint on investment, and included in order to reflect, however inadequately, the possibility of credit rationing by banks. Fourth, multiplicative seasonal dummy variables outperform linear seasonal dummys for the plant and equipment equation but not for the other two investment categories. The final specification reflects this asymmetry.

In explaining fixed investment by firms, the capital-stock adjustment principle requires some measure of productive capacity. For this purpose, an indicator of potential output was constructed by dividing GNP by a current utilization rate of capacity.[12] This variable was introduced as a deviation from lagged GNP, and it produced the expected negative coefficient. That is, given current GNP, the higher is potential GNP, the less is the incentive to invest in plant and equipment. As for the interest rate variable, both the long rate and the short rate were tried in both a linear and a multiplicative (with Y) form. While producing uniformly negative coefficients, they were never significant by the (inappropriate) conventional tests. Equation (4) reports the best of these attempts.

The same set of explanatory variables was tried for $F2$, the residual investment category.[13] There are two significant differences in equation (5), compared with equation (4). The coefficient of the potential GNP variable is only a small fraction of its standard error; but as $F2$ consists mainly of residential construction, this

---

is measured as manufacturing inventory investment, but $F2$ is constructed as gross private domestic investment less $F1$ less total nonfarm inventory investment. The consequences of this for our later multiplier calculations are likely to be negligible.

[12] The reader is reminded that the real variable Y/K differs from the variable Y^* only in that Y/K is seasonally unadjusted, and hence Y/K is exogenous. See the discussion below of equation (50).

[13] The movements in $F2$ reflect those in residential construction and not much else.

finding is not disturbing. The other difference is that the interest rate is now significant in multiplicative form.[14]

The inventory equation is a simple version of the flexible accelerator model which makes ΔH a function of lagged inventories, sales, and the change in sales.[15] The last variable enters if expected sales are taken to be a function of past sales (or, as is more common, a linear combination of current and past sales). To implement this equation, sales were measured by "final sales" ($Y - \Delta H$), so as to avoid the introduction of a new variable. In addition, the change (lagged) in unfilled orders and the capacity utilization rate were included as explanatory variables. The inclusion of unfilled orders can be justified on a variety of grounds, e.g., production-smoothing considerations, as a measure of market tightness, or as an indication of the increase in goods-in-process inventories (dominating over decreases from raw materials and finished goods) induced by unfilled orders.[16] Production-smoothing and market-tightness considerations can similarly justify the inclusion of a capacity variable.[17] Both variables proved to be of importance in explaining inventory investment. Finally, while the change in commercial loans yielded a positive coefficient that was twice its standard error, the interest rate variables did not improve the results in any way.

Since government expenditure and net foreign investment are taken as exogenous to the model, equations (1) through (6), together with equation (49), determine the level of GNP in money terms. Given GNP, identities (13) and (16) yield personal income and personal disposable income, respectively.[18] Thus, the equa-

---

[14] A multiplicative specification can result from a model in which the desired capital stock is a capital coefficient times output and the capital coefficient is a simple function of an interest rate. See Goldfeld, *Commercial Bank Behavior*.

[15] For a discussion of this, see Michael C. Lovell, "Determinants of Inventory Investment," in National Bureau of Economic Research, *Models of Income Determination* (Princeton University Press, 1964).

[16] *Ibid.*, Goldfeld, *Commercial Bank Behavior*, and references in both publications. In principle, unfilled orders should be treated as an endogenous variable. On this point, see Gerald L. Childs, "Linear Decision Rules for Explaining Finished Goods Inventories and Unfilled Orders" (Ph.D. dissertation, Massachusetts Institute of Technology, 1963).

[17] Of course, high capacity utilization may increase the difficulty of obtaining inputs, and this could exert a negative influence on inventory investment. The empirical evidence above, and also in Goldfeld, *Commercial Bank Behavior*, suggests that the positive relationship dominates.

[18] These identities are slightly different from those used by OBE because of (a) the absence of statistical discrepancy and (b) our treatment of federal taxes on the liability basis, as explained below.

tions in groups (7) through (18) attempt to explain items appearing in these two identities. Note here that A_1 and A_2 are taken as exogenous to the model. Some variables included in A_1 and A_2, particularly some state and local government revenues and expenditures, may be quite responsive to economic activity and money market conditions and probably should be made endogenous.[19]

Equation (7), the dividend equation, is a simple adaptation of the well-known formulation by Lintner.[20] One peculiar feature of the dividend equation is that the data available before and after the 1965 revision by OBE gave quite different results. Two differences were particularly noteworthy. First, the seasonally unadjusted data on the revised basis gave such poor fits that the attempt to work with them eventually had to be abandoned.[21] Second, when the unrevised data were used, some significant negative influence of investment expenditure on dividends was detected; when the revised data were used, this influence disappeared completely.[22]

Equation (8) expresses corporate profits including inventory valuation adjustment[23] as a function of current GNP, GNP lagged,

---

[19] Two recent studies tend to confirm the notion. See R. E. Bolton, "Predictive Models for State and Local Government Purchases" (Brookings Institution, Working Paper in Econometric Model Project, 1965) and E. M. Gramlich, "State and Local Governments and Their Budget Constraints" (unpublished paper by staff member of Board of Governors of the Federal Reserve System).

[20] John Lintner, "Distribution of Incomes of Corporations Among Dividends, Retained Earnings, and Taxes," *American Economic Review*, Vol. 46 (May 1956).

[21] As explained in the Appendix, OBE does not prepare seasonally unadjusted data on dividends. We constructed approximate data by using monthly seasonally unadjusted figures on publicly reported dividends and adjusting them to the annual total of the national income figures.

[22] The result using the older data was as follows:

$$V = .820V_{-1} + .199(\pi - TC) - .077(F1 + \Delta H) - .0015S_1(Y - \Delta H)_{-1}$$
$$\quad (.046) \qquad (.043) \qquad\qquad (.025) \qquad\qquad (.0010)$$
$$\quad - .0013S_2(Y - \Delta H)_{-1} + .0060S_4(Y - \Delta H)_{-1} + .025$$
$$\quad\;\; (.0007) \qquad\qquad\quad (.0007) \qquad\qquad (.022)$$
$$R^2 = .96, \qquad DW = 2.75$$

When a similar equation was estimated by using revised data, the results were totally unsatisfactory. We cannot pass judgment on the merits of the revision on this basis. We merely note that the statistical and conceptual changes (in the treatment of mutual companies and of dividends paid by foreign corporations) in the 1965 revision resulted in a substantial modification, both in level and in movement over time, in the dividend series.

[23] Since equation (8) is only an empirical approximation of a complex behavioral pattern, we let it represent inventory valuation adjustment in addition to corporate profits. We have no obvious excuse for this procedure other than that of expedience.

and corporate profits lagged. It is a traditional *ad hoc* equation for profits, which seems to work fairly well.[24] As in the dividend equation, when the analogous formulation was tried on seasonally unadjusted data, it gave an extremely poor fit.[25] Both equation (7), the dividend equation, and equation (8), the equation for corporate profits, were estimated by ordinary least squares.

Equation (9), indirect business taxes other than property taxes, is a straightforward formulation, in which total consumption expenditure acts as a proxy for the tax base. The rate of tax, ρ_i, was computed as a weighted average of all excise tax rates, both of federal and state, using the tax bases for 1960 as weights, as explained in the Appendix. The fact that the elasticities of both consumption expenditure and the rate are somewhat less than unity suggests that the approximation is not perfect; however, it seems generally satisfactory.

Equation (10) deals with contributions to Old Age and Survivors Insurance (OASI). The pattern of actual cash payments under the OASI program is rather complex. The contribution of the individual ceases as his earnings reach the maximum taxable income during the year. Under these circumstances, the seasonal pattern depends on the level, as well as the distribution and the annual pattern, of wages and salaries and on the maximum taxable income. In addition, OASI contributions of self-employed persons until very recently were largely paid in the following year at the time when these individuals filed their final tax returns. Partially because of these difficulties, but, more importantly, in order to be consistent with the treatment of the federal personal income tax as explained below, we decided to work with the liability of OASI contributions rather than with the cash payment. Liability, of course, is not very well defined except on an annual basis. Hence, equation (10) was estimated by using annual data, and the figures for quarterly liabilities were generated by the substitution of quarterly income for the income variable in equation (10). The coefficient of ρ_0 was restricted to be unity, and X's represent the changes in the coverage

[24] Edwin Kuh, "Profits, Profit Mark-Ups, and Productivity," in *Employment, Growth, and Price Levels*, Study Paper No. 15, Joint Economic Committee, 86 Cong. 1 sess. (1960); Charles L. Schultze, "Short-Run Movement of Income Shares," in National Bureau of Economic Research, *The Behavior of Income Shares* (Princeton University Press, 1964); and Ando and Brown, in *Stabilization Policies*.

[25] Seasonal adjustment made much less difference in terms of data before the 1965 revision by OBE.

that occurred during the period covered by the study. One serious defect of this equation is that it does not contain any variable representing the maximum taxable income, which should have an important influence on the liability. A variety of proxies for it were tried; but no usable result was obtained.[26]

Equation (11) for unemployment insurance contributions is analogous to equation (10), except that the coverage of the program is represented by the ratio of the covered labor force to the total labor force, and the rate is a weighted average of the state contribution rates. The weighted average rate is fairly crude, and perhaps this is the reason for the very low elasticity of income.

The equation for unemployment insurance benefits, (12), is a straightforward approximation to the legal structure of the system, giving the benefits as the product of maximum weekly benefits and unemployment. Here again, another logical variable, the ratio of the covered labor force to the total labor force, does not contribute to the explanation.[27]

Identity (13) defines the relationship between GNP and personal income in current dollars. As is well known, OBE does not collect the data on personal income on a seasonally unadjusted basis. Therefore, we constructed our own seasonally unadjusted personal income series through identity (13). In the process we made one approximation and three changes in definitions. The approximation was for dividends, as discussed earlier.[28] The changes in definitions were as follows: (1) contributions to OASI were changed to a liability basis; (2) contributions to unemployment insurance also were changed to a liability basis; (3) the statistical discrepancy was ignored. For the other items in the identity, including the components of A_1, the seasonally unadjusted data were readily available from OBE.

The relationship among the federal personal income tax liability, the effective rate of taxes, and taxable income is defined by (14). The data for this identity are meaningful only on an annual basis.

---

[26] For an additional discussion of OASI contributions, unemployment insurance contributions, and benefits, see Ando and others, in *Brookings Quarterly Econometric Model*.

[27] One reason for this difficulty is that, under the present system, newly covered workers will not receive benefits until substantial time has elapsed and they have accumulated sufficient credits on which to draw.

[28] See footnote 21, above.

This identity plus equation (17) for taxable income explains the federal personal income tax liability. Equation (17) is discussed below; our remarks here are limited to the effective rate, ρ_{fp}. In principle, ρ_{fp} is a complex function of the statutory tax rates, distribution of income, and the status of families. However, between 1954 and 1963, a period in which the statutory rates were constant, the effective rate was practically unchanged at 23 percent. Thus, for this period, the tax liability could readily be predicted, once taxable income was predicted. This led to the suggestion that the effective rate is fairly insensitive to changes in income distribution, and therefore, if the rate structure is changed, the effective rate could be easily predicted through the sample returns for earlier years.[29] However, preliminary indications are that, under the Revenue Act of 1964, more careful attention will have to be paid to the relation between income distribution and the rate structure in order accurately to predict the effective rate.[30]

Equation (15) describes state personal income taxes. The dependent variable here was taken from OBE national income statistics and is, therefore, on a cash collection basis. To be consistent with our treatment of other taxes, particularly the federal personal income tax, we should have worked with the liability rather than cash collections in this instance also. However, the lack of data on liabilities for state personal income taxes, even on an annual basis, prevented us from doing so. Since data for the weighted average rate were available only on an annual basis, the equation was estimated on an annual basis and then quarterly income figures were substituted to obtain quarterly tax payments. The independent variables were lagged one year because, in many states, income taxes paid in one year are those for the preceding calendar year.

Identity (16) defines disposable personal income. It differs from the one used by OBE in that federal personal income is treated on a liability basis rather than on a cash collection basis. This change was made because the quarterly cash collection of the federal personal income tax is exceedingly complex, and also because there is some evidence suggesting that the income concept defined on a

[29] Joseph A. Pechman, "Individual Income Tax Provisions of the Revenue Act of 1964," *Journal of Finance*, Vol. 20 (May 1965).

[30] Ando and Brown, in this volume.

liability basis explains consumer expenditure as well as, if not better than, the income concept defined on a cash collection basis.[31]

Equation (17) explains taxable income for the federal personal income tax. The rationale for this equation was discussed extensively by Brown and Kruizenga, and it was tested again by Ando and Brown.[32] The estimate here was based on annual data, and quarterly income was then substituted in the equation to obtain quarterly taxable income. This equation, together with identity (14), gives the federal personal income tax liability.

Equations estimated on an annual basis—(10), (11), (15), and (17)—were not incorporated into the two-stage estimation procedure; therefore, the estimates reported here are the results of ordinary least squares estimation. In addition, equations (9) and (12) were estimated by ordinary least squares procedure.

Identity (18) gives corporate tax liability, both federal and state, as the product of the effective tax rate and corporate profits. The effective rate was computed through this identity for the past. Since the effective rate appears to be very stable, given the statutory rates, it is fairly easy to predict the change in the effective rate corresponding to any reasonable contemplated change in statutory rates.

Equations (23) through (32) explain the public's demand for financial assets. The estimated equations for currency (23), demand deposits (24), and time deposits (27) are all of the same basic form, i.e., the flow of the asset depends on the lagged stock, some measure of income, and various interest rates entered multiplicatively with GNP.[33] The currency equation includes, for example, GNP and the Treasury bill rate times GNP. It also includes the percentage rate of change of prices on the grounds that the more prices are increasing, the less attractive are assets whose values are fixed in monetary terms.[34] Since the variable has the dimensions of an in-

---

[31] *Ibid.*

[32] E. Cary Brown and R. J. Kruizenga, "Income Sensitivity of a Simple Personal Income Tax," *Review of Economics and Statistics*, Vol. 41 (August 1959); also Ando and Brown in this volume.

[33] For a rationale for this multiplicative form, see Goldfeld, *Commercial Bank Behavior*. We might also note that multiplicative seasonals were tried in equation (24); but as they worked no better than the linear variables, we retained the simpler form.

[34] The same variable did not prove important in the equations for demand deposits or time deposits. This variable was also utilized in T. C. Liu, "An Exploratory Quarterly Econo-

terest rate, it was introduced multiplicatively with Y. Finally, the currency equation includes a weighted GNP variable analogous to the one utilized by deLeeuw.[35] It can be interpreted as a measure of expected or normal income, and its apparently puzzling negative coefficient can be explained if the two income coefficients are written as follows:

$$.077Y - .072\overline{Y} = .077(Y - \overline{Y}) + .005\overline{Y}.$$

The variable $(Y - \overline{Y})$ represents unexpected income and hence equation (23) implies a positive response to both unexpected and expected income.

The equations for demand and time deposits follow the same basic framework. In particular, demand deposits respond negatively to the Treasury bill rate and the yield on time deposits, while time deposits respond negatively to the long-term government bond rate and positively to the time-deposit yield. It should be noted that, if the bill rate, instead of r_{10}, is used in the time deposit equation, a significant negative coefficient is obtained. The final choice was somewhat arbitrary and rested on the finding of a slightly better fit when the long-term rate was used. A similar choice resulted in the inclusion of the weighted GNP variable, $\overline{Y}$, instead of Y, in the time deposit equation. On the whole, then, both money and time deposits appear to be significantly interest elastic. Furthermore, the interest and income elasticities are different for currency and demand deposits, suggesting that disaggregation of money demand is a reasonable procedure.

Commercial loans held by the public are the last financial asset represented in the model. Unfortunately, the market for commercial loans does not fit simply into a standard demand-supply formulation. The literature abounds with discussions of credit rationing as a source of imperfection in the loan market. In addition, various writers have emphasized the importance of nonprice elements and have cast doubt on the relevance of the reported loan rate as an indicator of market conditions.[36] The position adopted in

metric Model of Effective Demand in the Postwar U. S. Economy," *Econometrica*, Vol. 31 (July 1963).

[35] Frank deLeeuw, "A Model of Financial Behavior," in *Brookings Quarterly Econometric Model*.

[36] See discussion in Goldfeld, *Commercial Bank Behavior*.

this paper, while not fully satisfactory, does attempt to take account of these problems. First, the possibility of credit rationing is reflected by the inclusion of ΔCL as a variable in each investment equation. Next, on the demand side, it is assumed that the demand for commercial loans is a function of business needs for funds, the relative cost of loans, and a variable which hopefully captures some of the nonprice effects. In equation (30), the demand for commercial loans is explained by the lagged stock of loans, the volume of inventory investment, the differential of the loan rate over the bill rate, and D^*, a potential deposit variable.[37] Other types of investment were tried but they did not materially add to the explanation of ΔCL. The dominant role for inventory investment is in accord with much of the literature.[38] The coefficient of the cost variable implies that the demand for loans depends negatively on the price of loans and positively on the price of an alternative source of finance. The potential deposit variable is itself a function of open-market operations and can be interpreted as reflecting an availability effect. Thus a fall in D^*, given other money market conditions, may be thought of as indicating a tighter monetary policy and stronger nonprice rationing, and through the relationships expressed in equation (30) will result in a lower volume of commercial loans.

These equations describing the public's demand for financial assets refer to total volumes held at all commercial banks. Since our bank behavior equations require that these assets be disaggregated according to the classes of banks issuing them, it is necessary to distribute them among classes of commercial banks. Some thought was given to making endogenous the distribution of these assets between country and noncountry banks and member and nonmember banks. However, some pilot calculations suggested that this would be a rather difficult task.[39] Consequently, in equations

---

[37] D^* is defined by equation (45), and discussed below.

[38] See references cited in Goldfeld, *Commercial Bank Behavior*.

[39] For example,

$$(DT^N + DT^C)/DT = \gamma_6 = .810 + .0091S_2 + .0083S_3 + .0176S_4 - .0021r_s$$
$$(.0036)\quad (.0038)\quad (.0059)\quad (.0011)$$

$$- .0020\Delta D^* + .0148d_3$$
$$(.0009)\quad\quad (.0022)$$

$$R^2 = .38.$$

(25), (26), (28), (29), (31), and (32), the γ's are taken as exogenous variables.

Equations (21), (22), and (34) through (43) describe the behavior of commercial banks. The emphais is on commercial banks' attitudes toward holdings of assets and liabilities, and toward the setting of time deposit and commercial loan rates. These equations, together with a few identities discussed below, define the supply conditions of the financial assets for which demand conditions have been discussed above.

These equations, with one exception, are simply updated versions of some earlier work,[40] and all are based on a set of simple assumptions. First, it is assumed that in each period banks partially adjust their portfolios to a desired portfolio which in turn depends on the yields on all bank assets. In addition, flows of deposits, reserves, and commercial loans are taken as constraints on bank portfolio adjustments.[41] For demand deposits and reserves the assumption seems straightforward, but for time deposits and commercial loans the situation is less clear. For time deposits, as a first approximation, we conceive of banks as setting a rate and accepting deposits at that rate. While this view was probably appropriate prior to 1962, the development of the certificate of deposit (C of D) market has undoubtedly changed the situation.[42] Ideally, one could separate out this market and adjust the bank equations accordingly. Data limitations, however, prevented us from doing this and, as a result, we attempted to deal with the problem by the use of dummy variables in equations (21), (22), (38), (39), (42), and (43).

This suggests, reasonably enough, that member banks had more time deposits relative to nonmembers after the certificate-of-deposit market emerged and the easier was monetary policy. For the other γ's, however, no equation as satisfactory as this was found.

[40] See Goldfeld, *Commercial Bank Behavior*. One focus of this earlier study was the behavioral differences among classes of banks. Although, in the present study, we are not concerned with this aspect, we have retained the same classification, for purposes of comparison.

[41] By constraint, we mean that the bank equations have as explanatory variables the change in deposits, loans, etc. For a more detailed discussion of all these assumptions see deLeeuw, in *Brookings Quarterly Econometric Model* and Goldfeld, *Commercial Bank Behavior*.

[42] For a description of the market for negotiable certificates of deposits, see R. C. Fieldhouse, "Certificates of Deposit," in Federal Reserve Bank of New York, *Essays in Money and Credit* (1964).

The proper treatment of commercial loans is even more problematical. What we would have liked to assume is that there exists a
category of bank "customers" whose loan requests are necessarily
serviced and to whom banks feel committed. As the concept of a
"customer" is unobservable at the aggregate level, the only reasonable alternative was to assume that banks view the entire volume
of commercial loans largely as a constraint. It was not assumed
that banks supply a given quantity of loans, but, rather, that they
set a loan rate which is gradually adjusted toward an optimum
(given demand conditions). This, it is recognized, does not adequately cope with the problem of credit rationing. However, as
nonprice effects are allowed for on the demand side, this seems to
be a reasonable first approximation.

The actual results show that bank holdings of excess reserves—
equations (34) and (35)—depend on the opportunity cost of holding
these reserves (taken to be the yield on Treasury bills), the rate of
injection of new reserves, and the reserve-requirement ratios. These
last two were combined in D^*, the potential deposit variable, but,
in addition, reserve requirement variables were tried directly in
the form of q^N and q^C.[43] Only the latter proved to be significant.
Finally, the city-bank equation for excess reserves contains a dummy variable which is designed to take account of the influence of the
Treasury-Federal Reserve accord.[44]

Equations (36) and (37), the equations for borrowings, are of
the same form as equations (34) and (35), with the addition of the
discount rate and an excess-profits tax dummy as explanatory variables.[45]

In addition to the variables mentioned earlier, the equations for
short- and long-term securities—(38), (39), (40), and (41)—include
$\Delta\bar{S}$ and $\Delta\bar{O}$, the total supply of government debt (in private hands)
with maturity of 0–5 years and more than 5 years, respectively.
The purpose of these variables is to take account of the timing
problems created by the arbitrary choice of a dividing line between
short- and long-term securities. Aside from the flow constraint

---

[43] See identities (46) and (47).

[44] For a more complete discussion, see Goldfeld, *Commercial Bank Behavior*.

[45] The excess-profits tax during the Korean war made it profitable for banks to borrow
funds even if they did not use them. As a result, borrowing expanded greatly in that period.
Ibid.

variables, the equations for S^N and S^C include the reserve-requirement variables and a dummy variable to deal with problems created by the C of D market. It should be mentioned that no interest rate effects were discernible in the equations for short-term securities. They were, however, important in the equations for long-term securities.

The equations for bank holdings of municipal securities—(42) and (43)—include the total supply of municipals; it was believed that this would allow for certain nonprice effects (e.g., community relations) entering into bank decisions. In these equations, the flows of time deposits appear to be particularly important variables. In keeping with this, there seems to have been a marked increase in the volume of municipals held after the emergence of the C of D market. This is reflected in the significant coefficient of the dummy variable d_3, in both country and city bank equations.[46]

As for the two rates determined by the banks, r_t and r_e, both are explained by a partial-adjustment model and both were affected to a considerable extent by the emergence of the C of D market. The rate on commercial loans—equation (21)—depends on the lagged rate, the quantity of commercial loans (in the form of a loan-deposit ratio), and the Treasury bill rate. The last variable is included with various lags to take account of the lag in response of the loan market to changing money-market conditions. Finally, the equation includes the C of D dummy variable, d_4, which obtains a significant negative coefficient. This, sensibly enough, suggests that

---

[46] Put another way, the emergence of the C of D market reduced the need for short-term securities for liquidity purposes and, consequently, the released funds have been channeled, in part, into increased municipal holdings. It will be observed that no interest rate variables appear in the municipal equations. Various attempts were made to include one or more such variables but none proved completely satisfactory. For example, let r_m be the yield on municipals; then

$$\Delta MUN^C = \text{seasonals} - .011 MUN^C_{-1} + .019 \overline{\Delta MUN} + .220 \Delta T^C$$
$$\phantom{\Delta MUN^C = \text{seasonals}} (.018) \phantom{MUN^C_{-1}} (.009) \phantom{\overline{\Delta MUN}} (.072)$$

$$+ .101 \Delta D^C + .180 d_3 + .134 r_m - .151 r_e$$
$$(.035) (.058) (.058) (.064)$$

$$R^2 = .677$$

While at first glance this appears all right, in that it has two significant interest rate coefficients, the R^2 including the interest rates is considerably lower than the R^2 excluding them (.758). This suggestion of statistical difficulties in the context of a simultaneous equations system led us to use the simpler formulation.

as the C of D market grew (d_4 increased gradually from zero in 1961-I) there was less pressure on the loan rate to increase, since banks had a new source of loanable funds.

The equation for the yield on time deposits, (22), is an adaptation of the one presented by deLeeuw.[47] The variable r_t is available on only an annual basis; hence, equation (22) was estimated with only 15 observations. It differs from deLeeuw's formulation by the addition of ΔD^* and the dummy variable d_5. The former obtains a negative coefficient, which implies that a tighter monetary policy will force the banks to raise r_t by a greater amount. The significance of the d_5 variable is undoubtedly connected with the C of D market. Its negative coefficient suggests that r_t increased by less than it would have if the C of D market had not emerged. As the development of the C of D market enabled banks to capture some funds which previously would have been earmarked for the short-term security market, this seems to be a reasonable finding.

In addition to these estimated equations, five identities relate to the commercial banking sector: (33) defines the loan-deposit ratio; (44) indicates the distribution of required reserves; and (46) and (47) define the changes in the average required reserve ratios for the two classes of banks.[48] The variable D^* is defined by (45); it represents the maximum amount of demand deposits which could be held at member banks, given the volume of unborrowed reserves and the time deposit "drain."

The banking sector plays a number of important roles in the linkage between the monetary and real sectors. For one, given the volume of reserves supplied by the Federal Reserve, the decisions of the banks with respect to their holdings of excess and borrowed reserves serve, in part, to make the money supply an interest-elastic endogenous variable.[49] Second, the bank loan rate is a determinant in the demand function for commercial loans and thus

[47] In *Brookings Quarterly Econometric Model.*

[48] For the earlier years of the sample period, the Federal Reserve made a distinction between the two classes of banks—Reserve City and Central Reserve City. The reserve requirement on demand deposits differed for the two classes. This was taken into account in constructing q^N, q^C, and D^*; but since the distinction has now been abandoned, we present the equations in their simpler form.

[49] Although there is no explicit money supply equation in our model, the set of equations (19), (25), (26), (28), (29), and (44) does imply such a relation. For an example of an explicit derivation, see deLeeuw, in *Brookings Quarterly Econometric Model,* and Goldfeld, *Commercial Bank Behavior.*

feeds back to investment expenditures. Finally, the time deposit rate is an important element in the equilibration of the money market, which likewise feeds back into the real sector.

In this connection, one other feature of both the earlier and the present model should be noted. While we have equations explaining bank holdings of short-term, long-term, and municipal securities, the impacts of these decisions are not reflected elsewhere in the model.[50] This results from the elimination of the bank balance-sheet identity (and the residual asset items) from the model. A more desirable procedure might be to utilize the balance-sheet identity directly in the estimation of the model.[51]

Of the remaining four equations, two are in the nature of market equilibrium conditions, one explains the formation of prices, and the fourth defines the capacity utilization rate. Equation (20) explains the term structure of interest rates. Theoretically, we should have specified demand functions for both short- and long-term securities, equated demand to supply, and thus determined the relevant rates of interest. This task was clearly beyond our scope and we relied instead on a term-structure equation.[52] The form of the equation essentially follows the work of Modigliani and Sutch,[53] who argue that the differential of the long-term rate over the bill rate should depend on the bill rate and past values of the long-term rate. We estimated the dependence on the lagged values of r_{10} in a rather simple way, but the fit appears to be reasonable.

Equation (19) is the open-market equilibrium condition which indicates that Federal Reserve credit (Z) must be exactly exhausted by required reserves, excess and borrowed reserves, and currency.

---

[50] In more technical language, the model can be put in block recursive form with two blocks, the second containing the six equations for S^N, S^C, O^N, O^C, MUN^N, and MUN^C. These six equations, of course, do contain useful information. For example, they indicate how banks have financed the expansion of commercial loans.

[51] We are informed by deLeeuw that he is currently attacking a related problem along these lines. There is another way in which bank security decisions could feed back to the rest of the model. For example, demand functions for all groups that hold government securities could be estimated, and the sum of these demands could be equated to (an exogenous) supply. This would determine the interest rates on government securities, incidentally eliminating the need for a term-structure equation, and would allow bank behavior to influence interest rates directly.

[52] See the preceding footnote.

[53] Franco Modigliani and R. Sutch, "Innovations in Interest Rate Policy," in *American Economic Review*, Vol. 56 (May 1966).

We treated Z, the sum of unborrowed reserves and currency, as an exogenous policy variable.[54]

The price equation, (49), is a rather poor-fitting first approximation, but it produces coefficients with sensible interpretations. In particular, prices will rise by greater amount, the closer is actual output to full capacity output, the more expansive is monetary policy, and the greater is the change in unfilled orders. This equation is minimally satisfactory; more work is clearly called for to improve the price relationships in the model.

The last equation, (50), defines the capacity utilization rate used in this model. Y^*, real potential maximum output, was constructed by fitting a trend through seasonally adjusted GNP in 1958 dollars for the two quarters (fourth quarter, 1955, and first quarter, 1966) for which the Wharton School capacity utilization index was a maximum. These quarters were used as bench marks to interpolate and extrapolate linearly in logarithms. Given the values of Y^*, the definition of K is self-evident. We used this definition of K, rather than the Wharton index, primarily because, if we did not do so, we had to introduce an equally *ad hoc* explanatory equation for the Wharton index. We chose our procedure as the lesser and simpler of two evils.

Endogenous Variables[55]

1. Y GNP
2. CN Nondurable consumption expenditure
3. CD Durable consumption expenditure
4. $F1$ Gross investment in plant and equipment
5. $F2$ Gross private domestic investment less $F1$ less ΔH
6. ΔH Change in inventory stock
7. V Dividends
8. π Corporate profits plus inventory valuation adjustment
9. TI Indirect business taxes (other than property tax)

---

[54] See deLeeuw in *Brookings Quarterly Econometric Model*, and Goldfeld, *Commercial Bank Behavior*. A more careful examination of the Federal Reserve policy-making process might make untenable our assumption of the exogeneity of Z.

[55] All flow variables are in billions of current dollars (quarterly totals, not annual rates, unless otherwise stated). Interest rates are in percentages, and tax rates are in actual fractions. The endogenous variables are numbered and ordered so that their order of appearance in this list corresponds, as far as possible, to the order of equations explaining these variables.

10. TO Contribution to Old Age and Survivors Insurance (liability)
11. TU Contribution to unemployment insurance (liability)
12. TB Unemployment insurance benefits
13. YP Personal income
14. TFP Federal personal income tax liability
15. TSP State personal income tax
16. YD Disposable personal income
17. TY Taxable income (for federal personal income tax)
18. TC Corporate profit tax liability
19. r_s Interest rate on 3-month Treasury bills
20. r_{10} Interest rate on 10-year government bonds
21. r_e Interest rate on commercial and industrial loans at commercial banks
22. r_t Interest rate on time deposits at commercial banks
23. DR Currency outside banks
24. DD Demand deposits adjusted
25. DD^N Net demand deposits at city banks
26. DD^C Net demand deposits at country banks
27. DT Time deposits at commercial banks
28. DT^N Time deposits at city banks
29. DT^C Time deposits at country banks
30. CL Commercial and industrial loans by commercial banks
31. CL^N Commercial and industrial loans by city banks
32. CL^C Commercial and industrial loans by country banks
33. CL^* Loan-deposit ratio (including savings deposits)
34. E^N Excess reserves of city banks
35. E^C Excess reserves of country banks
36. B^N Borrowings of city banks from Federal Reserve Banks
37. B^C Borrowings of country banks from Federal Reserve Banks
38. S^N Short-term government security holdings of city banks
39. S^C Short-term government security holdings of country banks
40. O^N Long-term government security holdings of city banks
41. O^C Long-term government security holdings of country banks
42. MUN^N Municipal security holdings of city banks
43. MUN^C Municipal security holdings of country banks

44. R^R Required reserves

45. D^* Potential demand deposits

46. q^N Change in the average required reserve ratio (city banks)

47. q^C Change in the average required reserve ratio (country banks)

48. EM Employment, in millions

49. P GNP deflator, 1958 = 1.00

50. K Ratio of actual GNP to full employment GNP, $1966 - I = 1$

Exogenous Variables[56]

1. A_1 Capital consumption allowance + indirect business taxes other than excise taxes − government transfer payments other than unemployment insurance + contributions to social insurance other than OASI and unemployment insurance − subsidies less current surplus of government − interest paid by government and consumers

2. A_2 Federal personal taxes other than income taxes plus state and local personal taxes other than income taxes

3. COV Ratio of covered employment to total labor force under state unemployment insurance system

4. d_1 Dummy variable: 1 from third quarter 1950 to second quarter 1953; 0 otherwise

5. d_2 Dummy variable: 1 in third and fourth quarter of 1952; 0 otherwise

6. d_3 Dummy variable: 1 from first quarter 1962 to fourth quarter 1964; 0 otherwise

7. d_4 Dummy variable: 0 from third quarter 1950 to first quarter 1961; subsequently it is the ratio of negotiable certificates of deposit of New York City banks to the sum of DD^N and DT^N

8. d_5 Dummy variable, annual: 0 from 1950–62; 1 from 1963–64

---

[56] Arranged alphabetically.

9. EX Per capita exemption for federal personal income tax computation, in hundreds of current dollars

10. G Government expenditure (federal, state and local) and net exports

11. k_1 Required reserve ratio for demand deposits of member banks in reserve cities

12. k_3 Required reserve ratio for demand deposits of country member banks

13. k_4 Required reserve ratio for time deposits of member banks

14. L Labor force, in millions

15. $\Delta \overline{MUN}$ Change in supply of municipal securities

16. $\Delta \overline{O}$ Change in supply of long-term government securities

17. Pop Population, in millions

18. r_d Federal Reserve rediscount rate

19. r_{max} Regulation Q maximum on time deposit rates

20. ρ_c Effective rate of federal corporate tax

21. ρ_{fp} Effective rate of federal personal income taxes

22. ρ_i Indirect business tax rate

23. ρ_o OASI contribution rate

24. ρ_{sp} Index of state and local personal income tax rates, $1950 = 1.00$

25. ρ_u Unemployment insurance contribution rate

26. $\Delta \overline{S}$ Change in supply of short-term government securities

27. S_i Seasonal dummies: 1 in ith quarter; 0 otherwise

28. UO Unfilled orders, in billions of current dollars

29. W Net worth of households, in billions of current dollars

30. WB Weekly maximum benefits of unemployment insurance in current dollars

31. X_1 1 for 1947, '48, '49; 0 otherwise

32. X_2 1 for 1950; 0 otherwise

33. X_3 1 for 1951, '52, '53; 0 otherwise

34. X_4 1 for 1954; 0 otherwise

    (These X's represent changes in coverage of OASI program)

35. Y^* Full employment GNP

36. Z Federal Reserve credit (unborrowed reserves + currency)

Estimated Equations and Identities[57]

1. Components of Gross National Product

$$Y = CN + CD + F1 + F2 + \Delta H + G$$

2. Nondurable Consumption Expenditure (real)

$$CN = -3.49 + 6.27S_2 + 4.42S_3 + 8.61S_4 + .207YD$$
$$ (.79) \quad\;\; (.67) \quad\; (1.08) \quad\;\; (.060)$$
$$+ .647CN_{-1} + .0027W$$
$$ (.096) \qquad\quad (.0013)$$
$$R^2 = .997 \qquad DW = 2.70 \qquad S_e = .44$$

3. Durable Consumption Expenditure (real)

$$CD = -8.04 + 2.14S_2 + .85S_3 + 2.29S_4 + .074YD$$
$$ (.39) \quad\;\; (.30) \quad\;\; (.51) \quad\;\; (.018)$$
$$+ .462CD_{-1} + .140\Delta Y^s + .044(DD + DR)$$
$$ (.117) \qquad\quad (.080) \qquad\;\; (.027)$$
$$R^2 = .873 \qquad DW = 2.36 \qquad S_e = .62$$

4. Investment in Plant and Equipment (real)

$$F1 = -.424 + .314S_2(F1)_{-1} + .166S_3(F1)_{-1}$$
$$ (.023) \qquad\qquad (.016)$$

$$+ .246S_4(F1)_{-1} + .625(F1)_{-1} - .032\left(\frac{Y}{K} - Y_{-1}\right)$$
$$ (.028) \qquad\qquad (.059) \qquad\qquad (.010)$$

$$+ .022Y + .209\Delta CL - .157\left[\frac{\sum_{i=1}^{10}(r_s)_{t-i}}{10}\right]$$
$$ (.007) \quad\; (.053) \qquad\;\; (.121)$$
$$R^2 = .971 \qquad DW = 1.93 \qquad S_e = .19$$

5. Investment, Other Than Plant and Equipment, and Change in Inventory (real)

$$F2 = -1.65 + 1.89S_2 + 1.48S_3 + .20S_4 + .629(F2)_{-1}$$
$$ (.34) \quad\;\; (.20) \quad\;\; (.30) \quad\;\; (.124)$$

[57] All stock variables are in billions of current dollars, and all flow variables are in billions of current dollars—quarterly totals, not annual rates, except in those equations which are marked "real." In the latter cases, variables are individually deflated by P of the corresponding period [e.g., real $\Delta X = (X/P - X_{-1}/P_{-1})$]. Superscript "$s$" denotes seasonally adjusted values.

$$+ .038Y - .0027(r_s Y) + .349\Delta CL$$
$$(.013) \quad (.0012) \quad (.168)$$
$$R^2 = .887 \quad DW = 1.06 \quad S_e = .453$$

6. Inventory Investment (real)

$$\Delta H = -6.137 + 2.790S_2 + 1.530S_3 + 3.987S_4$$
$$(1.184) \quad (.904) \quad (1.392)$$
$$- .070H_{-1} + .133\Delta UO_{-1} + .019(Y - \Delta H)$$
$$(.045) \quad (.025) \quad (.013)$$
$$+ 5.87K - .237\Delta(Y - \Delta H) + .392\Delta CL$$
$$(3.61) \quad (.073) \quad (.195)$$

$$R^2 = .799 \quad DW = 2.17 \quad S_e = .52$$

7. Dividends

$$V^s = .169(\pi^s - TC^s) + .709V^s_{-1} - .233$$
$$(.044) \quad (.073) \quad (.167)$$
$$R^2 = .88 \quad DW = 2.7 \quad S_e = .28$$

8. Corporate Profits Including Inventory Valuation Adjustment

$$\pi^s = .350Y^s - .331Y^s_{-1} + .702\pi^s_{-1} + 1.058$$
$$(.050) \quad (.043) \quad (.066) \quad (.389)$$
$$R^2 = .93 \quad DW = 2.3 \quad S_e = .63$$

9. Indirect Business Taxes

$$\ln TI = .863 \ln (CN + CD) + .768 \ln \rho_i + .097S_2$$
$$(.043) \quad (.222) \quad (.027)$$
$$- .114S_3 + .320S_4 - 3.508$$
$$(.031) \quad (.032) \quad (.308)$$
$$R^2 = .98 \quad DW = 2.0 \quad S_e = .039$$

10. OASI Contribution Liability

$$\ln TO = \ln \rho_0 + .937 \ln YP - .283X_1 - .297X_2$$
$$(.061) \quad (.044) \quad (.044)$$
$$- .120X_3 - .130X_4 - .382$$
$$(.028) \quad (.034) \quad (.364)$$
$$R^2 = .995 \quad DW = 1.82 \quad S_e = .028$$

11. Unemployment Insurance Contribution Liability

$$\ln TU = \ln \rho_u + .572 \ln YP + .826 \ln COV + 1.207$$
$$\qquad\qquad (.039) \qquad\quad (.282) \qquad\qquad (.368)$$
$$R^2 = .99 \qquad DW = 1.54 \qquad S_e = .018$$

12. Unemployment Insurance Benefits

$$\ln TB = .241 \ln WB + .441 \ln (L - EM) + .544 \ln TB_{-1}$$
$$\quad (.113) \qquad\qquad (.104) \qquad\qquad\qquad (.088)$$
$$- .374 S_2 - .415 S_3 - .326 S_4 - 1.458$$
$$\quad (.068) \quad\ (.062) \quad\ (.058) \quad\ (.505)$$
$$R^2 = .93 \qquad DW = .94 \qquad S_e = .143$$

13. Relation Between GNP and Personal Income

$$YP = Y - TI - \pi - TO - TU + V + TB - A_1$$

14. Federal Personal Income Tax Liability

$$TFP = \rho_{fp} \cdot TY$$

15. State Personal Income Taxes

$$\ln TSP = .531 \ln \rho_{sp, -4} + 1.679 \ln YP_{-4} - 4.858$$
$$\qquad\ (.306) \qquad\qquad (.195) \qquad\qquad (.979)$$
$$R^2 = .95 \qquad DW = .99 \qquad S_e = .091$$

16. Relation Between Personal Income and Disposable Income

$$YD = YP - TFP - TSP - A_2$$

17. Taxable Income for Federal Personal Income Tax

$$\ln \left(1 - \frac{TY}{YP}\right) = -.310 \ln \frac{4YP}{Pop} + .330 \ln EX - .943$$
$$\qquad\qquad\qquad\quad (.017) \qquad\quad (.049) \qquad\qquad (.087)$$
$$R^2 = .96 \qquad DW = 2.06 \qquad S_e = .011$$

18. Corporate Profit Tax Liability

$$TC = \rho_c \pi$$

19. Uses of Federal Reserve Credit

$$R^R + E^N + E^C - B^N - B^C + DR = Z$$

20. Differential of Long-Term and Short-Term Interest Rates

$$r_{10} - r_s = .431 - .172(r_d - r_s)$$
$$(.107)$$

$$+ .379 \frac{\sum\limits_{i=1}^{5} (r_{10})_{-i}}{5} + 1.130 \frac{\sum\limits_{i=1}^{10} (r_{10})_{-i}}{10}$$
$$(.173)$$

$$- .749 \frac{\sum\limits_{i=1}^{15} (r_{10})_{-i}}{15} - .807r_s$$
$$(.242) \qquad\qquad (.045)$$

$$R^2 = .939 \qquad DW = 1.42 \qquad S_e = .13$$

21. Commercial Loan Rate

$$\Delta r_e = - .161 - .350(r_e)_{-1} + 7.01CL^* + .092\Delta r_s$$
$$(.074) \qquad (1.39) \qquad (.032)$$

$$+ .063(\Delta r_s)_{-1} - 4.69d_4 + .082 \left[\frac{\sum\limits_{i=1}^{10} (r_s)_{-i}}{10} \right]$$
$$(.029) \qquad (1.42) \qquad (.040)$$

$$R^2 = .612 \qquad DW = 1.44 \qquad S_e = .081$$

22. Rate on Time Deposits

$$\Delta r_t = - .312 - .059(r_t)_{-1} + .065r_{10} - .100(r_{10} - r_{max})$$
$$(.025) \qquad (.041) \qquad (.022)$$

$$+ 1.310CL^*_{-1} - .070d_5 - .028\Delta D^*$$
$$(.325) \qquad (.020) \qquad (.019)$$

$$R^2 = .828 \qquad DW = 2.41 \qquad S_e = .056$$

23. Demand for Currency

$$\Delta DR = - .815 + .026(S_2 DR_{-1}) + .027(S_3 DR_{-1})$$
$$(.003) \qquad\qquad (.003)$$

$$+ .028(S_4 DR_{-1}) - .007(DR_{-1}) + .077Y$$
$$(.005) \qquad\qquad (.031) \qquad (.012)$$

$$- .072\overline{Y} - .0009(r_s Y) - .199 \left(\frac{\Delta P}{P} Y \right)$$
$$(.012) \qquad (.0004) \qquad (.080)$$

$$R^2 = .940 \qquad DW = 1.82 \qquad S_e = .15$$

24. Demand for Demand Deposits

$$\Delta DD = 3.587 + 2.476S_2 + 3.516S_3 + 6.355S_4 - .207DD_{-1}$$
$$(.733) \qquad (.710) \qquad (1.190) \qquad (.089)$$
$$+ .193Y - .0063(r_s Y) - .014(r_t Y)$$
$$ (.096) \quad (.0021) \qquad (.011)$$
$$R^2 = .923 \qquad DW = 1.36 \qquad S_e = .90$$

25. Distribution of Demand Deposits Between Classes of Member Banks

$$\frac{DD^N}{DD^C} = \gamma_2$$

26. Distribution of Demand Deposits Between Member and Non-member Banks

$$DD^N + DD^C = \gamma_5 DD$$

27. Demand for Time Deposits

$$\Delta DT = .256 - .0098(S_2 DT_{-1}) - .0165(S_3 DT_{-1})$$
$$(.0039) \qquad\qquad (.0039)$$
$$- .0200(S_4 DT_{-1}) - .025DT_{-1} + .045\overline{Y}$$
$$ (.0041) \qquad\qquad (.023) \qquad (.024)$$
$$+ .025(r_t Y) - .019(r_{10} Y)$$
$$ (.006) \qquad (.004)$$
$$R^2 = .791 \qquad DW = 1.77 \qquad S_e = .68$$

28. Distribution of Time Deposits Between Classes of Member Banks

$$\frac{DT^N}{DT^C} = \gamma_3$$

29. Distribution of Time Deposits Between Member and Non-member Banks

$$DT^N + DT^C = \gamma_6 DT$$

30. Demand for Commercial and Industrial Loans

$$\Delta CL = -7.480 + 1.67S_2 + 1.42S_3 + 2.20S_4$$
$$(.36) \qquad (.37) \qquad (.52)$$

$$- .040CL_{-1} - .577(r_e - r_s) + .436\Delta H + .091D*$$
$$(.027) \qquad (.289) \qquad\quad (.112) \qquad (.047)$$
$$R^2 = .609 \qquad DW = 1.91 \qquad S_e = .57$$

31. Distribution of Commercial Loans Between Member and Non-member Banks

$$CL^N + CL^C = \gamma_1 CL$$

32. Distribution of Commercial Loans Between Classes of Member Banks

$$\frac{CL^N}{CL^C} = \gamma_4$$

33. Definition of Loan-Deposit Ratio

$$CL* = \frac{CL^N + CL^C}{DD^N + DD^C + DT^N + DT^C}$$

34. Demand for Excess Reserves by City Banks

$$\Delta E^N = .134 + .049S_2 + .003S_3 + .025S_4$$
$$\qquad\quad (.031) \quad (.028) \quad (.041)$$
$$- 1.086E^N_{-1} - .00025r_s(DD^N + DT^N) + .116d_1$$
$$(.116) \qquad (.00007) \qquad\qquad\qquad\quad (.019)$$
$$+ .0044\Delta D* + .0083\Delta D*_{-1}$$
$$(.0066) \qquad (.0032)$$
$$R^2 = .672 \qquad DW = 2.22 \qquad S_e = .042$$

35. Demand for Excess Reserves by Country Banks

$$\Delta E^C = .205 + .024S_2 + .045S_3 + .022S_4$$
$$\qquad\quad (.029) \quad (.027) \quad (.047)$$
$$- .389E^C_{-1} - .00034r_s(DD^C + DT^C)$$
$$(.148) \qquad (.00015)$$
$$+ .0131\Delta D* + .0031\Delta D*_{-1} - 4.742q^C$$
$$(.0078) \qquad (.0026) \qquad\qquad (1.995)$$
$$R^2 = .610 \qquad DW = 2.09 \qquad S_e = .034$$

36. Borrowings by City Banks from Federal Reserve Banks

$$\Delta B^N = .201 + .147S_2 + .146S_3 - .301S_4 - .560B^N_{-1}$$
$$\qquad\quad (.100) \quad (.114) \quad (.175) \quad (.097)$$

$$- .237(r_d - r_s) + .308d_2 - .052\Delta D^* - .106\Delta DT^N$$
$$\quad (.118) \qquad\qquad (.121) \quad\quad (.027) \qquad\quad (.032)$$
$$R^2 = .562 \qquad DW = 2.31 \qquad S_e = .15$$

37. Borrowings by Country Banks from Federal Reserve Banks

$$\Delta B^C = .015 + .062S_2 + .007S_3 + .059S_4$$
$$\qquad\quad (.018) \quad\quad (.020) \quad\quad (.030)$$
$$- .247B^C_{-1} - .037(r_d - r_s) + .047d_2$$
$$\quad (.062) \qquad\quad (.018) \qquad\qquad (.022)$$
$$- .0088\Delta D^* - .017\Delta DT^C + 2.92q^C$$
$$\quad (.0048) \qquad\quad (.011) \qquad\quad (1.47)$$
$$R^2 = .613 \qquad DW = 2.36 \qquad S_e = .026$$

38. Holdings of Short-Term Government Securities by City Banks

$$\Delta S^N = 3.21 - 1.984S_2 - .813S_3 - 2.01S_4 - .139S^N_{-1}$$
$$\qquad\qquad (1.16) \quad\quad (.972) \quad\quad (1.60) \quad\quad (.052)$$
$$+ .089\Delta \bar{S} - .244\Delta \bar{O} + .767\Delta DD^N + .883\Delta DT^N$$
$$\quad (.076) \qquad (.087) \qquad\quad (.248) \qquad\qquad (.438)$$
$$- .833\Delta CL^N - 210.0q^N - 26.2d_4$$
$$\quad (.398) \qquad\qquad (60.64) \quad\; (33.9)$$
$$R^2 = .683 \qquad DW = 2.38 \qquad S_e = 1.15$$

39. Holdings of Short-Term Government Securities by Country Banks

$$\Delta S^C = .86 - .22S_2 + .25S_3 + .19S_4 - .101S^C_{-1}$$
$$\qquad\qquad (.38) \quad\; (.55) \quad\; (.60) \quad\; (.048)$$
$$+ .082\Delta \bar{S} - .114\Delta \bar{O} + .359\Delta DD^C$$
$$\quad (.041) \qquad (.046) \qquad\quad (.280)$$
$$+ 1.342\Delta DT^C - .263\Delta CL^C - 63.3q^C - 22.5d_4$$
$$\quad (.501) \qquad\qquad (.829) \qquad\quad (35.3) \quad\; (15.5)$$
$$R^2 = .733 \qquad DW = 2.28 \qquad S_e = .564$$

40. Holdings of Long-Term Government Securities by City Banks

$$\Delta O^N = - .543 + .422S_2 + .367S_3 + .660S_4 - .002O^N_{-1}$$
$$\qquad\qquad\quad (.225) \quad\quad (.242) \quad\quad (.259) \quad\quad (.023)$$
$$+ .180\Delta \bar{O} - .107\Delta \bar{S} + .239(r_{10} - r_s)$$
$$\quad (.037) \qquad (.034) \qquad\quad (.176)$$
$$R^2 = .786 \qquad DW = 1.90 \qquad S_e = .563$$

41. Holdings of Long-Term Government Securities by Country Banks

$$\Delta O^C = 0.314 + .385S_2 + .340S_3 + .561S_4 - .0100^C_{-1}$$
$$(.159) \quad (.146) \quad (.171) \quad (.023)$$
$$+ .111\Delta\bar{O} - .092\Delta\bar{S} - .483\Delta CL^C + .236(r_{10} - r_s)$$
$$(.022) \quad (.021) \quad (.319) \quad (.109)$$
$$R^2 = .848 \quad DW = 2.53 \quad S_e = .33$$

42. Holdings of Municipal Securities by City Banks

$$\Delta MUN^N = -.034 - .342S_2 - .061S_3 - .290S_4$$
$$(.070) \quad (.079) \quad (.068)$$
$$- .063MUN^N_{-1} + .078\Delta\overline{MUN} + .442d_3$$
$$(.018) \quad (.022) \quad (.131)$$
$$+ .138\Delta DT^N + .115\Delta DT^N_{-1} + .014S^N_{-1}$$
$$(.063) \quad (.044) \quad (.008)$$
$$R^2 = .776 \quad DW = 2.46 \quad S_e = .171$$

43. Holdings of Municipal Securities by Country Banks

$$\Delta MUN^C = .110 - .067S_2 - .108S_3 - .157S_4 - .016MUN^C_{-1}$$
$$(.038) \quad (.055) \quad (.060) \quad (.011)$$
$$+ .018\Delta\overline{MUN} + .147d_3 + .160\Delta DT^C + .081\Delta DD^C$$
$$(.007) \quad (.035) \quad (.064) \quad (.028)$$
$$R^2 = .758 \quad DW = 1.67 \quad S_e = .060$$

44. Distribution of Required Reserves

$$R^R = k_1 DD^N + k_3 DD^C + k_4(DT^N + DT^C)$$

45. Definition of Potential Demand Deposits

$$D^* = \frac{Z - DR - k_4(DT^N + DT^C)}{\dfrac{k_1 DD^N + k_3 DD^C}{DD^N + DD^C}}$$

46. Change in Required Reserve Ratio for City Banks

$$q^N = \Delta\left(\frac{k_1 DD^N + k_4 DT^N}{DD^N + DT^N}\right)$$

47. Change in Required Reserve Ratio for Country Banks

$$q^C = \Delta\left(\frac{k_3 DD^C + k_4 DT^C}{DD^C + DT^C}\right)$$

48. Employment (real)

$$EM = .067Y + .632EM_{-1} + .048(S_2 EM_{-1}) + .042(S_3 EM_{-1})$$
$$(.012) \quad (.065) \qquad (.004) \qquad\qquad (.002)$$
$$+ .007(S_4 EM_{-1}) + 14.716$$
$$(.002) \qquad\qquad (2.879)$$
$$R^2 = .99 \qquad DW = 1.41 \qquad S_e = .39$$

49. Rate of Change of GNP Implicit Deflator

$$\frac{\Delta P}{P_{-1}} = .015 - .00045 \left(\frac{Y}{KP} - \frac{Y_{-1}}{P_{-1}} \right) + .00027 \left(\frac{UO_{-1}}{P_{-1}} - \frac{UO_{-2}}{P_{-2}} \right)$$
$$\qquad\qquad (.00012) \qquad\qquad\qquad (.00017)$$
$$- .00016 \frac{UO_{-1}}{P_{-1}} + .254 \frac{\Delta P_{-1}}{P_{-2}} + .0014 \Delta D^*$$
$$(.00005) \qquad (.127) \qquad (.0004)$$
$$R^2 = .368 \qquad DW = 2.11 \qquad S_e = .004$$

50. Definition of Capacity Utilization Rate

$$K = \frac{Y^s}{Y * P}$$

Implications of the Stabilization Policies

As stated earlier, the primary purpose of the model presented here is to investigate in some detail the implications of various stabilization policies. Our view is that the model is too preliminary to conduct a detailed simulation analysis (a major undertaking because of the nonlinearity of the model), but that it contains enough meaningful economic content to warrant attention short of such an extensive analysis. As a compromise, "dynamic" multipliers were calculated and used for analyzing impacts of various policy measures.

The strategy was first to linearize the model by expanding each nonlinear term in the system by a Taylor's series around the average values for 1965 of all variables.[58] By use of the linearized model, the changes in the endogenous variables were computed for the four quarters of 1965, relative to their values in the fourth quarter, 1964, corresponding to various changes in monetary and fiscal policies instituted in the first quarter of 1965.[59] Implicit in this procedure was

---

[58] For complete details, see the Appendix.

[59] The multipliers on GNP and its components are expressed in money terms; see Appendix. Also, in the tables below the information is confined to the more interesting endogenous and exogenous variables.

the assumption that, for four quarters of 1965, all exogenous variables (except, of course, lagged endogenous variables and seasonal dummies) maintained the values which they actually took in the fourth quarter of 1964.

The most common (and major) policy measures will be discussed first. They are (1) changes in government expenditure, G; (2) changes in the effective rate of federal personal income taxes, ρ_{fp}; (3) changes by the Federal Reserve System in the reserve base, Z, or open market operations of the traditional type; and (4) changes in the required reserve ratios, k_1 and k_3. For purposes of presentation of the tables in this section, the units of the reserve requirement ratios, the tax rates, and the unemployment insurance coverage were adjusted to percentages.

The summary of responses to changes in federal government expenditure is given in Table 1A (p. 263). To illustrate clearly the proper interpretation of this and the other multiplier tables, let us examine portions of Table 1A with some care. Two rows, corresponding to Y and TFP, respectively, in that table, are reproduced below, in billions of dollars:

	First quarter	Second quarter	Third quarter	Fourth quarter	Cumulated change
Y	1.000	0.711	0.346	0.272	2.329
TFP	0.079	0.066	0.042	0.035	0.223

The policy we shall consider is an increase in G of $1 billion in the first quarter of 1965 (relative to the fourth quarter of 1964), with G being maintained at this new level thereafter.[60] The first row (Y) above indicates that in the first quarter GNP increases by $1 billion and that in the second quarter there is a further increase of $0.711 billion. This latter increase is relative to the first quarter of 1965 so that to obtain the increase relative to the fourth quarter of 1964 the two changes must be added together. These cumulated changes are as follows, in billions of dollars:

	First quarter	Second quarter	Third quarter	Fourth quarter	Average quarterly change
Y	1.000	1.711	2.057	2.329	1.774
TFP	0.079	0.145	0.187	0.223	0.159

[60] The tables are set up so that a $1 billion increase or a change of 1 percentage point can be read easily. Actually, the impact of a change in G in either direction and of any amount can be computed by simply adjusting the appropriate elements in the table. Because of the linearization, however, the results may be unreliable for large changes.

Thus, by the fourth quarter of 1965, GNP increases by $2.329 billion over its value in the fourth quarter of 1964. However, it should be emphasized that this is not the average quarterly change. That figure is $1.774 billion, as shown above. This is the number that would be recorded by national income statisticians.

Similar comments apply to the entries for TFP (federal personal income tax liability). The increase in G increases TFP by $79 million in the first quarter and by an additional $66 million in the second quarter. Hence, in the second quarter the government is collecting $145 million more than it was in the fourth quarter of 1964. For the year as a whole, the government collects, on the average for each quarter, $159 million more than it did in the fourth quarter of 1964.

As already noted, GNP in money terms increases by $1 billion in the first quarter, so that with G increasing by $1 billion gross private domestic demand remains unchanged. This does not mean, however, that all components of GNP other than government expenditure remain constant, The entries immediately below GNP (or Y) in Table 1A reveal that nondurable consumption expenditures (CN) increase by $83 million, durable consumption expenditures (CD) by $206 million, and the two components of investment ($F1$ and $F2$) are virtually unchanged. These changes are, however, offset by the inventory decumulation (ΔH) of $253 million. In subsequent quarters, nondurable consumption increases more substantially—by $161 million, $203 million, $217 million, respectively—to the annual total of $664 million. Durable consumption, on the other hand, increases mildly in the second quarter and then levels off, with the annual total increase amounting to $280 million. Investment in plant and equipment ($F1$) rises slowly to the annual total of $177 million, while residential housing construction ($F2$) actually declines a little.[61] Inventories, however, increase in the second quarter by $382 million (more than the decline in the first quarter), and continue to rise mildly in the third and fourth quarters, with the annual net increase amounting to $276 million.

Since all our calculations terminate after four quarters, they may not adequately indicate the equilibrium or long-run impact of policy changes. While many variables seem to be converging, others

---

[61] This decline is caused by the rise in interest rates, as noted below.

give indications of increasing changes (e.g., CN) at the end of four quarters. The consequences of speeding up some of the partial adjustments are examined later.

Our study of the multipliers for G shows that all government revenues rise as the result of higher levels of various components of GNP and of income. The major items, of course, are federal personal income tax liability and corporate tax liability. The pattern of reaction over time for one is, however, quite different from that for the other. The corporate tax liability (TC) rises very quickly in the first quarter ($147 million) and in the second quarter ($72 million) and then remains essentially steady. On the other hand, federal personal income tax liability (TFP) rises gradually in the four quarters ($79 million, $66 million, $42 million, and $35 million, respectively), so that the rise for the year is $223 million. When revenues from other sources (OASI contributions, unemployment contributions, indirect business taxes, and reduction in unemployment benefits) are added, the pattern of total government revenues and transfers is $274 million, $181 million, $72 million, and $57 million, respectively, in four quarters, and the annual total is $587 million.[62] To compute the average quarterly tax increase, however, the four quarterly figures must be cumulated; when this is done, the average increase is $460 million. Thus, with an additional government expenditure of $1 billion the average quarterly budget deficit would increase by $540 million.

Under this experiment, the increase in G raises the level of GNP and hence the demand for money. However, as Z is unchanged, the tighter conditions in the money market should tend to increase interest rates. Table 1A shows that all interest rates rise, with the most conspicuous increase, .28 percent, occurring in the Treasury bill rate (r_s). The rate on long-term government bonds (r_{10}) increases by .13 percent for the year, and those on commercial loans (r_e) and time deposits (r_t) also rise, but not so dramatically.

Currency in circulation (DR) increases substantially (by $266 million for the year), but demand (DD) and time (DT) deposits decline (by $202 million and $466 million, respectively). These changes result from the higher interest rates and the greater interest-

---

[62] The annual total may differ from the sum of the four quarterly values because of rounding.

sensitivity of the demand and time deposit equations. Thus, the total money supply increases by only $64 million for the year.

The commercial banks adjust their portfolios in the manner more or less expected of them under the circumstances. Commerical loans (CL), over which the banks have least control, first decline with the fall in inventories, then gradually rise, and the net annual increase is $143 million. To offset this increase in commercial loans and the decrease in both demand and time deposits, banks decrease their holdings of excess reserves, short-term government securities, long-term government securities, and municipal securities by $43 million, $615 million, $230 million, and $78 million, respectively. Borrowings from the Federal Reserve increase by $180 million by the end of the year, thus creating a decline of $223 million in free reserves.

Because of the unsatisfactory nature of the price equation in the model, too much significance cannot be attached to the results for prices. They do not seem to move at all under this particular policy measure, which seems unreasonable to us.

The multipliers implied by Table 1A and discussed above are somewhat on the small side. In their paper in this volume, Ando and Brown suggest that there is a possibility of seriously underestimating the speed of adjustment of consumption to income changes, because of the simultaneous presence of serially correlated residuals and the use of lagged dependent variables as explanatory variables. To deal with this problem adequately in the context of a simultaneous equations system is not very easy; we have resorted to some *ad hoc* adjustments in order to see how much difference this bias, if present, would make in our results. We have altered the coefficients of the consumption functions to give them considerably faster speeds of adjustment, while keeping unchanged the equilibrium relations implied by these equations.[63] Using the original model but substituting the consumption functions given in footnote 63 for the two functions in the model, we recomputed the various multipliers. The results, relating to the same change in G

[63] The coefficients of CN_{-1} and CD_{-1} in the linearized version of equations (2) and (3) were originally .653 and .466, respectively. This implies percentage adjustments in the first period of roughly 35 percent and 53 percent, respectively. The coefficients were changed to .217 and .233 implying adjustments of 78 percent and 77 percent, respectively. All other coefficients were adjusted accordingly. These choices are quite arbitrary; for some basis for the order of magnitudes, see paper by Ando and Brown in this volume.

as before, are given in Table 1B. A comparison of Tables 1A and 1B shows, as expected, that the increases in consumption are much more substantial and prompt in Table 1B than in Table 1A. As a consequence, GNP now rises by $1,232 million, $998 million, $572 million, and $456 million, respectively, in the four quarters, with a total annual increase of $3,259 million. The average quarterly rise of GNP is $2,381 million, which seems to be a more reasonable order of magnitude for the GNP multiplier. The general pattern of Table 1B is very similar to that of Table 1A, except that the former multipliers are generally greater. This seems to be more pronounced for items that are closely associated with consumption (such as indirect business taxes) relative to other items (such as investment in plant and equipment and commercial loans). Somewhat interestingly in Table 1B the change in nondurable consumption expenditures (CN) in the fourth quarter is less than that in the third quarter. This contrasts with the steady increase shown in Table 1A. The average quarterly increase in endogenous government revenues is $641 million, so that the increase in the government deficit is $359 million.

The second experiment to be considered is a 1 percent increase in the effective rate of federal personal income tax. The relevant results are presented in Tables 2A and 2B.[64] Since taxable income in 1965 is roughly $63 billion (quarterly total, not annual rate), this amounts to a federal income tax increase of roughly $0.63 billion if income remains constant. Income, of course, does not remain constant, as shown in Tables 2A and 2B.

From Table 2A it is seen that federal personal income tax liabilities (TFP) increase by $613 million in the first quarter, but then decline slightly, because of the decline in income, and that the annual total increase is $560 million. In terms of an annual quarterly average, the gain in TFP is $587 million. When the speed of adjustment of consumption is increased as before (Table 2B), the increase in the quarterly average tax yield is $553 million, reflecting the fact that income declines faster in this case. Other endogenous tax revenues decline and unemployment benefit payments increase, so that the gain in total government revenue, in terms of a quarterly

---

[64] Hereafter, "A" always refers to the model as estimated, and "B" to the model with "speeded up" consumption expenditures.

average, is $540 million according to Table 2A and only $359 million according to Table 2B. Disposable income declines accordingly, and with it consumption expenditure. The GNP loss, in terms of an average quarterly decrease, is $477 million according to Table 2A and $954 million according to Table 2B. The multiplier in the usual sense is not well defined in this context, but the ratio of the GNP loss to the increase in TFP, again in terms of quarterly averages, is 0.81 according to Table 2A and 1.72 according to Table 2B. The model underlying Table 2B is probably closer to reality.

The rest of the story is fairly similar to that of changes in G, and the reader may examine Tables 2A and 2B in detail according to his particular interest. Attention may be called, however, to one other calculation that has received some attention from economists in the past. What are the results of a fiscal policy which keeps the government deficit constant? If this question means the GNP that results from an increase of $1 billion each in government expenditure and government revenue,[65] the increase in GNP is $1.245 billion according to the original model and $1.400 billion according to the "speeded-up model." Thus, a balanced budget multiplier of slightly greater than unity for a year appears to be a good rule of thumb. The reason the balanced budget multiplier is not exactly equal to unity is fairly clear from the structure of the model.

Turning now to the consequences of monetary policy measures, we first consider an increase of $1 billion in the reserve base (Z). Table 3A shows that an immediate effect of this action is an increase in potential demand deposits (D^*) by as much as $7.384 billion in the first quarter; but as banks make their adjustments, the deposits decline gradually in the following three quarters, and by the end of the year the net increase is $3.112 billion. The commercial banks reduce their borrowings from the Federal Reserve Banks $(B^N + B^C)$ by $688 million in the first quarter, but then gradually increase them over the year, and for the year as a whole the net decrease of borrowings is only $94 million.[66] The excess reserves of banks $(E^N + E^C)$

---

[65] The budget is balanced in terms of the average quarterly changes. The number in the text is derived by computing the change in ρ_{fp} that is necessary to make up the deficit from the increase of $1 billion in G (e.g., $540 million for Table 1A). By revenue, we mean $TI + TB + TFP + TC + TO + TU$.

[66] One potential difficulty with this result should be noted. Borrowings cannot drop below zero; therefore, if the initial outstanding borrowings are less than the implied reduction, in this case $688 million, then, clearly, a reduction in borrowings of this amount cannot

rise substantially in the first quarter ($182 million) but then decline during the year and by the year-end actually show a slight net decline ($16 million). Commercial banks make other adjustments in their portfolios, very substantially increasing their holdings of short-term government securities, and also their holdings of long-term government securities and municipal securities, though to a lesser extent. Commercial loans also increase substantially, as bank reserves expand and greater demand is created by increased investment. For the year as a whole, the increase is $1.112 billion, with the expansion amply accommodated by an inflow of deposits.

Demand deposits (DD) increase by $1.578 billion in the first quarter and continue to increase until the fourth quarter, when there is a slight decline; for the year as a whole, the net increase is $2.76 billion. Currency holdings (DR), on the other hand, decline slightly in the first quarter but gradually increase thereafter and show a net increase of $500 million for the year. The initial decline in currency is brought about by a first quarter increase of roughly 1 percent in prices.[67] For the remainder of the year, prices remain, essentially, at this higher level. For the entire year, then, the money supply ($DR + DD$) increases by $3.25 billion, a money multiplier of the right order of magnitude. Time deposits increase by only $184 million in the first quarter but the increase for the year is a significant $1.24 billion.

The increase in Z has a substantial influence on interest rates. The rate on Treasury bills (r_s) declines drastically in the first quarter,[68] then recovers gradually to the end of the year, with a net decline for the year of 0.119 percent. The long-term rate (r_{10}) follows a similar pattern, but with a less drastic decline in the first quarter and a much smaller recovery during the following quar-

---

take place, However, as the expansion of $1 billion in Z is a rather large *ceteris paribus* change, this problem need not concern us. It should be acknowledged that a less likely possibility of violating a non-negativity or other constraint (e.g., ceiling on time deposit rate) exists for other variables as well. To take care of this, one might estimate the equation in a way that insures the constraint is satisfied. For example, deLeeuw, in *Brookings Quarterly Econometric Model*, has done this with a borrowing equation. Alternatively, one could make some assumptions about what happens when borrowing hits zero.

[67] It will be recalled that one of the explanatory variables in the currency equation is $(\Delta P / P_{-1} \cdot Y)$.

[68] The large initial decline in interest rates, especially in the bill rate which drops by .84 percentage point, was also found by deLeeuw; see Frank deLeeuw, "Financial Markets in

ters; by the end of the year, the decline of 0.151 percent is greater than the change in r_s. The rate on commercial loans (r_e) declines by 0.077 percent in the first quarter, but recovers completely during the following quarters so that at the end of the year it is virtually the same as at the beginning. This recovery of interest rates is due to the substantial increases in GNP and income.

The initial decline in interest rates has a substantial influence on investment in residential housing ($F2$), which increases by $433 million in the first quarter. The increase in prices and the expansion of commercial loans contributes to an increase of $470 million in inventory investment (ΔH), while investment in plant and equipment ($F1$) rises only moderately ($66 million). With the multiplier effect increasing consumption substantially, GNP rises by $1.911 billion in the first quarter. In the second quarter, investment in plant and equipment begins to increase materially ($223 million); it continues to rise in the following quarters at an increasing rate, and by the end of the year it has risen by $842 million. Housing investment also increases in the second quarter, but the advance loses momentum as interest rates rise again, and the total increase for the year ($694 million) is less than that for plant and equipment investment. Inventory investment quickly adjusts itself, actually declining in the second and third quarters, showing virtually no change in the fourth quarter, and ending the year slightly lower than at the beginning. Thus, GNP by the end of the year shows an increase of $2.656 billion—an average quarterly gain of $2.274 billion.[69]

The increases in GNP and its components, and in the various concepts of income, raise government revenues substantially; the average quarterly gain, as calculated from Table 3A, is $596 million.

Business Cycles; A Simulation Study," *American Economic Review*, Vol. 54 (May 1964). His estimated decline of 1.5 is even larger than ours. He explained this result in terms of his relatively slow speeds of adjustment for currency and demand deposits. Subsequently, Tucker provided a more detailed analysis, substantiating deLeeuw's argument; see D. P. Tucker, "Income Adjustment to Money-Supply Changes," *American Economic Review*, Vol. 56 (June 1966). For curiosity, we substituted a "speeded-up" demand deposit equation (comparable to the consumption experiment described above) and recalculated the multipliers. As expected, the first-quarter interest rate response was considerably reduced. Although this speed-up has some intuitive appeal, unlike the case of the consumption function, there seems to be no evidence that it is justified in terms of the statistical biases involved.

[69] It has been pointed out by deLeeuw that the economy adjusts faster in response to monetary policy than to fiscal policy. In terms of GNP, this point is illustrated in Table A.

The pattern of influence of the increase in Z, shown in Table 3B (with a faster speed of adjustment for consumption), is essentially the same as that shown by Table 3A, except, of course, that the movements of GNP and its components are magnified. The average quarterly gain in GNP for the year is $3.362 billion, compared with $2.274 billion in Table 3A.

Table A. Reactions of GNP to Change in ρ_{fp} and to Change in Z

| | Change per Quarter | | | | First Quarter Change as Percent of Total Annual Change |
	I	II	III	IV	
Basic Model					
Tax change (ρ_{fp})	−0.2	−0.2	−0.2	−0.2	25
Open market purchase (Z)	1.9	0.3	0.1	0.4	70
"Speeded-up" consumption model					
Tax change (ρ_{fp})	−0.4	−0.4	−0.3	−0.2	31
Open market purchase (Z)	3.1	0.5	−0.4	0.2	91

This feature of the model is certainly at variance with the generally accepted notion and needs some explanation.

The major reason for the rather unsatisfactory behavior is the inclusion of the term ΔD^* in the price equation. Because D^* reacts immediately and automatically to a change in Z, the price level goes up sharply when Z is increased, while the reaction of the price level to a tax change is very mild and slow. Thus, a large part of the change in GNP that is due to a change in Z, reported in the tables in the text and reproduced above, reflects changes in the price level. In terms of the real GNP, the pattern of reaction to a change in Z is given in Table B.

Table B. Reactions of GNP to Change in Z

| | Change per Quarter | | | | First Quarter Change as Percent of Total Annual Change |
	I	II	III	IV	
Basic model	0.2	0.0	0.3	0.6	19
"Speeded-up" consumption model	1.4	0.3	−0.2	0.3	79

Since the price level changes very little when ρ_{fp} is changed, Table B can be compared with the rows showing tax changes in Table A. The reaction pattern for the basic model in Table B is almost "reasonable," while the reaction pattern produced by the "speeded-up" consumption model is still too fast.

This in turn is due to two factors. First, the lag structure in investment functions with respect to the interest rate is probably too fast. Second, the presence of the commercial loan variable in both the plant and equipment equation and the inventory equation, together with the presence of the potential demand deposit variable (D^*), provides a very fast channel through which monetary policy can affect the output of the economy. Both of these problems are currently the subject of intensive investigation in the Federal Reserve-MIT project referred to earlier in this paper.

A comparison of Tables 1 and 3 show that the major differences in expansive fiscal and monetary policy actions are as follows: (1) interest rates decline under expansive monetary policy and rise under expansive fiscal policy; (2) the increase in investment is much more substantial under expansive monetary policy than under expansive fiscal policy; (3) the increase in consumption is more heavily weighted in favor of durables under expansive monetary policy; and (4) the price rise is much more substantial under monetary policy.

The last experiment to be analyzed in any detail is a simultaneous increase of 1 percent each in the required reserve ratio for demand deposits of member banks in reserve cities (k_1) and of country member banks (k_3). To facilitate the reading of Tables 4A and 4B, it is helpful to remember that demand deposits in city and country member banks in 1965 were about $70 billion and $46 billion, respectively; therefore, a change of 1 percent in both k_1 and k_3 implies roughly a reduction of $1.2 billion in available member-bank reserves. Thus, when Table 4 is compared with Table 3, the figures in Table 4 should be reduced by a factor of 1.2 to make them roughly comparable. These tables show that increases in the k's and an equivalent reduction in Z have very similar effects on all aspects of the economy represented in this model, with one noticeable exception. The holdings of short-term securities by commercial banks ($S^N + S^C$) decrease much more substantially under the change in k's than under the change in Z. A similar result was obtained by deLeeuw,[70] and the reasons for this difference have been discussed in the literature.[71] It should also be noted here that, if this result does represent the actual behavior of the commercial banks, it may be that its effects on the economy elsewhere are much more widespread than our results indicate. As noted above, a characteristic of our model is that the bank portfolio equations form a separate block, and variations of the variables within this block do not feed back into the rest of the system.[72]

Tables 5A and 5B present results similar to those reported in Tables 1 through 4 for ten additional fiscal and monetary policy measures. Because of space limitations, the organization of Tables

[70] In *American Economic Review.*

[71] J. Aschheim, "Restrictive Open-Market Operations Versus Reserve-Requirement Increases: A Reformulation," *Economic Journal*, Vol. 73 (June 1963).

[72] See p. 233, above.

5A and 5B is slightly different from that of Tables 1 through 4. There is now a single table for each period, which contains all multipliers with respect to all policy measures under consideration.

The first column of Table 5 refers to the consequences of changing exogenous taxes and government transfers, such as property taxes and OASI benefit payments. A comparison of this column with column 1 in Table 2 reveals that in our model the effects of increasing A_1 and A_2 and of increasing the effective rate of federal personal income tax are very similar, except that, of course, personal income is more directly affected by changes in A_1 and A_2 than by changes in ρ_{fp}. The effects on disposable personal income, however, are almost the same.

The second column deals with changes in the per capita exemption in the federal personal income tax. Again, a comparison with Table 2 confirms our expectations that the effect of changes in exemption should be very similar to that of changes in the effective rate.[73] If an often expressed hypothesis that changes in income distribution lead to a changed consumption-income ratio has any substance, a model which does not take the income distribution into account would not be an accurate description of reality. However, we know of no convincing evidence for this proposition.

The three items, changes in the rate of excise tax (ρ_i), the OASI contribution rate (ρ_o), and unemployment insurance contribution rate (ρ_u), presented in columns 3, 4, and 5, generate patterns of reactions so similar to that of changes in ρ_{fp} that only very brief comments are necessary. If our model contained a more satisfactory description of price variations which, among other things, took explicit account of cost-price relationships, then the effect of changing ρ_i would, in principle, be different from that of changing ρ_{fp} through a different behavior of prices. However, without a detailed mechanism for price variations, the effect of changing ρ_i is mainly to change personal income, given GNP. Under these circumstances, the interesting question of the comparative study of variations in ρ_i and in ρ_{fp} must be left to later work.

On the other hand, there is no reason to believe that variations

---

[73] Per capita exemption is measured in terms of $100 in our model, and hence, according to our equations for taxable income and tax liability, a change of one unit in *EX* would induce, roughly, a change of $3.5 billion in taxable income and of $0.7 billion in tax liability. This is a slightly stronger policy action than a change of 1 percent in the effective tax rate, which induces a change of roughly $0.6 billion in tax liability.

in ρ_o and ρ_u should be significantly different in their effects from that of changing ρ_{fp}, and the results given in Table 5 tend to confirm this supposition.

The effects of changes in corporate tax rates are shown in column 6 of Table 5. It must be stated at once that our model does not contain two essential features of the economy necessary to analyze the effects of corporate profit tax variations, namely, the mechanism of corporate tax shifting and the relation between the expected rate of return and the corporate tax rate, except for the very indirect route through the effects of the corporate tax rate on market rates of interest. Thus, column 6 should largely be ignored. This is one of the most unsatisfactory aspects of our model.

Column 7 deals with the effects of variations in the ratio of covered employment to total labor force under the state unemployment insurance system. Here again, the results given by our model are not reliable, because we have been unable to detect statistically significant effects of the variation of this ratio on the benefit payments; therefore this variable does not appear in our benefit equation (12). Consequently, the figures reported in column 7 reflect only the effects of the variation of this ratio on unemployment insurance contributions. Since, in principle, the benefit payments should also be affected by changes in this ratio and since our inability to detect the effect must be due to statistical problems, this column should also be considered unsatisfactory.[74]

Column 8, the consequences of a change in the required reserve ratio for time deposits of member banks (k_4), is very similar to variations in k_1 and k_3, discussed in relation to Table 4, except that the variation in k_4 has a stronger influence on the amount of savings deposits at commercial banks. This is reasonable because the direct effect of changing k_4 or k_1 and k_3 is to change the excess reserves of member banks, and there is no reason to believe that commercial banks should react differently to the same changes in excess reserves whether they are caused by a change in k_4 or in k_1 and k_3. A one-unit change in k_4 and a one-unit change in k_1 and k_3 have about the same quantitative effect on excess reserves, since in 1965 the volume of time deposits at member banks was about the same as the volume of demand deposits.

[74] See, however, footnote 27, above.

Column 9 describes the effects of a change in the maximum rate on time deposits under Regulation Q (r_{max}). The most direct effect of changing r_{max} is to change r_t, the rate paid on time deposits at commercial banks. This in turn induces consumers and other holders of deposits to shift their holdings from demand deposits and other financial assets to time deposits at commercial banks. And this in turn reduces the volume of demand deposits plus currency in the economy; and since this latter variable appears with a positive sign in the equation for consumer durables, consumption expenditure on durables declines, leading to some reduction in GNP. In the meanwhile, member banks invest in short-term securities, and to a lesser extent in municipal securities, the funds that result from the increase in time deposits.

These developments are reasonable up to a point. However, due to an insufficiently developed formulation of credit rationing in our model, one important aspect of the role that r_{max} may play in the money market is not caught in our analysis. When conditions in the money market are very tight, and r_t is already very close to r_{max}, raising r_{max} would enable commercial banks to bid for additional funds in the form of negotiable certificates of deposit, and to meet additional demand for commercial loans. This in turn might increase investment. However, neither of these effects is observed in our multipliers. Thus, while our model does introduce rationing practices to a minor extent, evidently it is not sufficient to yield this result.

The last column in Table 5 exhibits the impacts of a change in the Federal Reserve rediscount rate (r_d). The first and most obvious effect of this action is to raise the interest rate on Treasury bills, and this in turn reduces the amount of demand deposits, currency, and time deposits. The reduction of the last two items increases potential demand deposits (D^*), and this, plus the fact that the commercial loan rate, which adjusts only slowly, is now more attractive relative to the rate on treasury bills (r_s), tends to increase the volume of commercial loans. The increase in commercial loans, through the interaction of commercial loans and inventory investment, moderately increases inventories in the first quarter. This leads to a somewhat unexpected, though small, rise in GNP, in that quarter.

The rise in inventory investment ceases in the second quarter, however, and a decline begins in the third quarter. The higher rates of interest begin to exert their influence on investment, both in plant and equipment and in housing, and this leads to a fall in GNP, beginning in the second quarter. In the fourth quarter, the decrease in plant and equipment investment is still substantial, and it will be some time before investment will reach a new equilibrium level. The fall in investment occurs despite the fact that commercial loans keep increasing throughout the four quarters because of their relative attractiveness compared with alternative borrowings in the short-term market. These movements of commercial loans and investment show that in our model—at least in the situation discussed here—interest rates rather than the availability of commercial loans dominate the behavior of investment in plant and equipment. Commercial banks finance the increases in commercial loans through a reduction in their holdings of short-term, long-term, and municipal securities. They also repay a substantial amount of their borrowings from the Federal Reserve.

Throughout this section, the consequences of a variety of fiscal and monetary policy measures implied by this model have been considered. The discussion has been confined largely to situations in which one specific policy is undertaken while all other policy variables are held constant. It is possible, however, to investigate the implications of any combination of two or more policy actions —as described earlier in the discussion of a simultaneous increase in G and ρ_{fp}—so as to keep the government deficit constant. For example, the situation might be considered in which a change in either G, ρ_{fp}, or some other fiscal parameter, or any combination of them, is undertaken, while monetary policy is designed to keep the interest rate on bills constant, Or, a monetary policy might be designed to increase investment by a specific amount, and then fiscal policy might be used to reduce consumption so that total GNP, in real terms, might be kept constant. The data needed for these inquiries are given in Tables 1 through 5, and may be used to study the consequences of any particular policy combination. When the data are used, however, all the qualifications resulting from the limitations inherent in the structure of this model (discussed throughout this paper) must be kept in mind.

Concluding Remarks

As pointed out throughout this paper, the model on which the analysis is based has a number of defects that must be remedied before the model can be considered a reliable policy instrument. A more careful formulation of price-wage behavior; a more systematic introduction of capacity, production, and their relationship with investment, labor-force participation, and technical change; a more explicit treatment of the influence of the expected rate of return and of the cost of capital on investment, together with recognition of tax-shifting behavior of corporations; and more detailed attention to the behavior of state and local governments—these are probably the major improvements that are most urgently called for.

In addition, the estimation procedure must be improved, in order that biases in the estimates are removed as much as possible. In particular, it is essential to devise a better procedure than the one used in this paper for estimating the lag structure in the context of a simultaneous equations system, in which residuals are serially correlated as well as correlated with each other.

Unreliability of the analysis because of these defects in the model is not equally serious for all policy measures that have been discussed. On the one hand, the model is practically useless for predicting the effects of changes in corporate income taxes; but, on the other hand, it is useful for determining the effects of changes in federal personal income taxes and of open market operations by the Federal Reserve System.

Since the model was linearized by using the annual average values for 1965 of all variables, the conclusions are valid, strictly speaking, only in the neighborhood of 1965, say one or two years on both sides of 1965 provided that no drastic change in the economy takes place. In particular, 1965 was a year of near full employment, and some policy measures whose effects are crucially dependent upon employment conditions—such as a change in weekly maximum benefits under a state unemployment insurance system—must be analyzed by using other periods with different employment conditions before their impacts can be fully understood. In the end, when most of the more serious shortcomings of the model are remedied, extensive simulation analysis, using the model as estimated rather than the linearized version, must be carried out before any model can be reliably used to assess the impacts of all policy measures.

In spite of all these qualifications, we believe that the results reported in this paper supply some useful additions to the growing body of knowledge of how the U. S. economy functions and how it reacts to various aggregative policy measures. In particular, the analysis allows some detailed comparison of fiscal policy measures and monetary policy actions for stabilization.

In their exchange with Friedman and Meiselman in 1965, Ando and Modigliani insisted that, insofar as indicated by any evidence then available to them, both fiscal and monetary policy measures contribute significantly to the determination of the levels of output, income, and employment, and that it was useless to argue which of them was the more important.[75] The evidence reported in this paper provides much more convincing support for their contention than that given by them at the time. The difference between the effects of fiscal and of monetary policies, at least in a period of reasonably full employment, is not that one influences aggregate income and output and the other does not. They both are capable of producing similar changes in aggregate income and employment. Differences arise, however, in the manner in which these changes are brought about, in the composition of changes in aggregate income and employment, and in emphasis on different sectors of the economy.

From the point of view of the national welfare, these details can be as important as aggregate income and employment, and in choosing alternative policies designed to produce similar aggregative effects, the policymaker must evaluate their impacts in detail.

In addition to providing, hopefully, more accurate estimates of aggregative impacts of stabilization policy measures, the advantage and the strength of structural econometric models are that they should at best generate useful information on these important details, with which more *ad hoc* procedures, by their nature, cannot deal. The results reported in this paper are presented as a modest contribution in this direction.

[75] Albert Ando and Franco Modigliani, "The Relative Stability of Monetary Velocity and the Investment Multiplier," *American Economic Review*, Vol. 55 (September 1965).

TABLE IA. Effects of Changing G at Beginning of 1965: Original Model

Variable	First Quarter	Second Quarter	Third Quarter	Fourth Quarter	Annual Total
Y	1.000	0.711	0.346	0.272	2.329
CN	0.083	0.161	0.203	0.217	0.664
CD	0.206	0.086	−0.002	−0.009	0.280
F1	0.004	0.075	0.066	0.032	0.177
F2	−0.040	0.007	−0.014	−0.022	−0.068
ΔH	−0.253	0.382	0.093	0.054	0.276
π	0.343	0.167	0.000	−0.026	0.484
TI	0.017	0.016	0.011	0.017	0.061
TO + TU	0.023	0.019	0.012	0.010	0.066
TB	−0.008	−0.008	−0.007	−0.006	−0.029
YP	0.644	0.538	0.343	0.285	1.810
TFP	0.079	0.066	0.042	0.035	0.223
YD	0.564	0.472	0.300	0.250	1.587
TY	0.409	0.342	0.218	0.181	1.150
TC	0.147	0.072	0.000	−0.011	0.208
r_s	0.087	0.089	0.064	0.038	0.279
r_{10}	0.032	0.037	0.033	0.028	0.130
r_e	0.005	0.012	0.011	0.010	0.039
r_t	0.012	0.012	0.006	0.001	0.032
DR	0.070	0.087	0.065	0.045	0.266
DD	−0.004	−0.045	−0.079	−0.074	−0.202
DT	−0.034	−0.082	−0.143	−0.206	−0.466
CL	−0.106	0.058	0.089	0.102	0.143
$E^N + E^C$	−0.014	−0.018	−0.009	−0.002	−0.043
$B^N + B^C$	0.054	0.060	0.041	0.025	0.180
$S^N + S^C$	0.031	−0.147	−0.228	−0.272	−0.615
$O^N + O^C$	−0.013	−0.058	−0.076	−0.082	−0.230
$MUN^N + MUN^C$	−0.004	−0.013	−0.024	−0.036	−0.078
R^R	−0.002	−0.009	−0.016	−0.017	−0.043
D^*	−0.469	−0.570	−0.410	−0.256	−1.704
EM	0.067	0.093	0.086	0.073	0.319
P	−0.001	−0.000	0.000	0.001	−0.000

TABLE IB. Effects of Changing G at Beginning of 1965: "Speeded Up" Consumption Model

Variable	First Quarter	Second Quarter	Third Quarter	Fourth Quarter	Annual Total
Y	1.232	0.998	0.572	0.456	3.259
CN	0.224	0.363	0.389	0.366	1.342
CD	0.363	0.101	−0.034	−0.022	0.407
F1	0.005	0.092	0.090	0.052	0.240
F2	−0.049	0.004	−0.019	−0.030	−0.094
ΔH	−0.311	0.438	0.146	0.090	0.363
π	0.422	0.250	0.041	−0.011	0.702
TI	0.035	0.030	0.019	0.028	0.112
TO + TU	0.028	0.026	0.019	0.016	0.090
TB	−0.010	−0.010	−0.010	−0.010	−0.039
YP	0.780	0.732	0.523	0.447	2.481
TFP	0.096	0.090	0.065	0.055	0.306
YD	0.684	0.641	0.459	0.392	2.176
TY	0.495	0.465	0.333	0.284	1.577
TC	0.182	0.108	0.018	−0.005	0.302
r_s	0.108	0.121	0.095	0.063	0.387
r_{10}	0.039	0.050	0.047	0.042	0.178
r_e	0.007	0.016	0.016	0.015	0.053
r_l	0.015	0.017	0.010	0.004	0.045
DR	0.086	0.115	0.095	0.071	0.367
DD	−0.005	−0.056	−0.103	−0.104	−0.268
DT	−0.042	−0.106	−0.188	−0.277	−0.613
CL	−0.130	0.058	0.110	0.135	0.173
$E^N + E^C$	−0.017	−0.024	−0.014	−0.005	−0.060
$B^N + B^C$	0.067	0.080	0.061	0.042	0.250
$S^N + S^C$	0.039	−0.176	−0.296	−0.370	−0.804
$O^N + O^C$	−0.017	−0.073	−0.102	−0.114	−0.306
$MUN^N + MUN^C$	−0.005	−0.016	−0.032	−0.049	−0.102
R^R	−0.002	−0.011	−0.020	−0.024	−0.057
D^*	−0.577	−0.759	−0.602	−0.416	−2.355
EM	0.083	0.123	0.121	0.108	0.435
P	−0.001	−0.001	0.000	0.001	−0.001

TABLE 2A. Effects of Changing ρ_{fp} at Beginning of 1965: Original Model

Variable	First Quarter	Second Quarter	Third Quarter	Fourth Quarter	Annual Total
Y	−0.173	−0.223	−0.193	−0.161	−0.751
CN	−0.142	−0.118	−0.109	−0.105	−0.473
CD	−0.081	−0.056	−0.030	−0.014	−0.182
F1	−0.001	−0.013	−0.019	−0.017	−0.050
F2	0.007	0.003	0.004	0.006	0.021
ΔH	0.044	−0.040	−0.039	−0.032	−0.067
π	−0.059	−0.065	−0.038	−0.016	−0.179
TI	−0.013	−0.011	−0.007	−0.010	−0.042
TO + TU	−0.004	−0.005	−0.005	−0.005	−0.020
TB	0.001	0.002	0.002	0.003	0.008
YP	−0.102	−0.149	−0.150	−0.138	−0.539
TFP	0.613	−0.018	−0.018	−0.017	0.560
YD	−0.715	−0.131	−0.131	−0.121	−1.099
TY	−0.065	−0.095	−0.095	−0.088	−0.343
TC	−0.026	−0.028	−0.016	−0.007	−0.077
r_s	−0.015	−0.024	−0.025	−0.022	−0.086
r_{10}	−0.006	−0.010	−0.011	−0.012	−0.038
r_e	−0.001	−0.003	−0.004	−0.004	−0.011
r_l	−0.002	−0.003	−0.003	−0.002	−0.011
DR	−0.012	−0.022	−0.024	−0.022	−0.081
DD	0.001	0.008	0.018	0.024	0.051
DT	0.006	0.018	0.035	0.056	0.115
CL	0.018	0.001	−0.014	−0.026	−0.021
$E^N + E^C$	0.002	0.005	0.004	0.003	0.014
$B^N + B^C$	−0.009	−0.016	−0.016	−0.014	−0.056
$S^N + S^C$	−0.005	0.022	0.052	0.077	0.146
$O^N + O^C$	0.002	0.011	0.020	0.026	0.060
$MUN^N + MUN^C$	0.001	0.003	0.006	0.010	0.019
R^R	0.000	0.002	0.004	0.005	0.011
D^*	0.081	0.146	0.157	0.137	0.521
EM	−0.012	−0.023	−0.028	−0.029	−0.092
P	0.000	0.000	0.000	−0.000	0.000

TABLE 2B. Effects of Changing ρ_{fp} at Beginning of 1965: "Speeded Up" Consumption Model

Variable	First Quarter	Second Quarter	Third Quarter	Fourth Quarter	Annual Total
Y	−0.429	−0.434	−0.290	−0.219	−1.371
CN	−0.361	−0.200	−0.177	−0.164	−0.903
CD	−0.191	−0.075	−0.005	0.007	−0.263
F1	−0.002	−0.032	−0.038	−0.026	−0.098
F2	0.017	0.002	0.007	0.012	0.039
ΔH	0.108	−0.130	−0.077	−0.047	−0.146
π	−0.147	−0.119	−0.039	−0.003	−0.307
TI	−0.033	−0.018	−0.010	−0.013	−0.073
TO + TU	−0.009	−0.011	−0.009	−0.007	−0.036
TB	0.003	0.004	0.004	0.004	0.016
YP	−0.251	−0.303	−0.246	−0.207	−1.007
TFP	0.595	−0.037	−0.030	−0.026	0.502
YD	−0.846	−0.266	−0.216	−0.181	−1.509
TY	−0.160	−0.193	−0.156	−0.132	−0.640
TC	−0.063	−0.051	−0.017	−0.001	−0.132
r_s	−0.037	−0.050	−0.043	−0.031	−0.161
r_{10}	−0.014	−0.020	−0.021	−0.019	−0.073
r_e	−0.002	−0.006	−0.007	−0.006	−0.021
r_t	−0.005	−0.007	−0.005	−0.002	−0.019
DR	−0.030	−0.046	−0.043	−0.033	−0.152
DD	0.002	0.020	0.040	0.044	0.106
DT	0.015	0.040	0.074	0.112	0.240
CL	0.045	−0.011	−0.040	−0.055	−0.061
$E^N + E^C$	0.006	0.010	0.007	0.003	0.026
$B^N + B^C$	−0.023	−0.033	−0.028	−0.020	−0.104
$S^N + S^C$	−0.013	0.058	0.115	0.152	0.312
$O^N + O^C$	0.006	0.027	0.041	0.048	0.122
$MUN^N + MUN^C$	0.002	0.006	0.012	0.019	0.040
R^R	0.001	0.004	0.008	0.010	0.023
D^*	0.201	0.305	0.273	0.201	0.980
EM	−0.029	−0.049	−0.052	−0.048	−0.178
P	0.000	0.000	0.000	−0.000	0.000

TABLE 3A. Effects of Changing Z at Beginning of 1965: Original Model

Variable	First Quarter	Second Quarter	Third Quarter	Fourth Quarter	Annual Total
Y	1.911	0.318	0.071	0.356	2.656
CN	0.754	0.065	−0.090	−0.029	0.701
CD	0.188	0.048	0.086	0.123	0.446
F1	0.066	0.223	0.240	0.313	0.842
F2	0.433	0.258	0.074	−0.071	0.694
ΔH	0.470	−0.276	−0.240	0.019	−0.027
π	0.655	−0.059	−0.120	0.009	0.485
TI	0.056	0.007	−0.000	0.008	0.071
TO + TU	0.044	0.014	0.007	0.012	0.077
TB	−0.015	−0.009	−0.006	−0.006	−0.037
YP	1.208	0.386	0.195	0.337	2.125
TFP	0.149	0.048	0.024	0.042	0.262
YD	1.059	0.339	0.171	0.295	1.863
TY	0.767	0.245	0.124	0.214	1.351
TC	0.282	−0.025	−0.052	0.004	0.208
r_s	−0.836	0.295	0.111	0.311	−0.119
r_{10}	−0.305	0.065	0.007	0.081	−0.151
r_e	−0.077	−0.003	0.046	0.036	0.002
r_l	−0.196	0.051	0.064	0.052	−0.029
DR	−0.094	0.159	0.230	0.205	0.500
DD	1.578	0.852	0.415	−0.083	2.762
DT	0.184	0.201	0.451	0.405	1.241
CL	0.439	0.371	0.137	0.164	1.112
$E^N + E^C$	0.182	−0.018	−0.131	−0.050	−0.016
$B^N + B^C$	−0.688	0.265	0.171	0.157	−0.094
$S^N + S^C$	0.704	0.137	0.208	−0.126	0.923
$O^N + O^C$	0.199	0.097	0.075	−0.037	0.334
$MUN^N + MUN^C$	0.069	0.064	0.081	0.071	0.286
R^R	0.224	0.124	0.072	0.002	0.422
D^*	7.384	−1.126	−1.663	−1.483	3.112
EM	0.128	0.108	0.078	0.074	0.388
P	0.011	0.002	−0.002	−0.002	0.009

**TABLE 3B. Effects of Changing Z at Beginning of 1965:
"Speeded Up" Consumption Model**

Variable	First Quarter	Second Quarter	Third Quarter	Fourth Quarter	Annual Total
Y	3.136	0.513	−0.396	0.157	3.410
CN	1.895	−0.347	−0.333	−0.025	1.190
CD	0.626	−0.118	−0.121	0.123	0.510
F1	0.071	0.314	0.271	0.276	0.931
F2	0.384	0.295	0.070	−0.090	0.660
ΔH	0.161	0.368	−0.282	−0.127	0.119
π	1.075	−0.101	−0.375	−0.084	0.515
TI	0.150	−0.030	−0.024	0.008	0.103
TO + TU	0.070	0.024	0.000	0.008	0.102
TB	−0.024	−0.015	−0.008	−0.006	−0.054
YP	1.926	0.669	0.007	0.220	2.822
TFP	0.237	0.082	0.001	0.027	0.348
YD	1.689	0.586	0.006	0.193	2.474
TY	1.224	0.425	0.004	0.140	1.794
TC	0.462	−0.043	−0.161	−0.036	0.222
r_s	−0.729	0.346	0.094	0.276	−0.013
r_{10}	−0.266	0.089	0.010	0.078	−0.090
r_e	−0.071	0.009	0.049	0.035	0.023
r_l	−0.181	0.058	0.058	0.044	−0.021
DR	−0.008	0.218	0.222	0.179	0.611
DD	1.573	0.801	0.351	−0.102	2.622
DT	0.142	0.123	0.345	0.284	0.894
CL	0.310	0.515	0.253	0.209	1.287
$E^N + E^C$	0.165	−0.030	−0.124	−0.039	−0.028
$B^N + B^C$	−0.621	0.302	0.158	0.136	−0.026
$S^N + S^C$	0.742	−0.065	0.014	−0.248	0.443
$O^N + O^C$	0.182	0.034	0.026	−0.063	0.180
$MUN^N + MUN^C$	0.064	0.052	0.061	0.048	0.225
R^R	0.221	0.114	0.060	−0.005	0.391
D*	6.810	−1.507	−1.587	−1.282	2.434
EM	0.210	0.177	0.093	0.070	0.550
P	0.010	0.001	−0.001	−0.001	0.010

TABLE 4A. Effects of Changing k_1 and k_3 at Beginning of 1965: Original Model

Variable	First Quarter	Second Quarter	Third Quarter	Fourth Quarter	Annual Total
Y	−2.136	−0.356	−0.088	−0.418	−2.998
CN	−0.845	−0.067	0.105	0.033	−0.773
CD	−0.212	−0.059	−0.103	−0.143	−0.517
F1	−0.068	−0.252	−0.277	−0.365	−0.962
F2	−0.495	−0.293	−0.082	0.082	−0.788
ΔH	−0.516	0.314	0.269	−0.025	0.042
π	−0.732	0.066	0.131	−0.016	−0.551
TI	−0.063	−0.008	0.000	−0.009	−0.080
TO + TU	−0.049	−0.016	−0.008	−0.014	−0.087
TB	0.017	0.010	0.007	0.007	0.042
YP	−1.350	−0.432	−0.223	−0.390	−2.396
TFP	−0.166	−0.053	−0.028	−0.048	−0.295
YD	−1.183	−0.379	−0.196	−0.342	−2.100
TY	−0.858	−0.275	−0.142	−0.248	−1.523
TC	−0.315	0.028	0.056	−0.007	−0.237
r_s	0.978	−0.338	−0.132	−0.357	0.151
r_{10}	0.357	−0.074	−0.009	−0.092	0.182
r_e	0.092	0.006	−0.051	−0.039	0.008
r_t	0.219	−0.060	−0.073	−0.059	0.027
DR	0.099	−0.186	−0.266	−0.238	−0.591
DD	−1.811	−0.977	−0.471	0.099	−3.159
DT	−0.256	−0.281	−0.565	−0.512	−1.614
CL	−0.468	−0.389	−0.127	−0.159	−1.142
$E^N + E^C$	−0.231	0.030	0.155	0.060	0.014
$B^N + B^C$	0.800	−0.300	−0.195	−0.181	0.123
$S^N + S^C$	−2.277	−0.027	−0.123	0.238	−2.190
$O^N + O^C$	−0.238	−0.121	−0.094	0.036	−0.417
$MUN^N + MUN^C$	−0.085	−0.098	−0.114	−0.100	−0.397
R^R	0.931	−0.144	−0.084	−0.003	0.700
D^*	−8.285	1.330	1.937	1.732	−3.286
EM	−0.143	−0.121	−0.088	−0.084	−0.436
P	−0.012	−0.002	0.002	0.002	−0.010

TABLE 4B. Effects of Changing k_1 and k_3 at Beginning of 1965: "Speeded Up" Consumption Model

Variable	First Quarter	Second Quarter	Third Quarter	Fourth Quarter	Annual Total
Y	−3.510	−0.568	0.440	−0.198	−3.836
CN	−2.124	0.404	0.380	0.025	−1.315
CD	−0.703	0.127	0.130	−0.145	−0.591
F1	−0.074	−0.353	−0.311	−0.323	−1.062
F2	−0.440	−0.335	−0.078	0.104	−0.749
ΔH	−0.169	−0.410	0.319	0.141	−0.119
π	−1.203	0.115	0.418	0.086	−0.584
TI	−0.168	0.035	0.027	−0.010	−0.116
TO + TU	−0.078	−0.027	−0.000	−0.009	−0.115
TB	0.027	0.017	0.009	0.007	0.060
YP	−2.155	−0.746	−0.009	−0.261	−3.171
TFP	−0.266	−0.092	−0.001	−0.032	−0.391
YD	−1.890	−0.654	−0.008	−0.228	−2.780
TY	−1.370	−0.474	−0.006	−0.166	−2.015
TC	−0.517	0.049	0.180	0.037	−0.251
r_s	0.858	−0.394	−0.112	−0.319	0.034
r_{10}	0.313	−0.100	−0.011	−0.088	0.113
r_e	0.084	−0.007	−0.055	−0.038	−0.016
r_t	0.203	−0.068	−0.067	−0.051	0.017
DR	0.003	−0.252	−0.257	−0.209	−0.715
DD	−1.805	−0.919	−0.399	0.121	−3.002
DT	−0.209	−0.194	−0.447	−0.377	−1.227
CL	−0.323	−0.552	−0.255	−0.208	−1.338
$E^N + E^C$	−0.211	0.044	0.146	0.048	0.027
$B^N + B^C$	0.725	−0.341	−0.181	−0.157	0.046
$S^N + S^C$	−2.320	0.200	0.093	0.373	−1.655
$O^N + O^C$	−0.220	−0.051	−0.039	0.065	−0.245
$MUN^N + MUN^C$	−0.079	−0.084	−0.092	−0.074	−0.329
R^R	0.933	−0.133	−0.070	0.004	0.735
D^*	−7.641	1.754	1.848	1.507	−2.533
EM	−0.235	−0.198	−0.104	−0.080	−0.617
P	−0.011	−0.001	0.001	0.001	−0.010

TABLE 5A(1). Effects of Selected Policy Measures Taken at Beginning of 1965: Original Model, First Quarter

Variable	$A_1 + A_2$ (1)	EX (2)	ρ_i (3)	ρ_o (4)	ρ_u (5)	ρ_c (6)	COV (7)	k_4 (8)	r_{max} (9)	r_d (10)
Y	−0.256	0.189	−0.195	−0.156	−0.086	−0.008	−0.025	−2.236	−0.044	0.267
CN	−0.209	0.155	−0.160	−0.128	−0.070	−0.006	−0.021	−0.878	−0.014	0.075
CD	−0.120	0.089	−0.092	−0.073	−0.040	−0.004	−0.012	−0.218	−0.015	0.008
F1	−0.001	0.001	−0.001	−0.001	0.000	0.000	0.000	−0.086	−0.003	0.081
F2	0.010	−0.007	0.008	0.006	0.003	0.000	0.001	−0.487	−0.003	−0.093
ΔH	0.064	−0.048	0.049	0.039	0.022	0.002	0.006	−0.567	−0.009	0.197
π	−0.087	0.065	−0.067	−0.054	−0.029	−0.003	−0.009	−0.766	−0.015	0.092
TI	−0.019	0.014	0.818	−0.012	−0.007	−0.001	−0.002	−0.065	−0.002	0.005
TO + TU	−0.023	0.004	−0.033	0.639	0.352	−0.001	0.104	−0.051	−0.001	0.006
TB	0.002	−0.001	0.002	0.001	0.001	0.000	0.000	0.017	0.000	−0.002
YP	−0.632	0.111	−0.919	−0.734	−0.404	−0.036	−0.119	−1.413	−0.028	0.172
TFP	−0.078	−0.668	−0.113	−0.090	−0.050	−0.004	−0.015	−0.174	−0.003	0.021
YD	−1.054	0.779	−0.806	−0.644	−0.354	−0.031	−0.105	−1.239	−0.024	0.151
TY	−0.402	−3.445	−0.584	−0.466	−0.257	−0.023	−0.076	−0.898	−0.018	0.109
TC	−0.037	0.028	−0.029	−0.023	−0.013	0.182	−0.004	−0.330	−0.007	0.039
r_s	−0.022	0.017	−0.017	−0.014	−0.008	−0.001	−0.002	0.901	−0.002	0.489
r_{10}	−0.008	0.006	−0.006	−0.005	−0.003	0.000	−0.001	0.329	−0.001	0.006
r_e	−0.001	0.001	−0.002	−0.001	0.000	0.000	0.000	0.081	−0.002	0.060
r_l	−0.003	0.002	−0.002	−0.002	−0.001	0.000	0.000	0.229	0.103	−0.017
DR	−0.018	0.013	−0.014	−0.011	−0.006	−0.001	−0.002	0.119	0.003	−0.085
DD	0.001	−0.001	0.001	0.001	0.000	0.000	0.000	−1.763	−0.248	−0.449
DT	0.009	−0.006	0.007	0.005	0.003	0.000	0.001	−0.127	0.438	−0.088
CL	0.027	−0.020	0.021	0.016	0.009	0.001	0.003	−0.556	−0.015	0.388
$E^V + E^C$	0.003	−0.003	0.003	0.002	0.001	0.000	0.000	−0.232	−0.002	−0.021
$B^V + B^C$	−0.014	0.010	−0.011	−0.008	−0.005	0.000	−0.001	0.790	0.018	0.172
$S^V + S^C$	−0.008	0.006	−0.006	−0.005	−0.003	0.000	−0.001	−2.000	0.304	−0.559
$O^V + O^C$	0.003	−0.003	0.003	0.002	0.001	0.000	0.000	−0.204	0.002	−0.276
$MUN^V + MUN^C$	0.001	−0.001	0.001	0.001	0.000	0.000	0.000	−0.068	0.047	−0.024
R^R	0.000	0.000	0.000	0.000	0.000	0.000	0.000	0.903	−0.020	−0.065
D^*	0.120	−0.089	0.092	0.073	0.040	0.004	0.012	−8.587	−0.119	0.601
EM	−0.017	0.013	−0.013	−0.010	−0.006	−0.001	−0.002	−0.150	−0.003	0.018
P	0.000	0.000	0.000	0.000	0.000	0.000	0.000	−0.013	0.000	0.001

TABLE 5A(2). Effects of Selected Policy Measures Taken at Beginning of 1965: Original Model, Second Quarter

Variable	$A_1 + A_2$ (1)	EX (2)	ρ_i (3)	ρ_o (4)	p_u (5)	ρ_c (6)	COV (7)	k_4 (8)	r_{max} (9)	r_d (10)
Y	−0.329	0.243	−0.252	−0.201	−0.111	−0.015	−0.033	−0.334	−0.105	−0.036
CN	−0.173	0.128	−0.132	−0.106	−0.058	−0.009	−0.017	−0.076	−0.034	0.069
CD	−0.082	0.061	−0.063	−0.050	−0.028	−0.005	−0.008	−0.046	−0.033	−0.068
F1	−0.019	0.014	−0.015	−0.012	−0.006	−0.001	−0.002	−0.246	−0.011	−0.013
F2	0.004	−0.003	0.003	0.003	0.001	0.000	0.000	−0.303	−0.009	−0.032
ΔH	−0.059	0.044	−0.045	−0.036	−0.020	0.000	−0.006	0.338	−0.019	0.008
π	−0.096	0.071	−0.074	−0.059	−0.032	−0.005	−0.010	0.083	−0.034	−0.037
TI	−0.016	0.012	−0.013	−0.010	−0.006	−0.001	−0.002	−0.008	−0.004	0.000
TO + TU	−0.008	0.006	−0.006	−0.005	−0.003	−0.001	−0.001	−0.015	−0.002	0.000
TB	0.003	−0.002	0.002	0.002	0.001	0.000	0.000	0.011	0.001	−0.001
YP	−0.220	0.163	−0.168	−0.134	−0.074	−0.030	−0.022	−0.428	−0.067	0.004
TFP	−0.027	0.020	−0.021	−0.017	−0.009	−0.004	−0.003	−0.053	−0.008	0.000
YD	−0.193	0.142	−0.147	−0.118	−0.065	−0.027	−0.019	−0.375	−0.059	0.003
TY	−0.140	0.103	−0.107	−0.085	−0.047	−0.019	−0.014	−0.272	−0.043	0.002
TC	−0.041	0.031	−0.032	−0.025	−0.014	−0.002	−0.004	0.036	−0.015	−0.016
r_s	−0.036	0.026	−0.027	−0.022	−0.012	−0.001	−0.004	−0.276	−0.009	−0.090
r_{10}	−0.014	0.010	−0.011	−0.009	−0.005	−0.001	−0.001	−0.055	−0.003	−0.032
r_e	−0.004	0.003	−0.003	−0.002	−0.001	0.000	0.000	0.005	−0.005	0.032
r_t	−0.005	0.004	−0.004	−0.003	−0.002	0.000	0.000	−0.059	0.100	−0.012
DR	−0.032	0.024	−0.025	−0.020	−0.011	−0.001	−0.003	−0.181	0.005	−0.087
DD	0.012	−0.009	0.009	0.007	0.004	0.000	0.001	−1.002	−0.436	−0.236
DT	0.026	−0.019	0.020	0.016	0.009	0.001	0.003	−0.213	0.855	−0.034
CL	0.001	−0.001	0.001	0.001	0.000	0.001	0.000	−0.432	−0.045	0.361
$E^N + E^C$	0.006	−0.005	0.005	0.004	0.002	0.000	0.001	0.026	−0.002	0.010
$B^N + B^C$	−0.023	0.017	−0.018	−0.014	−0.008	−0.001	−0.002	−0.300	−0.029	−0.111
$S^N + S^C$	0.032	−0.024	0.025	0.020	0.011	0.001	0.003	−0.004	0.673	−0.264
$O^N + O^C$	0.017	−0.012	0.013	0.010	0.006	0.001	0.002	−0.113	0.009	−0.244
$MUN^N + MUN^C$	0.004	−0.003	0.003	0.002	0.001	0.000	0.000	−0.081	0.116	−0.021
R^R	0.002	−0.002	0.002	0.002	0.001	0.000	0.000	−0.145	−0.032	−0.034
D*	0.215	−0.159	0.164	0.131	0.072	0.009	0.021	1.277	−0.227	0.602
EM	−0.033	0.025	−0.026	−0.021	−0.011	−0.001	−0.003	−0.124	−0.009	0.010
P	0.000	0.000	0.000	0.000	0.000	0.000	0.000	−0.002	0.000	0.001

TABLE 5A(3). Effects of Selected Policy Measures Taken at Beginning of 1965: Original Model, Third Quarter

Variable	$A_1 + A_2$ (1)	EX (2)	ρ_i (3)	ρ_o (4)	ρ_u (5)	ρ_c (6)	COV (7)	k_4 (8)	r_{max} (9)	r_d (10)
Y	−0.284	0.210	−0.217	−0.173	−0.095	−0.019	−0.028	−0.062	−0.157	−0.183
CN	−0.160	0.119	−0.123	−0.098	−0.054	−0.011	−0.016	0.108	−0.053	0.023
CD	−0.045	0.033	−0.034	−0.027	−0.015	−0.005	−0.004	−0.098	−0.048	−0.073
FI	−0.027	0.020	−0.021	−0.017	−0.009	−0.001	−0.003	−0.265	−0.018	−0.101
$F2$	0.006	−0.005	0.005	0.004	0.002	0.000	0.001	−0.091	−0.015	0.010
ΔH	−0.057	0.042	−0.044	−0.035	−0.019	−0.002	−0.006	0.285	−0.023	−0.041
π	−0.056	0.042	−0.043	−0.034	−0.019	−0.005	−0.006	0.145	−0.044	−0.077
TI	−0.011	0.008	−0.008	−0.007	−0.004	−0.001	−0.001	0.001	−0.005	−0.003
$TO + TU$	−0.008	0.006	−0.006	−0.005	−0.003	−0.001	−0.001	−0.008	−0.004	−0.004
TB	0.003	−0.002	0.003	0.002	0.001	0.000	0.000	0.007	0.001	0.000
YP	−0.221	0.163	−0.169	−0.135	−0.074	−0.028	−0.022	−0.211	−0.110	−0.103
TFP	−0.027	0.020	−0.021	−0.017	−0.009	−0.003	−0.003	−0.026	−0.014	−0.013
YD	−0.193	0.143	−0.148	−0.118	−0.065	−0.025	−0.019	−0.185	−0.096	−0.091
TY	−0.140	0.104	−0.107	−0.086	−0.047	−0.018	−0.014	−0.134	−0.070	−0.066
TC	−0.024	0.018	−0.018	−0.015	−0.008	−0.002	−0.002	0.062	−0.019	−0.033
r_s	−0.037	0.028	−0.029	−0.023	−0.013	−0.002	−0.004	−0.120	−0.011	−0.103
r_{10}	−0.017	0.012	−0.013	−0.010	−0.006	−0.001	−0.002	−0.006	−0.005	−0.041
r_e	−0.005	0.004	−0.004	−0.003	−0.002	0.000	−0.001	−0.049	−0.010	−0.004
r_t	−0.004	0.003	−0.003	−0.003	−0.002	0.000	0.000	−0.074	0.096	−0.006
DR	−0.036	0.026	−0.027	−0.022	−0.012	−0.002	−0.004	−0.264	0.005	−0.084
DD	0.027	−0.020	0.021	0.017	0.009	0.001	0.003	−0.500	−0.580	−0.083
DT	0.052	−0.038	0.040	0.032	0.017	0.002	0.005	−0.512	1.238	0.070
CL	−0.021	0.016	−0.016	−0.013	−0.007	0.000	−0.002	0.158	−0.082	0.322
$E^N + E^C$	0.006	−0.005	0.005	0.004	0.002	0.000	0.001	0.157	−0.001	0.006
$B^N + B^C$	−0.024	0.018	−0.018	−0.015	−0.008	−0.001	−0.002	−0.193	−0.035	−0.087
$S^N + S^C$	0.077	−0.057	0.059	0.047	0.026	0.003	0.008	−0.115	1.062	−0.002
$O^N + O^C$	0.029	−0.022	0.022	0.018	0.010	0.001	0.003	−0.092	0.016	−0.208
$MUN^N + MUN^C$	0.008	−0.006	0.006	0.005	0.003	0.000	0.001	−0.103	0.180	−0.003
R^R	0.005	−0.004	0.004	0.003	0.002	0.000	0.001	−0.086	−0.039	−0.009
D^*	0.231	−0.171	0.177	0.141	0.078	0.013	0.023	1.910	−0.312	0.554
EM	−0.042	0.031	−0.032	−0.025	−0.014	−0.002	−0.004	−0.088	−0.017	−0.006
P	0.000	0.000	0.000	0.000	0.000	0.000	0.000	0.002	−0.001	0.001

TABLE 5A(4). Effects of Selected Policy Measures Taken at Beginning of 1965: Original Model, Fourth Quarter

Variable	A_1+A_2 (1)	EX (2)	ρ_i (3)	ρ_n (4)	ρ_u (5)	ρ_c (6)	COV (7)	k_4 (8)	r_{max} (9)	r_d (10)
Y	−0.237	0.175	−0.181	−0.145	−0.080	−0.020	−0.024	−0.392	−0.207	−0.291
CN	−0.154	0.114	−0.118	−0.094	−0.052	−0.013	−0.015	0.040	−0.076	−0.028
CD	−0.021	0.015	−0.016	−0.013	−0.007	−0.004	−0.002	−0.141	−0.060	−0.066
F1	−0.025	0.019	−0.019	−0.015	−0.008	−0.002	−0.002	−0.351	−0.025	−0.168
F2	0.009	−0.007	0.007	0.006	0.003	0.001	0.001	0.078	0.021	0.024
ΔH	−0.047	0.035	−0.036	−0.029	−0.016	−0.002	−0.005	−0.018	−0.026	−0.054
π	−0.024	0.018	−0.018	−0.015	−0.008	−0.004	−0.002	−0.007	−0.048	−0.092
TI	−0.014	0.011	−0.011	−0.009	−0.005	−0.001	−0.001	−0.008	−0.011	−0.008
TO + TU	−0.007	0.005	−0.006	−0.005	−0.002	−0.001	−0.001	−0.014	−0.005	−0.007
TB	0.003	−0.003	0.003	0.002	0.001	0.000	0.000	0.007	0.002	0.002
YP	−0.204	0.151	−0.156	−0.124	−0.069	−0.029	−0.020	−0.374	−0.152	−0.196
TFP	−0.025	0.019	−0.019	−0.015	−0.008	−0.004	−0.002	−0.046	−0.019	−0.024
YD	−0.179	0.132	−0.137	−0.109	−0.060	−0.025	−0.018	−0.328	−0.133	−0.172
TY	−0.129	0.096	−0.099	−0.079	−0.044	−0.018	−0.013	−0.238	−0.096	−0.125
TC	−0.010	0.008	−0.008	−0.006	−0.003	−0.002	−0.001	−0.003	−0.021	−0.039
r_s	−0.032	0.024	−0.024	−0.019	−0.011	−0.002	−0.003	−0.356	−0.013	−0.083
r_{10}	−0.017	0.013	−0.013	−0.010	−0.006	−0.001	−0.002	−0.093	−0.006	−0.040
r_e	−0.005	0.004	−0.004	−0.003	−0.002	0.000	−0.001	−0.042	−0.016	0.007
r_l	−0.003	0.002	−0.002	−0.002	−0.001	0.000	0.000	−0.060	0.091	−0.002
DR	−0.032	0.024	−0.025	−0.020	−0.011	−0.002	−0.003	−0.236	0.002	−0.084
DD	0.035	−0.026	0.027	0.021	0.012	0.002	0.003	0.079	−0.686	−0.006
DT	0.083	−0.061	0.063	0.051	0.028	0.004	0.008	−0.464	1.582	0.179
CL	−0.037	0.028	−0.029	−0.023	−0.013	−0.001	−0.004	−0.185	−0.123	0.282
E^N+E^C	0.004	−0.003	0.003	0.003	0.001	0.000	0.000	0.061	0.001	0.007
B^N+B^C	−0.021	0.015	−0.016	−0.013	−0.007	−0.002	−0.002	−0.180	−0.038	−0.072
S^N+S^C	0.114	−0.084	0.087	0.070	0.038	0.005	0.011	0.253	1.451	0.187
O^N+O^C	0.038	−0.028	0.029	0.023	0.013	0.002	0.004	0.037	0.025	−0.181
MUN^N+MUN^C	0.014	−0.011	0.011	0.009	0.005	0.001	0.001	−0.091	0.238	0.018
R^R	0.007	−0.006	0.006	0.005	0.003	0.000	0.001	−0.005	−0.042	0.005
D^*	0.202	−0.149	0.154	0.123	0.068	0.015	0.020	1.705	−0.372	0.531
EM	−0.042	0.031	−0.033	−0.026	−0.014	−0.003	−0.004	−0.082	−0.024	−0.023
P	0.000	0.000	0.000	0.000	0.000	0.000	0.000	0.002	−0.001	0.001

TABLE 5A(5). Effects of Selected Policy Measures Taken at Beginning of 1965: Original Model, Total for Four Quarters

Variable	$A_1 + A_2$ (1)	EX (2)	ρ_i (3)	ρ_ρ (4)	ρ_u (5)	p_c (6)	COV (7)	k_t (8)	r_{max} (9)	r_d (10)
Y	−1.107	0.818	−0.846	−0.675	−0.372	−0.061	−0.110	−3.024	−0.513	−0.242
CN	−0.697	0.515	−0.533	−0.426	−0.234	−0.040	−0.069	−0.806	−0.176	0.138
CD	−0.268	0.198	−0.205	−0.164	−0.090	−0.017	−0.027	−0.504	−0.155	−0.199
F1	−0.073	0.054	−0.056	−0.045	−0.025	−0.003	−0.007	−0.949	−0.057	−0.200
F2	0.030	−0.022	0.023	0.019	0.010	0.002	0.003	−0.803	−0.048	−0.091
ΔH	−0.098	0.073	−0.075	−0.060	−0.033	−0.003	−0.010	0.037	−0.077	0.110
π	−0.264	0.195	−0.202	−0.161	−0.089	−0.016	−0.026	−0.545	−0.140	−0.115
TI	−0.061	0.045	0.786	−0.038	0.021	−0.004	−0.006	−0.081	−0.022	−0.005
TO + TU	−0.046	0.021	−0.051	0.625	0.344	−0.004	0.102	−0.088	−0.013	−0.004
TB	0.012	−0.009	0.009	0.007	0.004	0.001	0.001	0.043	0.004	−0.001
YP	−1.277	0.587	−1.411	−1.128	−0.621	−0.123	−0.183	−2.427	−0.356	−0.124
TFP	−0.157	−0.610	−0.174	−0.139	−0.077	−0.015	−0.023	−0.299	−0.044	−0.015
YD	−1.620	1.197	−1.237	−0.989	−0.544	−0.108	−0.161	−2.127	−0.312	−0.109
TY	−0.812	−3.142	−0.897	−0.717	−0.394	−0.078	−0.117	−1.542	−0.226	−0.079
TC	−0.113	0.084	−0.087	−0.069	−0.038	0.176	−0.011	−0.234	−0.060	−0.049
r_s	−0.127	0.094	−0.097	−0.078	−0.043	−0.007	−0.013	0.148	−0.036	0.213
r_{10}	−0.056	0.042	−0.043	−0.034	−0.019	−0.003	−0.006	0.175	−0.015	−0.106
r_e	−0.016	0.012	−0.012	−0.010	−0.005	−0.001	−0.002	−0.006	−0.033	0.095
r_t	−0.015	0.012	−0.012	−0.010	−0.005	−0.001	−0.002	0.036	0.391	−0.038
DR	−0.119	0.088	−0.091	−0.073	−0.040	−0.006	−0.012	−0.562	0.015	−0.341
DD	0.075	−0.056	0.058	0.046	0.025	0.003	0.007	−3.186	−1.950	−0.774
DT	0.107	0.125	0.130	0.104	0.057	0.007	0.017	−1.316	4.113	0.128
CL	−0.030	0.023	−0.023	−0.019	−0.010	0.000	−0.003	−1.331	−0.266	1.352
$E^N + E^C$	0.020	−0.015	0.016	0.013	0.007	0.001	0.002	0.012	−0.004	0.001
$B^N + B^C$	−0.082	0.061	−0.063	−0.050	−0.028	−0.004	−0.008	0.118	−0.120	−0.442
$S^N + S^C$	0.215	−0.159	0.165	0.131	0.072	0.009	0.021	−1.866	3.490	−0.637
$O^N + O^C$	0.087	−0.065	0.067	0.054	0.029	0.004	0.009	−0.372	0.052	−0.909
$MUN^N + MUN^C$	0.027	−0.020	0.021	0.017	0.009	0.001	0.003	−0.343	0.580	−0.030
R^R	0.016	0.012	0.012	0.010	0.005	0.001	0.002	0.667	−0.132	−0.102
D^*	0.768	−0.568	0.587	0.469	0.258	0.040	0.076	−3.694	−1.032	2.288
EM	−0.135	0.100	−0.103	−0.083	−0.045	−0.007	−0.013	−0.444	−0.053	−0.001
P	0.000	0.000	0.000	0.000	0.000	0.000	0.000	−0.010	−0.002	0.004

275

TABLE 5B(1). Effects of Selected Policy Measures Taken at Beginning of 1965: "Speeded Up" Consumption Model, First Quarter

Variable	$A_1 + A_2$ (1)	EX (2)	ρ_i (3)	ρ_v (4)	ρ_u (5)	ρ_c (6)	COV (7)	k_4 (8)	r_{max} (9)	r_d (10)
Y	−0.632	0.467	−0.483	−0.386	−0.212	−0.019	−0.063	−3.663	−0.073	0.383
CN	−0.532	0.394	−0.407	−0.325	−0.179	−0.016	−0.053	−2.207	−0.035	0.187
CD	−0.281	0.208	−0.215	−0.172	−0.095	−0.008	−0.028	−0.727	−0.030	0.044
F1	−0.002	0.002	−0.002	−0.002	−0.001	0.000	0.000	−0.092	−0.003	0.082
F2	0.025	−0.018	0.019	0.015	0.008	0.001	0.002	−0.430	−0.002	−0.098
ΔH	0.160	−0.118	0.122	0.098	0.054	0.005	0.016	−0.206	−0.002	0.167
π	−0.216	0.160	−0.165	−0.132	−0.073	−0.006	−0.021	−1.255	−0.025	0.131
TI	−0.048	0.036	−0.039	−0.030	−0.016	−0.001	−0.005	−0.174	−0.004	0.014
TO + TU	−0.031	0.010	0.796	0.634	0.349	−0.002	0.103	−0.081	−0.002	0.009
TB	0.005	−0.004	0.004	0.003	0.002	0.000	0.000	0.028	0.001	−0.003
YP	−0.853	0.274	−1.087	−0.869	−0.478	−0.042	−0.141	−2.250	−0.044	0.239
TFP	−0.105	−0.648	−0.134	−0.107	−0.059	−0.005	−0.017	−0.277	−0.005	0.030
YD	−1.248	0.922	−0.953	−0.762	−0.419	−0.037	−0.124	−1.973	−0.039	0.210
TY	−0.542	−3.342	−0.691	−0.552	−0.304	−0.027	−0.090	−1.430	−0.028	0.152
TC	−0.093	0.069	−0.071	−0.057	−0.031	0.180	−0.009	−0.540	−0.011	0.056
r_s	−0.055	0.041	−0.042	−0.034	−0.019	−0.002	−0.005	0.776	−0.004	0.499
r_{10}	−0.020	0.015	−0.015	−0.012	−0.007	−0.001	−0.002	0.283	−0.002	0.010
r_c	−0.003	0.002	−0.003	−0.002	−0.001	0.000	0.000	0.073	−0.002	0.060
r_t	−0.007	0.006	−0.006	−0.005	−0.003	−0.002	−0.001	0.212	0.103	−0.016
DR	−0.044	0.033	−0.034	−0.027	−0.015	−0.001	−0.004	0.019	0.001	−0.077
DD	0.003	−0.002	0.002	0.002	0.001	0.000	0.000	−1.757	−0.248	−0.450
DT	0.021	−0.016	0.017	0.041	0.007	0.001	0.002	−0.078	0.439	−0.092
CL	0.066	−0.049	0.051	0.041	0.022	0.002	0.007	−0.405	−0.012	0.376
$E^N + E^C$	0.009	−0.007	0.007	0.005	0.003	0.000	0.001	−0.212	−0.001	−0.023
$B^N + B^C$	−0.034	0.025	−0.026	−0.021	−0.012	−0.001	−0.003	0.713	−0.020	−0.165
$S^N + S^C$	−0.020	0.015	−0.015	−0.012	−0.007	−0.001	−0.002	−2.044	0.303	−0.555
$O^N + O^C$	0.008	−0.006	0.007	0.005	0.003	0.000	0.001	−0.185	0.003	−0.278
$MUN^N + MUN^C$	0.002	−0.001	0.002	0.002	0.001	0.000	0.000	−0.061	0.047	−0.025
R^R	0.001	−0.001	0.001	0.001	0.000	0.000	0.000	0.905	−0.019	−0.065
D^*	0.296	−0.219	0.226	0.181	0.099	0.009	0.029	−7.918	−0.106	0.547
EM	−0.042	0.031	−0.032	−0.026	−0.014	−0.001	−0.004	−0.245	−0.005	0.026
P	0.000	0.000	0.000	0.000	0.000	0.000	0.000	−0.012	0.000	0.001

TABLE 5B(2). Effects of Selected Policy Measures Taken at Beginning of 1965: "Speeded Up" Consumption Model, Second Quarter

Variable	A_1+A_2 (1)	EX (2)	ρ_i (3)	ρ_o (4)	ρ_u (5)	ρ_c (6)	COV (7)	k_4 (8)	r_{max} (9)	r_d (10)
Y	-0.640	0.473	-0.489	-0.391	-0.215	-0.031	-0.064	-0.556	-0.170	0.036
CN	-0.295	0.218	-0.226	-0.180	-0.099	-0.019	-0.029	0.404	-0.076	0.112
CD	-0.110	0.081	-0.084	-0.067	-0.037	-0.009	-0.011	0.152	-0.056	-0.096
FI	-0.047	0.035	-0.036	0.029	-0.016	-0.001	-0.005	-0.352	-0.013	-0.004
F2	0.003	-0.003	0.003	0.002	0.001	0.001	0.000	-0.347	-0.007	-0.031
ΔH	-0.191	0.141	-0.146	-0.117	-0.064	-0.003	-0.019	0.414	-0.018	0.055
π	-0.175	0.129	-0.134	-0.107	-0.059	-0.010	-0.017	0.133	-0.055	-0.022
TI	-0.026	0.020	-0.020	-0.016	-0.009	-0.002	-0.003	0.036	-0.009	0.001
TO+TU	-0.016	0.012	-0.012	-0.010	-0.005	-0.001	-0.002	-0.027	-0.004	0.002
TB	0.006	-0.004	0.005	0.004	0.002	0.000	0.001	0.018	0.001	-0.002
YP	-0.446	0.330	-0.341	-0.273	-0.150	-0.041	-0.044	-0.755	-0.108	0.060
TFP	-0.055	0.041	-0.042	-0.034	-0.019	-0.005	-0.005	-0.093	-0.013	0.007
YD	-0.391	0.289	-0.299	-0.239	-0.132	-0.036	-0.039	-0.662	-0.094	0.052
TY	-0.284	0.210	-0.217	-0.173	-0.095	-0.026	-0.028	-0.480	-0.068	0.038
TC	-0.075	0.056	-0.057	-0.046	-0.025	-0.004	-0.007	0.057	-0.024	-0.009
r_s	-0.073	0.054	-0.056	-0.045	-0.025	-0.003	-0.007	-0.335	-0.016	-0.080
r_{10}	-0.029	0.022	-0.023	-0.018	-0.010	-0.001	-0.003	-0.083	-0.006	-0.028
r_e	-0.009	0.007	-0.007	-0.005	-0.003	0.000	-0.001	-0.009	-0.006	0.034
r_l	-0.010	0.007	-0.008	-0.006	-0.003	0.000	-0.001	-0.067	0.099	-0.011
DR	-0.068	0.050	-0.052	-0.042	-0.023	-0.003	-0.007	-0.249	-0.001	-0.078
DD	0.029	-0.022	0.022	0.018	0.010	0.001	0.003	0.942	0.435	-0.241
DT	0.058	-0.043	0.045	0.036	0.020	0.002	0.006	-0.123	0.859	-0.043
CL	-0.015	0.012	-0.012	-0.010	-0.005	0.001	-0.002	0.601	-0.042	0.369
E^N+E^C	0.014	-0.010	0.011	0.009	0.005	0.001	0.001	0.041	-0.001	0.008
B^N+B^C	-0.048	0.036	-0.037	-0.029	-0.016	-0.002	-0.005	-0.342	-0.033	-0.105
S^N+S^C	0.086	-0.064	0.066	0.053	0.029	0.002	0.009	0.232	0.676	-0.281
O^N+O^C	0.039	-0.029	0.030	0.024	0.013	0.001	0.004	-0.040	0.011	-0.250
MUN^N+MUN^C	0.009	-0.006	0.007	0.005	0.003	0.000	0.001	-0.067	0.116	-0.023
R^{lR}	0.006	-0.004	0.005	0.004	0.002	0.000	0.001	-0.134	-0.031	-0.035
D^*	0.449	-0.332	0.343	0.274	0.151	0.019	0.045	1.719	-0.190	0.541
EM	-0.071	0.053	-0.055	-0.044	-0.024	-0.003	-0.007	-0.204	-0.015	0.020
P	0.000	0.000	0.000	0.000	0.000	0.000	0.000	-0.002	0.000	0.001

277

TABLE 5B(3). Effects of Selected Policy Measures Taken at Beginning of 1965: "Speeded Up" Consumption Model, Third Quarter

Variable	A_1+A_2 (1)	EX (2)	ρ_i (3)	ρ_o (4)	ρ_u (5)	ρ_c (6)	COV (7)	k_4 (8)	r_{max} (9)	r_d (10)
Y	−0.427	0.316	−0.326	−0.261	−0.144	−0.034	−0.042	0.489	−0.251	−0.223
CN	−0.261	0.193	−0.199	−0.159	−0.088	−0.021	−0.026	0.398	−0.113	−0.014
CD	−0.007	0.006	−0.006	−0.005	−0.003	−0.006	−0.001	0.143	−0.072	−0.110
F1	−0.055	0.041	−0.042	−0.034	−0.019	−0.003	−0.006	−0.301	−0.023	−0.094
F2	0.010	−0.008	0.008	0.006	0.004	0.001	0.001	−0.086	−0.013	0.011
ΔH	−0.113	0.084	−0.087	−0.069	−0.038	−0.005	−0.011	−0.335	−0.030	−0.016
π	−0.057	0.042	−0.044	−0.035	−0.019	−0.008	−0.006	0.444	−0.069	−0.105
TI	−0.014	0.011	−0.011	−0.009	−0.005	−0.001	−0.001	0.029	−0.010	−0.007
TO+TU	−0.013	0.010	−0.010	−0.008	−0.004	−0.001	−0.001	0.000	−0.006	−0.004
TB	0.006	−0.005	0.005	0.004	0.002	0.000	0.001	0.009	0.002	0.000
YP	−0.363	0.268	−0.277	−0.222	−0.122	−0.040	−0.036	0.012	−0.175	−0.112
TFP	−0.045	0.033	−0.034	−0.027	−0.015	−0.005	−0.004	0.002	−0.022	−0.014
YD	−0.318	0.235	−0.243	−0.194	−0.107	−0.035	−0.032	−0.011	−0.153	−0.098
TY	−0.230	0.170	−0.176	−0.141	−0.077	−0.025	−0.023	0.008	−0.111	−0.071
TC	−0.024	0.018	−0.019	−0.015	−0.008	−0.004	−0.002	0.191	−0.030	−0.045
r_s	−0.064	0.047	−0.049	−0.039	−0.022	−0.004	−0.006	−0.099	−0.022	−0.103
r_{10}	−0.030	0.022	−0.023	−0.018	−0.010	−0.002	−0.003	−0.008	−0.009	−0.040
r_e	−0.010	0.007	−0.008	−0.006	−0.003	−0.001	−0.001	−0.053	−0.011	−0.004
r_t	−0.007	0.005	−0.006	−0.004	−0.002	−0.001	−0.001	−0.068	0.095	−0.007
DR	−0.063	0.046	−0.048	−0.038	−0.021	−0.004	−0.006	−0.255	−0.005	−0.082
DD	0.058	−0.043	0.045	0.036	0.020	0.002	0.006	−0.425	−0.575	−0.091
DT	0.108	−0.080	0.083	0.066	0.037	0.005	0.011	−0.390	1.247	0.057
CL	−0.059	0.044	−0.045	−0.036	−0.020	−0.001	−0.006	−0.292	−0.082	0.339
E^N+E^C	0.010	−0.007	0.008	0.006	0.003	0.001	0.001	0.149	0.001	0.006
B^N+B^C	−0.041	0.030	−0.031	−0.025	−0.014	−0.003	−0.004	−0.178	−0.041	−0.087
S^N+S^C	0.169	−0.125	0.129	0.103	0.057	0.006	0.017	0.110	1.074	−0.029
O^N+O^C	0.060	−0.045	0.046	0.037	0.020	0.003	0.006	−0.035	0.022	−0.215
MUN^N+MUN^C	0.018	−0.013	0.014	0.011	0.006	0.001	0.002	−0.080	0.181	−0.005
R^R	0.011	−0.009	0.009	0.007	0.004	0.000	0.001	−0.072	−0.038	−0.011
D^*	0.402	−0.297	0.307	0.245	0.235	0.025	0.040	1.817	−0.250	0.547
EM	−0.077	0.057	−0.059	−0.047	−0.026	−0.004	−0.008	−0.105	−0.027	−0.002
P	0.000	0.000	0.000	0.000	0.000	000.0	0.000	0.001	−0.001	0.001

278

TABLE 5B(4). Effects of Selected Policy Measures Taken at Beginning of 1965: "Speeded Up" Consumption Model, Fourth Quarter

Variable	$A_1 + A_2$ (1)	EX (2)	ρ_i (3)	ρ_o (4)	ρ_u (5)	ρ_c (6)	COV (7)	k_4 (8)	r_{max} (9)	r_d (10)
Y	−0.322	0.238	−0.246	−0.197	−0.108	−0.034	−0.032	−0.152	−0.320	−0.400
CN	−0.242	0.179	−0.185	−0.148	−0.081	−0.023	−0.024	0.043	−0.153	−0.109
CD	0.011	−0.008	0.008	0.007	0.004	−0.004	0.001	−0.141	−0.081	−0.093
F1	−0.039	0.029	−0.030	−0.024	−0.013	−0.003	−0.004	−0.307	−0.033	−0.170
F2	0.018	−0.013	0.014	0.011	0.006	0.001	0.002	0.100	−0.017	0.025
ΔH	−0.070	0.052	−0.053	−0.043	−0.023	−0.005	−0.007	0.153	−0.036	−0.053
π	−0.004	0.003	−0.004	−0.003	−0.002	−0.006	0.000	0.104	−0.072	−0.134
TI	−0.019	0.014	−0.014	−0.012	−0.006	−0.002	−0.002	−0.008	−0.019	−0.017
TO + TU	−0.011	0.008	−0.008	−0.007	−0.004	−0.001	−0.001	−0.008	−0.008	−0.009
TB	0.006	−0.005	0.005	0.004	0.002	0.000	0.001	0.007	0.003	0.002
YP	−0.305	0.226	−0.233	−0.186	−0.103	−0.040	−0.030	−0.232	−0.234	−0.256
TFP	−0.037	0.028	−0.029	−0.023	−0.013	−0.005	−0.004	−0.029	−0.029	−0.032
YD	−0.267	0.198	−0.204	−0.163	−0.090	−0.035	−0.027	−0.203	−0.205	−0.224
TY	−0.194	0.143	−0.148	−0.118	−0.065	−0.025	−0.019	−0.147	−0.149	−0.162
TC	−0.002	0.002	−0.002	−0.001	−0.001	−0.002	0.000	0.045	−0.031	−0.058
r_s	−0.045	0.034	−0.035	−0.028	−0.015	−0.004	−0.005	−0.315	−0.027	−0.093
r_{10}	−0.027	0.020	−0.021	−0.017	−0.009	−0.002	−0.003	−0.088	−0.012	−0.042
r_e	−0.009	0.007	−0.007	−0.006	−0.003	−0.001	−0.001	−0.042	−0.018	0.007
r_i	−0.003	0.003	−0.003	−0.002	−0.001	0.000	0.000	−0.051	0.090	−0.004
DR	−0.049	0.036	−0.038	−0.030	−0.017	−0.004	−0.005	−0.205	−0.010	−0.092
DD	0.065	−0.048	0.050	0.040	0.022	0.004	0.006	0.101	−0.677	−0.010
DT	0.164	0.121	0.126	0.100	0.055	0.008	0.016	−0.323	1.600	0.166
CL	−0.081	0.060	−0.062	−0.049	−0.027	−0.003	−0.008	−0.238	−0.126	0.298
$E^N + E^C$	−0.004	−0.004	0.004	0.003	0.002	0.001	0.000	0.048	0.003	0.009
$B^N + B^C$	−0.030	0.022	−0.023	−0.018	−0.010	−0.003	−0.003	−0.154	−0.047	−0.079
$S^N + S^C$	0.224	−0.166	0.172	0.137	0.075	0.011	0.022	0.393	1.474	0.166
$O^N + O^C$	0.071	−0.053	0.054	0.043	0.024	0.004	0.007	0.066	0.034	−0.184
$MUN^N + MUN^C$	0.028	−0.021	0.022	0.018	0.010	0.001	0.003	−0.064	0.241	0.015
R^R	0.014	0.011	0.011	0.009	0.005	0.001	0.001	0.003	−0.040	0.004
D^*	0.297	−0.219	0.227	0.181	0.100	0.026	0.029	1.465	−0.292	0.587
EM	−0.071	0.052	−0.054	−0.043	−0.024	−0.005	−0.007	−0.077	−0.039	−0.028
P	0.000	0.000	0.000	0.000	0.000	0.000	0.000	0.001	−0.001	0.001

279

TABLE 5B(5). Effects of Selected Policy Measures Taken at Beginning of 1965: "Speeded Up" Consumption Model, Total for Four Quarters

Variable	A_1+A_2 (1)	EX (2)	ρ_i (3)	ρ_o (4)	ρ_u (5)	ρ_c (6)	COV (7)	k_4 (8)	r_{max} (9)	r_f (10)
Y	-2.022	1.494	-1.545	-1.234	-0.679	-0.118	-0.201	-3.882	-0.815	-0.204
CN	-1.331	0.984	-1.017	-0.812	-0.447	-0.079	-0.132	-1.361	-0.377	0.176
CD	-0.388	0.287	-0.296	-0.237	-0.130	-0.028	-0.039	-0.573	-0.239	-0.255
F1	-0.144	0.107	-0.110	-0.088	-0.049	-0.007	-0.014	-1.052	-0.073	-0.186
F2	0.057	-0.042	0.043	0.035	0.019	0.003	0.006	-0.763	-0.040	-0.093
ΔH	-0.215	0.159	-0.164	-0.131	-0.072	-0.007	-0.021	-0.132	-0.086	0.154
π	-0.453	0.335	-0.346	-0.277	-0.152	-0.030	-0.045	-0.575	-0.222	-0.130
TI	-0.108	0.080	0.751	-0.066	-0.036	-0.007	-0.011	-0.117	-0.041	-0.008
TO+TU	-0.071	0.040	-0.070	0.610	0.336	-0.006	0.099	-0.117	-0.020	-0.002
TB	0.023	-0.017	0.018	0.014	0.008	0.001	0.002	0.062	0.007	-0.002
YP	-1.968	1.098	-1.939	-1.549	-0.853	-0.163	-0.252	-3.225	-0.561	-0.068
TFP	-0.242	-0.547	-0.239	-0.191	-0.105	-0.020	-0.031	-0.398	-0.069	-0.008
YD	-2.225	1.644	-1.700	-1.358	-0.748	-0.143	-0.221	-2.827	-0.492	-0.060
TY	-1.250	-2.818	-1.232	-0.984	-0.542	-0.104	-0.160	-2.049	-0.357	-0.043
TC	-0.195	0.144	-0.149	-0.119	-0.065	0.170	-0.019	-0.247	-0.095	0.056
r_s	-0.238	0.176	-0.182	-0.145	-0.080	-0.013	-0.024	0.028	-0.068	0.222
r_{10}	-0.107	0.080	-0.082	-0.066	-0.036	-0.006	-0.011	0.104	-0.028	-0.100
r_c	-0.031	0.023	-0.024	-0.019	-0.011	-0.002	-0.003	-0.030	-0.037	0.097
r_t	-0.028	0.021	-0.022	-0.017	-0.010	-0.002	-0.003	0.026	0.387	-0.038
DR	-0.224	0.166	-0.171	-0.137	-0.075	-0.012	-0.022	-0.690	-0.014	-0.330
DD	0.156	-0.115	0.119	0.095	0.052	0.007	0.015	-3.022	-1.935	-0.792
DT	0.353	-0.261	0.270	0.216	0.119	0.016	0.035	-0.914	4.146	0.088
CL	-0.089	0.066	-0.068	-0.054	-0.030	-0.001	-0.009	-1.536	-0.263	1.382
E^N+E^C	0.037	0.028	0.029	0.023	0.013	0.002	0.004	0.025	0.002	0.000
B^N+B^C	-0.153	0.113	-0.117	-0.094	-0.052	-0.008	-0.015	0.039	-0.141	-0.436
S^N+S^C	0.460	-0.340	0.352	0.281	0.155	0.019	0.046	-1.309	3.527	-0.699
O^N+O^C	0.179	-0.132	0.137	0.109	0.060	0.008	0.018	-0.194	0.070	-0.928
MUN^N+MUN^C	0.058	-0.043	0.045	0.036	0.020	0.002	0.006	-0.273	0.586	-0.037
R^R	0.033	-0.025	0.025	0.020	0.011	0.001	0.003	0.703	-0.128	-0.106
D^*	1.444	-1.067	1.103	0.882	0.485	0.079	0.143	-2.917	-0.839	2.222
EM	-0.262	0.193	-0.200	-0.160	-0.088	-0.013	-0.026	-0.632	-0.085	0.016
P	0.000	0.000	0.000	0.000	0.000	0.000	0.000	-0.011	-0.002	0.004

APPENDIX

Technical Notes and Sources of Data

Procedure for Linearization of the Model

With the residual error terms ignored, our system can be represented by

(A.1) $$F(Y_t, Y_{t-1}, Y_{t-2}, \cdots; Z_t, Z_{t-1}, Z_{t-2}, \cdots) = 0$$

where Y is the vector of endogenous variables and Z the vector of exogenous and policy variables. Since the structure of our system is such that F is differentiable in the neighborhood of the annual average value of Y and Z for 1965, we can write

(A.2) $$dF = \frac{\partial F}{\partial Y_t} dY_t + \frac{\partial F}{\partial Y_{t-1}} dY_{t-1} + \frac{\partial F}{\partial Z_t} dZ_t + \frac{\partial F}{\partial Z_{t-1}} dZ_{t-1} + \cdots = 0$$

or

$$dY_t = - \left(\frac{\partial F}{\partial Y_t}\right)^{-1} \left(\frac{\partial F}{\partial Y_{t-1}}\right) dY_{t-1} - \left(\frac{\partial F}{\partial Y_t}\right)^{-1} \left(\frac{\partial F}{\partial Y_{t-2}}\right) dY_{t-2} - \cdots$$
$$- \left(\frac{\partial F}{\partial Y_t}\right)^{-1} \left(\frac{\partial F}{\partial Z_t}\right) dZ_t - \left(\frac{\partial F}{\partial Y_t}\right)^{-1} \left(\frac{\partial F}{\partial Z_{t-1}}\right) dZ_{t-1} - \cdots$$

The partial derivatives are evaluated at the average values of the variables for 1965. Let the matrices of partial derivatives so evaluated (therefore constant) be denoted by

281

$$\left(\frac{\partial F}{\partial Y_t}\right) = -A, \quad \left(\frac{\partial F}{\partial Z_{t-\tau}}\right) = B_\tau, \quad \tau = 0, 1, 2, \cdots$$

$$\left(\frac{\partial F}{\partial Y_{t-\tau}}\right) = D_\tau, \quad \tau = 1, 2, \cdots$$

Since interest here is in the effects of once-for-all policy changes taking place in the first quarter of 1965, isolated from all other variations in exogenous variables and other disturbances, we can write, identifying t to represent the first quarter, 1965,

$$dY_t = A^{-1} B_0 \, dZ_t$$
$$dY_{t+1} = A^{-1} D_1 \, dY_t + A^{-1} B_1 \, dZ_t$$
(A.3) $dY_{t+2} = A^{-1} D_1 \, dY_{t+1} + A^{-1} D_2 \, dY_t + A^{-1} B_2 \, dZ_t$
$$dY_{t+3} = A^{-1} D_1 \, dY_{t+2} + A^{-1} D_2 \, dY_{t+1} + A^{-1} D_3 \, dY_t + A^{-1} B_3 \, dZ_t$$

In using (A.3) actually to compute "dynamic multipliers", account was taken of the variations over quarters of some elements of A's and D's, which were due to the presence of seasonal factors, as discussed below.

Equations in real terms were first multiplied by the current price before they were linearized, so that, for example,

$$\frac{CN}{P} = \alpha + \beta \frac{CN_{-1}}{P_{-1}} + \cdots$$

was transformed into

$$dCN = \left(\alpha + \beta \frac{\overline{CN}_{-1}}{\overline{P}_{-1}}\right) dP + \beta \left(\frac{\overline{P}}{\overline{P}_{-1}}\right) dCN_{-1} - \beta \frac{\overline{CN}_{-1}}{(\overline{P}_{-1})^2} \overline{P} \, dP_{-1} + \cdots$$

After the linearization was carried out, for a few equations in which the nonlinearity was particularly pronounced, the actual values for the first two quarters of 1962 were substituted for variables in the linearized equations, and the residuals obtained from the linearized equations were compared with the residuals in the original equations to see how close the linear approximations were over the two- or three-year interval. The results suggest that errors introduced through the linearization were almost negligible in these equations individually for the interval, though they by no means imply that errors due to linearization for the system as a whole would also be negligible.

Problems of Seasonality

Seasonal factors were introduced into the model in three ways: (1) in some equations, seasonal dummies were introduced as additive terms;

(2) in some others, they were introduced by multiplying the lagged values of the dependent variables of the equation; and (3) a few variables were seasonally adjusted in some equations but not in others.

The variables that were both seasonally adjusted and unadjusted are GNP, dividends, corporate profits before taxes and inventory valuation adjustment, and corporate profits after taxes. We examined the ratio of seasonally adjusted values to unadjusted figures over the period covered by our study, and concluded that the seasonal variations of these variables were sufficiently constant so that we could define meaningful multiplicative seasonal factors for each variable. Thus, for instance, for GNP,

$$(A.4) \qquad\qquad Y^s = \sigma_i Y; \quad i = 1, 2, 3, 4$$

where σ_i's are seasonal factors which differ from variable to variable but remain constant for any variable for all years.

To understand the implications of seasonal factors on the dynamic characteristics of the system, it is convenient to start from the equilibrium position of the system for a given set of values for the exogenous variables. At equilibrium, the system must satisfy the following relationships:

$$(A.5) \qquad \begin{aligned} A_1\bar{Y}_1 &= C_1 + B\bar{Z} + D_1\bar{Y}_4 \\ A_2\bar{Y}_2 &= C_2 + B\bar{Z} + D_2\bar{Y}_1 \\ A_3\bar{Y}_3 &= C_3 + B\bar{Z} + D_3\bar{Y}_2 \\ A_4\bar{Y}_4 &= C_4 + B\bar{Z} + D_4\bar{Y}_3 \end{aligned}$$

where $\bar{Z}$ is the given vector of exogenous variables, $\bar{Y}_i$ is the corresponding equilibrium vector of Y for the ith quarter, A_i, B, and D_i are matrices of coefficients of Y, Z, and Y_{-1} appropriate for the ith quarter.[76] Note that, of the three types of seasonal variations listed above, the first is reflected by the presence of four C matrices, the second by the presence of four D matrices, and the third by the presence of four equation systems.

In equilibrium, the system (A.5) implies that there will be a purely seasonal change in Y from quarter to quarter. The change from the fourth quarter to the first quarter is then given by

$$(A.6) \qquad \begin{aligned} \bar{Y}_1 - \bar{Y}_4 &= \left[A_1^{-1}C_1 - A_4^{-1}C_4\right] + (A_1^{-1} - A_4^{-1})B\bar{Z} \\ &\quad + \left[A_1^{-1}D_1\bar{Y}_4 - A_4^{-1}D_4\bar{Y}_3\right]. \end{aligned}$$

If the value of Z is changed from $\bar{Z}$ to $\bar{Z} + \Delta Z$ in the first quarter, then the value of Y in the first quarter is given by

[76] While, for convenience of exposition, we write (A.5) as involving first order lags in Y and no lag in Z, our formulation can be trivially generalized to any order lag in both Y and Z by reinterpreting Z and Y_{-1} to include all lagged values of Z and Y.

(A.7) $\qquad Y'_1 = A_1^{-1}C_1 + A_1^{-1}B(\bar{Z} + \Delta Z) + A_1^{-1}D_1\bar{Y}_4$
$\qquad\qquad = \bar{Y}_1 + A_1^{-1}B\Delta Z$

so that the change from the fourth quarter to the first quarter is

(A.8) $\qquad Y'_1 - \bar{Y}_4 = [A_1^{-1}C_1 - A_4^{-1}C_4] + (A_1^{-1} - A_4^{-1})B\bar{Z}$
$\qquad\qquad\qquad + [A_1^{-1}D_1\bar{Y}_4 - A_4^{-1}D_4\bar{Y}_3] + A_1^{-1}B\Delta Z.$

Hence, the change in Y that is due to the change in Z, net of purely seasonal variation, is

(A.9) $\qquad\qquad (Y'_1 - \bar{Y}_4) - (\bar{Y}_1 - \bar{Y}_4) = A_1^{-1}B\Delta Z.$

Similarly, the purely seasonal change in Y from the first quarter to the second quarter, if Z is kept at $\bar{Z}$, is

(A.10) $\qquad \bar{Y}_2 - \bar{Y}_1 = [A_2^{-1}C_2 - A_1^{-1}C_1] + (A_2^{-1} - A_1^{-1})B\bar{Z}$
$\qquad\qquad\qquad + [A_2^{-1}D_2\bar{Y}_1 - A_1^{-1}D_1\bar{Y}_4]$

whereas the value of Y in the second quarter when Z is changed to $\bar{Z} + \Delta Z$ in the first quarter and kept at the new value thereafter is

(A.11) $\qquad Y'_2 = A_2^{-1}C_2 + A_2^{-1}B(\bar{Z} + \Delta Z) + A_2^{-1}D_2Y'_1$
$\qquad\qquad = \bar{Y}_2 + [A_2^{-1} + A_2^{-1}D_2A_1^{-1}]B\Delta Z.$

Thus, the change in Y from the first quarter to the second quarter is given by

(A.12) $\quad Y'_2 - Y'_1 = \bar{Y}_2 - \bar{Y}_1 + A_2^{-1}B\Delta Z + A_2^{-1}D_2A_1^{-1}B\Delta Z - A_1^{-1}B\Delta Z$

and the net change in Y from the first quarter to the second quarter excluding purely seasonal variation is

(A.13) $\quad (Y'_2 - Y'_1) - (\bar{Y}_2 - \bar{Y}_1) = (A_2^{-1} - A_1^{-1})B\Delta Z + A_2^{-1}D_2A_1^{-1}B\Delta Z.$

If $A_2 = A_1 = A$, $D_2 = D$, i.e., if there is no seasonal factor, then the expression (A.13) reduces to

(A.14) $\qquad\qquad (Y'_2 - Y'_1) - (\bar{Y}_2 - \bar{Y}_1) = A^{-1}DA^{-1}B\Delta Z.$

This expression is equivalent to the corresponding expression in (A.3).

Expressions similar to equations (A.9) and (A.13) can easily be derived for the following two quarters.

The first term on the right-hand side of equation (A.13) represents the change in the seasonal variation induced by the change in Z, while the second term represents the change in Y net of seasonal variation induced by the change in Z. The term $(A_2^{-1} - A_1^{-1})B\Delta Z$ is only a transient term, and the system will eventually exhibit a new equilibrium seasonal variation which can be obtained by substituting $\bar{Z} + \Delta Z$ for $\bar{Z}$ in (A.5).

The purely additive seasonal factors (those incorporated in C_i's) do not appear in (A.9) and (A.13); therefore, they can be ignored in the calculation of multipliers. Furthermore, the terms $(A_2^{-1} - A_1^{-1})B\,\Delta Z$ and $A_2^{-1}D_2A_1^{-1}B\,\Delta Z$ in (A.13), and their equivalents in equations for subsequent quarters, do not interact with each other in the dynamic process of the system; therefore, the variation in Y due to these two terms can be considered separately.

Under these circumstances, we decided to abstract as far as possible from seasonal variations in our multiplier analysis, and the figures reported in Tables 1 through 5 were computed by using only the term $A_2^{-1}D_2A_1^{-1}B\,\Delta Z$ in equation (A.13) and its equivalents in equations for subsequent quarters, ignoring the term $(A_2^{-1} - A_1^{-1})B\,\Delta Z$. Since the variation in A arises from the seasonally adjusted variables and there are only four variables of this type, our results are unlikely to be very different from those obtained by following equation (A.13) exactly.

Sources of Data

INCOME AND OUTPUT DATA

All components of national income statistics used in this paper were supplied by the Office of Business Economics (OBE), U. S. Department of Commerce, through the courtesy of its director, Mr. George Jaszi. They represent seasonally unadjusted versions of the national income statistics revised and published in the August 1965 and subsequent issues of the *Survey of Current Business*. There are several exceptions to this general statement.

1. OBE does not prepare seasonally unadjusted data on personal income, and we constructed this series by starting from seasonally unadjusted GNP and working through the definitional relationships of GNP, national income, and personal income. All data are available from OBE except (a) capital consumption allowance, which we assumed to have no seasonal variation; (b) dividends, for which we used the "publicly reported dividends" series from the *Survey of Current Business*, adjusted proportionately to equal national income figures on an annual basis; and (c) statistical discrepancy, which we assumed to be identically zero on a seasonally unadjusted basis.

2. Federal personal income tax, OASI contributions, and unemployment insurance contributions were computed on a liabilities basis. (a) Liabilities for federal personal income tax, which were obtained from *Statistics of Income*, include the liabilities of fiduciaries. The data on liabilities are available on an annual basis, so that the equation was estimated on

an annual basis. The quarterly figures required for our multiplier analysis were then generated through equations (14) and (17) in the text, using quarterly data on personal income and the effective tax rates. Data on taxable income, also obtained from *Statistics of Income*, include taxable income of fiduciaries. (b) OASI contributions on an annual basis, except for the self-employment tax, as reported by OBE, were considered to be on a liabilities basis; and the self employment tax liabilities, as reported in *Statistics of Income*, were added to obtain total liabilities. Equation (10) was then estimated on an annual basis, and quarterly data were obtained through this equation by substituting in (10) quarterly personal income and the rate of contribution. (c) Annual figures for unemployment contributions as reported by OBE were considered to be a satisfactory approximation of the liabilities. Equation (11) was estimated on an annual basis, and quarterly data were generated in the same way as above.

3. Disbursements under the Federal Temporary Unemployment Compensation Program for 1958–62 were subtracted from unemployment insurance benefits and treated as exogenous in the model.

4. $F1$ was taken to represent investment in plant and equipment as reported by the Securities and Exchange Commission—Department of Commerce, rather than the figures in national income statistics.

5. Inventory investment is inventory investment by manufacturers rather than the total given in national income statistics.

TAX RATES AND RELATED ITEMS

1. For the effective rate and per capita exemption for federal personal income tax, see Brown and Kruizenga in *Review of Economics and Statistics*, p. 264, and Ando and others in *Stabilization Policies*, p. 98. For the discussion of estimating the rate for 1964 and 1965, see Ando and Brown, in this volume, and Pechman in *Journal of Finance*.

2. The rate for indirect business tax used in our model is a weighted average of all excise tax rates, both federal and state, weighted by the approximate tax base for each tax in 1959–60. All rates were first converted to an ad valorem basis, using price indices which are as close to the item concerned as practicable. The computation of this average rate is extremely laborious; the basic data for the calculation are available at the Brookings Institution.

3. The rate of state personal income tax is a weighted average of rates for major states having personal income taxes.

4. For the federal corporate income tax rate, see *Brookings Quarterly Econometric Model*, p. 542. We treated the state corporate income tax rate in a manner similar to that followed for the federal rate and combined the two into a single rate in this model.

LABOR FORCE, EMPLOYMENT, AND UNEMPLOYMENT

Data for these three items were taken directly from the *Survey of Current Business*, where they are reported as civilian labor force, employment, and unemployment, on a seasonally unadjusted basis.

INTEREST RATES AND OTHER VARIABLES RELATED
TO THE MONETARY SECTOR

All these variables are defined and explained in detail in Goldfeld, *Commercial Bank Behavior*, with the following exceptions:

Some of the series were discontinued by the Comptroller of the Currency in Quarterly Call Reports; subsequently they were available only semi-annually. Estimates of quarterly data were made available by the Board of Governors of the Federal Reserve System.

The maximum interest rate on savings deposits that commercial banks are allowed to pay under Regulation $Q(r_{max})$ is published in the *Federal Reserve Bulletin*. When the rate changed in midyear, an average was computed. The actual numbers used in the paper are as follows: for 1950–56, 2.5 percent; for 1957–61, 3.0 percent; for 1962, 3.8 percent; for 1963, 3.9 percent; for 1964, 4.2 percent.

Selected References

Ando, Albert, and Franco Modigliani, "Growth, Fluctuations, and Stability," *American Economic Review*, Vol. 49, May 1959.

———, and Franco Modigliani, "The Relative Stability of Monetary Velocity and the Investment Multiplier," *American Economic Review*, Vol. 55, September 1965.

———, E. Cary Brown, John Kareken, and Robert M. Solow, "Lags in Fiscal and Monetary Policy," in Commission on Money and Credit, *Stabilization Policies*. Englewood Cliffs, New Jersey: Prentice-Hall, Inc., 1963.

Aschheim, J., "Restrictive Open-Market Operations Versus Reserve-Requirement Increases: A Reformulation," *Economic Journal*, Vol. 73, June 1963.

Baumol, W. J., "Pitfalls in Contracyclical Policies: Some Tools and Results," *Review of Economics and Statistics*, Vol. 43, February 1961.

Beveridge, William, *Full Employment in a Free Society*. New York: W. W. Norton and Co., Inc., 1945.

Bolton, Roger E., "Predictive Models for State and Local Government Purchases." Brookings Institution, Working Paper in Econometric Model Project, 1965.

Brittain, John A., *Corporate Dividend Policy*. Washington: Brookings Institution, 1966.

Brown, E. Cary, "Comments on Tax Credits as Investment Incentives," *National Tax Journal*, Vol. 15, June 1962.

———, "Fiscal Policies in the Thirties: a Reappraisal," *American Economic Review*, Vol. 46, December 1956.

———, "Fiscal Policy in a Growing Economy: a Further Word," *Journal of Political Economy*, Vol. 64, April 1956.

———, "Fiscal Policy in the Post-war Period," in Ralph Freeman, ed., *Post-war Economic Trends in the United States*. New York: Harper and Bros., 1960.

———, "The Policy Acceptance in the United States of Reliance on Automatic Fiscal Stabilizers," *Journal of Finance*, Vol. 14, March 1959.

———, "The Static Theory of Automatic Fiscal Stabilization," *Journal of Political Economy*, Vol. 63, October 1955.

———, and R. J. Kruizenga, "Income Sensitivity of a Simple Personal Income Tax," *Review of Economics and Statistics*, Vol. 41, August 1959.

Brownlee, O. H., and Alfred H. Conrad, "Effects upon the Distribution of Income of a Tight Money Policy," *American Economic Review*, Vol. 51, May 1961.

Burns, A. F., "Progress Towards Economic Stability," *American Economic Review*, Vol. 50, March 1960.

Chase, Samuel B., Jr., "Tax Credits for Investment Spending," *National Tax Journal*, Vol. 15, March 1962.

Childs, Gerald, *Unfilled Orders and Inventories: A Structural Analysis.* Amsterdam: North Holland Publishing Company, 1967.

Clement, M. O., "The Quantitative Impact of Automatic Stabilizers," *Review of Economics and Statistics*, Vol. 42, February 1960.

Cohen, Leo, "An Empirical Measurement of the Built-in Flexibility of the Individual Income Tax," *American Economic Review*, Vol. 49, May 1959.

———, "A More Recent Measurement of the Built-in Flexibility of the Individual Income Tax," *National Tax Journal*, Vol. 13, January 1960.

Colm, Gerhard, "Comments on Samuelson's Theory of Public Finance," *Review of Economics and Statistics*, Vol. 38, November 1956.

Commission on Money and Credit, *Money and Credit: Their Influence on Jobs, Prices, and Growth.* Englewood Cliffs, New Jersey: Prentice-Hall, Inc., 1961.

Conrad, Alfred H., "The Multiplier Effects of Redistributive Public Budgets," *Review of Economics and Statistics*, Vol. 37, May 1955.

deLeeuw, Frank, "The Demand for Capital Goods by Manufacturers: A Study of Quarterly Time Series," *Econometrica*, Vol. 30, July 1962.

———, "Financial Markets in Business Cycles: A Simulation Study," *American Economic Review*, Vol. 54, May 1964.

Duesenberry, James S., Otto Eckstein, and Gary Fromm, "A Simulation of the United States Economy in Recession," *Econometrica*, Vol. 28, October 1960.

———, Gary Fromm, Laurence R. Klein, and Edwin Kuh, eds., *The Brookings Quarterly Econometric Model of the United States.* Chicago: Rand McNally & Company; Amsterdam: North-Holland Publishing Company; 1965.

Eckstein, Otto, "Federal Expenditure Policy for Economic Growth," *Journal of Finance*, Vol. 17, May 1962.

Economic Report of the President, together with *The Annual Report of the Council of Economic Advisers.* Washington: Government Printing Office, annually.

Eilbott, Peter, "The Effectiveness of Automatic Stabilizers," *American Economic Review*, Vol. 56, June 1966.

Fellner, William, *et al.*, "The Economics of Eisenhower: A Symposium," *Review of Economics and Statistics*, Vol. 38, November 1956.

Fels, Rendigs, "The Recognition-Lag and Semi-Automatic Stabilizers," *Review of Economics and Statistics*, Vol. 45, August 1963.

Fleming, J. M., "Domestic Financial Policies Under Fixed and Under Floating Exchange Rates," *Staff Papers* (International Monetary Fund), Vol. 9, November 1962.

Friedlaender, Ann F., *The Interstate Highway System: A Study in Public Investment.* Amsterdam: North Holland Publishing Company, 1965.

Friedman, Milton, "A Monetary and Fiscal Framework for Economic Stability," *American Economic Review*, Vol. 38, June 1948.

———, *A Theory of the Consumption Function*. Princeton, New Jersey: Princeton University Press, 1957.

Galbraith, J. K., "Market Structure and Stabilization Policy," *Review of Economics and Statistics*, Vol. 39, May 1957.

Gallaway, L. E., and P. G. Smith, "A Quarterly Econometric Model of the United States," *Journal of the American Statistical Association*, Vol. 56, June 1961.

Goldberger, A. S., *Impact Multipliers and Dynamic Properties of the Klein-Goldberger Model*. Amsterdam: North-Holland Publishing Company, 1959.

Goldfeld, Stephen M., *Commercial Bank Behavior and Economic Activity*. Amsterdam: North-Holland Publishing Company, 1966.

Goldsmith, Raymond W., Robert E. Lipsey, and Morris Mendelson, *Studies in the National Balance Sheet of the United States*. Princeton, New Jersey: Princeton University Press, 1963.

Goode, Richard, "Critique of Public Finance Based on the Report of the Commission on Money and Credit," *Harvard Business Review*, Vol. 40, May–June 1962.

———, "Special Tax Measures to Restrain Investment," *Staff Papers* (International Monetary Fund), Vol. 5, February 1957.

Gordon, R. A., "Alternative Approaches to Forecasting: The Recent Work of the National Bureau," *Review of Economics and Statistics*, Vol. 44, August 1962.

Gramlich, E. M., "The Behavior and Adequacy of the United States Federal Budget, 1952–1964," *Yale Economic Essays*, Vol. 6, Spring 1966.

———, "State and Local Governments and Their Budget Constraints." Unpublished paper by staff member of Board of Governors of Federal Reserve System.

Hansen, A. H., "Some Reflections on the Annual Report of the Council of Economic Advisers," *Review of Economics and Statistics*, Vol. 44, August 1962.

Hansen, W. Lee, and Charles M. Tiebout, "An Intersectoral Flows Analysis of the California Economy," *Review of Economics and Statistics*, Vol. 45, November 1963.

Harris, Seymour, *et al.*, "Economic Policies Under Kennedy in 1962 and 1963: A Symposium," *Review of Economics and Statistics*, Vol. 44, February 1962.

Holmans, A. E., *United States Fiscal Policy: 1945–1959*. New York: Oxford University Press, 1959.

Holt, Charles C., "Linear Decision Rules for Economic Stabilization and Growth," *Quarterly Journal of Economics*, Vol. 76, February 1962.

———, Franco Modigliani, John F. Muth, and Herbert A. Simon, *Planning Production, Inventories, and Work Force*. Englewood Cliffs, New Jersey: Prentice-Hall, Inc., 1960.

Klein, L. R., and A. S. Goldberger, *An Econometric Model of the United States*. Amsterdam: North-Holland Publishing Company, 1955.

Koyck, Leendert, *Distributed Lags and Investment Analysis*. Amsterdam: North-Holland Publishing Company, 1954.

Kuh, Edwin, "Cyclical and Secular Labor Productivity in U. S. Manufacturing," *Review of Economics and Statistics*, Vol. 47, February 1965.

————, "Profits, Profit Mark-Ups, and Productivity," in *Employment Growth, and Price Levels*. Study Paper No. 15, Joint Economic Committee. 86 Cong. 1 sess. Washington: Government Printing Office, 1960.

Leontief, Wassily W., and Marvin Hoffenberg, "The Economic Effects of Disarmament," *Scientific American*, Vol. 240, April 1961.

Lerner, A. P., "The Burden of the Debt," *Review of Economics and Statistics*, Vol. 43, May 1961.

Levinson, Harold M., *Postwar Movement of Prices and Wages in Manufacturing Industries*. Study Paper No. 21, Joint Economic Committee. 86 Cong. 2 sess. Washington: Government Printing Office, 1960.

Levy, Michael E., *Fiscal Policy, Cycles and Growth*. New York: National Industrial Conference Board, 1963.

Lewis, Wilfred, Jr., "Automatic Fiscal Stabilizers in the 1957–58 Business Contraction: A Comment," *Review of Economics and Statistics*, Vol. 42, November 1960.

————, *Federal Fiscal Policy in the Postwar Recessions*. Washington: Brookings Institution, 1962.

Lintner, John, "Distribution of Incomes of Corporations Among Dividends, Retained Earnings, and Taxes," *American Economic Review*, Vol. 46, May 1956.

Liu, T. C., "An Exploratory Quarterly Econometric Model of Effective Demand in the Postwar U. S. Economy," *Econometrica*, Vol. 31, July 1963.

Lovell, Michael C., "Determinants of Inventory Investment," in National Bureau of Economic Research, *Models of Income Determination*. Princeton, New Jersey: Princeton University Press, 1964.

————, "Manufacturers' Inventories, Sales Expectations, and the Acceleration Principle," *Econometrica*, Vol. 29, July 1961.

Meade, James E., *Consumers' Credits and Unemployment*. New York: Oxford University Press, 1938.

Meyer, John, and Robert Glauber, *Investment Decisions, Economic Forecasting, and Public Policy*. Boston: Division of Research, Graduate School of Business Administration, Harvard University, 1964.

Minsky, H. P., "Employment, Growth and Price Levels," *Review of Economics and Statistics*, Vol. 43, February 1961.

Modigliani, Franco, "Long-run Implications of Alternative Fiscal Policies and the Burden of the National Debt," *Economic Journal*, Vol. 71, December 1961.

————, and R. Sutch, "Innovations in Interest Rate Policy," *American Economic Review*, Vol. 56, May 1966.

Moore, Geoffrey H., ed., *Business Cycle Indicators*. Princeton, New Jersey: Princeton University Press, 1961.

————, "Measuring Recessions," *Journal of the American Statistical Association*, Vol. 53, June 1958.

Mundell, R. A., "Growth, Stability, and Inflationary Finance," *Journal of Political Economy*, Vol. 73, June 1965.

Musgrave, R. A., "On Measuring Fiscal Performance," *Review of Economics and Statistics*, Vol. 46, May 1964.

————, "Tax Policy," *Review of Economics and Statistics*, Vol. 46, May 1964.

———, "Tax Reform: Growth With Equity," *American Economic Review*, Vol. 53, May 1963.

———, *The Theory of Public Finance*. New York: McGraw-Hill Book Co., 1959.

National Bureau of Economic Research and Brookings Institution, Conference Report, *The Role of Direct and Indirect Taxes in the Federal Revenue System*. Princton, New Jersey: Princeton University Press, 1964.

Neumark, F., *Tax Harmonization in the Common Market*. Chicago: Commerce Clearing House, 1963.

Oakland, William, "The Theory of the Value-Added Tax: I—A Comparison of Tax Bases; II—Incidence," *National Tax Journal*, Vol. 20, June and September 1967.

Okun, Arthur, "Measuring the Impact of the 1964 Tax Reduction," *Review of Economics and Statistics*, forthcoming issue.

———, "On the Appraisal of Cyclical Turning-point Predictors," *Journal of Business*, Vol. 33, April 1960.

Peacock, A. T., and D. G. M. Dosser, "Regional Input-output Analysis and Government Spending," *Scottish Journal of Political Economy*, Vol. 6, November 1959.

———, and I. G. Stewart, "Fiscal Policy and the Composition of Government Purchases," *Public Finance*, Vol. 13, No. 2, 1958.

Pechman, Joseph A., "Individual Income Tax Provisions of the Revenue Act of 1964," *Journal of Finance*, Vol. 20, May 1965.

Peck, Merton J., and Frederick Scherer, *The Weapons Acquisition Process: An Economic Analysis*. Boston: Harvard University Press, 1962.

Perry, George L., "The Determinants of Wage Rate Changes and the Inflation-Unemployment Trade-off for the United States," *Review of Economic Studies*, Vol. 31, October 1964.

———, *Unemployment, Money Wage Rates, and Inflation*. Cambridge, Massachusetts: Massachusetts Institute of Technology Press, 1966.

Phelps, Charlotte P. D., "The Impact of Tightening Credit on Municipal Capital Expenditures in the United States," in Commission on Money and Credit, *Impacts of Monetary Policy*. Englewood Cliffs, New Jersey: Prentice-Hall Inc., 1963.

Phillips, A. W., "Stabilisation Policy and the Time-Forms of Lagged Responses," *Economic Journal*, Vol. 67, June 1957.

———, "Stabilisation Policy in a Closed Economy," *Economic Journal*, Vol. 64, June 1954.

President's Advisory Committee on a National Highway Program, *A 10-Year National Highway Program: A Report to the President*. Washington: Government Printing Office, 1955.

Prest, A. R., "The 'Economic Efficiency' of Taxation: a Note," *Economic Journal*, Vol. 70, June 1960.

Salant, William A., "Taxes, Income Determination, and the Balanced Budget Theorem," *Review of Economics and Statistics*, Vol. 39, May 1957.

Samuelson, Paul A., "Aspects of Public Expenditure Theories," *Review of Economics and Statistics*, Vol. 40, November 1958.

———, "Diagrammatic Exposition of a Theory of Public Expenditure," *Review of Economics and Statistics*, Vol. 37, November 1955.

———, "Full Employment vs. Progress and Other Economic Goals," in Max Millikan, ed., *Income Stabilization for a Developing Democracy.* New Haven: Yale University Press, 1953.

———, "Principles and Rules in Modern Fiscal Policy," in *Money, Trade, and Economic Growth: Essays in Honor of John Henry Williams.* New York: Macmillan & Co., 1951.

———, and R. M. Solow, "Analytical Aspects of Anti-inflation Policy," *American Economic Review*, Vol. 50, May 1960.

Schultze, C. L., "Economic Outlook and Policy Evaluation," *Review of Economics and Statistics*, Vol. 44, February 1962.

———, "Short-Run Movement of Income Shares," in National Bureau of Economic Research, *The Behavior of Income Shares.* Princeton, New Jersey: Princeton University Press, 1964.

Smith, W. L., "Monetary-Fiscal Policy and Economic Growth," *Quarterly Journal of Economics*, Vol. 71, February 1957.

Solow, Robert M., "Distribution in the Long and Short Run." Palermo, Italy: International Economic Association, Conference on the Distribution of National Income, September 1964.

Stanford Research Institute, *The Industry-Government Aerospace Relationship*, Vol. 2. Menlo Park, California, 1963.

Strotz, R. H., "Two Propositions Related to Public Goods," *Review of Economics and Statistics*, Vol. 40, November 1958.

Stuvel, G., "A Systematic Approach to Macroeconomic Policy Design," *Econometrica*, Vol. 33, January 1965.

Suits, D. B., "Forecasting and Analysis with an Econometric Model," *American Economic Review*, Vol. 52, March 1962.

Theil, Henri, *Optimal Decision Rules for Government and Industry.* Amsterdam: North-Holland Publishing Company, 1964.

Tobin, James, "The Business Cycle in the Postwar World: A Review," *Quarterly Journal of Economics*, Vol. 72, May 1958.

———, "Economic Growth as an Objective of Government Policy," *American Economic Review*, Vol. 54, May 1964.

Tucker, D. P., "Income Adjustment to Money-Supply Changes," *American Economic Review*, Vol. 56, June 1966.

U. S. Congress. House. Committee on Public Works. *Hearings, Highway Amendment Act.* 86 Cong. 1 sess. Washington: Government Printing Office, 1959.

U. S. Congress. Joint Economic Committee. *The Federal Budget as an Economic Document.* 87 Cong. 2 sess. Washington: Government Printing Office, 1962.

———. *Federal Expenditure Policy For Economic Growth and Stability.* Papers Submitted by Panelists Appearing Before the Subcommittee on Expenditure Policy. 84 Cong. 1 sess. Washington: Government Printing Office, 1955.

———. *Federal Tax Policy for Economic Growth and Stability.* Papers Submitted by Panelists Appearing Before the Subcommittee on Tax Policy. 84 Cong. 1 sess. Washington: Government Printing Office, 1955.

———. *Hearings, January 1961 Economic Report of the President and the Economic*

Situation and Outlook. 87 Cong. 1 sess. Washington: Government Printing Office, 1961.

———. *Inventory Fluctuations and Economic Stabilization.* 87 Cong. 1 sess. Washington: Government Printing Office, 1961.

———. *State of the Economy and Policies for Full Employment.* Hearings Before the Joint Economic Committee, August 1962. 87 Cong. 2 sess. Washington: Government Printing Office, 1962.

U. S. Congress. Senate. Committee on Finance. *Revenue Act of 1963.* Hearings. 88 Cong. 1 sess. Washington: Government Printing Office, 1963.

Weidenbaum, Murray L., "The Economic Impact of the Government Spending Process," *Business Review of the University of Houston,* Spring 1961.

———, "The Expenditure of Governmental Funds in the United States," *Public Finance,* Vol. 15, No. 2, 1960.

———, "The Timing of the Economic Impact of Government Spending," *National Tax Journal,* Vol. 12, March 1959.

Weston, J. Fred, ed., *Defense-Space Market Research.* Cambridge, Massachusetts: Massachusetts Institute of Technology Press, 1964.

Williams, A., "Fiscal Policy and Interregional Resource Allocation," *Public Finance,* Vol. 16, No. 2, 1961.

Index